Whither Pakistan

Dictatorship or Democracy?

VANI PRAKASHAN

21-A, Darya ganj New Delhi-110002

Ph. : 011-23273167, 23275710

Fax : 011-23275710

e-mail : vaniprakashan@gmail.com

website : www.vaniprakashan.com

Whither Pakistan

Dictatorship or Democracy?

Benazir Bhutto

Edited and Compiled by

Dr. Iqbal Narejo

Vani Prakashan's logo is a creation of
the strokes from the paintbrush of the
veteran artist M.F. Husain

I: ISBN : 978-93-86799-93-7

VANI PRAKASHAN
21-A, Daryaganj New Delhi-110002
First Edition : 2007

Cover Design : Vani Chitrankan
Printed by : Jai Bharat Press Delhi-110032

Rs. : 225.00

**WHITHER PAKISTAN
DICTATORSHIP OR DEMOCRACY?**
by : Benazir Bhutto
Edited and Compiled by Dr. Iqbal Narejo

Dedication

I dedicate this book to those unknown political soldiers whose sacrifice, sufferings and contributions made it impossible for a succession of tyrants to stamp out the desire for democracy and justice in our land.

— **Benazir Bhutto**

Contents

Foreword

My thoughts often go back to the first day of my present exile. I was in London on that day. I could see the same blue sky as the one over Moenjodaro in my ancestral hometown of Larkana. The trees were green and the flowers glowed with the same red, lilac, pink, violet and yellow colours. The colours were the same as in Karachi, Peshawer, Lahore, Quetta and Islamabad. Yet they seemed faded and had lost their power to enchant.

A voice seemed to carry over through the centuries, the voice of the blind Greek poet Homer, who lived 3000 years earlier, and whispered the words from The Odyssey in my ear : 'I, for one, know of no sweeter sight for a man's eyes than his country.'

I, a woman, was born three thousand years after Homer's immortal character Odysseus and the battle of Troy. But for my motherland, for my people, my heart yearned like his. My eyes thirsted for the sight of the wild cactus plants growing in the desert sands.

The Greeks were the wisest of writers, poets and philosophers! It was Euripides who once said: '*There is no sorrow above the loss of a native land*'. I travel on a jet plane around the world, visiting countries far and wide on distant shores. Yet I cannot freely travel to my own motherland'. First one military tyrant of the eighties denied me the water, air and sunlight of the Indus Valley civilisation. Then another dictator abused power to force me out of my own land to live in exile to carry on the dreams that I nurtured since I was a child.

These dreams were born in my early academic years as I learnt of the great founding principles that brought together the Muslims of the South Asian Sub Continent to struggle for an independent homeland of their own. They were strengthened, as I saw my Father fight one military dictatorship after another with enormous courage, determination and perseverance. They were nurtured when as a student I lived in democratic countries and learnt for myself the power of people to change the course of history.

It is my desire to serve the downtrodden people of Pakistan, the heirs of the Indus Valley civilisation, as well as the larger Muslim community and humanity that give me the strength to face the state power unleashed against my Party, my family and myself.

I belong to that generation of South Asians, proud of my heritage and culture, which seeks to emancipate our people from backwardness, exploitation and oppression.

My Grandfather Sir Shah Nawaz Bhutto successfully separated Muslim Sindh from Hindu Bombay in the nineteen thirties. By so doing he laid the foundation for Pakistan whose clarion call for which was given on March 23, 1940. My Father as a student wrote to Quaid-e-Azam that he was ready to give his life for Pakistan, the dream of the pure state where every citizen lived in liberty, equality and fraternity, free to practice their faith without prejudice or discrimination. When the time came, he did indeed give his life for the values he believed in.

I was born in the first decade after Pakistan was created in 1947. I dreamt of our soil flourishing under the framework devised by our Founding Father promoting Federalism, provincial autonomy and social emancipation of our people. I naively believed that the land for whose freedom for which my grandfather and father had struggled and loved each particle would transform into an earthly paradise.

My father had started the Pakistan People's Party to fulfill the aspirations of our people and provinces for a proud, dignified, self reliant and independent country where the flower of freedom would blossom, where the majesty of justice would extend its golden hand to rich and poor equally, where an unfettered, representative parliament would enact laws addressing the problems of the people including poverty, inflation, lack of clean water, good schools and hospitals.

Quaid-e-Awam Zulfikar Ali Bhutto strove to eradicate poverty, hunger, illiteracy and unemployment from our country with the help of the PPP workers and the pro democracy forces. He believed that a Federal Pakistan had the potential for a great future. When the dark cloud of military dictatorship overtook the sun of democracy in the land of the pure, when young men were lashed and women dragged by their Dupattas to prison, when the screams of the youth being tortured filled the torture chambers, when the hand raised to defend our country was raised to inflict the whiplash and tie the hangman's noose, my Father sacrificed his life. He preferred death to dishonour and walked proudly to the gallows knowing that ideas live on when coup makers turn to dust.

My Father's faith in the people of Pakistan never wavered. His faith in doing what was right, what was just, what was in keeping with the principles of the PPP gave me the strength to face the tyrants when they came after me. When they tried to seize my liberty or that of my husband and Party colleagues I thought of the dank and squalid death cell where I had bid my Father farewell before they took his life. They took his life and came after me because the people of the four federating units of Pakistan had reposed their trust and confidence in Father and daughter. Nearly forty years after the PPP was formed, there are only two forces that can independently form a government in Pakistan. One is the PPP and its allies. The other is the military establishment.

And even though the PPP has served the defence of the country better than any tin pot military dictator, the military establishment has never forgiven it for being a rival centre of power. It has done everything in its power over decades to crush the party of the masses. It has failed because the masses have had the political awareness to recognize the conspiracy against them and defeat it by stubbornly supporting the PPP.

I inherited from my martyred father the will to fight for freedom, justice and equality until my last breath, to be prepared to shed the last drop of my blood in the fight to change the destiny of my people.

But there are many lands other than Pakistan in the world, many countries, many peoples with their own history, languages and cultures.

At first I had dreams for my own country alone and for our region, to live in peace internally and externally. However, after the events of September 11, my thoughts began to change, to go beyond frontiers, boundaries and limitations. During exile, the reality dawned upon me that love only for our own land and people, limits us like still water in a pool in a world that is increasingly global. The world has become a global village and problems are now multifaceted. I came to the realisation that my desire to see humanity share a secure, peaceful and prosperous future was similar to the Indus River. Wherever the Indus flows, it brings with it fertility and prosperity.

We live in an interconnected world. News travels faster than the speed of light. If the wings of a butterfly fluttering in one country can change the weather in another through a ripple affect, the politics, environment, economics of each country have a ripple effect on others on earth. We may yet fail to recognise, it but I believe that harmony is indivisible as is pain, sorrow, and happiness. Everybody's pain is my pain and my happiness as it is yours. Except few realise it.

Realising this connection has given me the courage and strength to struggle for justice, peace, democracy and human rights and to fight against, poverty, terrorism, extremism and injustice.

A helpless village woman of Pakistan and I, Benazir Bhutto, are connected through this thread of pain.

My life mirrors the larger Pakistani canvas of the last half-century of law, politics and a politicized judiciary. Contrary to globally accepted values, Pakistan is one of the few nations where today the military rules, where judges are sacked, arrested and made to swear new oaths of allegiance. The generals claim they are experts on freedom, and will take the country from "sham democracy" to "true democracy".

When the press is critical of generals, it comes in for a battering. As dictatorship continues, the crisis deepens. Even as it does so, it weakens the political structure, political parties, the judiciary, administrative framework of the country and even the Constitution with arbitrary amendments passed by decree. By so doing, dictatorship, when it withdraws, sows the seeds of its own return. And Pakistan falls victim to repeated military interventions.

I am banned from my country. I am banned from contesting for premiership of my country and banned from contesting as an ordinary member. For eight long, lonely and torturous years I was banned from seeing my husband who was imprisoned in Pakistan. He was nearly killed under torture. I was banned from entering my ancestral homes, banned from praying at the graves of my martyred father and brothers.

During these years of exile, when I brought up my small children as a single Mother, fought legal battles in foreign jurisdictions as well as national, ran the largest political party of the country, kept a hectic schedule meeting the press, diplomats, other political parties, think tanks, I survived on the spiritual and political nourishment I received as a child of the Indus Valley civilisation.

Spiritually I recalled my Islamic history. I recalled how the Prophet of Islam (PBUH) had been forced to leave Mecca and go into exile in Medina. I recalled how he had returned triumphantly to his home. This example sustained me in days that were bitter, harsh and sometimes appeared hopeless. There were so many naysayers, those who said that the regime in power was too powerful, that like Suharto of Indonesia and Mubarak of Egypt the rulers would continue forever and ever.

But I recalled my political upbringing. As a young student I heard my Father speak before the United Nations in December 1971. As the darkest chapter in our Nation's history unfolded and the country disintegrated, when fear stalked the land that the whole of Pakistan would collapse, my Father's voice rang out in the halls of the United Nations where the diplomats of the world heard him mesmerized into silence. "Realities change", he said. "The reality was that Hitler's troops were at the gates of Leningrad but realities change".

I was brought up to believe that realities do change and ultimately truth prevails over injustice and that good prevails over evil. This simple belief has sustained me through my life.

I also remembered my Father's wisdom passed on to me in the dark days of his solitary confinement in the death cell at Rawalpindi District Jail. There he told me that, "Nothing lasts, neither good nor bad. These days in prison will pass too, It is important only that we pass them in dignity for victory or defeat lie in the hands of God".

I therefore am not guided by short-term considerations of winning of losing. I put my trust more in the success of ideas, of values and of principles. Sometime short-term compromises have to be made. However, while showing flexibility one should never lose sight of the goal, which is to be achieved, and the mission, which is to be accomplished. Perhaps it is done in our lifetime. Perhaps it is done in another. But each individual must do what is right for in the end we live with our conscience and we take to the grave none of the material pleasures of the world. We take to it only our name and reputation.

In life, an individual makes choices. I made mine on the last day of my father's life in a prison that our colonial masters built in the city of Rawalpindi. That was the choice to continue the mission for which my Father gave his life, a democratic Pakistan and to fight for human dignity that must come when people can combat hunger, poverty and illiteracy.

This book 'The Vision of an Exile' is a collection of articles that I wrote often in the early hours of the morning when all other work was completed. Some of them are lectures that I presented at different forums around the world. They were penned or delivered during the uncertain, lonely and painful days that mark the life of an exile. However, I am proud to say that despite the pressures that I was subjected to, I always strove to keep a smile on my face.

I remember as a child being told that, "when you laugh the world laughs with you. When you cry, you cry alone".

The world has become an unsafe place after 9/11. Terrorists aimlessly target innocent citizens all over the world in ghastly conspiracies of bombing and butchering. Pakistan is not safe either. Our Masjids have been attacked, as have Churches and Temples as well as diplomatic missions and bazaars. These terrorists remind one of the nine-headed monster of Greek mythology, Hydra, which developed two heads when one of its heads was cut off.

The fact now is that the whole world is in the grip of a great turmoil, which does not discriminate between Hindu and Muslim, Christian and Jew. Everybody feels threatened by the other person. People are afraid of their own shadow and are impatient to wield and show their power and strength. Those who take interest and study world affairs know these are very special times. These are very dangerous times. These are times of misperceptions and confusion.

In the West, there is often talk about the "Muslim Street". The Street most often seen here on television is the street of fanaticism whipped into frenzy. But there is another Muslim street. It is a silent street of women who suffer discrimination in every aspect of life. It is a silent street of students who are not educated. It is a silent street of businessmen and businesswomen who are not allowed to compete freely. It is a silent street of human rights activists who are jailed, political parties that are decimated, and political leaders who are either prisoners or exiles. It is the street of the people constrained by the totalitarian powers of the state. It is the street of the future in the chains of present-day intolerance, ignorance and dictatorship. And it is the street far more likely to explode than the street of religious extremists.

There appear to be groups in both the Muslim and non-Muslim worlds who believe that a clash of civilisations is needed for religious reasons.

This political scenario is threatening to undo the entire global social fabric built since the end of the second World War – one based on the tolerance betweens different faiths, races, genders and cultures.

Professor Samuel Huntington of Harvard wrote of an inevitable clash of civilisations between the West and the Islamic world. I argue that this clash is far from inevitable, unless we make it so. Terrorism and fanaticism will not succeed unless we fall into the psychopaths' trap. A clash of civilisations can lead to the Armageddon, where there will be no winners on earth. But perhaps the religious extremists are not searching for winners on earth.

At this time of continuing crisis, the Asian people need to understand those who use violence in the name of Islam. They are not clerics. They are criminals. Their actions are contradictory to the teachings of Islam. Even in war, Islam does not permit the killing of non-combatants and especially not of women, children and old men.

Moreover, Islam is committed to tolerance and equality, and it is committed to the principles of democracy. It is ironic that despite the strong commitment to democracy, most Muslims are living in dictatorships. The Muslim people want freedom. They want modernity, diversity and democracy. They want the rights to debate, discuss and dissent.

Autocrats rule many parts of the Muslim world. But those autocrats reflect their own ambition and power. The do not represent, and cannot reflect, the sentiments of the people of the Muslim world.

At present two different political earthquakes shake the Muslim world. One crosses the battle lines in the fight between democracy and dictatorship. The second battle is one between political modernization and theocracy.

Human dignity and respect is at the heart of Islam. If there are political prisoners in Pakistan and elsewhere, if there are witch-hunts against women and minorities, that is not Islam. It is discrimination. Regarding discrimination, I would like to tell you that the ruling classes in Pakistan practice discrimination against all citizens. Be it our minorities, our women, farmers or workers, all are deprived of their rights. The money, which should have been spent on human development, has been diverted to the defence budget. While PPP supports a strong defence it disagrees with the concept of a rapacious military class above all laws, without accountability, overstretching the resources of the state and colonising land that belongs to the poor people of the concerned area.

American and British soldiers are killed in Iraq and Afghanistan but they do not get plazas and plots nor plunder the land. They get two months' salary. They fight for their country and are proud to sacrifice their lives. Our soldiers have given their lives too for internal and external security. Yet that sacrifice is not as widely acknowledged because of the industrial empire, parallel state structure and usurpation of the constitutional rights of the people which has repeatedly taken place since the country was founded.

We need to study veteran programmes in other Nations and bring ours in accordance with the modern armies and nation states. Now the time has come when the Nation as a whole must, with one voice, unite to prevent further militarization of Pakistan and the devitalisation of the civil society resulting from the rape of democracy through military intervention. Politicians cannot be blamed when a democratic government gets three years or less and the present military rule has been continuing since 1999 consecutively.

Once I cautioned President George Bush 41's administration about "creating a Frankenstein" in reference to the most fanatic Afghan groups that had been put together to fight the Soviets in Afghanistan. Today I caution his son the 43rd President of the United States to beware of the danger of a military dictatorship in Pakistan. This dictatorship is squeezing the democratic political parties and presiding over the rise of militant groups. It is astonishing that the Pakistani military is signing treaties through tribal maliks with militants of the Taliban and Al-Qaeda who are Afghan and Arab. The question arises whether our territory is or is not in our control and if we cede control of our territory in one place, can we stop such forces from making us cede control of our territory elsewhere?

Washington made a huge miscalculation in Iran under the Shah of Iran. It did not pressure him to reform society and allow the moderates to flourish. By the time the Shah fell, the moderates were in no position to control the situation, which fell to the religious parties. Until today, more than a quarter of a century after the Shah fell, the international community is still at odds with Teheran and sowing the seeds of a wrong policy that alienated the Iranian people. Dictatorship breeds the forces of terrorism. It is of little surprise that many of the areas where there are fanatic groups happen to be countries like the Philippines and Pakistan and Indonesia, which suffered long periods of dictatorship when the will of the people was stifled, and jungle law prevailed leading to a culture of lawlessness and militancy.

The future of our coming generations is at stake. The time has come to rethink. Only by returning to the values of democracy, the will of the people, a broad-based government and by building institutions that can respond to the people, can the social malaise be addressed.

At the end of the twentieth century, I had said that it is a confluence of energy committed to universal social, economic and political values – this triad defines comprehensive human rights for the future.

It is a confluence of ideology that must shape a world free from exploitation and maltreatment of women, a world in which women have opportunities to rise to the highest level in politics, business, diplomacy, and other spheres of life. The new century must, for once and for all, exclude even the notion of battered women.

It must be an era where honour and dignity are protected in peace, and in war, where women have economic freedom and independence, where women are not defined by their fathers or husbands, but by their own achievements, where they are equal partners in peace and development.

We have inherited an ancient and great civilisation, so rich in culture, so full of diversity and populated with a hard working and talented people. It is tragic that this sub-continent, so full of history, has remained for so long the most likely site for a nuclear exchange on our planet.

South Asia must begin its search for a peace dividend. We can think of a peace dividend as the sum of resources no longer devoted to the military, and available to the social sector. The peace dividend can be traditional guns for butter trade-off. In the longer term, a peace dividend is defined by investment. We must invest in technology. We must invest in infrastructure. Above all we must invest in human capital – specifically in education and health.

We can attain a thriving society through democracy, through justice. We can achieve our past and lost glory. Greatness rests on a sense of justice. Talk of a just leadership, a just society, a just war echoes through the corridors of history. It echoes because every great society and leadership flowed from the perception of justice done, of right triumphing over wrong, of the weak challenging the mighty because Right empowered them to do so.

My country is rich in weapons of mass destruction, a country that nearly went to a nuclear war over the frozen wastelands of an area called Kargil. A country where bomb blasts ruin lives and desperate young men commit suicide because they cannot afford to live.

It is unethical when a regime is deaf, dumb and blind to the agonies of its own people. All of us, as Asians, can raise our voice when rules we set, in the ink of humanity, are violated.

Many of us gave years of our lives battling dictatorship. I congratulate the Asian countries that have won that battle of freedom. But freedom is still under assault in parts of Asia, including Burma and my own country Pakistan.

Winning freedom is the start of another journey – the journey for our people to lead a life, free from want and hunger, from slums and squalour. The people of Pakistan are victims of crushing poverty, destitution and helplessness. Most nations of the world are moving towards a better future but the tomorrow of our people is under the shadow of hopelessness. The promise of our tomorrows awaits fulfilment.

Globalisation has placed us in a new political storm. Today Asia declares its readiness to face the brave new world dominated by regional trading blocs. While the goal of an Asian parliament, an Asian trading currency and an Asian monetary fund appear a distant dream, there is a will to adjust to globalisation forces dictating the pace of change.

The French philosopher Rousseau said that we were all born free. Yet our societies, cultures, politics and militaries, keep our people chained to illiteracy, ignorance, intolerance, infant mortality, malnutrition and disease. It is to break those chains of backwardness that the PPP was working from the Simla Summit to the Islamabad Summit for peace.

At the Islamabad Summit, I proposed that the South Asian Association of Regional Countries (SAARC) adopt a South Asian Preferential Tariff Agreement. This was done in December 1988. When I returned to office in 1993, the PPP ratified SAPTA. It was in Islamabad that I successfully proposed that we increase travel and trade in the region by allowing groups of people, beginning with judges and parliamentarians, to travel without visas and to advance trade to build a huge market that could invite investment, create jobs, create opportunities and harness the energy of our people to build a bright future for the people of South Asia.

I am proud of my South Asian heritage. I read the stories of the great Kings and rulers that came down the centuries through the Khyber Pass in the North and Sindh in the South. History tells us of how rich South Asia once was, of its silks and spices, of its jewels and treasures that built the Taj Mahal, the Shalimar Gardens and the Grand Trunk Road. History lights the path for us to seek redemption by turning swords into ploughs to harvest a tomorrow that can bring light to lives now darkened in the night of misery.

The cold war is over. The strategic compulsions for keeping Nation-states intact no longer exist. Nations will rise and fall on the will of the people. Force can no longer glue together those that want to go their separate ways. It is common endeavour, common purpose and common goals that will unite different ethnic and religious groups into entities that are viable and can flourish. Human rights, international courts, crimes against humanity, laws against disappearances are markers on the horizon of how the ways of the past will simply not do.

Pakistan was created as an expression of the free will of the Muslims of the Subcontinent in general and of the free will of the people of Sindh, Punjab, Balauchistan and the Frontier as expressed by their representatives. It can be kept together, in unity and strength, through this free will. It cannot be kept together through the barrel of a gun. Therefore the sooner we turn towards our survival, the sooner we turn towards the universal values to which we signed up at the United Nations in the Human Rights Declaration, the sooner we can strengthen the foundations on which the Federation of one hundred and sixty million people rests. The time is now.

In my father's last letter to me before he was murdered by one of Pakistan's early tyrants, he quoted Tennyson:

"Ah, what I shall be at fifty if I find the world so bitter at twenty.' So, be strong but do not be bitter."

Today there is terror, war, death, destruction and fear.

I dream of a world where we can live in peace, a world without violence. That is what I dream of : a world free of fear, a world at peace. I believe each one of us, regardless of our race, our colour, our beliefs have an important role to play in building a world free from fear.

Let us be truthful, the world will be a fair place when each and every human being on our planet is treated equally.

Democracy is the first step towards humanity's liberation. But it is not an end in itself. Liberty depends on social and economic justice, and above all on the universal, non-selective application of human rights to all citizens of the world.

I believe a democratic Pakistan is the best guarantee of respect and dignity for the people of Pakistan. I believe a democratic Pakistan living by the rule of law, within and without, is the best guarantee of the triumph of moderation and modernity amongst one billion Muslims at the crossroads of our history. These are difficult times. We stand at the crossroads of a new world order.

We can remember that the future is in our hands. As the European philosopher Goethe once wrote:

"Freedom must be reinvented in every generation."

The clock is ticking and I plan to return to Pakistan believing the time is now right to fight for democracy from my home soil. Through the long nights and days of exile, when each moment seems an hour and each hour a day. I dreamt of freedom and through my writing and speeches, strived to reinvent it for my generation. It is my prayer that my generation will pass on to the coming generations the torch of freedom which will never again be snuffed out by the forces of tyranny.

I would like to record my deep appreciation and gratitude to Dr. Iqbal Narejo. Many people proposed that I put together some of my writings and speeches. However, it was Dr. Iqbal Narejo who concretely supported me. He went to the trouble of collecting what had been written, putting it together and helping me edit it. It took one full year's hard work and research sifting through the newspapers and magazines all over the world for him to compile this selection of my writings, lectures and speeches. I believe that Dr. Narejo single handily has accomplished what only an institution could do.

Dr. Narejo showed great patience when my schedules changed or when I travelled and our meetings were postponed. I can honestly say that this work would not be possible without his help and support for which I remain grateful. He worked selflessly never seeking any return.

I hope Dr. Narejo's example can inspire others of the importance in life of contributing selflessly for a cause that one believes in. Human success is often built on the unsung, unknown heroes who worked behind the scenes to make the impossible possible. We have monuments in many countries to the Unknown Soldier. There are many unknown political soldiers whose sacrifices, sufferings and contributions made it impossible for a succession of tyrants to stamp out the desire for democracy and justice in our land. The dream of our Founding Fathers survives because of them. And this book is dedicated to them.

— Benazir Bhutto

Without A War on Poverty We Will Never Defeat Terror

While the world focuses on the war against terror, the war against poverty slides on to the backburner. Since the bombing of the World Trade Centre in 2001; three developments have become decisive on a global scale. The first is the fight to root out militants, the second is the political rise of those on the religious margins and the third is the growing gap between the rich and the poor.

Pakistan is a frontline state in the war against terrorism. Most of the leading terrorists have been arrested in Pakistan. Khalid Sheikh Mohammed, once described as the CEO of Al-Qaeda, was arrested in Rawalpindi. Other important leaders continue to be caught in dribs and drabs every six months, including Ahmed Khalfan Ghailani, a Tanzanian, who was arrested in the Pakistani city of Gujrat last month.

This is good and bad news for Islamabad's military ruler. The positive part is that General Pervez Musharraf gets to play good cop and earn Washington's pleasure to continue his dictatorship. The bad part is that eyebrows are raised as to why leading Al-Qaida militants found it necessary to hide in a land run by Washington's "key ally" in the war against terror.

Unfortunately for Pakistan, assassinations and suicide bombings have also been increasing domestically. Scores of Pakistanis and many foreigners have been killed. Many political leaders have been gunned down in the streets - from Rawalpindi in the north to Karachi in the south.

None of the assassins has been arrested. Instead, public attention has been focused on five apparent assassination attempts against high-profile targets that have taken place since last December: two attacks on Gen Musharraf, and one each on the Karachi corps commander, the prime minister-designate, Shaukat Aziz, and the Balochistan chief minister.

While the regime insists these were genuine assassination attempts, their pattern suggests something different. At most, they seem to have been attempts to frighten the targets. At worst, if the cynics are to be believed, the attacks were stage-managed for external consumption.

For example, in each case, the bombers used low intensity explosives. None of the people hurt or killed was of political value - though they were, of course, of personal and national value. These included innocent people escorting the apparent targets. The main targets escaped without a scratch. While it is welcome news that they survived, the larger issue needs resolving.

The drivers in the corps commander's and prime minister-designate's cars were killed, but the other passengers escaped unscathed. It is difficult to believe that bombers would repeatedly use low-intensity explosives so that only one occupant of the car being attacked - or a person outside the car - would die. A public commission into these attacks is needed.

The second crucial development since September 11, 2007 has been the rise of religious extremists. There appear to be groups in both the Muslim and non-Muslim worlds who believe that a clash of civilisations is needed for religious reasons. The Christian fundamentalists believe that Christ will be resurrected once the people of the Jewish faith are resettled on the banks of the Euphrates. The Muslim extremists believe that the Mahdi will arrive when the battle between Muslims and non-Muslims intensifies.

This political scenario is threatening to undo the entire global social fabric built since the end of the Second World War - one based on the tolerance between different faiths, races, genders and cultures. A clash of civilisations can lead to the Armageddon, where there will be no winners on earth. But perhaps the religious extremists are not searching for winners on earth.

The challenge for the world community is to emphasize the values of tolerance, moderation and inter-faith understanding, on which rest the pillars of a less violent world. However, the bombing of the World Trade Centre and the events in Iraq have made that more difficult. The former led to suspicion against Muslims and a loss of civil liberties; the latter to a counter-suspicion from Muslims as to the real purposes of the war. The inability to find weapons of mass destruction and the Abu Ghraib abuses undermined the reasons given for the Iraq war.

While global attention is focused on terrorism, the crisis of poverty is effectively disregarded. Today, big business seems to be in the driving seat. One recent report found that while 20 years ago CEO's made an average of 40 times more than factory workers, last year it was 400 times more, and is now climbing to a multiple of 500.

This staggering rise in the fortunes of those on top, while those below suffer, is a festering sore that has the potential to erupt. The recent Indian elections showed that a stock-market economy alone could not make India shine. The Indian electorate went against all predictions, as peasants, labourers and the middle classes voted for change. Similarly, in Pakistan the talk of stock market rises and foreign exchange increases hides a more troubling picture. This is one of increasing poverty, hunger, misery and frustration. The numbers of young people killing themselves because of hunger was 1,200 in six months. These are the officially recorded figures - the real figures are believed to be much higher.

In Pakistan, the average income has been shrinking. The cost of living is rising sharply. It is becoming increasingly difficult for the ordinary citizen to pay fat utility bills and buy the basic necessities of life. The Pakistan Economic Survey admits that poverty has increased since democracy was derailed in 1996. The gap between the rich and the poor is growing at an alarming rate. The war against terrorism is primarily perceived as a war based on the use of force. However, economics has its own force, as does the desperation of families who cannot feed themselves. A more stable world depends on the ability to use force when necessary - and to seek political solutions when possible. After all, force is the prelude to achieving a more favourable negotiating position in a political settlement.

Militancy and greed cannot become the defining images of a new century that began with much hope. As the body count rises in Iraq, as a leading NGO pulls out of Afghanistan and as a suicide attack takes place against Pakistan's prime minister designate, the time has come to rethink. By returning to the values of democracy, the will of the people, broad-based government and building institutions that can respond to the people, the social malaise can be addressed.

The neglect of rising poverty against the background of religious extremism can only complicate an already difficult world situation.

Dictatorship and religious extremism are fuelled by gross inequality.

— The Guardian
Monday, August 9, 2004

VICTIMS OF TERRORISM

I am pleased to come before you at the time of the year when Christmas, Eid and Hanukah coincide. Maybe in this week of holidays that celebrate renewal, hope, faith and peace, we can begin to move away from the precipice of disaster that I fear the world finds itself in this December of 2002.

I know you are here primarily to learn from my experiences throughout my career that you may be able to apply to your own lives, responsibilities and careers. I intend to address those points.

But these are very special times. These are very dangerous times. These are times of misperceptions and confusion. I want to share with you some thoughts about the extraordinary state of the world we live in.

First let us address the issue of terrorism, Islam and the West. Terrorism and fanaticism will not succeed unless we fall into the psychopaths' trap. Professor Samuel Huntington of Harvard wrote of an inevitable clash of civilization between the West and the Islamic world.

I argue that this clash is far from inevitable, unless we make it so.

There is nothing in the precepts of Islam that make it inconsistent with Judeo-Christian values. In our Holy Book, Abraham is our father, just as Moses and Jesus are our prophets. There will only be a clash of civilizations if we allow ignorance and fanaticism to take control, to shape the agenda and to shape the debate. Osama and his men use commercial airliners as bombs against cities and symbols to provoke the clash of cultures under which they will thrive. I am not unfamiliar with the terrorists of Al-Qaeda. I know them well; I know how they operate, how they think and I know what they want.

As Prime Minister of Pakistan, I stood up to them. I battled with many of these same criminals, including Osama Bin Laden himself. I took them on, and often paid a price. During the Afghan-Soviet war, my country became the breeding ground for their psycho-political religious manipulation and exploitation. Hiding under the cloak of religion, they preached a message that would enslave not liberate, teach children not to write but rather to hate, keep people hopeless and desperate, bitter, xenophobic and paranoid. I closed their so-called universities. I disarmed their Madressahs, their sham primary schools that do not teach children literature, science or mathematics but rather turn children into fanatics and criminals. I tried to restore law and order to our cities under incessant assault from terrorist attack. My government tracked down and extradited the terrorists, like Ramzi Youseff, who had exported death and destruction to New York in the 1990s. They struck back at my allies and me. They destroyed the Egyptian Embassy in Islamabad. They burned our National Assembly, hijacked school buses, gunned down diplomats and businessmen in the streets of Karachi and Lahore, and organized and financed schemes to topple my government.

As a woman, I was their enemy. As a democrat, I was their opposite. But above all, as someone who offered hope to our people — education, jobs, communication and modernity — I was a dangerous obstacle to the forces of hate. I took them on with my eyes open. I knew they would strike back, just as we expect or these fanatics to try and strike again in America. Despite the personal and political price I paid over the years, my only regret is that we were unable to destroy them completely, before they rained terror on America. Peace is often difficult to achieve, and even more difficult to maintain. The words on the Korean War Memorial on Washington's great mall never have rung more true — "Freedom is not free.". These terrorists' greatest fear is the spread of information, social equality and democracy. These three principles suffocate terrorism. These three goals guided my years as prime minister. May be this could explain the two assassination attempts against me by Al-Qaeda. My government heralded the information age by introducing fax machines, digital pagers, optic fibre communications, cellular telephones, satellite dishes, computers, Internet, e-mail and even CNN into Pakistan. Under my government Pakistan integrated into the global economy that the fanatics so fear. We became one of the ten emerging capital markets of the world, attracting billions of dollars in foreign investment, particularly in power generation. We eradicated polio in our country. We dramatically reduced infant mortality.

Despite the constraints of a political system rigged against democrats, and a social system biased against women, as Prime Minister of Pakistan I used my office to reverse centuries of discrimination against women. My tenure was a textbook affirmative action programme against gender discrimination. We increased literacy by one-third, even more dramatically among girls. We built over 30,000 primary and secondary schools, targeting rural Pakistan. Our education program targeting girls and rural areas has been dismantled by the military junta. We brought down the population growth rate by establishing women's health clinics in thousands of communities across our Nation. We outlawed domestic violence and established special women's police forces to protect and defend the women of Pakistan. We appointed women judges to our nation's benches for the first time in our history. We instituted a new programme of hiring women police officers to investigate crimes of domestic violence against the women of Pakistan. That special police force has been dismantled. We systematically appointed women judges to the courts of the land. That affirmative action programme for women in the judiciary has been dismantled.

I condemned, as state policy, the honour killing, by members of their own families, of women who had been raped. The military junta is now silent to these abominations. I condemned and sought to reverse the unspeakable prosecution of women raped and then tried for the crime of adultery, a perversion of justice that affronts the civilized world. The military junta uses this abomination as a means to solidify support among extremists. I encouraged women's and girls' participation in sports, nationally and internationally by lifting the ban on women's participation in sport. I persuaded the armed forces and security services to hire women in their institutions and as pilots in PIA, Pakistan's National Airline as Pilots.

I created a special Women's Development Bank to guarantee small business loans to women entrepreneurs, because I firmly believed that economic justice would build political justice. It was a bank run by women for women- although men were allowed to keep their money in it.

Case-by-case, issue-by-issue, policy-by-policy, the military junta that rules Pakistan with an iron fist undermines the policies aimed at ameliorating the role and rights of women in Pakistani society. The women of Pakistan cannot be expected to struggle alone against the forces of discrimination, exploitation and manipulation.

I recall the words of Dante who reminded us that "the hottest place in Hell is reserved for those who remain neutral in times of moral crisis." To the fanatics and the extremists, we became the enemy, the threat, and the obstacle. To Islam at the crossroads, a modern Pakistan was one fork in the road, fanaticism and ignorance the other. Islam is committed to tolerance and equality, and it is committed by Koranic definition to the principles of democracy. The Holy Book says that Islamic society is contingent on, and I quote: "mutual advice through mutual discussions on an equal footing."

Sadly, most Muslim countries are dictatorships, contrary to what Islam teaches. The denial of democracy shifts opposition from the political class to the mosque. This plays the into hands of militants and extremists. They can canvass to a captive audience. In Islam dictatorship is never condoned, nor is cruelty. Beating, torturing and humiliating women is unIslamic. Denying education to girls violates the very first word of the Holy Book: "Read." According to our religion, those who commit cruel acts are condemned to destruction.

Sometimes tragedy can lead to a resurrection of hope and spirit. As America and the civilized world respond to the most terrible terrorist attack in history, we must remember the lessons of history and not repeat the mistakes of the past. Osama Bin Laden did not emerge just like that from a nightmare. His depravity was long in the making, and there were errors — of omission and commission — that must never be repeated. Afghanistan is a tragic case in point of how retreating from the principles of human rights and democracy can have the most tragic unanticipated consequences. In the closing days of the Soviet occupation of Afghanistan, during a State Visit to America, I cautioned that US policy to defeat the Soviets had empowered and emboldened the most fanatical, extremist elements of the Afghan seven-faction Mujahedeen at the expense of the moderates, creating a "Frankenstein" that could come back to haunt us in the future.

The overall policy of standing against Soviet aggression in Afghanistan was right. Yet the early decisions to arm, train, supply and legitimize the most extreme fanatics sowed the seeds for the Twenty-first Century terrorism that is now swirling around us. In America and Pakistan's combined and admirable zeal to end the Soviet occupation, we failed to plan or work for a post-war Afghanistan built on democratic principles of coalition, consensus and cooperation. The fundamental mistake, which contributed to a long-term historical calamity, was that we were not consistently committed to the values of freedom, democracy, social equality and self-determination that ultimately undermine the basic tenets of terrorism. Short-term battlefield strategy is often myopic, as the anarchy, civil war and Taliban terror in Afghanistan so painfully proves.

Just as democracies do not make war against other democracies, democracies also do not sponsor international terrorism. The goal of the international community's foreign policy agenda must always be to simultaneously promote stability and to strengthen democratic values. Not selectively but universally. Not when it is convenient but rather because it is right. General Musharraf made the correct decision to stand with America at this moment of crisis. But the United States and the rest of the world must remember that Pakistan has an extra-constitutional military government with no democratic legitimacy. Elections that took place were exercises in fraud, a sad charade.

This is tragic, for a democratic Pakistan is America's best guarantee of the triumph of moderation and modernity among one billion Muslims at the crossroads of our history. The alternative of a long-term nuclear-armed Pakistani dictatorship has consequences that could make September 11 look like a mere prelude to an even more horrific future for the civilized world.

This is not the simple world we dreamed of with the end of the Cold War. And mine is not the simple life I dreamed of while growing up in Pakistan and going to school at Harvard and Oxford. The gauntlet of leadership was thrown down before me. I had no choice but to pick it up. But it has often been very difficult, often very sad. Leadership is not easy. It is never meant to be easy. It is born of a passion, and it is a commitment — a commitment to an idea, to principles, to fundamental human values. It has not always been an easy life for me, or for my family. But this is nothing new, really. Women have always had to make difficult choices, often choices that men are not been forced to make. And we must live with the consequences, for better or worse.

Those of us in positions of responsibility understand this special, unique and extraordinary moment in history. We fight for all the women who came before us who gave us this opportunity. And most of all, we do it for all women who will come after us — the baby girls yet unborn!

As a child of my age, in the late sixties, I was influenced by the social ferment around me. The worldwide students' movement, from Rawalpindi to Washington, were important factors in my youth. The fight against apartheid shaped the ferocity of my commitment to stand up for principle. The burgeoning movement for women's rights empowered and emboldened me. As an Asian at Harvard, I joined up with American students to protest a war that they thought was unjust and did not want to fight. These important steps helped shape my outlook on life, helped me focus on fighting injustice, promoting freedom and safeguarding the rights of the weak and dispossessed.

But above all, in America during the Watergate crisis I saw the awesome power of the people to change policies, change leaders, and change history. From Harvard I went to Oxford, where the British Politician Enoch Powell was threatening to throw all Asians into the sea. While I was at Oxford, the Conservative party chose a woman, Margaret Thatcher, as the Leader of Opposition. The idea of the first female British Prime Minister became an intense topic for student discussions.

At Oxford, I was the first female foreigner to be elected as President of the Oxford Union. The Oxford Union reflects the British Parliament. It was there that I learned to debate, slowly gaining confidence before an audience. I had been told that as a foreigner, I could not win the Presidency and should not run. I had been told that as a woman, I could not win, and should not run. But I did run and did win and overcame my fear of losing. I learned to overcome fear and to take risks. I learned never to give in when the task seemed formidable or impossible. What has always been clear to me is that the extraordinary educational opportunities I had, gave me a range of life and career options denied to most women, and certainly almost all women of the developing world.

My own experiences at Harvard and Oxford made it clear to me that only educational opportunity promotes empowerment for women. If women are truly to be defined by themselves and their own accomplishments and abilities, they need the level of education that empowers them. Education leads to the kind of financial independence that causes women to break the shackles of being only a man's daughter or a man's wife.

As the Prime Minister of Pakistan I appeared before a historic Joint Session of the United States Congress in 1989. In that address, the most meaningful line to me was my simple message to the woman of America, my message to the women of the world. Three simple, powerful words: YES YOU CAN!

I urge women all over the world not to accept the status quo, not to accept "no" for an answer. It is critical that women — whether in

London or in Kabul — refuse to accept traditional roles and traditional constraints. Acquiescing to a tradition dictated by men — a tradition of subjugation of mothers and daughters- can no longer be accepted. In the West and in the East we must stand up and reject the notion that leadership and femininity are contradictory. I recall the words of Lady Margaret Thatcher. "When a woman is strong, she is pushy. But when a man is strong...ah...he is a great leader!"

We have made progress; we have smashed many glass ceilings. But there are thousands left to break, many battles left to fight. The greatest obstacles to progress for women in the third millennium is the bigotry of men, and nowhere is that bigotry more venal than in the Taliban and the fanatics that have declared war on the civilized world. We fight against terrorism, and the bigotry and intolerance that will confine and constrain and victimize us in the generations ahead. Victimization of significant elements of society and the concept of long-term peace are mutually exclusive. The denial of human rights is a bomb that ultimately explodes.

These are difficult times. Freedom is under assault. Democracy is under assault. Criminal terrorists hijack my religion just as they hijack America's planes. The solutions will not be quick or simple. But if we maintain our commitment to the principles that define us — the principles of racial, gender and religious equality, the principles of political pluralism and tolerance, and the principle of peaceful change through democracy —we shall in the end prevail.

In addressing the new exigencies of the new century, we could translate dynamic religion into a living reality. Muslim societies need to learn to live by the true spirit of Islam, not only by its rituals. Those who are ignorant of Islam, could cast aside their pre-conceptions about the role of women in our religion. Contrary to what many believe, Islam embraces a rich variety of political, social and cultural traditions. The fundamental ethos of Islam is tolerance, dialogue and democracy. Just as in Christianity and Judaism, we must always be on guard for those who use the Muslim Holy Book for their own narrow political ends, who will distort the essence of pluralism and tolerance for their own extremist agendas. These manipulators, distorters and bigots exist all over the world, but nowhere were they more dangerous and destructive than the last years of the Taliban era in Afghanistan. And most central to the Taliban perversion was its concept and treatment of women. For the Taliban, and other extremists throughout the Moslem world, refute the central ethos of Islam which is equality, especially equality between the sexes. I find Islam in its writings respectful of the role of women in society. It is this tradition of Islam that empowered me, strengthened me, and emboldened me. It is this tradition of Islam that allowed me my battle for political and human rights. It strengthens me today in this hour of crisis for my family, my nation and myself.

Today in Pakistan, the veil of repression has descended across our people. The cause of human rights is being set back decades. But the cause of women's rights, I am sorry to say, is being set back a century. My immediate successor's attempt to turn back the clock on women's rights, on liberal society, on pluralistic democracy focused on me, on destroying me politically at home and destroying my reputation abroad. We have become accustomed to attempts to use the politics of personal destruction to turn back the course of democracy, human rights and women's rights in our homeland. It did not work then and it will not work now.

Despite the Musharraf regime's support of the international war against terrorism, this military junta, like its Martial law predecessors of the past, is attempting to use the teaching of Islam as an excuse to subjugate women, deny freedom, destroy a free press, dominate NGOs, break up political parties, decimate the Judiciary, and restore the iron hand of dictatorship to the land. For me, it is particularly heartbreaking, as the military regime dismantles the array of special programmes that I instituted in my two terms as Prime Minister to raise the quality of life of women in Pakistan.

Unfortunately hiding under the aura of international cooperation on terrorism, the current regime in Islamabad continues to terrorize its own women. A world focused on the destruction of the Al-Queda network has neither the interest nor the knowledge to investigate the human rights abuses in a "coalition" member. And thus the causes of women's rights, human rights, press freedom and democracy fall backwards into the dark chasms of a past era.

Yet I see great progress looming as the forces that shape the new century and the new millennium come together around the world. It is a confluence of energy committed to universal social, economic and political values — this triad definition of comprehensive human rights for the future. It is a confluence of ideology that must shape a world free from exploitation and maltreatment of women, a world in which women have opportunities to rise to the highest level in politics, business, diplomacy, and other spheres of life. The new century must, once and for all, exclude even the notion of battered women. It must be an era where honour and dignity are protected in peace, and in war, where women have economic freedom and independence, where women are not defined by their fathers or husbands, but by their own achievements, where they are equal partners in peace and development. Even as we catalogue, organize and hopefully attain our goals, step by step by step, all of those around the world who are committed to the common causes of human rights, women's rights and peace, must be vigilant. As in Pakistan today, repressive forces always stand ready to exploit the moment and push us back into the past. It seems that the words of Goethe continue to resonate: "freedom has been re-made and re-earned in every generation." Dear Guests, In the time it took for me to speak to you today, over one thousand children starved to death on this planet. As long as these basic violations of human rights are allowed to continue, none of us — regardless of where we live, regardless of how elegant or civilized our life-styles, regardless of our own personal circumstances and comforts — are free. My father, Prime Minister Zulfiqar Ali Bhutto, was toppled and ultimately murdered by the forces of dictatorship and extremism two decades ago. I recall vividly those dark and tragic days, with my father languishing in a dark prison, living in the most inhumane conditions, with the world helpless to stop his murder. But he remained courageous to the end, even in the hours before his death. I want to end this monograph with the words with which he ended his last letter to me, quoting Robert F. Kennedy, himself a victim of assassination, commenting on the poetry of Alfred Tennyson. Despite the crisis we live under today, these words set the tone for a new and brighter future. In 1979, from the horror of his death cell, my father wrote: "Every generation has a central concern, whether to end war, erase racial injustice, or improve the conditions of working people. The people demand a government that speaks directly and honestly to its citizens. The possibilities are too great, the stakes too high, to bequeath to the coming generations only the prophetic lament of Tennyson — "Ah, what shall I be at fifty…if I find the world so bitter at twenty." If there is anything that I can truly share from my life that applies to yours, it is the classic quote from Shakespeare's Hamlet, "to thine own self be true." In politics and business, in art and in the academia, there will always be pressures to do what is convenient, the path of least resistance, what is safe and conservative. But leadership is not rooted in safety; it rather is a product of boldness. Do not be timid. And do not surround yourself with those who are timid. Do not do what is necessarily popular, do what is right. It is sad that modern leaders often take public opinion polls to decide on courses of policy. Sixty years ago, a truly great leader, American President Franklin Delano Roosevelt, also took polls. But he did not take polls to determine what course to follow. On the contrary, he took polls to find out where the people were so that he would know how to educate them to stand with him to do what was right. Leaders lead, remember that. Convince, educate, bring people around to do what is moral, to do what is right, to do what is necessary. Whether it is in politics or business, do not be afraid to stand out and stand up. Ladies and gentlemen, go forth and lead. Good luck.

— London
16-Dec-2002

The Terror Attack

The long arm of terror struck deep into America's heart. Its reach and extent was astounding, unprecedented and worse than Pearl Harbour. The two mightiest symbols of global US economic and military might were savaged. President Bush described the ghastly tragedy as the first war of the Twenty-first century. The terror attacks were a crime against humanity. Most Muslims mourned with the USA as it grieved for the innocent dead and missing. Muslim countries condemned the terrorism. The finger of suspicion pointed at Osama Bin Laden, the Saudi dissident sheltered by the Taliban regime in Afghanistan. He, and those who harbour him, are in the dock. This makes it a matter of concern and introspection for the entire Islamic World. It is wrong to suspect the entire Islamic World of being complicit in the crime of a few. Of nearly 1.2 billion Muslims on this planet, most condemned the attack. Only a small fraction of Muslims can be called militant. But Islamic states share a collective responsibility to keep their societies free from the stigma of militancy. With few exceptions, Muslim countries oppose the use of terror to redress even what are perceived as legitimate grievances in the Middle East or elsewhere. They too are victims of international terrorists bent on destabilising the World Order. The terrorist crime of epic proportions on US soil hurt Muslims individually and it hurt the image of Islam. Muslims will mostly pay the price of the colossal political fallout as the crescendo rises to exact revenge for this brazen strike at the heart of America. The expected Western backlash could be devastating.

It is doubtful if the conspirators predicted the swift and robust reaction of the Bush Administration in support of freedom. NATO, spanning the western world, threw its weight behind the US. Even Russia rapidly came on board. A formidable alliance was quickly formed. The sheer scale of it is staggering, bringing together the US, NATO and Russia. The rallying point was the 'menace' of 'militant Islam'. Battle lines were quickly drawn to prepare for a real showdown with Islamic militants. The Muslim world, in contrast, was in disarray, demonstrating an absence of direction in its camp. The inability of the Muslim world to deal with challenges arising out of it showed its disunity. It was unable to stop two devastating fratricidal wars in the last two decades. The first was the Iran-Iraq War and the second, the occupation of Kuwait by Iraq. The tussle for supremacy between the Taliban and their opponents was another debilitating bloodletting. The bottom line, as the terror acts in America showed, was an Islamic world that is unable to safeguard its own interests and image. Militancy in the ranks of Muslims is as much a threat to Islamic societies in the world as it is to Western values. Sadly, there is little concern in the Islamic countries to address the problem. We are yet to come to grips with what prompts a Muslim to become a radical, embrace violence and give up his life. We are yet to come together in guiding young, aggrieved Muslims on the responses possible as meaningful and acceptable forms of protest. The act of terror, of suicide bombing, is abhorrent. It is also an act of desperation, pessimism and of surrender.

The unipolar world has thrown up its own power parameters. The bipolar world allowed militarily and politically weaker countries to exploit the rivalry to their benefit. Now they can no longer do so, they appear to have gone into shell shock. The vacuum created is being filled with the suicide bombers and the practitioners of terror. After the human cost of the suicide bombings for humanity, comes the political cost for the Islamic world. The first casualty is the Palestinian and the second is the Kashmiri freedom struggle. India will use the terror attacks to bolster its own political position. The third casualty will surely be the Taliban although few tears will be shed for them. The fourth casualty is the image of Islam and the effect on Muslims living in the western world.

Perhaps the terror attacks in America are a wake up call to the Muslim community to build a consensus on basic issues. This includes promoting the image of Islam as one of peace disassociated with acts of terrorism. Second, that Islam emphasizes sanctity to the right to life. Third, that Muslims respect fundamental rights and are tolerant to those of other faiths and sects. Living in the United Arab Emirates, it gives me great joy as a believer to see the tolerance allowed to religious worship. People of different faiths built places of worship even though they are not citizens. This is true of other Muslim countries too. Here people worship without fear.

Sadly, this is no longer true in Pakistan. Even as I write, Muslims of the Shia faith are gunned down in the streets of Karachi in the name of militancy. Those of minority faiths, as the Christians, worship in fear. The schools which teach Pakistani Muslims to hate grow, when for me, the message of Islam is of peace, love and tolerance. Those of us who believe in peace, love and tolerance find it hard to reconcile to the Taliban message. This is a movement where cultural heritage is destroyed and the way a woman or a man dresses is dictated. This is a movement that cares little for its children starving in refugee camps. It is a movement that can risk its soil, endanger its friend Pakistan and destabilise the region in the name of giving sanctuary to one man who is not even an Afghan.

America reacted quickly when confronted with a threat to its citizens. Now it is time for Pakistan, to react to the threat to its society from armed groups and their supporters instilling fear.

— The Nation
25-Sep-2001

TERRORISM : THE THREAT OF ASIA

Dear Delegates :

It is a special privilege for me to represent the Pakistan Peoples Party on this occasion: the second Asian Political Parties Conference. I thank the Thai Rak Party and its leader the Prime Minister, for giving us this opportunity to share views and shape the future of our continent. I thank Speaker Jose De Venecia for his efforts to promote Asian unity and thought of action, by bringing us together.

We meet in Thailand at a time of tension, turmoil and terrorism. Terrorism has struck repeatedly over the last month across different parts of Asia, from Indonesia to Kuwait. The era of peace for which we prayed, became a time of war. Tolerance was replaced by terrorism. Democracy in Pakistan was replaced by dictatorship. The reality of suicide bombings has struck my homeland — Christian churches, Muslim mosques, hotels, diplomatic missions are all targets. Scores were murdered. The fanatics struck innocents in Bali. They struck against the French in Yemen. They killed Americans in Kuwait. A military dictatorship in Pakistan failed to stop Al-Qaeda and its Taliban sympathizers from escaping during the bombing of Tora Bora.

Ladies and Gentlemen, the bombing of the World Trade Towers killed people of all races, ethnicities and religions. It killed Muslims, Christians, Hindus and Jews who were working together building worldwide trade communication and cooperation. The biggest challenge before the countries of Asia, indeed the countries of the world is to overcome the forces of terrorism that spread hate, religious intolerance, conflict and bloodshed. At this time of continuing crisis, the Asian people need to understand those who use violence in the name of Islam. They are not clerics. They are criminals. Their actions contradict the teachings of Islam. Islam is committed to tolerance and equality, and it is committed to the principles of democracy. It is ironic that despite the strong commitment to democracy, most Muslims are living in dictatorships. The Muslim people want freedom. They want modernity, diversity and democracy. They want the right to debate, discuss and dissent. Muslim women want to stop their discrimination. The businessmen and women dream of competing freely without the barriers of corruption and cronyism.

Our need is for judges who are not bribed or intimidated; of political parties that are not decimated through state sponsored factionalism. Of political leaders who are not political prisoners or exiles. This is the exact opposite of the fanatical and ignorant message spread by the Taliban and their allies in hate.

Ladies and Gentlemen, the Twenty-first century began with hopes of a golden era of human dignity and fundamental rights. But September 11 ended one period in time and heralded the birth of another. Asia became the new theatre of war. The war in Afghanistan. The threat of war in Baghdad. The violence in the Middle-East. The tension in South Asia. Muslims in Asia, and across the world, suffer because of Al-Qaeda and its war against the West. During the Afghan-Soviet war, Pakistan became the breeding ground for their religious manipulation and exploitation.

My government restored law and order to our cities under assault from terrorist attack. We restored the writ of government. We stopped Pakistan from being declared a terrorist state. We rescued it from bankruptcy and collapse. So they organized and financed schemes to topple my government. They destabilized democracy in Pakistan .

Ladies and gentlemen, these fanatics' greatest fear is democracy, diversity and modernization. It was to the cloisters of democracy and equality that I devoted my attention as Prime Minister of Pakistan. My government modernized Pakistan introducing optic fibre communications, cellular telephones, satellite dishes, Internet and computer literacy programmes. Pakistan integrated into the global economy that the fanatics fear. We became one of the ten emerging capital markets of the world, attracting billions of dollars in foreign investment, particularly in power generation. It was a transformation that was bringing Pakistan into the modern era as a model of what moderate, enlightened Islam could accomplish for its people. To Islam at the crossroads, a democratic Pakistan was one fork in the road, dictatorship the other.

With the eclipse of democracy in Pakistan in 1996, the Taliban seized Kabul. They invited in Al-Qaeda allowing it to raise, recruit and train disaffected Muslim Youth from across Asia. Two years after my overthrow , Bin Laden declared war on the West. I am afraid, Ladies and Gentlemen, that the consequences of that elimination of democracy in Pakistan continues to ripple across Asia.

Ladies and Gentlemen, Osama Bin Laden did not emerge suddenly. His movement was long in the making, and it is our responsibility that it must never be allowed to happen again. In our zeal to defeat the Soviets, we failed to work for a post-war Afghanistan built on the democratic principles of coalition, consensus and compromise. The fundamental mistake was that we were not consistently committed to the values of freedom, democracy and self-determination that undermine the basis tenets of terrorism. We must not repeat that mistake again. Democracy and human rights must be the centrepiece of Asian policy at home and abroad. Just as democracies do not make war against other democracies, democracies also do not sponsor terrorism. Those of us who are committed to human rights and democracy abhor terrorism in all of its murderous forms. At this time of political crisis in the world, I urge the Asian political parties to stand for the values and principles of freedom and the rule of law.

The October elections in Pakistan were a mockery of justice. The leaders of Pakistan's major political parties were banned from contesting. Significantly, Mullah Omar's teacher was allowed to contest and enter Parliament. The Pakistan Human Rights

Commission confirmed allegations of rigging. The European Union called the elections flawed. The Commonwealth refused to re-admit Pakistan amidst its members. The White House called this period a transition to civilian rule. The transition must give way soon to full democracy. It must give way to a full transfer of power from the military to the political parties to prevent a resurgence of militancy, extremism terrorism and suicide bombings. Muslim youth in Asia must be motivated to live, rather than kill and be killed.

The rigged elections in Pakistan made the religious parties contenders for power for the first time in Pakistan's history. Since the elections were rigged, I ask myself: why did the Generals permit the religious parties to sweep the Pakistani areas bordering Afghanistan? Perhaps the Generals wanted to tell the world that the choice in Pakistan is a choice between military dictatorship and religious constraint. But there is a third choice: the choice that the people want, the choice that a transparent election can give them: the choice of democracy and development.

Dictatorship does not constrain extremism, it provokes it. Building a moderate, stable and democratic Afghanistan would have marginalized the Taliban and the Osamas of this world before they embroiled parts of Asia in a new struggle shaped by the use of terror. Building a moderate, stable and democratic Pakistan can save South Asia from conflict, bloodshed, extremism, misery and despair. The military regime's October electoral farce must not be allowed to stand. A democratic Pakistan is the world's best guarantee of the triumph of moderation and modernity amongst the Muslims of Asia who stand at the crossroads of our history. Events over the last several months in Delhi, Islamabad and Srinagar underscore the danger.

Ladies and Gentlemen, Kashmir is long considered by the CIA as the most likely place for a nuclear confrontation. Since the overthrow of my government, India and Pakistan thrice came close to war. A military regime was the cinder block to the expansion of extremism in Afghanistan and to a possible nuclear conflict in South Asia. As I stated before, democracies do not go to war against other democracies and democracies do not allow terrorists to operate on their soil. The best and only control for the excesses of extremism, is accountability to the people.

Ladies and Gentlemen, in the dawn of this young century, we Asians fight against terrorism. We fight against dictatorship and intolerance that will confine and constrain and victimize us in the generations ahead. These are difficult times. Freedom is under assault. Democracy is under assault. Poverty, hunger and unemployment increase as terrorism hurts markets. Asian people suffer.

The solutions will not be quick or simple. But Asia shall overcome the obstacles to triumph. As an Asian leader in the Twentyfirst Century the greatest challenge I see is to overcome terrorism. Asians need peace, freedom and free markets to fight poverty, hunger, unemployment and conflict. A brighter future is anchored in peace, in freedom, in equal opportunity and in breaking the chains of fascism and dictatorship. These were the values our forefathers fought for in confronting colonialism. These are the values that can sustain and strengthen us in this new century.

At this historic Asia conference, I urge all Asian political parties to stand by the values of peace, of freedom and of equal opportunity.

Thank you, Ladies and Gentlemen.

— Political Parties Conference Bangkok
22-Nov-2002

Clash of Civilizations

It is a pleasure to meet you today on the island of Cyprus, which is a most appropriate venue to discuss the complex political, cultural, moral and religious intersections between Islam and the West. It was only four years ago that Harvard Professor Samuel Huntington shocked the world with his contentious monograph on the subject entitled "Clash of Civilizations".

As a Muslim woman who has been educated in the United States and the United Kingdom, I was initially appalled by the spectre of inevitable conflict that he outlined. I particularly disagreed with Huntington's unshakable pessimism about the emerging clash between the West and an increasingly self-confident and economically independent Islamic world.

Four years after I heard Prof. Huntington speak at Davos, I have moderated my own initial response to Prof. Huntington's thesis of a clash between civilizations. I do not subscribe to its inevitability, but his article has served as a useful mechanism to bring to the forefront of intellectual attention significant issues that warrant debate.

Whether we like it or not, whether it must be so or not, the world seems to be increasingly looking at the values and mores of the West, and the values and traditions of Islam, as mutually exclusive and confrontational. Let us explore these issues today. The world is a very different place now from what it was just ten years ago. At that point the nuclear threat was omnipresent. The Cold War raged on between the West and the Soviet bloc, reaching a boiling point in the battle for self determination for Afghanistan. It was the common stand of the Islamic world through the Fifties, up to the Eighties that was central to the containment of Communism on the Asian continent. It was the victory of Mujahideen, the Islamic freedom fighters, supported by the forces of freedom all over the world, that extinguished the fading embers of a dying system. Islamic resistance to the Soviets in Afghanistan proved, once and for all, that the Soviet Union could not, with all of its military might, suppress the forces of history and the forces of justice.

Afghanistan proved that might does not make right. Afghanistan proved that at least sometimes, and some place on this earth, right makes might.

I remember vividly my feelings on February 15, 1989 when as Prime Minister of the Islamic Republic of Pakistan I witnessed the final withdrawal of Soviet forces from Afghanistan. The Western and Islamic world jointly celebrated this victory for freedom and for democracy. Little did we realize at that glorious moment, that the victory in Afghanistan would be a catalyst to a curious corollary. The West's interest in, and need for alliance, with the Islamic world would steadily deteriorate with time! Interdependence gave way to indifference. Indifference has, in many ways, been replaced by contempt. Many in the west would like to think of us as terrorists and fanatics. We are neither. Muslims expect nothing from the West but basic respect.

Ladies and Gentlemen, the Communist threat united the Western and Muslim world. The Western world was rich, the Muslim world poor. The alliance between the West and the East led to the transfer of vast resources from one continent to another. In Pakistan alone, we received $4.2 billion worth of military and economic assistance, which sustained our economy. Other Muslim countries saw an influx of finances from one of the two Super Powers. The end of Super power politics heralded the end of the world of aid. Suddenly Muslim countries were economically at a disadvantage. The end of Super Power politics also heralded the end of an alliance. The West no longer needed the Muslim countries to contain communism. But the end of Super Power politics heralded something far more significant: a power vacuum. Each generation and each civilization needs to unite against a common threat. A vacuum cannot remain a vacuum for long. The power vacuum caused by the end of the cold war coincided with a historical economic shift. Since the end of World War II, newly emergent independent nation states had been involved in national reconstruction. While the economies of the West appeared to have reached saturation point, the economies of the Muslim and Confucian world seemed poised for an economic take off.

Resources are finite. Therefore the transfer of resources from one part of the world to another indicates the enrichment of one part at the expense of another. The demise of Communism lifted the strategic blinkers and opened the optic vision of a world of markets. Suddenly the West realized that the inexorable march of history would announce a reversal of roles. Whereas in the past era, the Muslim countries (and Confucian countries) were dependent on the West for territorial security, suddenly the West was on the brink of an era of dependence on Asian/Muslim/Confucian markets. Historical fears reared their heads, for the West meets Islam at the doorway of Europe. Irrespective of whether it looks East or West, it sees the world of Islam. A world that had once knocked on its doors and threatened conquest. The Islamic/Asian World on the other hand, feels let down at the unceremonious way in which the alliance and with it the concurrent economic assistance ended. Conscious of its economic potential, the world of Islam wonders whether the West will allow the principles of Free Trade to work when free trade could mean a disadvantage to a dominant West and an advantage to a rising East.

Many Muslim countries view global values such as child labour, Human Rights, Environment as attempts by the West to erect invisible barriers to prevent free competition. Of course, Muslim countries subscribe to the global values aimed at protecting human rights, promoting the environment and ending child labour. But when they see a West selective in its application of global values, they wonder whether the West wishes to promote a new global partnership or use these values as a tool to tame markets. This is a serious misgiving which needs tackling. Many Pakistanis wonder why the West is vocal about human rights violations in Burma, but silent about human rights violations in Pakistan, Kashmir and other parts of the Muslim world. The Muslim World embraced the economics of deregulation and privatization. Foreign funds were invested in its markets. But now there is a growing fear whether these foreign funds will be used for economic or political purposes - for instance, will contracts be given on merit or will countries be punished with withdrawal of foreign funds leading to erosion of balance of payments if a contract is not given to a favoured company in a favoured country.

I read an article in Vanity Fair (July 1997) that the rise of Kabila in Zaire had something to do with the grant of mining rights to a Western country. Let me give you the case of Pakistan. As Prime Minister I tried to diversify Pakistan markets between the West, the Gulf and East Asia. Although there was a quantum leap forward for Western companies during my stewardship of Pakistan, at least one diplomat considered me a threat to the commercial and agricultural interests of his country, although his country got billions more in contracts during my tenure than in any other. As an Asian and a Muslim I wanted the Gulf and East Asia to have a share of our market. And many in Pakistan believe I paid a heavy price for that.

The West has a vital stake in the markets of the Muslim World. That stake gives rise to fears and insecurities in the minds of Western analysts. The Muslim countries welcome deregulation but also see it as vulnerability, for themselves, to the powerful western companies to dictate contracts or to their countries to dictate a political agenda. This mutual suspicion is at an incipient stage. Prof. Huntington must be credited with scenting it so precisely at a time when the rest of us were caught up in the warm glow of global brotherhood, peace and harmony. To compound the rise of mutual suspicion is the rise of the Information Age. The Information age is dominated by Western cultural moves. These Western moves are at variance with the cultural taste of the Muslim countries. Many in the Muslim countries believe that Western culture is characterized by the indulgent individual. An indulgent individual who puts himself/herself above church, spouse, children. Divorce and drug rates are cited as examples of families falling apart. The East believes that the individual needs to sacrifice individual craving at the altar of the family or the community's needs.

Thus there is a gulf between the perceived roles of individuals in the West and the East. Then there is a threat to the concept of identity. Scholars have written that we are not only moving into a new millennium but into a new age. An age where individuals will be freed from the straitjacket of the nation state itself, where individuals will be able to access hospitals, schools, contacts and contracts through the computer. The global citizen is emerging from the chrysalis. This is change in a big way. And change is always resisted by the status quo.

Therefore the Western dominance in international media threatens the age-old traditions, identities and values in the Muslim world leading to another fault line of suspicion. Does this mean that the civilizations must clash? I believe the tension prints for a clash are there, but that a clash is not inevitable. This is an age of communication. We need better communication between the two worlds. We need not to dictate but to make concessions. We need to show greater sensibility on both sides and we need most of all to develop a universal morality for a global age where the global citizen will emerge. Leaders on both sides of the two civilizations need to show sensibility.

Let me give you an example. Muslims were horrified at the carnage in Bosnia; outraged that the West, which had acted so swiftly in the Gulf War to secure oil supplies, now watched silently as Muslim blood washed the streets of Sarejevo. As Prime Minister, I considered it my duty to help end the ghastly genocide and to reduce a potential gulf between the West and the East. With Prime Minister Ciller of Turkey, I flew to Bosnia to highlight, as Mothers, our concern for the innocent children of Bosnia. I took up the issue with European and American leaders.

I found them receptive, particularly Presidents Clinton, Chirac and Republican leader Bob Dole to my contention that delay in a cease-fire would lead to a backlash in Muslim countries. Our efforts paid off in the form of the Dayton Accord. When I met President Chirac upon his election, he mentioned Bosnia to me, and what I had said to him earlier. Europe and America alerted by a Muslim leader showed the sensibility required to act. Similarly in the case of the genocide in Jammu & Kashmir, my government highlighted the issue. And we were successful. President Clinton's Deputy National Security Advisor told me that when re-elected, President Clinton would focus more intently on South Asia. And that is what is happening now. Sensibility, communication, compromise are the key to building an understanding between the West and Islam.

Many Muslims are perturbed about the manner in which Prime Minister Mahathir has been portrayed in the Western dominated media. There is a perception, whether true or false is irrelevant, that the West is out to get Mahathir. It is no secret that many in the West viewed with dismay the rising deficit in Malaysia and the grandiose projects being undertaken by the government there. However the Muslim perception is not that the Western investors withdrew funds from Malaysia because of an economy going off track. The perception is that Mahathir led the ASEAN fight to include Burma on its economic frequency despite Western warning. And for that he had to be punished. So the signal went out for the Western investors to withdraw funds, send the Malaysian currency into a tailspin and rock the Malaysian economy. I could see the Malaysian storm breaking and had I been Prime Minister I would have tried for Pakistan to promote a greater understanding between the agenda of the West and the agenda of the East. I give this example to illustrate once again that sensibility, communication and a spirit of compromise are necessary to promote a better understanding between Islam and the West in an age of transition, in an age of transfer of resources and in the Information Age.

No doubt the West fears that a growing Muslim world will begin to flex its muscles in two to three decades. But attempts by the West to tame the Muslims through the tools of deregulation and free market vulnerabilities will surely backfire. Rapping the knuckles of leaders who do not fall into line will widen the gulf of understanding. Building bridges of understanding will lead to peace, harmony and stability. One billion Muslims stand at the crossroads today. One road leads to intolerance. Another leads to accommodation. There are voices of madness on both sides. There are those who say Muslims are barbarians who lock up their women. There are others who say the West is decadent, obscene and vulgar. In every society there is an extreme. Men and women of reason in the Information age need to tread the path of moderation for global understanding.

And I come to Cyprus to say that we in the West and in the Islamic World have a choice to make. For we are about to cross, together, into a new century, and into a new millennium. Whether we cross the millennium with acceptance, or fear, is very much in our control. For Islam and for the West, the forces of change, the thrust of modernity and technology, the strength of tolerance, the inevitability of freedom and liberty, and the sanctity of human rights, are all converging on this time — on our generation — providing an extraordinary opportunity to move the world.

In just 791 days from today, the calendar will mark the new millennium. We will have to determine whether this is just a change in date, or a change in attitude, in spirit, in hope. Let us determine to make that choice with reason and pragmatism in the light of an alliance that has ended with the Cold War but left behind the embers of a warm understanding upon which much can yet be built.

Thank you, Ladies and Gentlemen.

— The Centre for World Dialogue CYPRUS
30-Oct-1997

East and West : Can the two Meet?

It is said, "The East is the East and the West is the West. The two shall never meet". The conflicting perceptions on the Middle East highlight the differences between the two worlds. Seen from the prism of the West, as led by the US, the attention is on the Iraqi regime of Saddam Hussain. He is seen as the bad boy of the Middle East.

Following the events of September 11, which saw the worst attacks on the US since Pearl Harbour, US foreign policy is geared towards securing the homeland. Fears that Iraq is building weapons of mass destruction that could hurt US citizens and security is the driving force behind the "Get Saddam" Operation. Vice President Cheney is the latest in a series of US officials visiting the Middle East to secure support for the next US military action after Afghanistan. The signals from the Bush administration are clear. It is not a question of "if". It is a question of "when" the US begins its Middle-East action against Iraq. The lack of Arab support for such action failed to dampen the desire for "regime change" in Baghdad. The outlook in the East, led by the Arab world, is in sharp contrast. For the Arabs, and the larger Muslim world, the threat is Prime Minister Sharon. The Israeli Leader is seen fuelling the flames of fire. If Washington is looking for "regime change" in Baghdad, Tel Aviv is looking for "regime change" in the Palestinian Authority.

Sharon has called President Arafat "the enemy". His soldiers have stormed Arafat's headquarters. His tanks have moved into Palestinian territory. The message is clear: if he could get away with it, Sharon would assassinate the President of the Palestinian people. He says he regrets not doing it earlier. Only US pressure is holding him back so far. In an effort to halt the Middle East violence, President Bush nominated General Zinni as his Special Envoy. The Zinni mission was unable to stem the violent and bloody tide. There is little hope that it can. Maybe the US is waiting for the fighting to reach "exhaustion level" to set the stage for what it considers meaningful talks.

Much debated these days is the Saudi Peace Plan proposed by Crown Prince Abdullah. The Saudi Plan proposes that Israel go back to the 1967 borders in exchange for Arab recognition. The plan was endorsed at the Beirut Arab Summit and is based on the principle of land for peace. Israel is unlikely to accept the plan although it could be a face saving platform to bring the two sides to the negotiating table. Israel feels insecure with the 1967 borders. It dreads the return of the Palestinian refugees and sees its own death in them. Israel even fears its own Israeli Arab population. It seeks to protect the Jewish nature of the Israeli state. In fact, shortly after the Beirut Arab Summit on March 28, 2002 backed the Saudi Peace Plan, Israeli troops smashed into Arafat's Presidential power base. Room to room fighting broke out.

The Israelis are military giants compared to the armed strength of the Palestinian fighters. But the Israeli premise that its superior military force can bring the "regime change" so badly desired by the aging Sharon, floundered on the inability to read the Palestinian mind. It also floundered on the inability to read the Arab mind. The use of military force hardened Arafat's resolve. Offers of exile were spurned by him. He would die defying Israeli might. Arafat has lost his youth. But he has not lost his spirit. Sharon keeps calling the besieged, beleaguered leader "the problem". But for the Arabs, he is the solution. And they are standing behind Arafat. The Arab support for Arafat has yet to translate into international support of the kind that can restrain the Israelis. This is because a powerful segment in America shares Sharon's view that Arafat should go. They hold Arafat responsible for the failure of the Clinton-Barak initiative. They feel that Arafat is too stubborn. They back Sharon in finding a replacement who can be an Anwar Sadat.

Yet if Arafat goes, the future can be more dangerous. Arafat's departure can drive more men and women into the suicide bombing campaign. This can only endanger more Israelis and deny them the security they seek. Some wonder what Israel's goals are. Is it to drive out Arafat and bring regime change? Or is it to trigger a larger war to re-draw boundaries. Two aging men who fought many a battle in the past hold the fate of their people in their hands. One can win even if he dies. The other cannot, even if he kills his main prey. For the Arab world, Sharon's hands are stained with the blood of Sabra and Chattila. For the Israeli people, Sharon is the tough leader who promised them security. But the highest Israeli casualties in recent history characterise his tenure. Arafat was once a peace-maker. Sharon can become one if he gives up the gun for the negotiating table. Sharon's campaign against Arafat has united the Arab world. The Beirut Summit was a clear closing of Arab ranks on two fronts. First, the Arab nations rallied behind President Arafat and the Saudi Peace Plan. Second the Arab nations opposed "action against an Arab nation". Translated it means that the Arab countries are vetoing US goals over Iraq. Their aim is to keep the focus on Sharon's leadership of Israel. To the West, Saddam is the threat to peace. To the East, Sharon is the threat to peace. The Middle East is boiling.

As temperatures rise in the Middle East, it becomes more important to define terrorism. There is unanimity that the September 11 attack on America was an act of terror. There is little unanimity on terrorism in the Middle East. The answer is different depending on race and religion. That the race and religion determines the response makes the Middle East the real threat to world peace. Every action has a reaction that is equal and opposite. The West has military might at an unimaginable level. Smart bombs, Oxygen sucking bombs, predator planes, daisy cutters are new words in military terminology. Israel is depending on machines to protect and shield its interests and keep its casualties down. This has resulted in a reaction where the militarily weak are using the human body. When a person is beyond fearing death, he/she becomes the human bomb. The Palestinian refusal to wither away in the face of a superior military action rests on the willingness to die for the defence of Palestinian rights. They have the backing of a number of critical states.

It is time for the international community to review its policy before the world plummets into a graver crisis. To do that, the international community needs to come up with definitions of terrorism and definitions of wars of national liberation. It also needs to differentiate between conflicts recognised by the United Nations and others, which lack international legitimacy. Civilian deaths are abhorrent and must be rejected. But moral arguments, unfortunately, cut little ice when combatants are locked in mortal conflict. Peace in the Middle East will not come from the gun. Peace can only come through negotiations. Perhaps the Arab League could set-up a Middle East Contact Group to convince the world community. Otherwise the world may well wait for force to exhaust one side. And that would be too tragic.

— 11-Apr-2002

Islam Forbids Injustice Against People, Nations and Women

Madam Chairperson, Mr Secretary General, Distinguished Delegates, Sisters:

Pakistan is grateful to the Government and the people of China for hosting this Conference. We have been deeply touched by the warm welcome and gracious hospitality. I pay a special tribute to the Secretary General of the United Nations and Mrs. Gertrude Mongella, the Secretary General of the Conference, for their tireless efforts in organizing this meeting.

My dear Sisters, Ladies and Gentlemen, there is a moral crisis engulfing the world as we speak, a crisis of injustice and inaction, a crisis of silence and acquiescence. The crisis is caused by centuries and generations of oppression and repression. This conference, therefore, transcends politics and economics. We are dealing with a fundamental moral issue. This is a truly historic occasion. Some 40,000 women have assembled here to demand their rights; to secure a better future for their daughters; to put an end to the prejudices which still deny so many of us our rightful place in society. On this solemn occasion 1 stand before you not only as a Prime Minister, but as a woman and a mother - a woman proud of her cultural and religious heritage, a woman sensitive to the obstacles to justice and full participation that still stand before women in almost every society on earth.

As the first woman ever elected to head an Islamic nation, I feel a special responsibility towards women's issues and towards all women. And as a Muslim woman, I feel a special responsibility to counter the propaganda of a handful, that Islam gives women a second class status. This is not true. Today the Muslim world boasts three women Prime Ministers, elected by male and female voters on our abilities as people, as persons, not as women. Our election has destroyed the myth built by social taboo that a woman's place is in the house, that it is shameful or dishonourable or socially unacceptable for a Muslim woman to work. Our election has given women all over the Muslim world moral strength to declare that it is socially correct for a woman to work and to follow in our footsteps as working women and working mothers.

Muslim women have a special responsibility to help distinguish between Islamic teachings and social taboos spun by the traditions of a patriarchal society. This is a distinction that obscurantists would not like to see. For obscurantists believe in discrimination. Discrimination is the first step to dictatorship and the usurpation of power. A month ago, Pakistan hosted the first ever conference of Women Parliamentarians of the Muslim world. Never in the history of Islam had so many working women and elected representatives gathered together at one place to speak in one voice. As over a 100 delegates from 35 Muslim countries gathered together, I felt an enormous sense of pride that we women had each other for strength and support, across the globe and across the continents to face and oppose those who would not allow the empowerment of women. And, today, I feel that same sense of pride, that we women have gathered together at Beijing, at this ancient capital of an ancient civilization to declare; we are not alone in our search for empowerment, that women across continents are together in the search for self-esteem, self-worth, self-respect and respect in society itself. In distinguishing between Islamic teachings and social taboos, we must remember that Islam forbids injustice. Injustice against people, against nations, against women. It shuns race, colour, and gender as a basis of distinction amongst fellowmen. It enshrines piety as the sole criteria for judging humankind. It treats women as human beings in their own right, not as chattels. A woman can inherit, divorce, receive alimony and child custody. Women were intellectuals, poets, jurists and even took part in war. The Holy Book of the Muslims refers to the rule of a woman, the Queen of Sheba. The Holy Book alludes to her wisdom and to her country being a land of plenty. The Holy Prophet (peace be upon him) himself married a working woman. And the first convert to Islam was a woman, Bibi Khadija. Prophet Muhammad (peace be upon him) emphatically condemned and put an end to the practice of female infanticide in pre-Islamic Arabia. The Holy Quran reads: "When news is brought to one of them, of the birth of a female (child), his face darkens and he is filled with inward grief, with shame does he hide himself from his people because of the bad news he has had. Shall he retain it on sufferance and contempt, or bury it in the dust. Ah! what an evil choice they decide on." (Surah Al-Nahl, Ayat-57, 58, 59)

Ladies and Gentlemen, how true these words ring even today. How many women are still "retained" in their families "on sufferance and contempt" growing up with emotional scars and burdens. How tragic it is that the pre-Islamic practice of female infanticide still haunts a world we regard as modern and civilized. Girl children are often abandoned or aborted. Statistics show that men now increasingly outnumber women in more than 15 Asian nations. Boys are wanted. Boys are wanted because their worth is considered more than that of the girls. Boys are wanted to satisfy the ego: they carry on the father's name in this world. Yet too often we forget that for Muslims on the Day of Judgment, each person will be called, not by their father's name but by the mother's name. To please her husband, a woman wants a son. To keep her husband from abandoning her, a woman wants a son.

And, too often, when a woman expects a girl, she abets her husband in abandoning or aborting that innocent, perfectly formed child. As we gather here today, the cries of' the girl child reach out to us.

This Conference needs to chart a course that can create a climate where the girl child is as welcomed and valued as a boy child, that the girl child is considered as worthy as a boy child. When I was chairperson of the South Asian Association for Regional Cooperation, SAARC declared 1989 as the Year of the Girl Child. Six years later, the girl child's vulnerability continues. And it continues, not because of religion in the case of Pakistan, but because of social prejudice. The rights Islam gave Muslim women have too often been denied. And women are denied rights all over the world, whether developed or developing. All over the world women are subjected to domestic violence. Often a woman does not walk out for she has nowhere to go. Or she stays and puts up with the domestic violence for the sake of her children. We, in Pakistan, have started a public awareness campaign against domestic violence through the mass media to inform women that domestic violence is a crime and to alert men that they can be punished for it. Often women, in many a society are tortured, not only by men, but by women in-laws too, for financial benefits from the woman's family. Sometimes a wife is killed by her husband or in-laws so that they can gain another wife and more dowry.

Dowry system is a social ill against which we must raise our voices and create greater awareness. Women are not only victims of physical abuse, they are victims of verbal abuse also. Often men, in anger and frustration, indulge in the uncivilized behaviour of rude and vulgar language against women. Unfortunately, women at times also use vulgar language to denigrate another woman. So we have to work together to change not only the attitudes of men but the attitudes of men and women. Women have become the victims of a culture of exclusion, poverty, deprivation, and discrimination. Half a billion women are illiterate. Seventy per cent of the children who are denied elementary education are girls.

In Pakistan we are concentrating on primary education for girls to rectify this imbalance. We are concentrating on training women teachers and opening up employment avenues for women. It is my firm conviction that a woman cannot ultimately control her own life and make her own choices unless she has financial independence. A woman cannot have financial independence if she cannot work. The discrimination against women can only begin to erode when women are educated and employed. If my Father had not educated me or left me with independent financial means, I would not have been able to sustain myself or to struggle against tyranny or to stand here before you today as a special guest speaker.

If the girl child is to be valued, if the wife is to say "No" to domestic violence then we owe a special obligation to creating jobs for women. That is why we, in Pakistan, set up in 1989 the Women's Bank. A Bank run by women for women to aid and assist women in setting up their own enterprises, to gain financial independence and with it the freedom to make their own choices. Today 23 branches of the Women's Bank in Pakistan help working women. Our major cities are marked by enterprises set up by women: bakeries, restaurants, boutiques, interior decoration.

We have lifted the ban on Pakistani women taking part in international sporting events. In 1997 we host the Second Muslim Women's Olympics. Special sporting facilities are being set up to encourage participation by Pakistani women in sports. And Pakistani women are playing a significant role in defusing the population bomb in Pakistan. One hundred thousand women are to be trained to reduce Pakistan's population on growth levels and its infant mortality levels. When I visit poverty stricken villages with no access to clean drinking water, it gladdens my heart to see a lady health visitor, to see a working woman amidst the unfortunate surroundings. For it is my conviction that we can only conquer poverty, squalour, illiteracy and superstition when we invest in our women and when our women begin working. Begin working in our far flung villages where time seems to have stood still and where the bullock, not the tractor, is still used for cultivation. Where women are too weak from bearing too many children. Where the daughters are more malnourished than the sons, for the daughters get to eat the left overs. Where villagers work night and day with their women and children, to eke out an existence. Where floods and rain wash out crops and destroy homes. Where poverty stalks the land with an appetite that cannot be controlled until we wake up to the twin realities of population control and women's empowerment. And it is here that the United Nations and its Secretary General have played a critical role.

Distinguished Delegates, some cynics argue about the utility of holding this conference. Let me disagree with them. The holding of this conference demonstrates that women are not forgotten, that the world cares. The holding of this conference demonstrates solidarity with women. The holding of this conference makes us determined to contribute each in our own way, in any manner we can, to lessen the oppression, repression and discrimination against women. And while much needs to be done, each decade has brought with it its own small improvement.

When I was growing up, women in my extended family remained behind closed walls in village homes. Now we all travel to cities or abroad. When I was growing up, women in my extended family all covered themselves with the Burqa or veil from head to foot when we visited each other for weddings or funerals - the only two occasions for which we were allowed out. Now most women restrict themselves to the Dupatta or Chadar and are free to leave the house. When I was growing up, no girl in my extended family was allowed to marry if a boy cousin was not available, for fear of the property leaving the family. Now girls do marry outside the family. When I was growing up, the boy cousin inevitably took a second wife. Now girls do not expect their husbands to marry again. From the norm, it has become the exception to the norm. When I was growing up, women were not educated. I was the first girl in my family to go to university and to go abroad for my studies. Now it has become the norm for girls to be educated at university and abroad when the families can afford it.

I have seen a lot of changes in my lifetime. But I hope to see many more changes. And some of these changes I hope will flow from the Universal Declaration of Human Rights calling for the elimination of discrimination against women. I hope some of these changes will flow from Convention for the Elimination of all forms of discrimination which Pakistan signed last month. Of course there was resistance from many quarters. But we are determined to move forward in fulfilling our dream of a Pakistan where women contribute their full potential.

Distinguished Delegates, as women, we draw satisfaction from the Beijing Platform of Action which encompasses a comprehensive approach towards the empowerment of women. But women cannot be expected to struggle alone against the forces of discrimination and exploitation. I recall the words of Dante who reminded us that : "The hottest place in Hell is reserved for those who remain neutral in times of moral crisis."

Today in this world, in the fight for the liberation of women, there can be no neutrality. But my dear sisters, we have learned that democracy alone is not enough. Freedom of choice alone does not guarantee justice. Equal rights are not defined only by political value. Social justice is a triad of freedom, of equality, of liberty:

- Justice is political liberty;

- Justice is economic independence;

- Justice is social equality.

Delegates, Sisters, empowerment is not only a right to have political freedom. Empowerment is the right to be independent; to be educated ; to have choices in life.

Empowerment is the right to have the opportunity to select a productive career; to own property; to participate in business; to flourish in the market place.

Pakistan is satisfied that the draft Platform for Action of the Fourth World Conference on Women negotiated so far, focuses on the critical areas of concern for women and outlines an action-oriented strategy for the solution of their problems. However, we believe that the Platform needs to address the questions of new and additional resources, external debt, structural adjustment programmes, human rights for women, protection of women entrapped in armed conflicts and the realization of the right to self-determination of the territories still under foreign occupation and alien domination. It must also seek to strengthen the role of the traditional family as the bedrock of the society. Disintegration of the family generates moral decay. This must be arrested. The Platform is disturbingly weak on the role of the traditional family. This weakness can lead to misinterpretation, and even distortion by opponents of the women's agenda. We have seen much progress. The very fact that we convene in Beijing today is a giant step forward. But new clouds darken the horizon. The end of the Cold War should have ushered in peace and an era of progress of women. Regrettably, the proliferation of regional tensions and conflicts has belied our aspirations. As in the past, women and girls have again been the most direct victims of these conflicts-the most helpless, and thus the most abused. The use of rape as a weapon of war and an instrument of "ethnic cleansing" is as depraved as it is reprehensible. The unfolding of this saga in different parts of the world, including Jammu and Kashmir and Bosnia Herzegovina has shaken the conscience of the entire international community. The enormity of the tragedy dwarfs our other issues, urgent though they are. This conference must, therefore, express its complete solidarity with our sisters and daughters who are victims of armed conflict, oppression, and brutality. Their misfortunes must be our first priority.

Madam Chairperson, Ladies and Gentlemen, I come before you to speak of the forces that must shape the new decade, the new century, the new millennium. We must shape a world free from exploitation and maltreatment of women. A world in which women have opportunities to rise to the highest level in politics, business, diplomacy, and other spheres of life. Where there are no battered women. Where honour and dignity is protected in war and conflict. Where we have economic freedom and independence. Where we are equal partners in peace and development. A world equally committed to economic development and political development. A world as committed to free markets as to women's emancipation.

And even as we catalogue, organize, and reach our goals, step by step, let us be ever vigilant. Repressive forces always will stand ready to exploit the moment and push us back into the past. Let us remember the words of the German writer, Goethe : "Freedom has to be re-made and re-earned in every generation"

We must do much more than decry the past. We must change the future. Remembering the words of a sister parliamentarian Senator, Barbara Mikulski, that "demography is destiny", I believe time, justice and the forces of history are on our side. We are here in Beijing to proclaim a new vision of equality and partnership. Let us translate this vision into reality in the shortest possible time.

Thank you Madam Chairperson.

— Beijing
4-Sep-1995

Is Islam Compatible with the West

Honoured Guests, Ladies and Gentlemen,

I thank you for the invitation to return to the Oxford union and for the warm welcome. I am no stranger to this house. And it gives me great pleasure to be the guest of yet another woman president. I spent some of the happiest years of my life as a student at oxford. I was in England when Margaret Thatcher was the first woman to head a major political party, threatening to overthrow a male dominated preserve.

I was determined to do the same in Pakistan. I was told that the Oxford union was a mini house of commons. So I joined the Oxford union. I was told that politics, everywhere in the world, was summed up in two words: push and pull. So I did and became president of the oxford union. And then I went on to become Prime Minister. I see the deputy leader of the Conservative Party, Mr. Alan Duncan, in the audience. We were both at Oxford at the same time. I am grateful to him, and other Oxford friends, who together had my portrait painted for the union. And I see Dr. Charis Waddy, a dear and wise friend and mentor. Her works on Islam and women in Islam remain as my prized possessions.

Madam President, every generation has its secret of success. When I was at Oxford, our motto was, try and try again, unless it is a game of Russian roulette. It seems just like yesterday when I was here and I am tempted to say: Madam President, what are you doing in my chair? You, Madam President, have been unfairly criticized for inviting the famous designer, Stella MacCartney as a guest to the union. I, madam president, was criticized for holding a debate on the topic that this house would rather rock than roll.

By drawing up a menu of serious and lighter debates, Madam President, we have shown the common thinking, the compatibility between two women, of different races, of different cultures and of different continents.

Honourable members, the last time I spoke at the Oxford union, it was nearly twenty-five years ago. I spoke from the cross benches in my farewell debate on the motion that "this house likes dominating women." Today I return to speak on a much more serious issue. The motion before us, that this house believes that Islam is incompatible with the West, is an important one. Six years ago, a Harvard professor began the debate in a city called Davos. I was there when Samuel Huntington shocked the world with his thesis on the clash of civilizations. I did not believe it then. And I do not believe it today.

For fifty years, Islam and the West joined hands in their common struggle against communism. They were united in a common and compatible belief that state control was unacceptable; that the denial of individual liberty was unacceptable to the world community. They were united in a common and compatible belief for a free world and for free markets. My country, Pakistan, was in the forefront of this battle. When the Soviets occupied Afghanistan, Pakistan became a front line state in the battle against communism. Our cities were bombed and our country flooded with refugees. But Muslim Pakistan never wavered in the fight for freedom.

Honourable Members, I oppose this motion. And I oppose it for three reasons:

First, both worlds are built on religious faith and submission before God. Both religions share common features binding followers together: the belief in the day of judgment, in Jesus Christ, in the angel Gabriel, in Moses, in fasting, in meditation, in praying with beads, the rosary or the Tasbeeh. Both religions exhort followers to follow common commandments of good behaviour: to give charity, to stay clear of lying and cheating, to refrain from adultery, to show kindness to those who are disadvantaged.

The difference is that the Islam and the West are at different historical stages. Your battle between church and state has been resolved. Our battle is still to be won. And one billion Muslims are fighting that battle.

The second example I give of the compatibility of the West and Islam is the commitment to democratic values. Yes. To democratic values. I know my country Pakistan has fallen under the shadow of the military. I know that the military regime, like other dictators, is refusing to give a date for elections. But that has nothing to do with Islam. It has everything to do with despotism. Autocrats rule many parts of the Muslim world. But those autocrats reflect their own ambition and power. They do not represent, and cannot reflect, the sentiments of the people of the Muslim world.

Human dignity and respect is at the heart of Islam. If there are political prisoners in Pakistan and elsewhere, if there are witch-hunts against women and minorities, that is not Islam. It is discrimination.

The West cannot turn its back on the world of Islam. The West must support Islam in its battle for political emancipation just as Islam supported the West in its battle for a free world. The Oxford union is a prestigious debating club. Its name is known far and wide. Tonight the Oxford union can send a bold message across, by rejecting this motion.

The third argument I place in proving compatibility between our two worlds, the world of the East and the West, is our common approach to social issues. Issues of divorce, of child custody, of inheritance are as important to families in the West as in the East. In fact, Islam was the first religion to give the right of divorce to women and to ensure that daughters inherited along with the sons. The West came later in giving property rights to women and in recognizing divorce.

Now we lag behind. Poor literacy rates breed ignorance and with ignorance comes fear and superstition. We need the support and understanding of the West in meeting these challenges. In Pakistan and Afghanistan and other parts of the Muslim world, men still kill women in the name of male pride. Our women need the help and support of the West in securing their rights. The Taliban in Afghanistan do a great disservice to women and Islam when they ban women from working. Their ban has nothing to do with Islam. Their ban has much to do with ancient tribal customs and patriarchal values. The women of Afghanistan, and women in other parts of the Muslim world expect moral support from the rest of the world community in their struggle to work and to free choice.

The Afghan clerics and clerics elsewhere tell us that women must be locked behind four walls. But the prophet Mohammed, (peace be upon him) set the example by marrying a working woman. His wife was a successful businesswoman. Clerics tell us that a man can take four wives. They ignore the example of the prophet Mohammed who took but one wife until wife Khadija died. They ignore the example set by Hazrat Ali, who whilst wife Fatima lived, never took a second wife.

The Taliban are wrong when they drape women from head to foot forcing them to wear the purdah. Those who force women into purdah forget that the holy Prophet said that the best is the veil in the eyes.

I, as a Muslim woman, dispute those who say women are inferior to men in Islam. Like millions of other Muslim women, I place faith in the saying of the holy Prophet that men and women are as equal as the teeth in a comb.

I ask this house not to listen to the clerics.

I ask this house to reject a shrill minority that would launch a new crusade.

Honourable Members, this house would shrink in horror if Milosevic was described as the face of the West. Muslims shrink in equal horror when Osama bin Laden is described as the face of Islam. Muslims are affronted when they are rashly called terrorists. There is no such thing as a Muslim terrorist or a Christian terrorist. A terrorist is a terrorist irrespective of race or religion.

Now there are peace talks breaking out in Northern Ireland. But when I was studying here, all I heard was that the IRA were terrorists. Causes of conflicts arise when people of the same faith fight. They arise when people of different faiths fight. But we do not say that Catholics and Protestants are incompatible. We do not say that Germany and France are incompatible or Germany and Britain because they once had a conflict and fought a war. When I was a student, I did not hear Protestants call Catholics terrorists. And I do not like it when I hear Muslims called terrorists. I am a Muslim who risked her life with Christians fighting terrorists. I did that because I saw no incompatibility between us in building a world free of violence. I was Prime Minister when Ramzi Yusuf, the man who bombed the World Trade Center, was extradited from Pakistan. Ramzi Yusuf, the man who bombed the World Trade Center, twice tried to assassinate me. He did not make a distinction in trying to kill someone from the Islamic world or the Christian world. He would not need to do that if Islam and the West were incompatible. Honorable members: throughout my life, I have subscribed to universal values of love and brotherhood and harmony. I have friends in the East and the West. I see myself as a bridge between two cultures and two worlds. My world is a world united by common concerns. I see a world worried about gender issues, education, crime. And when my friends and I meet over coffee, whether in the East or in the West, we talk about the same issues: our children, our expanding waistlines, our rising blood pressure and other such important issues. Whether we like it or not, we are all cut from the same cloth. Wherever we live, our concerns are the same. Of course there are strident voices that we hear all too often in the media. But these are the voices of the extremists. These are not the voices of men and women of good will. I see Muslims here in England sit in the House of Lords and in the House of Commons. Would that be possible if Islam and the West were incompatible? I see Labour and Conservatives woo Muslim votes in Bradford, Birmingham, Manchester, Luton, Newham, Blackburn,

London. Would that be possible if the two were incompatible? I do not believe that we are incompatible. We are created by one God. Our religions tell us that we are the common descendants of Adam and Eve. Our love of Jesus and his mother Mary are a shared love. The prophet of the Muslims, Mohammed, (peace be upon him) preached the message of tolerance. Muslims are enjoined to greet each other with the words, peace be upon you. The search for peace is a universal search. It is your search and my search. It is a sign of our compatibility. Those who seek to construct walls of incompatibility do a great disservice. They are prisoners of an ugly past. This house is not. This house can, and should, pull down the walls of bigotry, intolerance and prejudice. And this house can do it tonight by rejecting the motion that Islam and the west are incompatible. I urge you to do so.

Thank you.

— London
20-Feb-2000

Attack on Iraq

Tony Jones: Benazir Bhutto, detailed plans of US led invasion of Iraq have now been leaked to the media. Were you Prime Minister of Pakistan still would you be bound to support a US invasion?

Benazir Bhutto, Former Pakistani Prime Minister: Well it would depend very much on what the Arab league decided. Pakistan tends to go with the Arab league, and if I were Prime Minister of Pakistan, I'd back the decision of the Arab league.

Tony Jones: Let me ask you this, if the US were to go it alone, without widespread support from the Arab league or other Islamic states, what would be the repercussions do you think in the Islamic world?

Benazir Bhutto: I think it's better for the US to plan its actions with the support of the United Nations. The United Nations is an international body and the United Nations has supported actions in Bosnia. It supported actions in Afghanistan. It supported the war against terror. So I think it's much better to go behind the tool or instrument of an international law and I think if the United States goes to the United Nations it will find it will make it much easier for its own friends to support its actions.

Tony Jones: How do you feel about the way the United States has co-opted General Musharraf, ostensibly a military dictator as a key ally?

Benazir Bhutto: Well obviously we are concerned and a little bit apprehensive that the co-option should not lead to the promulgation or sustenance of military dictatorship in our country, but we do understand that General Musharraf played a role in the events after September 11 and we do understand that the United States wants to send a message that it stands by its friends. We can understand that.

Tony Jones: You have suggested that America should be very careful here. That their support for Musharraf is something like their support in another era for the Shah of Iran?

Benazir Bhutto: Well there are concerns that we have- they're fears and they are unfounded fears at the present, but nonetheless, Pakistan had an experience with him. He used the US, he used the critical importance of Afghanistan to the United States to bolster his own dictatorship and Pakistanis fear that this history could repeat itself. We believe that democratisation can help Pakistan and the larger world community, including the United States.

After all, the democratisation of Pakistan will mean the success of the politics of moderation and of pluralism. Whereas, to our minds, dictatorship could produce a backlash. The world walked away from Afghanistan once before and we had in result the Taliban and al Qaeda. I think it's important for the world not to walk away from democracy in Pakistan. Otherwise we could have some terrible consequences.

Tony Jones: Are you essentially saying, like the Shah of Iran, General Musharraf may be in danger of being overthrown in Islamic revolution.

Benazir Bhutto: Partially, yes, partially I am saying that if the democratic process is stifled the underground militants could emerge as the only opposition to Musharraf. That there could be discontent, because he would be seen as a dictator bolstered by external forces. So I think that it's very important for the US to show appreciation for Musharraf, yes, but at the same time to stand by its very firm commitment to the democratic process and to transparent elections in Pakistan and not to put all its eggs in one basket.

Tony Jones: Let me ask you this, going back into history a bit, do you take any responsibility yourself for the rise of fundamentalist Islam in Pakistan? After all, it was during your second term as PM that Pakistan sponsored the birth of the Taliban, sent them into Afghanistan.

Benazir Bhutto: Yes, that's partially true and certainly there is a perception. In retrospect, having seen what the Taliban did, I would say that was a wrong decision by our part. At the same time, as PM of the Pakistan, I ensured the Taliban could not control the whole of Afghanistan. I persuaded them to sign an agreement, for a broad-based understanding, sponsored by the United Nations, but when my brother was killed and my government was going, my policies fell apart and I was thrown out soon after. Had I been in power, I doubt the Taliban would have taken Afghanistan or invited Al-Queda, or permitted it to use its territory for acts of terror overseas.

Tony Jones: But you do accept responsibility for allowing the Taliban to be born, for having them armed by Pakistan sent into Afghanistan to sponsor a revolution?

Benazir Bhutto: No, I would like to say that I never permitted the arming of the Taliban and if this was done, it would have been done against state policy and orders. I did make the error of allowing political support for the Taliban in Kandahar. I gave that political support because I thought it was important to influence them and prevent them from trying to take Kabul alone on their own. I encouraged them to hold negotiations with other key players, which they did, and they were about to sign an agreement on November 3 for a broad-based government, but my government was overthrown on November 4, and after that, the Taliban were never reined in.

Tony Jones: At the same time this was happening, once again during the years you were PM, Pakistan had a secret policy of developing nuclear weapons.

Now, were you aware of that when you were PM?

Benazir Bhutto: Pakistan did have a nuclear programme, and I worked very closely with President Bush senior to get a framework for that nuclear programme in place. Under the framework of that nuclear programme, Pakistan undertook not to make nuclear weapons unless its security was threatened.

That agreement of mine with the US was upheld and sustained by my successors. In 1998, that policy broke. India detonated nuclear devices and Pakistan followed suit, but until that time, the agreement that we reached with the United States, that Pakistan would not put together a nuclear device, did hold.

Tony Jones: But it takes a very long time indeed for a military industrial complex to develop a nuclear weapon. There's clear intelligence that was actually happening during your time in government. Were you not aware of it?

Benazir Bhutto: I was not aware of it. Never was a report put to me during my terms in office from 1993 to 1996 that such a device was being put together or a weaponisation was coming. I was in close touch with many leaders of the G8. They used to come and meet me and we used to discuss different issues, but this issue was not discussed at all during my second term.

Tony Jones: Was the military, do you believe at that time, the military intelligence out of control, out of your control in particular?

Benazir Bhutto: Yes, military intelligence was totally out of my control. I don't believe that power was ever transferred in Pakistan fully. The military and the military intelligence could plot and plan and conspire against the civilian PM and destabilise it. It could adopt individual policies of its own. I, as PM, if I came to know of something, I could restrain them and pull them in, but I was unable to promote or demote or punish any officer that was destabilising my government, leave alone violating government policy.

This is why I believe General Musharraf must not take us to the past. If decision-making in Pakistan is going to be confined to a few individuals, I'm afraid the hardliners will be calling the shots.

Tony Jones: The interesting thing here, if you look at Pakistan from today's perspective, if you look at it during that time, it could easily sound like a member of the axis of evil, secretly developing nuclear weapons, giving birth to the Taliban and sponsoring an Islamic insurgency in Kashmir.

Benazir Bhutto: Yes, it could appear like that, but that would be a very superficial perception.

I think one needs to look deeper at the issues. I agree that we in Pakistan face a lot of problems. There is the issue of nuclear proliferation. After the events of September 11, there's a great degree of concern about nuclear proliferation.

Pakistan needs to put into place checks to satisfy the international community that rogue elements or terrorists will not be able to access Pakistan's nuclear programme. We also have to have a clear direction about our future. Whether our future will be one where militants call the shots or whether our future will be one anchored in the principles of freedom, fundamental human rights and free markets. I think Pakistan needs the support of the international community in ensuring that we follow a path of moderation and progress, and what happens in Pakistan has a tremendous impact on the rest of the Muslim world. So I think that the battle that is taking place in Pakistan has echoes in the much larger world community.

Tony Jones: Let me ask you this. Have you given up any hope of going back to stand in the next elections in Pakistan?

Benazir Bhutto: No, I have not given up hope. I want to contest the elections in Pakistan. I believe my leadership changed much in the past and can change more in the future. I agree there were areas of weakness in my leadership. I've had 5.5 years to reflect on that. I have the experience. My party has the experience.

We've learnt from our mistakes and I think we could really contribute to Pakistan's well-being as well as to peace in the region and fighting terrorism overseas.

Tony Jones: One last question. Last week you failed to appear in court to answer corruption charges. You were sentenced to three years in jail. Can you imagine that being set aside to allow you to take part in these elections?

Benazir Bhutto: Well, General Musharraf made a new law with retrospective effect called the absentee law. He had me sentenced under the absentee law. That sentence was wrong. I was present in court through my defence lawyer. My defence lawyer wanted to answer the charges, which are politically motivated.

We were denied the right to defence and we'll be challenging that in a court of law. It depends what the court of law decides. I hope they will decide in my favour, but I'm concerned at the same time of the pressure that is put on the courts by the military regime. The military regime sacked the Chief Justice of Pakistan, and junior judges think they can be sacked too. I hope, though, one of them will have the conscience to put aside this grave injustice to me.

— Australian Broadcasting Corporation LATELINE
Late night news & current affairs TV Program Transcript
Broadcast: 17-7-2002

On Islam

The microcosm of America that was destroyed on September 11 – people of all races, ethnicities and religions – is everything the extremists abhor: men and women, working side by side as equals; Muslims, Christians, Jews and Hindus, together building worldwide trade and communications. America is a symbol of what can be to millions of oppressed people all over the world. America means everything to those deprived of human rights and the rule of law. America symbolizes modernity, diversity and democracy, and it is these three things which are the fanatics' worst fears.

At this time of continuing crisis, the American people and their leaders must understand that those who would use violence and terror in the name of Islam are heretics and hypocrites. They are criminals, not clerics. Their actions contradict the teachings of the Holy Prophet of Islam, about whom it is written, "Whenever the prophet of God sent forth a detachment, he said to it, 'Do not cheat or commit treachery, nor should you mutilate or kill children, women, or old men.'" And there is a specific prohibition in Islamic law that bans killing by stealth and targeting a defenceless victim in a way intended to cause terror in a society.

It grieves me that included in the list of the victims of the perfidy of September 11 is the image of Islam across the world. Our religion is not what these people preach; in fact, it is the opposite. Islam is committed to tolerance and equality, and it is committed by Koranic definition to the principles of democracy. It is ironic that despite the strong commitment to democracy in Islam, most Muslims today are living in dictatorships. The Muslim people want freedom, and they need support in their search for political, economic and social empowerment. Much like the people of the communist world of the past, the Muslim people today are hostages in totalitarian regimes that flourished during the days of the Cold War.

In the West, there is often talk about the "Muslim street." The street most often seen here on television is the street of fanaticism whipped into a frenzy. But there is another Muslim street. It is a silent street of women who suffer discrimination in every aspect of life. It is a silent street of students who are not educated. It is a silent street of businessmen and businesswomen who are not allowed to compete freely. It is a silent street of human rights activists who are jailed, political parties that are decimated, and political leaders who are either prisoners or exiles. It is the street of the people constrained by the totalitarian powers of the state. It is the street of the future in the chains of present-day intolerance, ignorance and dictatorship. And it is the street far more likely to explode than the street of the religious extremists.

As I said, in Islam, dictatorship is never condoned. Nor is cruelty. In fact, according to Islam, those who commit cruel acts are condemned to destruction. Irrespective of the ignorance reflected in the actions of fanatics, there are three key princples in Islam that point to democracy: consultation, known as shura; consensus, known as ijmaa; and independent judgement, known as ijtihad. Today the Muslim people are searching for freedoms that exist in other parts of the world. They are searching for forms of government that are representative and accountable. Just as Christians and Jews have the Bible to guide them, Muslims have the Holy Koran. The Koran makes it clear that the principal operations of the democratic process – consultation between elected officials and the people and accountability of leaders to the people — are fundamental to Islam. The Holy Koran says that Islamic society is contingent on mutual advice, through mutual discussions, on an equal footing. Consultation under the Koran demands that public decisions are made by representative officials. Consensus provides the basis for majority rule. And according to Muslim scholars, the legitimacy of the state depends upon the extent to which state organization and power reflect the will of the Muslim people.

Now this is the exact opposite of the fanatical, ignorant message that is spread by bin Laden, the Taliban and their allies in hate. These despots are the enemies of all civilizations. The terrorists who attacked America were not fighting for Islam. They were fighting for themselves. Their goal is to establish interlinked theocracies of ignorance that they can control for their own political ends. They are the enemies of Western principles, and they are the enemies of all humanity. In the end, they will be defeated. And, just as something more than arms defeated Communism, the terrorists will ultimately be defeated by basic and universal human nature. In the words of the former Czech president, Vaclav Havel, in his essay "The End of the Modern Era": "Communism was not defeated by military force, but by the human spirit, by conscience, by the resistance of man to manipulation."

Terrorism will fail unless we fall into the psychopaths' trap. Professor Samuel Huntington of Harvard wrote of an inevitable clash of civilizations between the West and the Islamic world. Ladies and Gentlemen, this clash is far from inevitable, unless we make it so...

The Military Crisis in South Asia, Terrorism and The Political Situation

Members of the Pakistani Community, Honoured Guests, Ladies and Gentlemen:

I thank Mr. Shahzaib Hassan for providing the opportunity for me to meet with you this afternoon.

I want to discuss with you the political situation in Pakistan, and Pakistan's position as we cross into a new political era. For those of us who fought and died for democracy in Pakistan, the events since November 1996 have been painful beyond comprehension. A democratic country has once again fallen prey to military rule. It was in November 1996, whilst the world concentrated on the American presidential elections, that democracy in Pakistan was derailed. On that November night, the President ordered the tanks to move and surround the Prime Minister's house. I was arrested along with my ailing mother and my three small children, all under the age of eight.

Parliament was dissolved. Midnight raids took place. Supporters were arrested and taken away to torture cells. Trumped up charges of corruption were used to justify the President's one man decision to overthrow the popularly elected government. A government elected by the people was overthrown despite enjoying the confidence of the people in the streets and the parliamentarians in the House. The brutal demise of an elected government was followed by a partisan interim administration. The people of Pakistan boycotted the sham elections held in 1997. Only eight percent voted for my successor. The dark road to military rule had begun. The presidential action of subverting democracy brought to power a government which lacked the support of the masses. Moreover, it reflected the views of the establishment rather than the provinces and people of Pakistan.

A controlled democracy was in place. Such a controlled democracy had been assiduously sought since General Zia lifted martial law and held non-party elections in 1985. Yet, the creation of artificial leaders through manipulation of the electoral process puts them at odds with the genuine representatives of the people.

This cycle of clash has been a part of our history since the fifties when Prime Minister Liaquat Ali Khan was killed. The artificial leadership, lacking democratic legitimacy always falters, giving way to military rule. The cost in social terms of this political manoeuvring has been extremely high. It has led to geographical disintegration, social chaos and fiscal collapse. When the fiscal or geographical collapse reaches a point of no return, there is a strategic withdrawal by the establishment and elections are held. As soon as the economic corner is turned, or unity strengthened, the genuine leaders are once again set aside and an artificial leadership created.

The Bhutto and Benazir cases are two examples in recent history. Sometimes the artificial leaders grow too big for their boots and they are thrown out too. The Junejo and Nawaz episodes are two recent examples. Both these leaders began to distance themselves from their political benefactors and found themselves out of power.

The right to govern ought to vest in the people of the country. Power can, and should shift to the people which, as the repositories of Allah's trust, are the rightful masters of the country.

The lesson of the twentieth century is that democracy works and the worst of democracies is better than the best of dictatorships. In Pakistan we hear that controlled democracy is better because real democracy brings back discredited politicians. I have little sympathy with this view. In democracies across the world, from the United States to Bangladesh and beyond, an election always brings back roughly the same number of elected representatives. In the United

States, Senators Kennedy, Brownback and Feinstein keep getting elected. Yet, those who disagree with their policies do not say that a law should be made in the name of anti corruption, which violates every principle of natural justice, to eliminate the winnable candidates with a view to bringing forward nonentities who cannot otherwise enter the Parliament. This is not democracy. This is tyranny.

We as a nation need to respect the human rights of ordinary Pakistanis, the poor and the wretched. It is they, rather than the elite, who have a right to determine the destiny of the country. If the people are allowed to run their own affairs, democracy will strengthen. Not overnight, but in due process. History cannot be rushed nor evolution expedited. Efforts to do so only delay the process further. Democracy is more than elections. Democracy is, first, a system where the judiciary is independent and impartial. It cannot function when a handful of judges disrupt the political process to fulfil a political agenda. It is hoped that the superior judiciary will rise to the challenge before it. Certainly the prayers of the nation are with them in enhancing the role of the justice system through fair and impartial dispensation of justice.

Yet, in the last decade that role has not been played by a few in the judiciary. I will give only three examples. First the legal grounds for upholding dissolution were changed on political grounds to achieve political purposes four times since 1985. Second, a crisis was created by Chief Justice Sajjad in collusion with President Leghari to undermine the PPP Government. Third, the assault of the Supreme Court of Pakistan was condoned to achieve a political objective.

Too often, the judiciary, instead of the electorate, has been seen as the arbitrator of political disputes. This has the unfortunate result of politicizing them for which they alone cannot be blamed. It is time for us to accept the people as the arbitrators of political disputes even if we do not like their verdict. Another challenge before the Bar and the Bench is to address issues of corruption when they arise with respect to some members within the judiciary. The judiciary is an independent organ of government and it is inappropriate for the

Executive to decide its propriety. However, there is a need for the Bar and the Bench to formulate a law which Parliament can pass addressing issues of appointments and accountability. Such a law, emanating from the heart of the judiciary, can help us build a better Pakistan.

First is the question of Accountability. This noble objective has too often been reduced to a farce in the country. Today a convicted criminal leads the prosecution for the military regime along with other aides convicted in the seventies for treason. Has any other country employed convicted criminals to prosecute elected leaders? I believe not. Can a process sullied by convicted criminals be credible? I believe not.

Second, the accountability law itself is a criminal law which seeks to rob the citizen of every fundamental right. The attempt to violate the basic principles of natural justice in the pursuit of politically motivated cases reeks of political persecution.

Third, the chief investigator has already prejudged politicians as corrupt. In the same breath, he confesses he has no evidence of wrongdoing. We must ask when, in a civilized society a person is innocent unless proved otherwise, we have allowed ourselves to degenerate to the savage state where elected leaders are prejudged and maligned.

The concept of justice is based on the due process of law. Unfortunately, in our country we have allowed intelligence leaks to the media about corruption to be treated as the gospel truth. When we have already tried and convicted innocent persons at the bar of public opinion, when we have demonized them immorally and inhumanly, how do we retreat when we discover that the stories were untrue?

We ought to withdraw in the face of absence of evidence. Instead we resort to obstructing the path of justice by torturing individuals to commit perjury or tampering with evidence. Accountability becomes a farce.

Which brings me to the fourth point: what then is the way forward? The way forward is to recognize that the Parliament is an independent organ of government and parliamentarians ought to submit themselves before a parliamentary investigation when questions of impropriety are raised. In this connection, the PPP had moved a bill in October 1996 asking Parliament to make lawful a committee of parliamentarians to examine questions of wrongdoing. To keep the balance, the government and opposition were to have equal representation with each side being provided access to investigators and prosecutors of their choice to examine allegations about the other side. An adverse finding was to be sent to the courts for trial.

This idea may or may not be acceptable. The important aspect is that parliamentarians need to come up with an equitable consensus that prevents witch-hunts but allows for proper investigation of allegations of wrongdoing. The cardinal principles of natural justice and due process must be upheld to end corruption and prevent political abuse.

This brings me to the fifth point with regard to the present accountability law. It is selective and a selective law is a bad law. Parliamentarians and the military may like to keep their friends outside the scope of investigation. Unfortunately, neither Islam, nor morality nor law provide for this. We live in an age of transparency and that means all in executive positions must submit themselves to accountability. Thus an accountability law for the executive needs to ensure that all officials, civil and military, are made accountable when allegations of wrongdoing are raised. It is not sufficient to blame civilian leaders for kickbacks in military purchases. Those who drew up the plans for such purchases have played the instrumental role and must bear responsibility.

I now come to a third aspect which needs national attention: this is an independent Election Commission. In the past, our people believed that when elections were held they would have the right to elect a leadership of their choice. Yet hope for tomorrow and confidence in the election process was killed with the brutal rigging in the elections of 1990 and 1997. This has led to a cynicism in Pakistan which is dismaying. It has also created a dangerous vacuum. It threatens the collapse of the political order and the rise of regional, ethnic and sectarian forces. It is a prescription for disaster. It began with General Zia's keenness for desired results. This is a keenness which has only grown with time and must be reversed if our country is to gain stability and to prosper.

First, we need to investigate charges that intelligence operatives bankrolled campaigns of favourites in the elections. Second, we need to ask why the electoral lists of 1995, stayed by the Supreme Court, have still not been decided. Third, we need to ask for an investigation into reports that results taken to the Election Commission are hacked into and changed. Fourth we need to insist on joint electorates, multi identification forms, computerized and printed electoral lists and polling stations and results announced by Returning Officers at the districts without interference by a central control. Results in 1988 were announced within two hours. Results in 1997 took two days. Fifth, we need to ask why cases before the courts, of election rigging, are not decided within six months as mandated by law. Those who should have decided these matters need to have a discussion about it with the Bench and the bar.

This brings me to the fifth aspect of our national trials: the role of the intelligence agencies. There is a perception that the intelligence agencies have their own domestic and foreign policy agenda. How far these perceptions are true cannot be said. Yet there are repeated reports of the intelligence having destabilized governments, interfered with state functioning, manipulated the electoral process and spread untrue stories of corruption. These perceptions need to be addressed.

Sixth, the end of the cold war has changed the regional picture. During the cold war, the West gave military and financial assistance to Pakistan to face the threat of communism. We took the money and the weapons to fight India. This resulted in a policy of parity. We did what India did. A bomb for a bomb and a missile for a missile.

A CTBT signature for a CTBT signature. The last decade has shown that policy is no longer valid. The end of Western financial and military aid has helped the Pakistani economy collapse. Today it is threatening the existence of the nation state itself. Nations rise and fall, not on outdated notions of military conquest, but on modern realities of economic viability. Pakistan is too great a nation to collapse because its elite was blinded to new realities.

It is time for us to build internal cohesion through an appraisal of our domestic and regional situation. In this connection, first, defence expenditure needs to be rationalized and submitted for parliamentary audit. If open audit is difficult, a closed audit by the parliamentary defence committee is necessary. Second, the centralized state needs to be stripped and power redistributed through provinces and local bodies. In this connection, the subjects of the concurrent list must be implemented as per the constitutional requirements. Moreover, a package and time frame prepared to accept the constitutional provision that GST is a provincial resource which is unfairly being taken by the Centre. There is much more which can be decided through a consensus between the political leaders of the four provinces, Azad Kashmir and Northern Areas. Third, local bodies can be made independent constitutionally so that a plurality of power is possible. Appointment of minorities and women to the judiciary is important as are the issues of joint electorates and increasing the indirect participation of women in Parliament through reserved seats. These are all issues which need a constitutional majority and it is my earnest hope that when the time is ripe the people should give the PPP one real chance at social reform.

The seventh message I would like to give is the message of brotherhood and harmony. Quaid-e-Awam Zulfikar Ali Bhutto had predicted that his assassination would bring about a vertical and horizontal polarization. That has happened. To overcome it, we Pakistanis, irrespective of who is in power and irrespective of which province or ethnic group we come from, need to reach out to each other and reconcile. We do not need to agree on issues. After all politics by its very nature is diverse. But we need to show a unity of approach in formulating amongst ourselves laws, which enhance justice and human dignity and policies which unite rather than divide.

Whether it is the military or the intelligence or the Muslim League or the Pakistan Peoples Party or one of the other parties, or the bureaucracy, the judiciary, we are all players in Pakistan. We need to leave the river of hate and climb upon the bank of confidence to appreciate that our hatred only breeds more hatred. I come from a land of Sufis and believe that love begets more love. When I look back upon the economic achievements of the PPP government, I often think it was achieved because we had the love of the people and were remembered in prayers.

Pakistan was a land of plenty but four years ago. There was so much money that the jobs of our people were safe and the youth had opportunities of employment. The ILO in its report concluded that the largest job generation increase took place under the PPP government. Literacy was increased by one third from 26 per cent to 35 per cent. Health facilities were improved for which the World Health Organization gave the PPP a gold medal.

The military were given whatever was required for defence, whether it was planes, or tanks or submarines. Our soldiers and officers won honour for Pakistan in the battlefields of Bosnia and other trouble spots of the world battling for peace. Per capita income increased. What was achieved in 12 years, PPP achieved in 3 years. Per capita income rose by $57 from $431 to $488. After the fall of the PPP government, per capita income fell by fifty dollars. Growth rate tripled during the PPP government reaching more than six percent. Now it is halved. The average rate of growth of investment reached its highest peak in 1995-96 at about 16.42 per cent. It fell to 4.5 per cent in 1998-99. Foreign Investment poured into the country in billions and now it has dried up to a few millions. Our stock exchanges, which once boomed with fifteen new issues annually, are now silent. Our bazaars, which hummed with activity, are caught in a deep recession. Our peasants, who saw the transfer of resources with good prices for their crops have seen poverty increase as their produce fails to get right prices.

Pakistan's foreign exchange reserves reached their highest peak in 1995. It increased to almost $ 3 billion from a low of $3 hundred million in 1993. If we take out rescheduled loan affects, currently it is minus $1.4 billion Pakistan's total reserve, consisting of gold, SDR and foreign exchange reached its highest peak ever in 1995. It was $3730 million which halved to $1737 in 1998. PPP government recovered Rs.18 billion bad debt in cash without arresting even one man. It restructured Rs. 17 billion with solid guarantees demonstrating that extreme methods, which destroy business confidence, are unnecessary.

It is proposed that a new credit rating system be introduced and a foreclosure law be passed for the purpose of bad debt and good debt.

Whilst we take satisfaction in the economic performance of the past, we look to the future. The future can improve by correcting the distortion of the national picture which took place on November 4, 1996. Derailed democracy needs to be back on track.

This has not been an easy time for the country, but I want you to know that it has not been an easy time for me, my family or my party. As a leader I may have committed mistakes but the politically motivated charges of corruption against my husband and myself are without substance. My daughter was three when my husband was arrested and taken away. Two days ago, she turned seven. In the last four years, I and many others, were stripped of our right to a good name, to a fair trial, to defence witnesses, to representation. Our basic rights were criminally snatched.

I derive great satisfaction from independent jurists, including two American former Chief Justices, who have opined that neither my husband nor I could have been convicted in an American Court. Is it not sad that American jurists have to say this about a Pakistani Prime Minister?

Let me give you but a small glimpse into the living hell in which we and our supporters were thrown. I read to you from the *Financial*

Times of November 12, 1999. It is the story of how a British citizen was kidnapped, tortured and threatened with death if he did not commit perjury against the parliamentary leader of the Opposition and her husband. According to the *Financial Times*, Ashby's " life was repeatedly threatened. He was deprived of sleep, beaten and spat upon. On one occasion, a revolver was held to his head; on another he was subjected to a game of Russian Roulette. During his detention, Mr Ashby said, he was taken on several occasions to see Senator Saifur Rehman. On one occasion, the senator threatened him and demanded a confession of corruption: "I want Benazir Bhutto. I want Asif Ali Zardari," he said. Mr. Ashby had never met Ms Bhutto or her husband. On another occasion, when Mr. Ashby refused to co-operate, the senator entered the room screaming, eyes blazing "looking like the devil ". "He threatened to throw me in jail, torture me, beat me. He said it would cost only 30 rupees (about forty pence) to get me killed," he said. This is just a glimpse of the wrong things which were done and have still not been corrected. Is it not time that we stopped criminalising every Prime Minister that takes office? I suffered immensely when Nawaz Sharif was Prime Minister. What he did to me was wrong and what is being done to him is wrong. Two wrongs do not make a right. Neither the PML nor the Nawaz family has contacted me. However, I do feel the sufferings of the women folk of the Nawaz family.

Ladies and Gentlemen, I worry for the country. We can hear the sound of the guns in the distance. Relations with India have plummeted. Guns are fired daily. Bomb blasts and incidents of sabotage have increased. There is a threat to Pakistan and we must awaken to it and save our country from calamity. General Musharraff is uniquely placed to do that. He can abandon the path of division and choose the path of unification. He can take the lead in inviting all the political parties to discuss a timetable for the restoration of Democracy and build a consensus. If he has the vision to look beyond the political orphans who surround him, he can win the approval of the Pakistani people and the international community. The euphoria which greeted his regime can be revived if he is able to give confidence to the people of justice, fairness, freedom and the rule of law.

For every ruler, an exit strategy is the most important strategy. General Musharraf, forced to seize power in circumstances beyond his control, needs to have the courage to call all political leaders to arrive at an agreement to restore democracy. In so doing, Pakistan can once again start its journey to recapture the lost dreams of its founding fathers.

— London
5-Feb-2000

The Difference Between Right and Wrong

Dictatorship breeds despair in society leading to a pessimistic outlook and a disenchanted people. Disenchantment, in turn, leads to despair, demoralisation and a defeatist attitude. This defeatist attitude is growing in Pakistan and in a number of countries that share, with Pakistan, a common history. A history of contradictions where freedom from colonialism was quickly replaced by domestic tyranny.

The movement against colonialism in the last century was led by brave and principled leaders. They created a resilient society inspiring people to greater heights and bigger sacrifices. Value systems seep through the body politic of a society.

In a dictatorship, the appeal is to benefit oneself for a plot, a permit or a post. It breeds a culture of corruption that erodes the nobility of the individual and the soul of the society. The pursuit of selfish materialism results in poverty of life where those who have everything have nothing.

By contrast, political parties ask followers to abandon self interest to help others. It is the act of abandonment of self interest for a greater cause that infuses the spirit of life into the soul of a Nation. Here the individual gives up the dearest possessions: life, liberty, youth, family, health and livelihood to further a cause larger than the self.

Prosperous societies are built around the majesty of law. Here judges overturn governmental excesses to protect the individual. The act of overturning a publicly perceived excess is an act of justice that crowns the rule of law with splendour. Once the dominant Muslim culture rested on the pillars of Adl and Insaaf—of being just and dispensing justice.

In the Twentyfirst Century, the danger is that leadership betrays the public confidence and dishonours its heroic past. The legacy of fighting for the rule of law and the emancipation of society is giving way to the use of force. Force is used by a few to get what they want irrespective of whether their community believes it is right or wrong. History is replete with examples of those marginalised because they thought wrong was right in the pursuit of an end they believed justified the means. This is where some Muslim societies started to stray after a period of greatness. Some Muslim schools began teaching that it was alright to commit a wrong (haraam) act if it was for a right (halal) end.

Greatness rests on a sense of justice. Talk of a just leadership, a just society, a just war echoes through the corridors of history. It echoes because every great society and leadership flowed from the perception of justice done, of right triumphing over wrong, of the weak challenging the mighty because right empowered them to do so.

Civilisations collapsed, and societies are collapsing, as the distinction between right and wrong, right and might is blurring. An ethical value system emphasises that right is stronger than might. Nations prosper where the weak and oppressed are considered equal to the rich and privileged. An ethical foundation brings individual prosperity irrespective of social background. To build ethical societies so many gave so much during the wave of anti-colonialism movements that in the Twentieth Century produced independent nations.

Today some of those independent nations in the arc from Aden in Yemen to the Straits of Malacca face dangers of disintegration. The danger comes from the form of governance resting on despotism. Dictatorial rulers use oppression, injustice, corruption to either bribe or terrorise otherwise good souls into debasing themselves into lower beings. In so doing, they corrupt an individual lacking the will to suffer. More dangerously, the fabric of society upon which, ultimately, rests the greatness of a Nation is destroyed. Fear begins to guide actions and reactions replacing the confidence that flows from the security that justice will be done.

Perhaps for this reason all the great religions of the world emphasised the importance of the word "just". God is always just. God created humanity in His image. When humanity is unable to act justly, humanity loses its divine spirit. Without spirit, life ebbs away until what is left is lifelessness or death.

Islamabad is a case study. As elections are rigged, Parliament mocked, parliamentarians pressured to sell themselves, the judiciary decried by the Pakistan Bar Council, the children of our generation suffer in Pakistan and elsewhere. Their upbringing is handicapped by the incapacity of society to differentiate between right and wrong.

The Middle East is also an example. Here the Israelis and Palestinians ceased to care about each other's children. The targets are not military. The targets are civilians randomly chosen to be killed. Hate generates hate and the fires of hate make rational thinking impossible. An Israeli leader threatens to assassinate the President of the Palestinians. It is a reflection of the times that such a shocking threat be made. Even more sadly that such a threat was silently received by the majority of nations.

If such a threat is permitted to materialise, a Palestinian may assassinate an Israeli Prime Minister in retaliation. The Israelis will retaliate by upping the ante. The vicious cycle of violence will continue.

Each action has an equal and opposite reaction. Of violence and of peace. Of right and of wrong. But somehow this lesson is forgotten. The belief is that might will crush the enemy and bring a one-sided victory.

A world that once condemned assassination as an evil act remains silent. The sacrosanct nature of human life seems to lose its sanctity. The changing values describe a world losing contact with the qualities of ethics and morality once considered the moving forces of human and societal behaviour.

Is the change continental? The dominant value of the past was spread by European powers where civil rights and compassionate tolerance were the hallmarks of greatness. Today it is America which is the undeclared new empire of the world. It is an empire born of a past where the maxim in the expansive wilderness was a raw and ready justice: "dead or alive".

This is in sharp contrast to the European ethos where each individual, even the most grotesque murderer, had rights and was entitled to an impartial trial. Previously a person was innocent before proven guilty. And that is what the United Nations Human Rights Convention still says. Yet the United Nations is no longer what it once was. A person is now presumed guilty and must battle to prove innocence. The changing ethos takes place against a more violent world.

It seems that the ones with might need not listen to representative bodies or submit to collective will. Thus Pakistan's dictator can remain President and Army Chief irrespective of what the Parliament thinks. And parliamentarians in Pakistan can switch sides for favours irrespective of what their constituents or parties think.

It must be asked: can such a value system produce societies that protect and nurture children, give pride to its youth and glory to its Nation? The answer rests on making that crucial difference which once was made when religion, society and great leaders taught the difference between right and wrong.

— 21-Sep-2003

Peace Conference

Ladies and Gentlemen:

I thought long and hard about whether to accept the gracious invitation to speak at this forum today. The politics of a former Prime Minister of Pakistan — and the leader of Pakistan's most popular party – travelling to India to discuss bilateral relations between our two Nations were truly complex.

In the end I decided to attend. I did this because the threat of a conflict in South Asia ending up in the first nuclear war since Hiroshima is real. Such a conflict could annihilate hundreds of millions without distinguishing whether they were Pakistanis or Indians or Kashmiris. The determination to make a contribution to avoid this nuclear nightmare far outweighed other arguments that could have crossed my mind.

We meet today with the world a different and more dangerous place than we expected when the Berlin Wall fell. The end of the Cold War promised to herald an era of global peace. The principles of Freedom and Free Markets promised to shake up sluggish economies. The prospect of a Peace Dividend was before us. It was not to be. The world is at war, not peace.

The U.S. led coalition occupies a major Islamic Nation, suffering daily attacks and many casualties. No one knows whether Iraq will survive the present phase. Both India and Pakistan are under pressure to send troops to Iraq. And both are considering that option separately. How much better it would be if countries in this South Asian region could consult each other on such important measures before taking a final decision.

And as I talk to you, the resurgent Taliban are mounting fresh attacks against the Karzai government in Afghanistan. They are mounting attacks against the Coalition forces and the NGOs working there. In Jammu and Kashmir, despite the present welcome ceasefire at the Line of Control, the intensity of violence has yet to decrease. We must ask ourselves: are we to condemn our future generations to a world of violence, of conflict, of bloodshed, of war, blood and destruction?

This conference, organized to explore peace initiatives, is an important step in building a different kind of world. A world of peace and harmony that protects the life, liberty and livelihood of every individual irrespective of race, religion, gender or political affiliation. This is an important responsibility on the shoulders of the leadership of South Asia. This responsibility is all the more grave as the world is involved in the war against terrorism.

Few nations or regions have been spared. Christian churches and Muslim mosques were targets of suicide bombers in Pakistan. Your own Parliament became a bloody target. Great Britain is a target. Saudi Arabia is a target. Turkey is a target. Indonesia is a target. Australia is a target. There are seemingly constant acts of terrorism in the Middle East, every day, every week. The world is threatened with carnage in many corners.

We owe it to ourselves and to our people, to all of South Asia, to make every effort, to strive, to seek, to pursue peaceful means for the resolution of outstanding disputes, for confidence building and for reduction of tension in our region. This is the part we can play in helping the world community deal with the threat of terrorism.

The Pakistan Peoples Party, which I lead, welcomed Islamabad's announcement of a unilateral ceasefire along the Line of Control inclusive of Siachen. This measure was taken in response to Prime Minister Vajpayee's recent twelve-point package of confidence building measures.

There are many who believe that in the context of Indo Pak relations, tension can only be reduced when both countries are truly democracies. I am one of those who believe that democracies do not go to war against other democracies. I say this on the basis of Indo-Pak history. Since Independence the three wars that took place between India and Pakistan took place under military dictatorships. And since the destabilization of the democratic government that I led in 1996, India and Pakistan have come close to war three times.

As a witness to the historic Simla Agreement, the agreement that prevented full-fledged war between our countries since 1971, my Party and I are committed to the Peace process between our countries. It is this commitment that led the PPP and myself to welcome talks between New Delhi and Islamabad despite the military dictatorship in my country.

We believe that the military rulers' overt statements for normalization of relations must be put to the test. If it is false, they will be exposed before the bar of public opinion. If it is true, the benefit will go to the people in the region. It is therefore important to communicate, to enter into dialogue and to test the intentions of each other.

It is to the credit of Prime Minister Vajpayee that he did not lose heart despite the undermining of Bus Diplomacy and the failure of the Agra Summit. But then he is a man of many surprises.

For the time being, the Indo Pak ceasefire has brought happiness and immediate relief on both sides of the Line of Control. Hundreds of villages with thousands of peaceful inhabitants are worst hit during a military standoff. Mines are laid maiming many. Constant firing denies villagers sustenance.

The atmosphere of congeniality has increased with the news that Prime Minister Vajpayee is to attend the forthcoming SAARC Summit in Islamabad in January 2004. A new year begins with new hopes and expectations.

The major impact of this ceasefire relates to Siachin area. Both India and Pakistan spend enormous amounts on maintaining their respective holds on this highest and coldest of battlegrounds. As Prime Minister, I have seen the transformation of the glaciers into formidable military camps. Estimates claim that the cost to both countries since 1985 is in the region of roughly twenty billion rupees annually. This huge amount is being spent to sustain and counter each other's confrontation in the icy peaks. The cost in lives, particularly during the Kargil fighting but also otherwise, and in those falling victim to cold induced injuries is immeasurable.

The announcement of the ceasefire serves as a deterrent to militancy. It minimizes the build up of a situation similar to that last year that could have erupted into a three-minute nuclear boom, and doom, massive destruction.

The United States, China and others have welcomed the much needed ceasefire in the hope that it will create conditions speeding up the peace process. Significantly, the ceasefire received wide acceptability in India and Pakistan igniting the hope that saner leadership will untie the Kashmir Gordian knot.

Prime Minister Vajpayee has indicated that his upcoming visit to Islamabad will include meetings with "everyone". This indicates that a meeting between General Musharraf, the man who wields the real power in Pakistan, and the Indian Prime Minister will take place. This is just as well as the Pakistani Premier's position is presently ceremonial and will remain so until power is transferred to the Parliament.

The support for the ceasefire rightly came from the Pakistan Peoples Party, the only Federal and broad based political party outside those created by the establishment. The PPP has the singular honour of making a breakthrough on Siachen during Indo Pak talks in 1989. It is the architect of the policy of soft borders on the disputed territories enunciated in 1999.

The PPP hopes that the ceasefire plan will be followed by greater travel links between the two countries as well as talks on how to lessen violence and use of force in the area. The PPP hopes that another ceasefire with militants and the Indian army can be reached as it was in the past. The lessening of violence in the valley can be calibrated to the reduction of Indian troops in the area giving a greater sense of security to the Kashmiri people as well as bolstering Indo-Pak relations.

While the borders were silent as the signs of a spring in relations dawned, militants tried to mar the spirit within Indian controlled Kashmir. New Delhi did not make these violent incidents an excuse to reject the ceasefire.

The frequent military standoffs contribute immensely to poverty in the region. The nuclear detonations in 1998 were a signal to awaken to new realities that changed the nature of a possible future Indo-Pak war.

Resultantly, public opinion in both countries was building up. Exchanges and visits by Parliamentarians, intellectuals, business community and women's groups took place. These visits indicated that public opinion was dissatisfied with the festering confrontation, exchanges of fire and the disruption in the normalization process. Public opinion was concerned about the despair, misery and abject poverty that marked the lives of those living in the shadow of the threat of conflict.

The renewed contacts between India and Pakistan are taking place against the backdrop of statements by key officials both in Washington and in London. The senior officials and politicians have raised New Delhi's concerns with General Musharraf. According to them, General Musharraf has assured them that he will stop cross border militant activity. This is a new strategic reality. It is arising out of the ashes of the Twin Towers that were brought down by the events of September 11.

Even as the world witnesses the emergence of a post September 11 world with zero tolerance for acts of violence, we must be ever vigilant for elements that would do their best to undermine the prospects of a breakthrough. These elements are the militants. They believe that without violence there will be no settlement of the Jammu and Kashmir issue. During their talks in Islamabad in January, the

Indo Pak leadership will need to discuss how to have borders that are soft and which are also safe. In war games and scenarios played out by think tanks fictitious volunteers are seen as the Achilles' heel of the normalization process. These war games have led security agencies to conclude that the region is "one of the most dangerous places on earth."

The worry is that a militant could spark a war that neither country really wants. For example, a dramatic act, similar to the attack on the Indian Parliament, could create intense public pressure on New Delhi to retaliate against Pakistan, triggering war. Perhaps this is why, on the eve of PM Vajpayee's visit, Islamabad banned some militant groups, froze their accounts and sealed their offices. It is hoped that such groups would not resurface once again when the snows of winter melt.

I take this opportunity to commend the All Parties Hurriyet Conference. Despite recent divisions, the APHC has kept the doors of dialogue open and back channels active. APHC has an important role to play in facilitating peaceful conditions in Srinagar as indeed in Muzzafarabad the parties of which are also part of the APHC.

In the past, New Delhi extended an invitation for unconditional dialogue to the APHC. Such measures, including the past ceasefire between militants and the Indian army, were innovative steps that gave momentum to the search for a solution that could end the threat of conflict from this ancient civilisation, so rich in culture, so full of diversity and populated with hard working and talented peoples.

It is tragic that this subcontinent, so full of history, has remained for so long the most likely site for a nuclear exchange on our planet. South Asia must begin its search for a peace dividend. We can think of the peace dividend as the sum of resources no longer devoted to the military and available for the social sector. The peace dividend can be the traditional guns for butter trade-off. In the longer term, a peace dividend is defined by investment. We must invest in technology. We must invest in infrastructure. Above all we must invest in human capital — specifically on education and health.

The 1990s began with falling defence budgets in the United States. But the United States quickly assumed its role as the world's only superpower. Now the US spends more on defence than during the Cold War. Another test of the peace dividend soon emerged following the Declaration signed by Israeli Prime Minister Rabin and Palestinian President Arafat on the White House lawn in September 1993. Foreign investment into Israel and Palestine soared. A Palestinian Development Bank was established funded by the IMF, the United States and the EU. All this finished with the Intifada.

We know that a South Asian peace dividend could dramatically increase the quality of life of our huge populations.

Scholars expect peace to break down poverty. A Harvard Professor, David Landes, writing in "The Wealth and Poverty of Nations" said, "poverty is inextricably linked to armed conflict." Poverty creates an atmosphere that encourages war for the purpose of national identification, national mobilization, and as a distraction from social inequality and hopelessness. Fighting poverty was a challenge in Pakistan with one of the highest population growth rates when I took office in 1988.

As Prime Minister I demonstrated with Prime Minister Rajiv Gandhi that men and women of good will, Indians and Pakistanis of good will, could make fundamental progress.

The nuclear confidence building treaty that we signed in 1988, a treaty by which we committed not to attack our respective nuclear facilities, was the most important peace accord between us since the Simla Agreement signed by our parents in 1972.

I am also proud that we were able to establish, for the first time, hot lines between the General Headquarters of both our countries modelled after the Hotline between Washington and the Kremlin.

Ladies and gentlemen,

We believed that these confidence building measures were an important prelude to moving along the cause of peace and in facing the challenge of differing perceptions on the issue of Jammu and Kashmir. We feel strongly on this issue, on both sides. Let us not be afraid to have two different points of view on the outstanding issues between us today. China and India have a border dispute but they do not threaten each other with war. In fact, relations between the two countries keep improving.

Beijing and Washington have a dispute over Taiwan yet they do not brandish nuclear weapons at each other. Instead they have excellent trade relations.

There are many countries with disputes and disagreements. Yet they manage their affairs in a way that enables their people to know each other through trade, travel and tourism. They share warm relations without prejudice to their differing positions and perceptions.

We can learn from such models of conflict management. We can make a meaningful attempt at resolution and reconciliation in South Asia to truly make progress across the board. And if we do make progress, the dividend before us is compelling.

Trade between our nations is ridiculously low, less than one per cent of our global trade. This has not always been the case. Immediately after Independence, India was Pakistan's most important trading partner. In the early years, 56 percent of Pakistan's total exports went direct to the Indian market. 32 per cent of its imports came from India. Lahore and Amritsar were important economic hubs when trade flourished with a free flow of goods and services. Then, as our political relations deteriorated in the 1950s, trade trickled away for fifty years.

As the Prime Minister who proposed a South Asian Tariff Agreement during the Islamabad Summit of 1988, and ratified the SAPTA agreement during her second tenure, I am surprised at how our nations see progress on trade as a favour to the other country. I see it as a benefit to the common man in each of our countries. Some suggest that the economic benefits of Indo Pak trading could be as much as $14 billion annually.

The greatest economic benefit of Indo Pak trade could occur in the sphere of energy cooperation. India is a rapidly growing energy market able to absorb new sources of supply as they materialize in the region. Pakistan's possible role is in fulfilling this need both as supplier and as a transit route from Iran and Central Asia. This requires construction of pipelines, a major capital investment that can come only in an environment of bilateral peace.

I suggest that expanding trade be a useful adjunct to the political process, instead of being constrained by it. Trade is but one of a great many potential benefits of peace that can change the face of the subcontinent.

Despite a growing middle class in both countries, the depth of poverty of our underclass defames our image. People from India and Pakistan go to America in search of the American Dream. They feel they have opportunities to succeed there that are missing in our region. We can offer our people the opportunity of an Asian dream. I dream of a time when our children's lives will be free of self-imposed limitations.

The French philosopher Rousseau said that we were all born free. Yet our societies, cultures, politics and militaries, keep our people chained to illiteracy, ignorance, intolerance, infant mortality, malnutrition and disease.

It is time to break those chains.

Ladies and gentlemen, India and Pakistan are nuclear powers. Despite the new cease-fire, we glare at each other across the LOC. Now is the time to move forward as the New Year in this new century approaches.

I commend the *Hindustan Times* for organizing this high powered conference. This is a conference that brings together political leaders, international diplomats, scholars, intellectuals and leading voices from the media. It is a conference that involves the public in a historic debate.

It is my hope that a leading Pakistani daily will follow the precedent set by the *Hindustan Times* in organizing a similar conference in Pakistan.

I thank the *Hindustan Times* for bringing together a galaxy of leaders to speak on one of the most important issues of our times impacting on the future of one fifth of humanity. And when a conference takes place in Pakistan, I hope I will be able to attend as I did here. For now, I am an exile.

I am banned from my country. I am banned from contesting for Premiership of my country, banned from contesting even as a backbencher, banned from seeing my husband who is in the eighth year of his imprisonment, banned from entering my ancestral homes, banned from praying at the graves of my Martyred Father and brothers.

I do not despair. In life, an individual makes choices.

I made mine on the last day of my Father's life in a prison that our colonial masters built in the city of Rawalpindi. That was the choice to fight for peace and democracy, to fight for human dignity that must come when people can combat hunger, poverty and illiteracy.

I know that realities change. That a person can go from Prime Minister to prisoner and from prisoner to Prime Minister. I have seen power from the time I was a child. I must tell you that the sense of satisfaction and joy that I felt never came from the chandeliered halls or the turbaned staff, or the pomp and power of governing a state.

It came from small acts. It came from giving a child polio drops knowing those small drops would change its life forever. It came from inaugurating a school, providing electricity and water to places that had none. It came from seeing the smile on the face of a boy or girl who got a job. The wheel of history turns. There was a time when Prime Minister Gujral could not visit Jehlum, the city he was born in because our two countries were at cross purposes. Now he, though an Indian, can visit Jehlum and I, though a Pakistani, cannot visit my Larkana.

The wheel of history turns. For individuals and Nations. And as the wheel of history turns for the children of Partition, I hope we bequeath them a better future than our bitter past.

Ladies and Gentlemen, I conclude with a quote from Alexander Pope, which I used during my last visit to New Delhi two years back. He said:

"What war could ravish,

Commerce could bestow

And he returned a friend

Who was a foe"

Thank you.

— New Delhi
13-Dec-2003

Restore Pakistani Democracy

My run-in with Osama bin Laden began before he achieved international infamy. He supported the pro-Taliban forces in Pakistan in their bid to control Islamabad as the centre for their battle against the civilized world. In 1989 bin Laden poured more than $10 million into an unsuccessful no-confidence move to bring down my government. Years later, after the attack on New York's World Trade Center in 1993, the bin Laden-backed mastermind, Ramzi Yousef, fled to Pakistan. Working with the FBI, my government's law enforcers apprehended Yousef near Islamabad. Before we extradited him, we learned the bin Laden apparatus had made two unsuccessful assassination attempts against me in 1993. During the tenure of my democratic government, we closed an important paramilitary training university in Peshawar and disarmed other forces. We arrested militants; they were on the run. We extradited wanted terrorists. They hit back by bombing the Egyptian Embassy in Islamabad, burning the National Assembly and hijacking a school bus. Of course, they were too busy fighting Democracy to fight the world. But when my democratically elected government fell in November 1996, the range of the militants increased. With oversight and constraint gone from the halls of government in Islamabad, the fanatics turned their attention to their agenda of international terrorism. The September 11 terror attacks, and their grim toll, climaxed in a call to end international terrorism. As America leads this fight, I caution that Pakistani Democracy not be sacrificed at the altar of Afghanistan. It is Pakistani Democracy that earlier contained the kind of terror and tragedy we witnessed in New York and Washington on Black Tuesday. It is Democracy that can help contain fanaticism and terror in the future.

It is right for America, as it battles international terrorism, to sow the seeds of stability. Democracy and debt reduction are two pillars on which the edifice of a political structure promising peace and stability can be raised. It is also right to rescind the discriminatory Pressler sanctions, which soured relations between our countries for a generation. It is also important for America and the rest of the world to keep their commitment to democratic values by continuing to press for party-based elections in Pakistan next year, open to all candidates and all parties. Democracies oppose terrorism. Democracies do not start wars. Democracy is the best safeguard against the Talibanization of Pakistan, a nuclear power.

Two of the most important long-term goals for our region should be the formation of a broad-based government in Afghanistan that gives confidence to the refugees to return to their land and, equally important, the restoration of true Democracy to Pakistan. We must ensure that the military and security apparatus of Pakistan that fought in the Afghan jihad in the 1980s come under civilian control. The militarization of Pakistan must end. Just as I once cautioned President George H.W. Bush's administration about "creating a Frankenstein", today I caution his son about the same danger. Save Pakistani Democracy from dictatorship in the name of anti-terrorism. Ultimately an anti-democratic Pakistan can become an anti-Western, fanatic threat to world peace.

— The Washington Post Page A19
24-Sep-2001

Guaranteeing the Rule of Law and Independence of the Judiciary in Pakistan

Distinguished Guests:

I am honoured to address this gathering of the Commonwealth Ethnic Bar Association.

I accepted the brief to carry coals to Newcastle in addressing issues of legal interest. I understand from Jeremy Bentham that, in certain cases, ignorance of law is not punished. I promise to speak the truth, the whole truth and nothing but the truth. I learnt from Lord Darling that Law 'is a very strange one; it cannot compel anyone to tell the truth…But what the Law can do is to give you seven years for not telling the truth'.

Friends, it is with a sense of nostalgia that I come to England's London, a country where I studied. I come to these Inns of Court where my Father, and my country's Father, walked and worked, spoke and studied, laughed and worried.

I speak here at a difficult time for my country, a country that has drifted rudderless in a sea of conflict and violence since Democracy was decapitated four years are in November 1996. The dismissal by decree of a democratic government enjoying the support of Parliament and the people set the stage for the decline of the rule of law. The flouting of the Constitution, which provides for fair elections by installing a partisan interim administration, the manipulation of the vote and a fraudulent mandate, set the stage for the rise of an insecure leader. A leader with paranoia as overwhelming as the mandate his party was given by the Generals. The criminalisation of the Parliamentary opposition, the mob attack on the Supreme Court and the terror unleashed against the press reduced the judiciary to a helpless and silent spectator.

Distinguished members of the Bar, my own life mirrors the larger Pakistani canvas of the last half- century of law, politics and a politicized judiciary. Contrary to globally accepted values, Pakistan is one of the few nations where the military today rules, where judges are sacked, arrested and made to swear new oaths of allegiance. The generals claim they are experts on freedom, and will take the country from "sham democracy" to "true democracy". When the press is critical of Generals, the press comes in for a battering. As dictatorship continues, the crisis deepens. Even as it does so, it weakens political structures, political parties, the judiciary, administrative framework of the country and even the Constitution with arbitrary amendments passed by decree. By so doing, dictatorship, when it withdraws, sows the seeds of its own return. And Pakistan falls victim to repeated military interventions. That cycle can be broken, if we learn from this experience, to stand up to the dismissal of democratic governments through edicts to declare that the first lesson for a lawful society is Democracy and more Democracy. Strong institutions strengthen the rule of law, giving birth to an orderly society, taking its place with pride in the world community.

I come here this evening as a citizen of a country that is far from ordinary. It is a nation that exploded six nuclear devices, in response to India's five, in a game of nuclear upmanship, in 1998. It fought 3 wars with neighbouring India in the last 50 years. Last spring, both countries nearly went to war again over the frozen glaciers of a place called Kargil. The ruling elite, with its contempt for the Constitution, has robbed the one hundred and forty million courageous citizens of their right to determine the direction of their destiny. The Commonwealth and Britain have rightly called for a restoration of the democratic process.

Leadership is about speaking out boldly. Leadership is about defending human values. It pains me to see Islamabad at odds with the prevailing international value system. Values that include freedom, human rights, minority, ethnic and gender rights. It pains me to hear of soldiers dying on the borders, of bomb blasts killing people at bus stops as they make their way to work. It pains me to see the regime pressured by militant organisations dictating an agenda of hate. An agenda that denies our people their rightful role as responsible citizens of a responsible country playing by the rules of the international game to gain peace, progress and stability.

The Generals are unable to grapple with the challenges of democratization, proliferation, terrorism, economic implosion and peace in the region. Their regime is prisoner to a myopic worldview, which died when the Cold War ended with the fall of the Berlin Wall. Increasingly, there is an international mantra being chanted about terrorism and Taliban and Islamabad. The people are restive and ready to rise. But the political class is divided between those seeking fresh elections, those seeking the restoration of the suspended assemblies, those seeking power through judicial elimination of their winnable rivals and fundamentalists who see themselves as King Makers. The challenge is to develop a consensus that the path to revival lies through a fair, free and impartial reference to the people through elections and the transfer of power to the people's representatives.

For much of my life, I thought fair, free and impartial elections could be easily conducted. But I have seen elections manipulated even as observers watched an orderly procedure. Unless the manner of the rigging of the 1990 and 1997 elections is determined and stopped, the fundamentalists will continue to play King Maker, ridding them of every unrepresentative puppet as he becomes unpopular, just to bring another. I deliberately use the word "he" for those brought in by extremist King Makers. In their vocabulary, there is little place for a "she". So an army chief who is on the ground can be sacked if the King Makers wish it so. An army chief in the air can become the chief executive if the King Makers agree. The Kings think they exercise power but the King Makers whisper when they are going even before the Kings know it. And when their manipulations bankrupt the process, the King Makers withdraw, handing over to politicians to pull the country out of the crisis. As soon as that happens, they move in again. And public hate is built by fuelling charges of corruption as the raison d'être of democratic death rather than an honest investigation allowing the law to determine the veracity of the accusations.

In all, five governments since 1985 were dismissed on unsubstantiated charges of corruption. I admit that we, the political parties, also made mistakes. One mistake was the inability to devise a mechanism for impartial investigation of corruption charges against members of a sitting government. But now we all pay the price. It is time for us to develop a consensus on impartial investigation, prosecution and trial of those charged with corruption in this age of transparency. In so doing, one major plank that permits King Makers to derail democracy, take power and undermine the judiciary, goes.

For much of my life, I believed that elections were a magic key which solved the Democracy problem and with it the rule of law. I thought: once we win elections truth will triumph over tyranny. How wrong I was. It took more than two decades to realize that elections are only one part of a pluralistic Democracy. I have seen election results become a farce to deny the people's mandate. I have seen my mandate mocked by elements within the military, judiciary and bureaucracy. I have heard them declare, "she can be Prime Minister of Islamabad, the capital, but we will stop her from governing Pakistan, the country". Whilst I should have been Tony Blair, I became Ken Livingstone. This gave rise to a state within a state where there was a government and there was not a government.

As twice Prime Minister, my government was largely denied the right to appoint judges by an entrenched establishment that saw some members of the judiciary as their key to killing Democracy. Ironically, the failure of the judiciary in resolving real or perceived grievances in a manner publicly beyond criticism, forced groups to look at the military as their saviour. The inability of the judiciary to protect the Opposition, press, and even itself, from the fascist assaults of the

Nawaz regime led to jubilation when the military intervened just one year back. The challenge is to build an independent judiciary. But how does one go about doing that when a handful of dishonest, politicized judges packed in during dictatorship, continue to sit, and are even promoted and rewarded? Technically, a Judge can be removed from office. Substantively that is a near impossibility except by the Generals.

Generals have formed political parties too. General Hameed Gul admitted forming the Opposition to my Party in the elections of 1988. General Durrani admitted skimming money off public sector banks to bankroll candidates against my Party in the General Elections of 1990. General Musharraf is on record stating that the last elections did not give the second Nawaz regime a mandate although the army was every polling booth. Political interference by the Generals led to the break up of the country in 1971. More dangerously, it weakens the very integrity of the country.

This month I wrote to the Chief Justice of the Supreme Court of Pakistan sending him copies of hand-written notes of the Chief Prosecutor asking accountability courts to "behave". By behave he presumably meant formalizing his disqualification of political leaders prejudged guilty. I understand that the hand-written note of the Prosecutor is available on the PPP web site. Those judges who "behave" will continue in office after Democracy is restored. Above accountability, they can fulfil their political agendas through judicial abuse. That deep is the rot that must be stemmed. It can be stemmed through judicial accountability. However, a consensus is presently missing. Another way is to change the present contempt for the law and allow free public scrutiny of judgments once delivered.

The international community can fund NGOs to scrutinize judgments in cases of political discrimination as well as that concerning discrimination against religious minorities and women. International financial institutions can focus on the law enforcement machinery constituted of investigators, prosecutors and judges. The entire machinery needs better funding for better performance.

Friends, I have seen the judge who butchered justice in ordering the judicial murder of my Father, Prime Minister Zulfikar Ali Bhutto, elected Senator. A Judge, who dishonestly legitimized the overthrow of my first government, was elected President of Pakistan. This same man stands accused by a former President of "taking briefcases of money" to bribe other judges in a famous 1997 case. The Election Commission rejected Justice Tarrar's nomination for the presidency. Justice Qayyum, on leave for his Mother's funeral, rushed back to grant a stay. And Tarrar was elected. As for the bribery charges, Tarrar, as a former Judge, like former generals, is immune to prosecution in real terms.

Last month, a key supporter of mine was brutally axed to death, burnt and his bones left to dissolve in a saline irrigation outfall. The killers admitted that they had been paid for and assured safety by a political opponent. The Inspector General Police rushed to Larkana to hush up the case. Larkana has been selected for the first round of local elections and those who oppose my party are to be supported, even if they are prime suspects in a murder most gruesome.

Four years ago, my brother Murtaza was gunned down in the streets of Karachi. I charged that he had been killed to overthrow my government. My opponents cruelly countered that I had had him killed. An independent British investigation team was stopped from investigating the murder. A judicial inquiry exonerating my husband was hushed up. Four judges, two magistrates and four investigators were changed to fabricate a case against my husband. One of the officers was asked to pervert the course of justice and be rewarded; in the event he declined, he was threatened with implications. He fled the country for England rather than bury justice. Today he has joined the British legal system.

But how many can do that? And that is why I ask the international community to step forward and assist the process of justice in Pakistan and everywhere else where it is under assault. The Twentieth Century was the century when freedom triumphed. But if we walk away now, the past could come back to haunt us once again. The international community can focus on better funding for law enforcement and judiciary, funding for NGOs prepared to scrutinize wrongful prosecution and trial, funding for the UN Rapporteur on Judges and Judiciary, and others established in regional forums, to hire independent investigators for independent scrutiny of judgments and prosecutions deemed politically motivated by parliamentarians.

Friends, Prime Ministers can be imprisoned, hanged and disqualified. Generals and Judges too in theory. The reality is different. Lord Acton said that power corrupts and absolute power corrupts absolutely. Unless Judges and Generals are accountable along with Prime Ministers and Parliamentarians, power can and will be abused. But honest Judges need protection too. Pakistan is a poor country. An accountability judge that refuses to "behave" can be sent home—and lose the fourfold increase in salary recently granted. Early this year, the Junta's Law Secretary, a sitting judge of the high court, hiding under a blanket, in the darkness of the night, went to secretly meet a Supreme Court Judge asking him to behave or be sacked.

Soon thereafter, the night of the long knives took place. Almost half the Judges of the Supreme Court were unceremoniously sent home. Judges can only be independent when they can do justice without fear and favour. And when they know that justice based on cronyism and disfavour will be punished.

My Party has written the United Nations Rapporteur on Judges and the Judiciary to investigate charges of judicial impropriety in the case in which I was judicially abused. Former British Attorney General, Sir John Morris, has expressed his reservations in the words, "Looking at the case as a whole, there are grounds for grave misgivings as to the fairness of the trial" Two American Chief Justices wrote, "An American court would not recognize the conviction as valid in the United States". A Queen's Counsel wrote, "An English court would hold that such flaws were so fundamental that the convictions should, for that reason alone, be quashed". A recently retired judge of Pakistan's Supreme Court opined "There is absolutely no case either against Mr. Zardari or Ms. Bhutto...both of them are entitled to acquittal" and "God may help us when judges become partisan".

Pakistani Human Rights Groups have suggested that Pakistan establish a constitutional court to deal with constitutional issues. A constitutional court could free the ordinary courts from the enormous political pressures that are brought to bear in a country that has spent half its existence under the Generals. Another proposal is for the law on conflict of interest. Under the present law, it is left to an individual judge to decide for himself whether he has a conflict of interest. In my case, the Supreme Court Chief Justice over whom I had raised no objections, declined to hear my case citing conflict of interest. Yet those judges against whom conflict of interest concerns had been raised insisted on trying my party, my family and myself. Two score and more cases were filed against my Mother, my husband and myself. Each case individually gave rise to other petitions and appeals. We were crushed under a mountain of litigation. The purpose was to mentally, physically and financially incapacitate us from performing our political duties, defending ourselves or even looking after our families.

Naively, the regime believed it could entrench itself by incapacitating the leader of Opposition through judicial abuse. I was shuttled back and forth from city to city spending whole days in court. Leaving to catch one plane after another. I was disoriented and would wake up at night wondering which city and roof I was in and under. I was totally unable to peruse documents against myself, to brief lawyers or to draw up a defence strategy. My funds were frozen and the state refused to fund my defence or release my own funds for the same purpose. The Government announced the order for freezing my accounts four hours before the Judge had signed it. During the course of the case, state funds were used for half page advertisements proclaiming my guilt before the verdict was delivered. The numerous contempt petitions I filed against the regime were allowed to gather dust. Judges sacked by my government and seeking revenge tried us. Their cruelty and how they mocked justice brutally and openly is before my eyes as I speak here tonight. Judges that had worked as legal retainers for the Prime Minister's family concerns tried me, as leader of the Opposition. Some of them, with bank loans from state banks were under pressure of business concerns going wrong if they did right by me. One Judge's son worked with a parliamentarian belonging to the ruling party. He assisted the prosecution. It was interpreted as the government paying cold cash to the Judge through his son to get my family and me. Another judge had been Deputy Attorney General for the dictator who had kept me behind bars for nearly six years. His Father had sentenced my Father to death. I had sacked him and his brother was elected a parliamentarian from the Prime Minister's home constituency. He chased me from city to city when the Supreme Court took my case away from him. He denied me the right to a single defence witness. He wrote the order convicting me before the trial was over. I have evidence that he discussed my sentence with the regime. I am prepared to prove it if the Pakistani authorities invite the United Nations Human Rights Commission to examine my allegations.

The nephew of the General who hanged my Father amidst international outrage and the unanimous recommendation of the Supreme Court was appointed to try my husband. One lawyer told me how he was called by the Judge and asked to become the prosecution lawyer. The lawyer declined citing the death sentence involved and said his conscience did not permit him to take the case. The Judge laughed and said, "If I am prepared to give the death sentence, why are you not prepared to argue it". I shiver as I recount the nightmare that my party, family and I have been subjected to even as the world celebrated the triumph of Democracy in the twilight of the Twentieth Century.

Women hater judges were lined up against us. Bigot judges with gender, political and theocratic bias against us. This same judge was the one who refused help when a woman was killed by her family in the name of male honour. Another Judge trying me was so biased against women that the Pakistan Human Rights Commission had complained about him. And here he was trying me even though he believed that women had no right to work.

An attempt was made to poison my husband by puncturing his toothpaste. When my husband made a judicial complaint, the complaint went uninvestigated. A junior police officer was promoted to Inspector General of Police and sent to kidnap my husband from prison on a weekend when the courts were shut. My husband was taken from judicial custody in violation of court orders. He was tortured and threatened that he would be killed if he did not implicate me, his wife. He was told that they could murder him and call it suicide. Three court orders ordering my husband transferred back to jail were ignored by the all-powerful executive. Ultimately my husband's life was saved by a hair's breadth by the cumulative efforts of the judiciary, the diplomats, the Governor and a General. A judicial inquiry later determined that his injuries were not self-inflicted.

Distinguished Guests, the concept of a public trial is rooted in the public judging judgments given by judges. In England, it is inconceivable that a person convicted by a court of law could be elected to Parliament. Pakistan is the opposite, indicating public perception that the judicial system is politicized. Judges can be pressured for none can protect them if they take on the State. However, the public has refused to be pressured by motivated judgments in giving up support to popular leaders. It is to deceive the public that trials have been conducted in camera in jail or through restricted trials. In restricted trials five or six press persons are assigned the beat. The lawyers, intelligence and a few close aides of the defendants are permitted entry. The proceedings are largely shrouded in secrecy. Huge police contingents with face and body plated with armour, guns and batons in hand with tear gas cylinders available would lay siege to the courtrooms. We had to cross three armed checkpoints to allow ourselves entry. Those seeking to enter with us would be beaten and left bleeding within earshot of the judges. The show of force was to intimidate our lawyers, the judges and us.

Once I was banned entry to my own hearing. Another time, elected Parliamentarians were banned entry elected President of a Bar Association was beaten until his back bled. When we finally persuaded the judge that he was entitled to enter as an officer of the court, the official showed his bruised and injured back. Instead of scolding the police, the judge admonished him for coming. During our trials, our lawyers were kidnapped, banned from travelling, imprisoned, their families received threatening calls and they were intimidated in different ways. Many top lawyers refused to take our case.

I have great praise for the International Parliamentary Union, the Pakistan Human Rights Organisation, for Mr. Fernandes of the International Bar Association and for the United Nations Special Rapporteur for Judges and the Judiciary. They were the few organizations that were prepared to listen to our complaints in the early days. I have been so inspired by the concept of the Special Rapporteur on Judges and the Judiciary, that I would like to recommend to the Commonwealth, and the South Asia SAARC to consider establishing similar Rapporteurs to examine complaints of judicial impropriety and judicially backed perversion of justice. For the time being, the UN Rapporteur can only visit a country after the government gives permission. This could change.

The Generals have packed the courts with politically motivated appointees. They can go on to destabilize Democracy even after the military goes back to the barracks. The Pakistani Human Rights Commissions and the elected Bar Associations can suggest how judicial appointments by the military can be scrutinized. The political parties can jointly back such a scrutiny. In doing so, the long shadow of the Generals through the judicial institution can be prevented.

Distinguished Listeners, Europe has a European Court of Justice. An aggrieved citizen can approach the European Court of Justice. Asia, particularly South Asia, can consider adopting the European example. But for that to happen, South Asians need to deal with the ghosts of the past that haunt peace in the present. For too long, South Asian countries have drawn the lines in hatred and blood. Our inability to manage conflicts has led to wars, arms build-ups and stockpiles of weapons of mass destruction. Even as we draw up huge arsenals meant to protect us against each other, even as we demonize each other, we neglect the human needs of our citizens. Vast numbers of our people live on the margins, without proper nourishment, clean water, health or educational facilities or due process. Our concept of greatness is tied to a bygone age rooted in military might. Even as we build weapons of mass destruction, hundreds of our people commit suicide because they can no longer afford to live.

During the Cold War, Super Powers rivalry subsidized our quest for such greatness. Now that the New World Order has begun, we extort from our people money to subsidize the machinery built in the hey day of the Cold War. By so doing, Islamabad has bled the economy and given birth to a frightening implosion. An implosion that could lead to fundamentalist takeover and the nightmare scenario of nuclear weapons in the hands of extremists and their politics of hatred. As a South Asian, I am worried when I see our efforts diverted to warmongering and weaponisation even as large sections of our people live in hunger and squalour.

My Party, too, was a prisoner of the precedent of power. It has taken a decade, and a threat to our very existence, to appreciate that the world has changed. The days of conquest heralded by the Caesars, Ghengiz Khan, Napoleon and others have gone away. Greatness in the third millennium is determined by the ability of a nation to allow its people material and spiritual growth through a framework of peace and equal economic opportunity.

Yes, India and Pakistan have a dispute over Kashmir. Yes, it is difficult for either to accept the solution posed by the other. But, yes, it is also incumbent upon both to manage the conflict. Too many lives have been lost. The lives of Kashmiris, Pakistanis and Indians. The Pakistan Peoples Party and I have proposed that India, Pakistan and the Kashmiris begin negotiations for safe and open borders along the disputed line of control in Kashmir without prejudice to the position of either party. Safe and open borders can herald a new era of peace and open up opportunities. Opportunities for all South Asians to build a community of common values based on freedom and free markets, of free travel and free trade. Conflict management can open up opportunities, open up markets and pave the way for a South Asian Court of Justice.

A South Asian Court of Justice will pressure host judicial systems to better performance. The very notion that a higher forum can challenge a judgment gives protection to victims of political, ethnic or gender discrimination even as it enhances the independence of the Judiciary. Peace and a just legal system can unleash the entrepreneurial skills of our people. Imagine a market of one fifth and more of humanity. Imagine the investment that could flow and the creation of jobs. Great opportunities for your people and for mine, for both our continents and for all continents that make up our planet.

Britain has rightly spoken up for an end to the night of the Generals. There is more that can be done. We can do it by watching out for civilian dictators who try to crush the opposition, creating a vacuum that draws the Generals in. Unsubstantiated corruption charges must fail to blind us to the needs of due process. Torture, arbitrary arrest, wrongful confiscation of property must be opposed in the absence of due process. The previous regime exploited religion to create a new political system. Afghanistan's Taliban system was officially praised. A proposed constitutional amendment sought subordination of the State before one individual giving him the powers to "prescribe what is right and what is wrong" in Islam.

Those of us, who opposed it, were called heretics. Citizens were incited to kill the heretics.

Islam preaches peace and power to the people as agents of God. Islam has little place for dictatorship. Yet fundamentalist dictatorship was being threatened in the name of religion. Democracy might have triumphed in the Twentieth Century but the rise of illiberal regimes, as the Pakistan model shows, can pose fresh threats to freedom and human dignity.

Friends, A word of caution about international treaties of assistance. They can be exploited by illiberal regimes to eliminate opponents and give international legitimacy to their cruel actions. The international community can and should resist cooperation when a request is bathed in perversion. I speak as an early victim of an order that allows cooperation without examining the merits of the charges. That is left to the host country. We have seen how fragile the judicial systems in host countries can be. If a request for international assistance is based upon the use of torture and if the state has tampered with evidence, that request must be rejected. To do otherwise would be to collude with and encourage the use of torture and the perversion of justice.

I come here to praise the British legal system that gave us refuge when all doors seemed shut. My husband, Senator Zardari judicially challenged Islamabad's request to the Home Office under assistance treaties. Shortly before the High Court decision, the Home Office allowed us our request to be informed of the grounds of the request. For the first time we learnt the nature of the charges. To our deep shock, we found a terrible narcotics related charge had been made to malign us in the eyes of the democratic countries of Europe. Even more shocking, we discovered, as we investigated further at home, that the case had been fabricated on the disputed statements of persons arrested and tortured. The High Courts of Pakistan in their orders had documented torture on those tortured. The charge had been concocted by the executive despite the refusal of the General heading the anti-narcotics force to sully his hands in the murder of justice. This incident shows that some Generals can be better than some civilians, that rules for good and bad are neither black nor white.

In Britain, the Mother of Democracy, we found the confidence to fight back. The Home Office, in acceding to Islamabad's request for assistance, has given us grounds for so deciding. These grounds can, and have been challenged, before British courts and so I shall say no more on that particular case. However, I do argue that torture is inhuman and degrading; that it is often used to pervert justice and that states using torture in preparing a request must be denied assistance. Torture was widely used to trump up charges against my Party and myself during my two stints in Opposition. The extract from the *Financial Times*, November 12, 1999, about the kidnapping and torture of a British citizen is an illustration of what happened to scores of Pakistani citizens. I am going to read from it:

"PAKISTAN: Expert swept up in political intrigue - By Stephen Fidler and Nancy Dunne in Washington. Richard Ashby did not expect a welcoming committee as he stepped off a British Airways jet in Islamabad on August 17 last year. The 33-year-old project finance expert was met at the foot of the aircraft steps by Pakistani federal police who took him to an unkempt private house in Islamabad for an interrogation that began a month-long ordeal. During this time, according to Mr. Ashby's account, his life was repeatedly threatened. He was deprived of sleep, beaten and spat upon. On one occasion, a revolver was held to his head; on another he was subjected to a game of Russian Roulette. His captors described to him in terrifying detail the layout of the interior of his home in Arlington, Virginia, where he lived with his wife and daughter. The Pakistani entity responsible for its side of the investigation was the Ehtesab, the "Accountability Bureau". During his detention, Mr. Ashby said, he was taken on several occasions to see the Head of the Bureau, Senator Saifur Rehman. On one occasion, the senator threatened him and demanded a confession of corruption: "I want Benazir Bhutto. I want Asif Ali Zardari," he said. Mr. Ashby had never met Ms Bhutto or her husband. There, he met two former Scotland Yard detectives. The two men said they were working for the Maxima Group, a London-based detective agency. The detectives said they wanted to hear how bribes were paid to Benazir Bhutto and her husband. When Mr. Ashby said he had no direct knowledge of any of this, he said that one of the detectives replied: "If you know what is good for you, you will say whatever and you can get out of here."

During his time in detention, Mr. Ashby was put under increasing pressure to admit to corruption and implicate others. The senator suggested Mr. Ashby's family in the US could be in danger. He made it clear that Mr. Ashby had been tailed for months before his detention, and his house had been entered. He described the house in minute detail - the location of his daughter's bedroom, his Toshiba television, his Sony stereo. "He knew I kept my files under the stairs," Mr. Ashby said.

On another occasion, when Mr. Ashby refused to co-operate, the senator entered the room screaming, eyes blazing "looking like the devil". "He threatened to throw me in jail, torture me, beat me. He said it would cost only 30 rupees (30 pence) to get me killed," he said. The US had launched a cruise missile attack on Afghanistan at about the same time. "He said he would blame my death on some of the Afghans floating around." If this could happen to a British citizen who could turn to his Embassy and Government for support, imagine what was happening to our supporters.

Given the widespread use of torture and perversion of justice to which the PPP was subjected in the last decade, it has proposed a Truth and Reconciliation Commission on the pattern of South Africa to investigate the charges and identify those responsible. I also propose that the United Nations assist the elected Government in establishing a Judicial Commission to examine cases of judicial impropriety made against politicised members of the Bar.

That Commission is unable to give to my children the seven years they lost when their Father was held hostage to their Mother's political career. It is unable to give back life to those who lost it, or sight, or health to those who still bleed from where they were tortured. But it can give to coming generations the assurance of safety from the brutalities meted out to others before them.

Pakistan's Founder, Jinnah, was cognizant that the real strength of American and British Democracy lay in their legal systems. Pakistan's inability to frame a Constitution acceptable to the people and the federating units is part of the crisis. The Generals seek concentration of power through a presidential system or local authorities dependent on handouts. The provinces demand autonomy and a parliamentary form of government. Pakistan's Founder proclaimed, "The Constitution of Pakistan can only be framed by the people." Half a century later that is still to be done.

Some say that there is a game of musical chairs in Pakistan where the military and the people alternate in power. Theocrats try to use the Generals to rewrite the Constitution. This game of musical chairs between the Generals and the people has played havoc with the country. Some academics are now describing Pakistan as a failed state.

The tide of decline can be reversed. But for that, we need to change too.

I accept my share of responsibility. Given power in a certain environment, my leadership was based in part on precedent. I was wrong in following bad precedents that had become conditioned behaviour. My appointment of a junior justice as chief of the Supreme Court was a mistake. It unleashed judicial discontent. It made the chief defensive and he turned on the government too. It pays little to indulge in favouritism, even if it is the pattern of the day. That is the easy way out and it is wrong.

Good intentions alone are insufficient. The means must justify the ends.

Tolerance poses its own challenge in Pakistan. Power to interpret religion and strike down laws repugnant to it has been given to the courts. Such power rightfully vests in the Parliament. We have had our economy rocked, and investment stalled, by judgments on fiscal systems pronounced by the justices in the name of religion.

Founder Jinnah had said, "You may belong to any religion or caste or creed—that has nothing to do with the business of the State..." Since Jinnah left, it has become increasingly the business of the state. My Party lacked a constitutional majority to change patriarchal structures. That is why I tell the people of Pakistan: Give us one real chance with a proper parliamentary majority and a government in the majority province of Punjab. Jinnah was a liberal and our supporters are liberals too. Jinnah died too soon and those who had opposed him gained increasing power. Jinnah sought Partition of India on four elemental grounds: First, that Partition would allow the Hindu and Muslim communities in the sub-continent to live in peaceful coexistence; second the Muslim majority units comprising the new state would unite in a federation based on the parliamentary system; third religious tolerance would be preached; fourth, women would be emancipated.

We lost Jinnah's dream in the game of global politics. Global politics placed Pakistan in the Western camp and India in the shadow of the Soviet Union. That put paid to peaceful co-existence. The Iron Curtain came down and compartmentalized our planet. The Berlin Wall divided Germany. Geography and Super Power game of chess made us a frontline state in the fight against communism when foreign forces invaded Afghanistan. Strategic concerns blinded western democracies to theocrats seizing power on the backs of Generals. As soon as the Soviets withdrew from Afghanistan, western largess dried up. We democrats have a right on the West too. Our people paid in lives, bomb blasts, military dictatorship and weak civil institutions in the fight to build a new world. There is much the West can do in helping build democracy in a country that was once its most close ally.

I am arguing that the West can underwrite the cost of peace in the sub-continent by writing off debt as it did in the Middle East. Britain rightly wrote off debt to some of the world's poorest countries in the twilight of the Twentieth Century. I am arguing that the debts the dictators ran up can and should be written off to show our people that the politics of peace pays dividends, that confidence building in proliferation matters is rewarded and democrats that practice good governance can be tangibly appreciated by the world community in its bid to foster global values.

It was James Bryce who said, and I paraphrase, "Law is respected and supported when it is trusted as the shield of the innocents". That shield is needed to protect Democracy, human rights, provinces and the rights of the weaker segments of society, including women, children and minorities in Pakistan. I know of some very good judges in Pakistan. I recall Justice Arif Iqbal Bhatti who acquitted a Christian in a false case of Blasphemy..Justice Bhatti was assassinated. I can recall the name of Justice Samdani, Justice Dorab Patel, Justice Safdar Shah and so many others whose names shine in gold in the pages of history.

But "the good that men do is interred with them", it is the evil that lives on. It is important for all of us, even as we recall the good, to determine to tackle the evil together. And evil lurks everywhere, just as good exists everywhere. Generals, Politicians, Judges, each one of us has our share of good and bad. There is little point in recrimination. Life, as my Father used to say, is too precious a gift to squander in bitterness or recrimination. I look to a future, letting go of the past. It is the future that is in our hands, yours and mine. In my life of triumphs and tragedies I learnt that you do not have to be strong or powerful to succeed. You just have to have the right ideas.

I recall a story about success that I want to share. One day, I got the opportunity to talk to the chief of the most powerful nation in the world. I asked him the secret of his success. He said, "Two words". I asked what those two words could be and he said, "Right decisions" I asked, "how do you make the right decisions" to which I got the reply, "Experience". I asked, "How do you get experience?" I was told, "Wrong decisions". Experience is a great teacher and in this remarkable era of peace and freedom where the dignity of an individual is acknowledged, I learn from experience to play my part for my people. I know you will play yours, for a future better than any of the yesterdays that we have known.

Thank you, Ladies and Gentlemen.

— **Commonwealth Ethnic Bar Association**
30-Oct-2000

Declarations are Difficult for Generals

It was drama at high noon when General Musharraf sped towards Agra airport even though the clock struck midnight on. After much expectation, and courtship, the so-called "historic summit" collapsed like a pack of cards. Even the cynics criticising Musharraf for making the journey to Agra without mandate expected a joint declaration. There was not even a joint statement.

Blaming Pakistani politicians for succumbing to army pressure, some in India believed it better to do business with the army instead. They found a self-confessing powerless army chief who claimed he would have to live in India in his old Neharwali house if he signed a declaration. The civilian leaders signed Simla, Islamabad and Lahore. All honourable agreements.

Diplomacy is the art of the possible. Political leaders are trained in the art of give and take. General Musharraf is a military dictator. When he speaks, others jump to attention. If they do not, they are locked away. Surrounded by unelectable yes men, Musharraf, despite proclaimed good intentions, stumbled at each key test: date for elections, political victimisation, economic revival and now foreign policy.

It was startling to witness the puerile brinkmanship where the Indians called the bluff. Time was always running short and then extended. First came the breakfast press ultimatum. Next delay after scheduled time for talks ended. The visit to Ajmer Sharif was postponed too. Islamabad got angry when, having called wolf once too often, Indian sources leaked that the talks would continue the next day. The minute preparations for the Summit came to nothing.

Even the ancient knowledge of spicing food with special mood enhancing herbs failed to deliver.

Musharraf made key errors in the trip. He failed to build an internal consensus of legitimate political forces. He went to India on the props of Pakistan's extremist parties, posing with them before his visit. He relied on an inefficient team which failed him previously. Had they given good advice, he would have stayed an extra day, matching Indian patience with greater patience of his own. Exhausting the other side is a pretty elementary diplomatic trick. Instead he left in a huff.

Apparently Islamabad was keen for a declaration and New Delhi knew it. This was revealed by a Pakistani delegate who told the *Gulf News*, "I went up to Jaswant Singh and told him he could write what he wanted, we would accept it". This is extraordinary. It is stunning in its crumbling of political will under pressure. It is little wonder that Foreign Minister Jaswant wanted another day of talks to put in his wish list, given the accommodation offered by Islamabad. It is also a case study of why Generals should look after borders and let politicians deal with diplomacy.

Kashmir is central to Pakistani thinking but the Indians have a different view. Narrowing the gulf was the purpose of the visit. If there is a legacy to this Summit, it is that Musharraf allowed New Delhi to match Pakistan's commitment to the Kashmir Dispute with an equally shrill and high profile repetition of "cross border terrorism". Since 1993, when the diplomat Dixit offered Pakistan Kashmir as a separate agenda item at the Cyprus Commonwealth Conference, the Indian side was willing to include Kashmir as the bone of contention. But the interpretation of that contention is different to Pakistan's. The lack of continuity in Pakistan's governments and foreign office allowed for ignoring this significant development.

Narrowing the focus to the words on a draft statement, usually successfully manoeuvred by diplomats, overlooks the larger picture. That picture involves tense relations between two nuclear capable states that have fought three wars and are daggers drawn at the Line of Control in the disputed Kashmir Valley. A nervous world community pushed both leaders towards the negotiating table to lessen tensions dangerous for a South Asia housing one-fifth of humanity.

Some hoped that Musharraf in sherwani would be a born again peacemaker. But he was hampered by his past and his dependence on a military constituency wedded to militancy since the Afghan Jihad days. He lacked a popular mandate and desired his Nation's highest constitutional posts. He carried the costly burden of the death of three thousand soldiers who died in the Kargil operation. Given his agenda, ambitions, army, America and Afghanistan, Musharraf played his cards well, except for the late night departure.

Camouflage is second nature to the commando and the camouflage came in handy. Landing in his sherwani, he hid the soldier who personally fought in two front lines with India courting death with every breath. Soon the sherwani was replaced with the informal short sleeved and tieless look. The message was, "I am at home and relaxed. You can trust me". The President of India did just that. In his banquet speech, he called the General "one of its (India's) distinguished sons on his first visit to the city after nearly half a century".

This was an amazing turnabout. The man, whose Kargil operation resulted in Indian soldiers losing their lives two years earlier, was quickly adopted as one of its "distinguished sons" when he indicated an overt willingness to transform. Given the opportunity, Musharraf played both constituencies. He met with the All Parties Hurriyat Conference in a show of solidarity. He also flattered the Indian premier emphasising "the respect and honour for his dignity and statesmanship". He said he was "prepared to go forward" and show "flexibility". Lacking internal support, under international financial pressure to play good cop in Delhi and with the UN sanctions heating the Afghan front, the General played the full gallery until his patience ran out at night. He bought international time and good will in the run up to the Summit. He used that goodwill to seize the Presidency, assume draconian powers under the National Security Council, get another tranche of the IMF loan and victimise his opponents.

In New Delhi, he extended an invitation to Premier Vajpayee which was accepted. The promise of another Summit helps his attempts to choreograph a domestic political scenario by October 2002. The potential Summit diverts attention from the growing Talibanisation in Pakistan and the sinking economy. The Indian Foreign Office planned well. But Musharraf beat them at their own game except at the last moment. They went out to woo him but he initially wooed them instead. He hogged the press headlines changing suits several times a day. A different man for every occasion. Disarmingly portraying himself as the "frank and simple soldier."

But the Summit revealed fatal flaws in the personality and background of the General, who today commands the fate of 140 million Pakistanis. First, his dramatic and impetuousness midnight departure for Islamabad. Second, the deep wounds he evokes in both India and Pakistan. The Indian Air Chief, representing his three armed forces, refused to salute him repaying the earlier Lahore refusal to salute Vajpayee and demonstrating solidarity with Indian troops in Kashmir.

In Pakistan, the ghosts of Kargil watch Musharraf. Kargil was Pakistan's biggest setback since Dacca's fall in 1971. Having conquered Indian held peaks, borne the relentless pounding of Indian guns, paid the ultimate sacrifice in lives when supply lines were cut and soldiers starved to death, the unilateral withdrawal insulted the soldiers. There is something undignified and unsavoury about Musharraf, the architect of the operation, scorning the lives lost. Therefore it was argued, far more dignified and honourable for the new government, unburdened by the cruel Kargil legacy, to enter negotiations after elections conclude in October 2002.

Musharraf had tea and cakes in Agra and posed at the Taj Mahal. Vajpayee is coming next to have tea and cakes and pose at the Quaid-e-Azam's Mazaar. These tea parties are yet to stop men and women dying in the blood soaked Kashmir valley. So what were the gains and losses? That two leaders from two nuclear capable states finally broke their silence was an achievement in itself. They sized each other up. They agreed to meet again. But the price was heavy. Two ceasefires broke: the unilateral Indian ceasefire in the Kashmir valley and the Indo-Pak ceasefire between the two countries. Even as Musharraf declared, "a military solution is not an option" at the grand presidential dinner where his delegates feasted, more than eighty people lost their lives in renewed violence. The sound of bullets never stopped. It was a grim reminder of the real dangers South Asia poses to peace and security. The failure of the Summit reinforces calls by Pakistani politicians for restoring democracy so representative governments can deal with diplomacy. More tellingly, the Summit showed that Politicians can come up with agreements but declarations are difficulties for Generals.

— The News
18-Jul-2001

Benazir Bhutto Addresses Woodrow Wilson Centre

Ladies and Gentlemen:

As part of the effort to build a safer world, the Pakistan Peoples Party has been calling for normalization of relations with India. In the context of Indo Pak relations, some believe that tension can only be reduced when both countries are truly democracies. I agree with that. Democracies do not go to war against other democracies. Indo Pak history proves this. Since the two countries won Independence in 1947, the three Indo-Pak wars that took place were under military dictatorships. And since the destabilization of the democratic government that I led in 1996, India and Pakistan came close to war three times.

As a witness to the historic Simla Agreement, the agreement which prevented full fledged war between our countries since 1971, my Party and I are committed to the Peace process between our countries. It is this commitment which led the PPP and myself to welcome talks between New Delhi and Islamabad despite the military dictatorship in my country. However, we do not believe General Musharraf has a vision for peace. He is a tactical leader who engages in short-term somersaults. His actions are to relieve momentary pressures. As soon as the pressure is off, he goes back to his basic nature. This is true of his actions relating to India, Taliban, the banning of militant groups and the regulations of political Madressahs.

It is the PPP which has the singular honour of making a breakthrough on Siachin during Indo-Pak talks in 1989. It was the architect of the policy of soft borders on the disputed territories enunciated in 1999. This policy flowed from a policy review undertaken after the Indo-Pak nuclear detonations of 1998. PPP in 2001, became first party in Pakistan to call for a ban on militant groups like Lashkar-e-Taiba and Jaish-e-Mohammad. Musharraf now adopts our policies, but on the ground his old policies are in place. I take this opportunity to commend the All Parties Hurriyet Conference. APHC has an important role to play in facilitating peaceful conditions in Srinigar as indeed in Muzzafarabad the parties of which are also part of the APHC.

As Prime Minister I signed with Prime Minister Rajiv Gandhi the nuclear confidence building treaty in 1988, a treaty by which we committed not to attack our respective nuclear facilities. It was the most important peace accord between us since the Simla Agreement signed in 1972. We were also able to establish hot lines between the General headquarters of both our countries modelled after the Hotline between Washington and the Kremlin. These confidence building measures were important to moving the cause of peace forward and facing the challenge of differing perceptions on the issue of Jammu and Kashmir. Other countries also have different points of view on issues. China and India have a border dispute but they do not threaten each other with war. In fact, relations between the two countries keep improving. We can learn from such models of conflict management. Progress can help build stronger economic ties. In the early years, 56 per cent of Pakistan's total exports went direct to the Indian market. However, as the political relations deteriorated in the 1950s, trade died down and became practically non-existent for fifty years. It was to revive this relationship that the PPP government under my leadership proposed a South Asian Tariff Agreement during the Islamabad Summit of 1988. The PPP government between 1993 and 1996 ratified the SAPTA agreement during my second tenure. Trade between our two countries benefits the common man. The politics of the PPP has always been the politics of the common man.

Despite a growing middle class in both countries, the depth of poverty of our underclass defames our image. The French philosopher Rousseau said that we were all born free. Yet our societies, cultures, politics and militaries, keep our people chained to illiteracy, ignorance, intolerance, infant mortality, malnutrition and disease. It is to break those chains of backwardness that the PPP was working from Simla to Islamabad to its vision of SAPTA and free travel for the countries of South Asia.

Ladies and Gentlemen, in 1988, my government and I worked closely with the world community on the issue of nuclear proliferation. My government convinced other major players in Pakistan's power structure of the importance of nuclear restraint. Following recent disclosures by Iran, Islamabad detained seven scientists attached to its nuclear facility at Kahuta. An investigation by our intelligence agency is underway. The recent proliferation accusations cover North Korea, Iran and Libya. Saif Gaddafi allegedly said Pakistan sold 'full bomb dossier' to Tripoli. The *New York Times* carried a sales brochure of nuclear components from Pakistan's AQ Khan Laboratories published in 2000 when Musharraf was the Chief Executive. Washington has indicated that it is willing to accept Musharraf's plea that this was "in the past". US officials said on January 16 that they are investigating a possible Islamabad connection in the export of trigger devices for nuclear weapons by a South African businessman of Israeli origin. *The New York Times* reports the paper trail leads to Pakistan. Islamabad faces an explosive situation. Pakistanis do not believe that their nuclear scientists could have sold nuclear technology on their own. There is a consensus that the scientists are being made scapegoats. Musharraf's go it alone attitude has left the public ignorant of developments relating to the proliferation inquiry. Most information has come from the American media.

It was from the US media that the people learnt that for the past two years, Musharraf suspected Abdul Qadeer Khan was free-lancing nuclear assets, while the Inter-Services Intelligence agency was in the dark. It was from the British paper that people in Pakistan learnt that Colin Powell had asked for the arrest of Qadeer Khan in 2002. Unless there is a transparent public inquiry into the chain of events leading to accusations against the scientists, a public backlash is likely. Few people are ready to believe that the scientists acted on their own.

Ladies and Gentlemen, I entered politics with the dream of helping my country prosper on democratic principles. Tragically, I found that the fanatics and the dictators fear the empowerment of the People of Pakistan — they fear literacy, equality and above all information. They demean political parties and democratically elected leaders to justify direct or indirect military rule. Concentrating power in one Institution has negative consequences. Iraq and Afghanistan are two recent examples. Both once key allies of the west, the Baathists and the Mujahideen had to be removed by force. Weakened political parties and structures make the task of reconstruction more difficult.

Ladies and Gentlemen, the terrorists of Al-Queda including Osama Bin Laden and Ramzi Yousef tried to get rid of the PPP government. Musharraf is also trying to get rid of the PPP. I ask myself why the common denominator between both of these apparently irreconcilable forces is the attempt to crush the PPP. I believe as a democrat, I am their opposite. As someone who offers hope to our people —education, jobs, communication and modernity instead of guns and disempowerment — I am an obstacle to the forces of hate.

Under the PPP government Pakistan integrated into the global economy. We became one of the ten emerging capital markets of the world. We invested in education and health. My government condemned honour killing, the murder of women who chose to marry without their guardian's permission. My party has moved a Bill in Parliament making these honour killings illegal. Sadly, but not unsurprisingly, Pakistan's military regime refuses to join us. General Musharraf did make the correct decision to stand with America following the attack on the World Trade Centres. But until he did so, his regime was the most ardent supporter of the Taliban even as it harboured Al-Queda. He learned his politics from the father of the Afghan Jihad, the religious despot Zia ul Haq. General Zia wanted the people of Pakistan to live under the strict interpretation of Islamic laws by the Muslim brotherhood just like the Taliban. Now Musharraf has promoted the politics of excluding the mainstream party, opening the way for the religious parties that, like Zia, wish to implement the

Muslim Brotherhood's interpretation of Islamic school of law. Musharraf is a leader who was best friends with AL-Queda harbourers and with the religious parties that recently bailed him out from his constitutional crisis. When pushed by President Bush to stand up and be counted as friend or foe, he dumped the Taliban. The US forgave him accepting that it was "in the past". Following Indian and Pakistani blasts, both countries nearly went to war in 2001. Musharraf banned militant groups following this attack and said "it was in the past". When Washington woke up to possible export of nuclear technology to North Korea, Musharraf assured the US Secretary of State that "it was in the past". But when it comes to pursuing his political opponents, it is never in the past. It is all about accountability.

It surprised people in Pakistan that as Washington talks of the importance of freedom in Iraq and Afghanistan, it coddles dictatorship in Pakistan. In Pakistan, those of us who are committed to human rights and democracy abhor terrorism in all of its murderous forms. At this time of political crisis in Pakistan, with a military dictatorship strangling our Constitution, America should stand for its values and principles, and reject tyranny. Pakistan's military dictator has given mixed signals at home and around the world. He denounces Osama, yet allows Taliban and Al-Queda leaders escaping from the Tora Bora mountain range. They are seen as his insurance policy to get continued support for his dictatorship. He knows that once the problem is resolved, he will no longer be needed. So he has to keep the pot boiling. The Taliban regrouped are now reasserting themselves. It is said that they have a parallel government in every province.

Musharraf professes pluralism abroad, while he smashes free expression, free association and free elections at home. The arrest of the French journalists and the trial of the reporter Rizvi are two recent examples. As the noted French author Bernard-Henri Levy recently observed in the *Washington Post*: "After September 11th, the war against terrorism had to be declared, and that it has to be carried on, with all the necessary alliances. But what is the real necessity, in this framework, of the US-Pakistan alliance? Was it necessary, after the most recent visit of Musharraf to Washington, to continue the massive funding of his regime?" People of Pakistan ask the same question. The United States is committing billions of dollars in military aid to Pakistan. It would make sense to tie this generous assistance to genuine political reform and social liberalization. General Musharraf presides over the most massive rise of religious parties that Islamabad has seen in its fifty-four year history.

"Pakistan", observed Arnold de Borchgrave, the UPI Editor in Chief, recently "is a nuclear power with two of its four provinces governed by six politico-religious parties whose leaders are friends of Taliban's Mullah Omar and Al-Queda's Osama bin Laden." These six parties are also friends of Musharraf whom they bailed out of the constitutional crisis. The October elections orchestrated in Pakistan in 2002 were a mockery of justice. The leaders of Pakistan's major political parties, including myself were banned from contesting. Taliban leader Mullah Omar's teacher was allowed to contest and did enter Parliament. We were stopped from contesting and campaigning.

Yet, after the polls closed, it seemed we won an overwhelming majority of parliamentary seats. But results were held off. Turnout, estimated at 20%, doubled, quadrupled, and in some areas exceeded 100%. Despite this rigging, my party won enough seats to form the government of Pakistan. But the session of the Parliament was postponed indefinitely. My party's majority was broken with the formation of a splinter group. The splinter group was formed by General Mehdi, Musharraf's appointee in charge of Paramilitary forces. He happens to be the brother-in-law of a former Air Chief Mushaf, another Musharraf appointee. That Air Chief, according to a recent American book "Why America Slept" was a supporter of Al-Queda who knew of the September 11 attacks before they took place. I believe those that believed they defeated one super power and could defeat another, who sympathise with Al-Queda and support Musharraf, sabotaged the chances of my party forming the government. This was despite the fact that I was banned from Parliament and would not have led the Government. This means that they oppose not just my leadership but they oppose the very ideas and policies of the PPP even as they pretend to adopt those policies. This is the disconnect between stated policy and the ground reality.

Ladies and Gentlemen, the European Union and the Colombo Observers, the Commonwealth found the October elections "flawed". Human Rights Watch said "The deck was stacked against the democratic parties". General Musharraf gave the religious parties control of the states bordering Afghanistan. He wants the people of Pakistan, and people all over the world, to believe the choice in Pakistan is between military dictatorship and religious dictatorship. He is saying that his military dictatorship alone stands in the way of the Talibanization of Pakistan, the creation of a nuclear-armed extremist Republic. A Powerful message. But a total fraud. Dictatorship does not constrain fundamentalism. It provokes it. The rise of religious parties to power in Pakistan under Musharraf proves this. The involvement of the military in the politics of Pakistan is undermining our institutions. Last February a Pakistan military officer fired on an American military officer. The America has dropped a 500lb bomb in retaliation. This is one of several clashes that took place at the Pak-Afghan border. The tribal areas are already tense with reports of a US Spring offensive in those parts, which according to the *Chicago Tribune* Musharraf has approved. However, Musharraf has denied the same in Pakistan. His policy is the policy of contradictions, duality, deceit—all tactical measures lacking vision or depth. Women's rights are thrown back a century as honour killings increase. Political leaders are arrested as part of the politics of revenge, sometimes for years. My own husband, hostage to my political career, is in Musharraf's custody as we speak tonight. He was arrested the night the PPP government was overthrown on November 4, 1996. Two American Presidents have completed their terms while he has been in prison. After he is released by the courts, he is charged again. Released, re-arrested. There is no justice under Musharraf's watch.

Blackmail of women politicians is openly indulged in. The husband of parliamentarian Farzana Raja was arrested and she was asked to switch sides. The electricity and telephone connections were cut and she was intimidated with the presence of intelligence hounds. Two other women did defect. One confided she was promised her brother would be promoted from Brigadier to Major General. The other presumably was offered both money and a ministry. This we know from those that rejected such offers. This kind of politics corrupts society and breaks down the professionalism of institutions. I am told that my husband will be freed if I announce my retirement from politics. I know that my duty to my people comes first, for the sake of my children and all the children of Pakistan. General Musharraf first staged an unconstitutional referendum to rubber-stamp his dictatorship. *The New York Times* called it a "dubious exercise". There were no other candidates, no voting lists, no fixed polling stations and eight year olds were pictured voting.

He passed 29 Constitutional Amendments in 2 minutes. It took America 250 years to pass 27 amendments. These amendments gave him unprecedented powers. Powers that Mullah Omar invested himself with in Afghanistan. And while he reaches agreement with the religious parties yielding his treasured uniform in the process, he refuses to make substantive concessions for a democratic Pakistan with the PPP which won the largest number of votes. The message is clear: He is willing to give in to the religious parties to promote them in society, while simultaneously tasking the intelligence to weaken democratic parties with fissures and desertions through tactics involving blackmail and bribe. Musharraf likes to call me corrupt although I have not been convicted by any court of law, despite seven years of trying by the military establishment. However, he refuses to investigate Saif Gaddaffi's claim that Libya paid forty million dollars for a "bomb dossier". Moreover, he included in his cabinet those of my Party charged with corruption. He made them Minister of Interior and Minister of Water and Power to give two examples. He refuses to let me return safely to my country even as he frees those charged and convicted for corruption taking them into his cabinet. A leading weekly recently asked: "Why does he hate Benazir Bhutto?" The dictator's attacks on me are really attacks on the policies my Party and I espouse, and the issues we advance. And thus in Pakistan the causes of women's rights, human rights, press freedom and democracy fall backwards into the dark chasms of a past era. General Musharraf uses Pakistan's importance to the United States in Afghanistan to further his own dictatorship. This is at the cost of the human and democratic rights of the people of Pakistan. He says he will contain terrorists and militants but they keep regrouping under different names. Now he is making Madrassahs flush with money from aid that Washington is giving while government institutes of education are starved for funds and government teachers poorly paid. He and his military dictator predecessors tasked the Intelligence to control the political process in the country. This politicisation is now tarnishing the image of the intelligence known as ISI. It is also tarnishing the image of Parliament. The new Prime Minister was elected after the ISI bussed in the parliamentarians to the ISI headquarters and ordered them to vote for Mr. Jamali who was until then being investigated for corruption charges.

How many more September 11s, how many more Danny Pearls, how many more wars where so many young people die before we realize that the greatest protection of freedom from terrorists, is replacing dictatorships with governments responsible to the people, governments based on the values of democracy and liberty. Democracies, must provide for the public welfare, must provide social services, and must provide education, health and housing. Dictatorships need not. More than one billion Muslims stand at the crossroads. They must not be left to choose between one dictatorship or another, between military dictatorship and religious dictatorship. History teaches us that when America turns against democracy, it turns against itself. This is what happened when Washington walked away from Afghanistan after the Soviets withdrew. Regrettably, Al-Queda made Afghanistan its base to launch a war against the West. Now, in this critical war against terrorism, America must keeps sight of its democratic values.

Islamabad rulers believe Washington will continue supporting them. They claim that Washington is tied down in Afghanistan and

Iraq, suffering daily casualties and will therefore sacrifice the cause of democracy. If General Musharraf is right in this assessment and his nuclear-armed military dictatorship continues exploiting the war on international terror to legitimize his illegitimate power, the threat from terrorists could build through this century. I empathize with the author Bernard Henry-Levi, who wrote: "I have become part of a growing club of those who cannot return to Pakistan, simply because they don't want to end up like journalist Daniel Pearl. But I am convinced that a harsher tone, a reformulation of the terms of alliance, is called for, so that our relationship with Musharraf will be more than a gullible, naïve embrace — and will conform to moral as well as political imperatives. And I would add that waiting for us is the other Pakistan —that which is liberal, democratic, secular, which fights, back against the wall, against mounting Islamicism, and which does not understand why, in this combat, [America] is not at its side."

Thank you, Ladies and Gentlemen.

— Woodrow Wilson Centre, Washington DC
9-Feb-2004

Democracy and Internationalism

With Iraq divided into American, British and Polish controlled zones, we gather together in Turin at an extraordinary and difficult time. Whatever our own views on the path leading to the recent Iraq War, it is time to look forward. It is time to assess the new world reality. The post Iraq international situation gives an opportunity to look for ways to promote the cause of democratization, human rights and the global community to which we are all committed. Many in the international community felt uncomfortable with a war without United Nations sanction. Demonstrations for peace broke out in the heart of Europe, at times larger than demonstrations within the Muslim world. No one likes war. No one likes Repression either.

Western societies absorb dissent. Non-Western societies are yet to deal with the challenge of those victimized, persecuted, imprisoned, tortured and exiled because of their political views. This community of the disaffected and the disenfranchised played a pivotal role both in Afghanistan and Iraq. In Kabul and Baghdad, popular voices of the people were denied political space. They formed the political front for a war to reclaim their own land. Countries descend into the darkness of international terrorism and state terrorism when pluralism is disrupted, when diversity is suppressed, when one man directs the destiny of millions, be ha Mullah Omar or Saddam Hussain or other dictators. America's President George Bush justified war claiming: "Men and women in every culture need liberty like they need food and water and air. Everywhere that freedom arrives, humanity rejoices; and everywhere that freedom stirs, let tyrants fear." Post Iraq, tyrants should fear.

It is troubling that some of those tyrants still feel little fear. Sadly, some of them are still close allies of Washington. In the case of Pakistan, a repressive regime exiles the popular opposition, imprisons dissidents and rigs elections. In the post Iraq world that dawned this April, the words rationalising the Iraq war can be used to press all nations, and especially Washington, to make consistent application of democratic principles the essence of internationalism in this new millennium. There were times in recent history where historic moments were squandered. When the moving finger of history writes of the end of the Twentieth Century, it will write of the international community's failure to reinforce the democratic breakthrough that the end of communism brought as the era's greatest missed opportunities. I recall speaking to European Parliaments, to the Congress of the United States proclaiming that the era of the dictator was over, that militaries all over the world had finally returned to their barracks, that democracy was blooming on every continent.

In retrospect, I fear it was merely a mirage. The forces of real politic were waiting to collide with the ideology of democracy. We proclaimed a new moral era, but actually constructed an era of moral relativity. And Ladies and Gentlemen, selective morality is by its very definition, immoral. Our standards are inconsistent and our policies selective. Those that decry dictatorship in Burma are silent about tyranny elsewhere. Those decrying dictatorship in Iraq, stay close to dictators in Pakistan. Many in this room rightfully demand self-determination in Palestine, but are less vocal about the rights of the Kashmiri people. In this age of moral relativism, political standards vary according to political expediency and economic imperatives. Democracy for Iraq, but dictatorship just miles away. Iraqi violations of UN resolutions bring a strong response. Violations of UN resolutions in the Middle East or in South Asia draw a less vocal reaction.

We evaluate national security by hardened borders and tanks and missiles. But true security is linked to the fight for economic justice that will liberate nations; true security is linked to the fight against famine and AIDs; true security means protecting the environment from pollution and desecration. No matter how great and powerful a nation may be, true leadership is more than military action. It is leading the fight against AIDS, against hunger, against poverty, against racism, and for women, the fight for justice.

Ladies and Gentlemen, the post Iraq world situation allows us to focus once again on the principle of freedom. This time it must be more than rhetoric that is exploited in pursuit of limited foreign policy objectives. I remember a time when the world walked from Afghanistan after the defeat of the Soviets in 1989. The fundamental mistake was that we were not consistently committed to the values of freedom, democracy and self-determination that ultimately undermine terrorism. The result was Taliban dictatorship, Al-Queda and terrorism. Dictatorship does not constrain fundamentalism or terrorism. It provokes it. The goal of rational foreign policy must always be to simultaneously promote stability and to strengthen democratic values. The stakes are high. Every war in the South Asian subcontinent, from where I come, started when my country was under a military dictator or one of its civilian surrogates. I do not know of a single case when a democratic country has gone to war against another democratic country. Dictators are not accountable and do not need a popular mandate behind their policies. The tragedy of Iraq is that Saddam Hussain spurned all offers of a peaceful transition from his regime to a democratic one. None dared tell him that he could not win a military war against American technology. None dared criticise his flawed strategy of a prolonged guerrilla conflict with house to house fighting in Iraq's cities to force Washington into a ceasefire while he remained in control. Dictators are cut off from reality by sycophants too scared to tell them the truth allowing for miscalculations that innocent people pay for in lives. Democracies are different. Democratic leaders are accountable before the Parliament, the Press and the People. Democratic governments must provide for the public welfare, must provide schools and hospitals, health and housing. Dictatorships need not. They rely on unaccountable secret services and are free to divert resources to schemes that parliamentary scrutiny simply would not permit. History has taught us the very hard lesson that when democratic states turn against democracy, they turn against themselves.

Ladies and Gentlemen, the international press has speculated about Islamabad's support to North Korea's nuclear program. Islamabad denies the charges. Even though Islamabad is a key ally of the US in the war against terrorism, Pakistani citizens are finger printed and photographed when they visit America. Military dictator General Musharraf promised the world community he would seal the borders with Afghanistan to prevent fleeing Al Queda from slipping into Pakistan. Yet scores made their way into the country as the recent arrests by the FBI demonstrate.

Ladies and Gentlemen, I believe a democratic Pakistan is the best guarantee of respect and dignity for the people of Pakistan. I believe that a democratic Pakistan living by the rule of law within and without is the best guarantee of the triumph of moderation and modernity amongst one billion Muslims at the crossroads of our history. These are difficult times. We stand at the crossroads of a new world order. We witness the dawn of a unipolar world environment where wars can take place with the coalition of the willing. We witness disunity in the United Nations Security Council, in NATO, in Europe and in the Muslim world. We can remember that the future is in our hands. As the European philosopher Goethe once wrote, "Freedom must be reinvented in every generation." Unipolarism can lead to unilateralism. As power shifts to new paradigms the challenge is to find ways where the voices of the rest of the world community can also be heard effectively. This is our turn to reinvent freedom. And we shall prevail.

Thank you ladies and gentlemen.

— The World Political Forum - Turin, Italy
19-Mar-2003

The Battle Between Dictatorship and Democracy

Thursday night I attended a brief interview session with former Pakistani Prime Minister Benazir Bhutto. She later spoke at Southwestern University in Georgetown, Texas– this year's Shilling Lecturer. Last year Bishop Desmond Tutu gave Southwestern's Shilling lecture.

Bhutto's lecture expanded on her answers in the interview section. South Western did an outstanding job with her lecture. No sound glitches, started on time, and the venue surprisingly intimate– especially since Bhutto gave the speech in the gymnasium. With heavy black wall drapes and a stage with podium it was a gym smartly transformed. South Western is an NCAA Division III school in a conference that includes other liberal arts colleges and universities like Sewanee, Rhodes, Trinity, and Oglethorpe. Georgetown is about thirty miles north of Austin. *The Austin American-Statesmen* reported the 1700 people attended the lecture– I can verify that the floor seats were packed.

Only two other reporters sat in on the media session– Camille Wheeler of the *American Statesman* and a student reporter from the Southwestern School paper– so we had an opportunity to get more than a sound bite. Here are two of Bhutto's intricate answers to several questions I asked her.

Bhutto (initial statement): I'll be talking tonight about what is needed for a more stable world and what is needed in Muslim countries; how democracy can be a better impetus to educational and gender reform. And how democracy undermines the forces of terrorism. I will speak about the reason for repeated military dictatorships, so many military dictatorships, Pakistan, Philippines, Indonesia, why these are the countries where we now have terrorist cells. You see them throughout Indonesia and Pakistan. I will argue that these military regimes relied on war and force, ruled by force, they raised a generation that believed power came through force and violent means. I will be speaking how the military dictatorships or authoritarian rulers would not tolerate mainstream political parties or democratic parties viewing them as a threat and therefore only parties that could approach the masses were the religious parties and the religious parties then had an open field for promoting their politics and modern democratic parties did not have their opportunity.

We have to give the people of the Muslim countries a choice, not a choice between a dictatorship and whether military dictatorship or religious dictatorship. And this is where the choice of democracy becomes so powerful for changing people's minds. We must educate the youth how change can come about peacefully. To educate the masses how they can change through the majesty of law and the constitution. I believe the Muslim people need to be saved from the militant groups that grew strong because of a particular past and the way to save the Muslim people in Muslim societies is through democracy and promoting justice through independence of the judiciary.

Bay: There's a democratic surge in the Middle East—what can stop it?

Bhutto: There is certainly a surge towards democracy. This year has been a remarkable one. In some ways like the year when the Berlin Wall fell and the momentum for freedom we've had elections, Afghanistan, Iraq, Palestine. And we've seen how the people of Lebanon are now on the streets and talking about their independence. However, the militants are still there and the beneficiaries of the old order are still there. We must remember that while the masses are on one side, there is also an entrenched vested interest that has been created through years of dictatorship or subjugation and these people are waiting to hit out at every single opportunity and they can hit out through several different ways and they can hit out with intrigue or conspiracy or hit out by violent means – beheadings, car bombs, assassination. In fact Iraq is very critical to the future direction of the Middle East. Success or failure in Iraq will have a profound impact of the future direction of the Middle East. And certainly those people who are carrying out the beheadings and the kidnappings and tape-recording with the videotapes of their victims.

The video tapes of the beheadings—[they are] trying to create terror at the horror, to lead to an early pullout, or diversion of the international community's attention so they [international community] leave. That must not happen. We've got to remember Germany and Japan. It took a generation to build the political and social institutions, the judicial system, the civil services that enable those countries to continue as vibrant successful democracies. We must remember after WWII, if the allied powers had turned their attention away after a year or two, well at that time the Nazi forces were still pretty entrenched. They may have tried a comeback. I think there needs to be a commitment to the promotion of freedom and patience and perseverance are required in knowing that people liberated from decades of repression and cruelty without any political institutions or political systems need the help of the international community. And while there may be voices that say why should the international community continue to stay, after all let the people sort it out for themselves, we must remember that this is one world now, a global village, this is one world and whatever happens in one part of the world affects another part of the world….We've seen that if peace is to be built and stability is to be built…We must have a common commitment to help humanity move to the road of modernity and progress in this century.

Bay: You mentioned the oppressed people that don't have political institutions to adapt to modernity. How has imprisonment shaped you as a political leader and how does that shape you now? You seem to have a direct understanding of that situation.

Bhutto: I fought against General Zia's military dictatorship in the 1980s. I was in prison for long periods of time. I was fortunate because I studied at Harvard on the East Coast. I saw freedom here, tolerance here, pluralism here. I saw people who could criticize the rulers without being arrested. I saw people gathering together for peace marches against the war in Vietnam. I was here at the Watergate crisis and I saw the President being brought down by people rather than the President crushing the people.

Throughout the years I was in prison despite the difficulties, trials illnesses, the solitary confinement, I was determined to make a difference in the lives of the people of my country. When I became Prime Minister of Pakistan there was the expectation that overnight Pakistan would become a democratic country. And so I saw first hand how there was this enormous surge in public opinion for democracy. But people who became powerful during dictatorship who had become politically or economically powerful were able [to undermine].

So I know that the expectations are great thinking victory has taken place, without realizing there is the morning after that the basis the reconstruction of a political system takes time, patience, perseverance. It takes time, time to train people, time for various institutions to come to grips. For example the people in the judiciary had all been appointed by the dictator. I feel this will be the same in Iraq, wherever there has been authoritarian rule. People have a particular mindset the elite have a particular mindset. [This takes time to change.]

The masses want the power but there is a struggle between the elite who want to take back their position and the ordinary people. Then I realized what happened in Germany and Japan. The allied powers made the commitment to Germany and Japan for military support and economic support that those two countries remained stable without once again being sucked into a horrific past.

I'll transcribe the rest of my notes and tape, possibly Sunday evening. Camille Wheeler asked Bhutto a superb question about women in senior leadership roles. I want to add Bhutto's response to my question about her role models as a leader– and I laced that question with references to Margaret Thatcher and Indira Gandhi. A hint of Ms. Bhutto's long and fascinating answer: Maggie, yes, Indira, no. I knew she is a Thatcherite of a certain stripe. Bhutto is a private-sector advocate, but knows how difficult it is to create the civic and governmental-judicial framework that encourages and protects private initiative.

The democratic surge in the Muslim Middle East was the centre of her interview and lecture. Bhutto argued that the revolution is on (and all of you know I agree). Afghanistan, Palestine, then Iraq have created the opportunities for democratizing the Middle East. Muslim countries world-wide (including Pakistan) have a chance to escape the yoke of dictatorship. She made the case that tyranny has distorted Muslim societies and distorted Islam.

I didn't ask her about nukes. I know about the nukes, I know she got missile plans for Pakistan from North Korea.

— Austin Bay Blog
3/11/2005

The Royal Institute of International Affairs

Ladies and Gentlemen:

It is a great pleasure for me to be with you in London today. As you may be aware, my family and I, and the leadership of the Pakistan Peoples Party are all under heavy assault from the current regime in Pakistan. This is a complex conspiracy to defame not only us, but the very concept of democracy in my besieged homeland. So lest you in the West think that the fight against fascism and totalitarianism lies in the past, remember what is going on in Pakistan, in Burma and in other parts of the world where the fight for freedom is not yet won.

This is consistent with the main point I would like to make to you today in our discussion of the Afghan situation in the context of big and small state relations. For the people of Britain and the United States and all of the West, the Cold War ended with the crumbling of the Berlin Wall. For countries of the developing world that were instruments and surrogates of the East and the West for forty years — and especially for my own country of Pakistan — we are still living with the profound and tragic consequences of the superpower confrontation. When the West correctly and bravely determined in the late forties to confront and contain communism's expansion, morality took on a bipolar configuration. Whether it was the Marshall Plan to economically rebuild Europe, or the creation of the NATO alliance to contain the Soviet Union, the world became a contest between "us" and "them." And the West strategically calculated, that any nations which would stand with the West against communism would be treated as friends and allies. Political systems became irrelevant. Due process became irrelevant. Human rights became irrelevant. Democracy became irrelevant. The enemy of my enemy became my friend.

The Greek junta. The Marcos dictatorship . The generals in Argentina. The Zia-ul-Haq bloodbath against democracy in Pakistan. The enemies of my enemy became my friends. And the victims of our friends became irrelevant.

A democratically elected government in Pakistan was overthrown in a military coup. A democratically elected Prime Minister was murdered. A political party was decimated, tortured, sent into exile. The press was destroyed. Unions were banned. Student organizations were prohibited. The cause of women was sent back into another century. And the world was silent. For in the polarity of the Cold War, the cooperation of the Pakistani dictator Zia-ul-Haq with the West's effort to dislodge the Soviet aggression in Afghanistan was sufficient justification to disregard the political and social abuse, the human rights travesties, the suppression of democracy.

For a long and bloody decade, from 1979 through 1989, the West — and particularly the United States — used Pakistan as a surrogate in its final confrontation with the Soviet Union. Billions of billions of covert aid was channelled through Pakistan to the Mujahideen. The Pakistan/Afghan border became a porous fiction. My country became the staging area for the West's final assault on the tottering Soviet empire. My country, which was totally unfamiliar to the drug culture, became a nation of heroin addicts. My country, which had no tradition of lawlessness, was so overridden with weapons in every neighbourhood, on every street, in almost every house, that a Kalashnikov mentality emerged and the rule of law disappeared. Our cities were overwhelmed with crime and violence, a situation that persists today. Millions of Afghan refugees, driven from their country by the civil war, took refuge in Pakistan and were housed, and educated, and provided with food and health care at extraordinary cost to Pakistani society. Almost two million of these refugees remain on Pakistani soil today. The consequences of the West's strategic effort in Afghanistan transcended the impact on my own country. For the confrontation with the Soviets, and the support of the Mujahideen itself became a symbol of the myopia of the Cold War.

When I visited the United States early in my first time as Prime Minister of Pakistan, in 1989, I vividly recall discussions with then President Bush about the political situation in Afghanistan. The United States had made a military decision to arm and strengthen the fiercest fighters in the Afghan resistance — the forces of Gulbuddin Hakmatyar. I cautioned Mr. Bush that he was creating a veritable Frankenstein by aligning the United States with the most extremist of the Mujahideen groups. I cautioned the West that by strengthening the most extreme and fundamentalist of the resistance, it was weakening the political position of the rest of the resistance coalition. The pragmatists and the moderates were shunned by the United State's single minded efforts to strengthen the most extreme of the seven Majahideen factions. And I cautioned that this element of the Mujahideen was not only religiously fanatic, but viscerally anti-Western

I warned that we must look beyond the inevitable military victory against the communist regime in Kabul, and work toward setting up a successor government that was broad-based and moderate. But because the United States chose not to opt for a political settlement involving all seven elements of the Mujahideen, peace was not restored to Afghanistan. Indeed in the decade since the Soviets withdrew in 1989, the people of Afghanistan have not seen a single day of peace. The extremists who were so emboldened by the United States during the eighties are now exporting their terrorism to other parts of the world. To the extent that they use heroin trafficking to pay for their exploits, international terrorism and international drug trafficking intersect. And as terrorism and drug trafficking pervade western society, the decision of the United States a generation ago has come full circle. For not only is stability in Afghanistan a victim, not only were the foundations and institutions of democracy in Pakistan destroyed in this process, but the recipients of the West's support and largesse have turned their venom against their benefactors. As

I predicted nine years ago in Washington, a true Frankenstein has been created.

I think there is a long-term, strategic lesson for all of us in this sad and continuing by-product of the Cold War: Whenever fundamental principles are sacrificed in the cause of expediency, danger follows. Whenever a dictator is cuddled, all democrats, all over the world, are weakened. Whenever human rights are abused, all of us become victims. Whenever the West sacrifices the political values that have made western democracy a model to the developing world, the chance for democratic change in Asia and Africa is tragically diminished. The principles of western democracy can never again be selectively applied, only when convenient, only in isolated cases. If a putsch is not to be recognized in Moscow, neither should it be in Islamabad. If fraudulent elections are not legitimized in Lagos, they should not be legitimized in Lahore. If human rights violations are not tolerated in Serbia, they should neither be tolerated in Karachi. If the lack of an independent judiciary is condemned by the West in Burma, the exploitation of the Courts to victimise the political opposition should not be tolerated in Pakistan. We have all learned a long and painful lesson from the lingering consequences of the Cold War. The selective application of morality is by its very nature immoral.

So Ladies and Gentlemen, as this conference ends and you return to your comfortable homes in this wonderful country at peace and prosperity, remember those all over the world who have paid a heavy price for the West's triumph against communism. For you the Cold War is over. For the drug addicts of Karachi, for the victims of lawlessness in Lahore, for the leaders of the Pakistan Peoples Party rotting in jails all throughout Pakistan — for us, my friends— the war continues.

Thank you, Ladies and Gentlemen.

— London, England
10-Sep-1998

Benazir Bhutto in BBC Programme

Here is the text of the question answer session:

BBC : Leaders of India and Pakistan have entered in a new phase in normalising the relations between the two countries. How sincere are the efforts this time in your view?

Benazir Bhutto: My understanding is that leaders of both the countries are under tremendous pressure from the peoples of South Asia. This region has serious problems which need to be addressed immediately - poverty, unemployment. The common man thinks unless these problems are addressed, this region would be left behind in the Twentyfirst century. It is this pressure, which has given a new hope of friendly relations between India and Pakistan.

BBC: How sincere is the present establishment of Pakistan in restoring friendly relations with India?

Benazir : I hope that this establishment in Pakistan has learnt lessons from the past. Earlier too, the Indian Prime Minister had made efforts to make peace with Pakistan with his Bus diplomacy and Agra Summit. Unfortunately, both failed, and I am extremely sorry to say that the media, newspapers and intellectuals blamed my country for failures on both occasions. But now I hope that Islamabad has learnt from the past, and the efforts being made by Gen Musharraf could yield good results, and my hope is based on the reason that peace is the need of the present time.

BBC listener from Singapore : Despite 55 years after Independence, Pakistan has been under the control of military dictators for the majority of the time. One Prime Minister was hanged in the past, and now two former Prime Ministers cannot enter the country. Is this because Pakistan has been obsessed with Kashmir and anti-India-ism ? Do you think Gen Musharraf would restore a civilian Government, or would he meet the same fate as those of his military ruler predecessors?

Benazir : There has been an impression that due to the tension in the region, the armed forces in Pakistan have managed considerable political clout, and therefore the democratic forces could not become strong. But now I hope, all this would become a part of history soon. So far, as Gen Musharraf is concerned, he has been under great pressure to start peace talks with India. I hope these efforts would reach some logical conclusion! When the democratic process would be restored in Pakistan, only at that time would I be satisfied, that a political consensus would lead to a durable peace process. In this regard, I have appealed to the Musharraf regime to allow both the exiled former Prime Ministers to return to the country and be a part of the peace process, so that the world can see this as a sincere effort of the army, civilian rule and people of all the four states of Pakistan, and not merely as a tactical manoeuvre!

BBC: You hope that the efforts being made by Gen Musharraf would be successful. Were the democratic governments in Pakistan in the past reluctant to have normal ties with India ?

Benazir : See, this world witnesses different scenarios and situations with the changing times. When the Berlin Wall was pulled down, a ray of hope arose that the people in other regions with similar walls could unite. It was at that time in 1989 that I felt that the struggle and sacrifices of the Kashmiri people would be highlighted at an international level. People were being killed on both sides - Kashmiri struggle and Indian army. That was one scenario, and the world had sympathy with such struggles. Then in 2001, after the attack on The World Trade Centre, the world saw another change, at that time the sympathy with such struggles and especially with the use of force ceased to exist. So it is the timing at a particular juncture that is important.

BBC: You were mentioning about the pressure on Gen Musharraf for peace talks with India. Who is pressurising him?

Benazir : He is under pressure from the entire world. On one hand is the internal pressure and, on the other is the external pressure. Washington clearly told Gen Musharraf to ban the militant groups within Pakistan. He promised to do so two years ago, but those groups started operating under different names. The US again told him that it was naming those groups as terrorist organisations, and they be banned, he says he would do it now, so he is under pressure from all sides!

BBC listener from Dubai : It has been 55 years now since the two countries have been fighting over territory and Kashmir. This time was the first, when both talked serious business, and decided to put controversial issues behind. You have ruled over Pakistan, tell us how much can the Musharraf regime be trusted, and does this regime have the power to implement what it promises?

Benazir : See, the issue of trust is an extremely sensitive one when we talk about Indo-Pak relations. We have to be clear that no particular individual can remain in power forever, and has to finally go one day! My understanding is, for Pakistan to be trusted internationally, there would have to be political consensus internally. Even if, today I were to say that a particular leader is sincere, he would not be there forever, and remember individual decisions are temporary, and not long-lasting. I feel that the people of South Asia are not ready to be cheated once again, we have to seize this opportunity and have an internal political consensus on the peace efforts with India.

BBC listener from Gujarat : In today's scenario, especially after 9/11 and the Iraq war, things have changed, and Gen Musharraf is accepted internationally. What is your and Nawaz Sharif's political future?

Benazir : You are right, both of us are out of the political process of the country. Gen Musharraf has himself been saying that the opposition in the National Assembly takes directions from those out of the country. If the opposition leadership is out of the country, then what sort of democracy is there in Pakistan ? I think it cannot be restored also like this.

Recently, Gen Musharraf sought a vote of confidence, he did not win that also. He struck an alliance with the MMA, and despite that had to resort to wrong counting. In Pakistan, the assemblies of the provinces have equal votes, but this time it was not the case, Punjab assembly was given more votes to ensure Musharraf's victory. Since we are out of the country, the civilian institutions are not being allowed to function properly, and the state of affairs is such that a powerful military ruler cannot win a vote of confidence, he has to resort to wrong practices to claim victory ! Only on our return can the things improve in Pakistan. Last time also, when I returned during Gen Zia's tenure, there was not a democratically elected government in Pakistan. Now I am looking for a chance to return to my country and serve the people !

See, the situation in Pakistan is very complex at the moment. On the one hand, rights of people have been snatched, and on the other, political leaders are facing persecution. But the situation is such, that due to the situation in Afghanistan, Gen Musharraf was able to cosy up to Washington, and has been able to divert attention from the internal situation in Pakistan. But myself, and Mian Nawaz Sharif want to return to Pakistan. Maybe both of us go together, maybe we go separately. So far as I am concerned, I am definitely planning my return !

BBC listener from Islamabad: Madam, you have blamed the previous governments of Pakistan for failures at Lahore and Agra, which is wrong. How can you be critical of Gen Musharraf who is supported by 99 percent Pakistanis? You are not in touch with reality as you have been out since last five-six years now.

Benazir : Supporters of Gen Musharraf think I have no credibility and he has the support of the majority of people in Pakistan. But the real situation is different. If his referendum was fair, then why did the European Union and other international bodies raise questions on it? If the General really had support, why did he have to rig the referendum? These are questions which have not been answered so far. Nawaz Sharif was my political rival, and the Lahore bus diplomacy took place during his tenure, and at that very time Kargil was being planned. You can point a finger and say I am wrong in saying that Pakistan was blamed for previous failures - Lahore and Agra ! But in the eyes of the world, the overwhelming opinion is - it was due to Kargil that the bus diplomacy failed ! I feel that the political leadership has the skills and experience to deal with different situations successfully!

BBC listener from Allahabad : Can India hope for better relations with Pakistan, given the interference of the army in every sphere of life, and the influence it has on the present Government in Islamabad?

Benazir : It is a fact that the army has interfered tremendously in the politics of Pakistan. Just have a look at the history of Indo-Pak relations. The two countries have fought three wars against each other, and during all three wars, there was a military ruler in Pakistan. On the other hand, look at civilian governments, after the Simla Agreement, there was no war between the two countries, this was a political achievement. Now look at the recent past, after the PPP government was destabilised in 1996, both the countries were close to another war on at least three occasions. Washington, London, different Muslim countries and even other neighbours in South Asia had to intervene to prevent the two nations from going to war against each other. Therefore, civilian governments bring peace, and it is a harsh reality that the military rule in Pakistan has not been able to build friendly relations with India.

BBC: But Madam, at the moment, peace efforts are being made by a military ruler.

Benazir : Yes the efforts are being made, and I hope they will be successful. But if political consensus is not evolved in Pakistan, it would mean these efforts are temporary, and it is being done under international pressure. You do not know what would be the situation tomorrow, therefore I repeat without political consensus, you do not know of the outcome!

BBC listener from Roorkee: Are Indo-Pak talks under any compulsion or is it an emotional issue for both sides. Why do both countries move and then stop suddenly?

Benazir: You are right, both the sides have raised hopes and then suddenly the peace process has stopped. Even now, there are certain doubts, that the hopes could be misplaced and, suddenly any development could spoil the entire show. But, let us not be held captive by the past. I could have easily said India should not talk to Gen Musharraf, as he is a military dictator, but I did not say so, because peace is so important for South Asia, that let us all keep the differences, rifts aside and give a momentum to the peace process. That is why I have welcomed the peace process, and let us now give a positive spin to the process. When we talk of a positive peace process, we should not make it an individual peace process, it should be a broad-based, institutional process.

BBC listener from Saudi Arabia: Madam, you are a leader of a political party, why don't you go to Pakistan to fight your cases and fight for Democracy, what are you achieving by sitting in London?

Benazir: I am in exile. See, the conspiracy bazaar is hot in Pakistan at the moment. These people would not allow me to do politics, meet my people and serve the country. They would like to see that my entire time goes in courts, one day in Karachi, another day in Lahore and so on. Therefore I am in exile. Every day I am looking for a chance to return to my country, and serve my people. I hope the day of my return would come very soon, and you would hear in Saudi Arabia, that I have returned back home. I would definitely go back one day!

BBC listener from Meerut : Whoever may rule in Pakistan, whether it be civilian or military, nobody is sincere in relations with India. When you were in the chair, you also did not make any sincere attempt to have friendly relations with India. Why is it so?

Benazir : See, there is a big constituency inside and outside Pakistan, which thinks that till the time the Kashmir issue is resolved, relations with India cannot be normalised. We have to keep this constituency in control, and send a message to Kashmiris that they are not being ignored. So far as the Pakistan People's Party is concerned, our stand is that the two countries should first concentrate on confidence building measures, as both of them would not agree on Kashmir due to huge differences in their respective stands. We feel once confidence building is done, friendship is there, then contentious issues could be solved. When I was the Prime Minister, I agreed with Rajiv Gandhi on trade, and both of us agreed that the two countries would not attack each other's nuclear facilities.

— Former Prime Minister Benazir Bhutto took part in a BBC program where she answered questions from viewers from across the world.
12-Jan-2004

New Regional Alignments

Decision making in Pakistan once took place in an institutional framework allowing debate between different governmental departments. This resulted in credible, legitimate, serious and acceptable policies based on consensus. No more. Since commando style politics reshaped Islamabad's foreign policy, impetuousness is the name of the game. Such impetuousness was displayed following the bombing of the World Trade Centres on September 11, 2001. As the call from Secretary of State Colin Powell came, Islamabad's military dictator leapt to attention. Much to the surprise of the American administration, disclosed in a book called "Bush at War", General Musharraf joined the international coalition against terrorism without naming a price, or consulting the institutions of government.

The foreign office, the security services, the National Security Council, the cabinet itself that would have supported the decision to join the war against terror were ignored. Impetuousness cost Pakistan consensus and perhaps debt relief that could relieve unborn generations of financial burdens. Other countries, including Egypt and Jordan, managed such relief when strategic regional situations developed. This summer the military dictator flew to Camp David for talks with President Bush, the most powerful leader of the unipolar world. His visit followed that of the President of the Philippines. She was treated to a resplendent state visit with a grand White House dinner while the Marine Band played in the background. He was treated to the lesser official visit, businesslike, simple and quickly over at Camp David.

Fresh from Camp David, the General decided on another display of impetuousness during a television talk show. He now wanted a "debate" on whether Pakistan should recognize the state of Israel. Although informal contacts between Islamabad and Tel Aviv existed since the days of General Zia in the seventies, Islamabad links recognition to the resolution of the Jerusalem and Golan Heights issues. Perhaps the General thought that all doors to Washington lead through Israel. Or perhaps he wanted to dangle a carrot for his continuation in office. In any event, this momentous announcement was made without consulting the cabinet, the national security council or even his brother officers that make up the corps commanders of the Pakistan army. Surprisingly, the General thought that a hard nosed state like Israel would bite a dangling carrot cutting its strategic relationship with India for a "debate" in Islamabad. Of course Prime Minister Vajpayee was listening. He swiftly invited Prime Minister Sharon to New Delhi to let those that were in the dark know that the Israeli-Indian nexus was safe and sound. The result of the General's commando gambit, throwing aside consensus for unilateral action, is a troubling backlash for Islamabad. Islamabad's foreign office expressed the depth of concern over the growing Indo-Israel defence cooperation. A Foreign Ministry spokesman said "It is an act directed against Pakistan and we would be most concerned as they are very negative developments."

The Israeli defence pact with New Delhi follows the Indo-Iranian defence agreement reached a few months back. Meanwhile Islamabad's relations with Kabul are hardly good as pro-Taliban militants regroup and attempt to destabilize the Karzai government. Against this background, the All Parties Hurriyet Conference, a grouping of Kashmiri leaders across the divide, sympathetic to Islamabad, split. Washington, which facilitated Indo-Pakistan talks in the past, has yet to suggest a summit meeting between Musharraf and Vajpayee during their September visits to the UN General Assembly in New York.

And Indian troops in Ladakh are carrying out military exercises which are "within the disputed territory" according to a foreign office briefing in Islamabad. These exercises are taking place with US Special Forces as part of new Indo-American military ties against the backdrop of Israeli Prime Minister Sharon's visit to New Delhi. Islamabad is helpless in the face of provocation even as it is Washington's most valued ally. The time calls for leadership to overcome the sorry pass of individual decision making although it seems that time and leadership are at odds with each other.

— **12-Sep-2003**

Global Free Trade and South Asia

Ladies and Gentlemen:

I am honoured to be asked to appear before this distinguished group, and thank the sponsors and this group of accomplished business executives, diplomats and Members of Parliament for extending me such warm hospitality.

As the world focuses on the atrocities of Kosovo, and makes attempts in fits and starts to respond as a cohesive global community to the bloodshed unleashed by the Serbian dictator, it is fitting that, as we stand on the threshold of a new century, such a diverse group is gathered in London discussing the future of Asian business, a city so far away from Asian realities yet becoming closer in trade and financial ties with each new treaty passage.

I know that all gathered here today are no strangers to either the business realities of present Asia, or the explosive growth in global economic integration we have experienced during this decade. All companies — and countries — are racing to keep pace with the revolutionary power that the new technologies of communications and transportation afford us. We are, in every sense of the word, entering a century to be dominated by the rules of a global market. And as we enter this new and exciting era, this new century, I am convinced that the new rules of the game are simple and concrete:

In the Twentyfirst Century, nations must uphold the principles of Democracy and the rule of law;

In the Twentyfirst century, governments must guarantee basic freedoms and liberties to their citizens;

In the Twentyfirst Century, regions must promote free trade with minimal state intervention, and with a policy of non-intervention and mutual respect in inter-state relations;

In the new century, the concerns of the state will be driven more by considerations of trade and commerce, rather than by our traditional military - territorial considerations. And the success of a Nation, as we head towards a new century, shall be based upon its level of exports, hard currency reserves, its per capita GNP, and the creative genius of its citizens. In our lifetime, achieving near complete free trade worldwide appears achievable, if not unstoppable.

GLOBAL FREE TRADE : EU LEADERSHIP

I came here to comment on trade and South Asia within the larger international context, and the halting but positive steps that we are taking to improve the business environment in our vibrant but still hampered region. Before focusing on South Asia, however, let me take a moment to look at the progress being made worldwide for free trade.

First and of precedent-setting importance is the example that you, the European Union, are providing to the rest of humanity. Let us not mince words: The EU is a revolutionary breakthrough in international relations, the ramifications of which are not yet fully understood. Many around the world have been watching with both astonishment and some envy as the European nations have been able to create one of the world's largest single markets in human history, and this without bloodshed or military conquest. Let us not underestimate the accomplishment of creating the European Common Market by states the entire history of which together, has been one of war, animosity and mistrust. The desire for the creation of 'super-economic zones' like the EC, was driven by smaller states seeking to effectively compete economically with the economic superpowers of the day, namely the United States and Japan. The GNP of America is (US$ 8 trillion) and of Japan (US$ 5 trillion). Only after combining the 10 'First World' European economies can the combined EC GNP compete (at US$ 7 trillion). All this has been accomplished without a single bullet being fired. Huge territories, nations and populations peacefully agreed to redefine their economic borders, and to co-exist with each other in the better interests of their future well being. The EC's formation is truly a model case of the new paradigm, where economically we enter an increasingly 'Borderless World' while maintaining our national sovereignty. In essence, the EC member states are 'pooling' their economic sovereignty in creating a free trade zone and a common currency, thus submerging their narrow national interests for the greater good of the whole European Community.

THE RACE FOR GLOBAL FREE TRADE

And, with the birth of the European Common Market and common currency, we are now witnessing the unleashing of a global race for ever-larger free trade blocs and trade zones, and at a pace and scale unprecedented in human history. On two fronts, the European Common Market itself is moving with utmost speed to expand its model on a global level. With the Far East, the EC and the ASEAN nations are in serious discussions to lower tariffs. This new development, know as ASEM (Asia-Europe Organization), just concluded its second year of high level discussions. The fruit bearing trees have been planted. At the most recent ASEM meeting in Berlin, EU President German Foreign Minister Fischer suggested a new Euro-Asia free trade zone, and through this, creation of "a stable world financial and monetary system". Asian nations now actively engaged in this process include Brunei, China, Indonesia, Japan, Malaysia, the Philippines, Singapore, South Korea, Thailand and Vietnam. In the opposite direction, the EU, under Spanish leadership, is moving quickly to establish free trade relationships between the EU and the South American nations. I understand that a multilateral summit to move forward this new free trade zone will be held next year, and it appears that unless the Americans can move at least as fast as the Europeans, South American trade may move more freely into European households than into those in America. The irony is not lost that in one short decade after the ending of the Cold War, American economic hegemony in its own hemisphere could be so severely challenged.

But the Europeans are not the only nations moving rapidly to dismantle old trade barriers. In Africa — all too often left out of the global economic debates — the nations of Southern and Eastern Africa are quickly moving to create their own version of the European Common Market. This new trading bloc, now known as the Common Market for Eastern and Southern Africa (or COMESA), has set an ambitious but achievable goal of eliminating tariffs within their bloc by the year 2000. For Africa as a whole, and the 21 nations participating in COMESA, this is indeed promising news.

In the Western Hemisphere, while there seems to be a delay in the expansion of NAFTA, I do not doubt that NAFTA, too, will expand throughout the Western Hemisphere. As the largest free trade bloc in the world, the economies of Canada, the U.S. and Mexico continue to seek expansion of their model throughout the entire Western Hemisphere. The new EC competition for South America may urge NAFTA to heightened urgency.

And even among the states of the former Soviet Union, high level talks within the former USSR are gaining momentum for a new free trade zone, led by the institution of the former Commonwealth of Independent States (CIS). For all of those nations, this is a needed and positive development, and should be given as much support and encouragement from the international community as are current IMF rescue packages.

THE SLOW PATH OF SOUTH ASIA

In this context of fierce global competition for the creation and expansion of free trade zones, I turn lastly to South Asia. South Asia has been for far too long a region teetering on the edge of catastrophe. For fifty years, we have been at each other's throats. We have fought four wars, and the last war dismembered my nation. Our troops, as we speak, fire at each other in the frozen wasteland called Siachen, which has become a metaphor for the senselessness that we have allowed to continue for half a century.

But there is hope. Six weeks ago in Islamabad, I was privileged to participate in the first Indian-Pakistan All Parliamentarians Conference. This historic meeting brought together parliamentarians from all parties from both India and Pakistan. Over the course of my lifetime — a few years less than the conflict between India and Pakistan — such a meeting between our two nations has been unprecedented. At that meeting, as our joint political leadership sought common ground for our regional problems, I unveiled an economic vision for South Asia. It is time for South Asia to fully participate in the explosion of global trade, and for our respective governments to set-aside territorial ambitions and seek economic progress for our peoples and our region. To the joint delegation, I proposed that the nations of South Asia now embark on an accelerated path of economic cooperation and follow the leadership of the European nations. I call this the Asian Free Zone. As you may notice, the word 'trade' is omitted, and for good reason, as it is time that we, one fifth of the world's population, tackle more than trade.

THE ASIAN FREE ZONE

But let us first start with trade. Based on our analysis, my recommendation is that the Asian Free Zone be created in two phases. In Phase I, the South Asian nations agree to form a free economic zone along the lines of NAFTA. This zone should comprise first all SAARC countries, with a secondary but not overly delayed inclusion of Iran, Turkey and the Muslim nations of the former CIS. Prior to coming here, and the disappointing recent SAARC ministers' meeting in Sri Lanka, I had proposed that a SAARC free trade zone would require one decade to fully establish. It has been my sense that a full decade was needed to allow the founding members to reach a critical phase in their economic development and in their per capita income. With the pace of free trade expansion globally, however, one decade is too long for this small step for South Asia. We must achieve a free trade zone among the SAARC nations by 2005, or the peoples of

South Asia will again be left on the sidelines of the global economic engine. Following a successful integration of the SAARC economies, Iran, Turkey and the Muslim CIS states, we propose entering Phase II, including the giant of China into our regional system, a goal that we must achieve by 2010. The states of the 'Asian Free Zone' would be independent sovereign nations sharing the pattern

Of the EC:

(1) a free economic trade zone

(2) a common Central Bank with a common trading currency

(3) a common security policy, and ultimately,

(4) a common revolving Presidency and Parliament (like the EC Presidency and Parliament).

Even the smallest member state, such as Sri Lanka through this cooperation could have a chance to be the President of the 'superpower' Asian Zone. In short, by 2010, I propose a free trade zone encompassing some 3 billion people with a GNP of US$ 7 trillion (based upon 1998 'Purchasing Power Parity').

The nations included in this new zone by that point could be the SAARC nations, with Afghanistan, Turkey, Azerbaijan, Kazakhstan, Kyrgyzstan, Tajikistan, Turkmenistan and Uzbekistan, and finally, China. This is a vision of an Asian Free Zone, roughly 2/3 of which would be China, and 1/3 SAARC and Muslim CIS States. Our Asian Free Zone could then be at the same level, in GNP terms, as the EC, US or Japan. With roughly 50% of the World's population located in the Asian Free Zone, we would have an economic market with considerable weight, influence and clout in the Twentyfirst Century.

FIRST WITH SAARC

First, however, our challenge is to solidify the SAARC nations. The South Asian region encompassing Pakistan, India, Bangladesh, Nepal and Sri Lanka has a common and shared history. We speak the same language. Our colour is the same. Our thinking, values, pre-1947 history and culture is the same. We have a multi-religious society with Muslims, Hindus, Sikhs, Christians, Parsees, Buddhists, and others. Each in our respective countries believes in freedom of religion, in safety and security resisting outside coercion or intervention. In Dubai, Singapore, or London, a representative sample of the entire gamut of our population and religious spectrum has learnt to co-exist peacefully. Within the SAARC nations, we have similar per capita income. We are in similar stages of economic development. We all share a common legal system based on English Law. We all have free market-based economies. We all share English as a common language for Government and business. And, perhaps most importantly, we all share a common history and culture.

NEW RULES FOR SOUTH ASIA

The essence of the new paradigm for South Asia is to organize government and economic affairs in a manner which delivers the maximum progress to the regional population in the shortest period of time, with the least wastage in resources. The fastest route to economic development and growth for our suffering people is the generation of critical economic mass through the formation of larger 'economic free zones'. Unless South Asia pulls itself out of the quagmire of poverty, prejudice and past conflicts, our people will remain slaves within the global economy, carrying-out menial low paying tasks for the richer citizens of the First World. The choice for us is stark and simple: either continue as warring sovereign states who continue to carry the "Third World" label for the next 100 years, or pool our resources to create an Asian economic powerhouse comparable to the EC.

STEPS FORWARD

And to achieve this new era for South Asia, we must make concrete steps on an urgent basis, or again be left behind:

(1) Cease abusing the trust and confidence of the international rules of commerce. In Pakistan specifically, there has been

perhaps no greater damage to our economy and our integration into the global economic system than the senseless and politically motivated attack on the Independent Power Producers. Foreign investors are rightly outraged, and many others have been scared off. Pakistan must uphold and value contracts signed.

(2) Accelerating the current SAFTA talks. We can not wait until 2002 to create the first small step for lowering tariffs among the SAARC nations. Let us move these timetables up at least one year.

(3) Entering immediately into free trade discussions with the EC and ASEAN nations. Free trade among larger trading blocs takes time. Just as the EC and the Far East have entered a long-term process, so too should South Asia.

Ladies and Gentlemen, I have already taken too much of your time this morning. In closing, I propose to you the notion that if the nations of South Asia continue to close our borders both among ourselves and towards the larger global economy, our region risks suffering a similar fate to that of the Soviet Union, Yugoslavia and other dismembered nations. If we are to be partners in the emerging global economy, we must act swiftly to open our borders, ease our trade restrictions and more fully integrate with our neighbours.

A new world is quickly taking shape, one where openness among nations is the path to survival and progress. The people of South Asia cannot afford to wait a full decade for free trade in our region. Indeed, we must be fully open with the world economy within a decade. This is my vision for an Asian Free Zone.

I invite your questions or comments.

— London Breakfast Club
16-Apr-1999

Indo-Pak Parliamentarians

Fellow Parliamentarians:

We meet at a time of hope, but also a time of despair. A time of opportunity, but also a time of peril. A time of change, but still a time of intractability.

Ladies and Gentlemen, South Asia has been far too long a region teetering on the edge of catastrophe. For fifty years, we have been at each other's throats. We have fought four wars, and the last war dismembered my nation. Our troops, as we speak, fire at each other in the frozen wasteland called Siachen, which has become a metaphor for the senselessness that we have allowed to continue for half a century. With the newly awakened nuclear capabilities of India and Pakistan, and what appears to be a deployment race well underway, we can ill-afford the luxury of ignoring the roots of our deep distrust towards each other. It is conventional wisdom that the roots of the Indo-Pak conflict, or more specifically, the enmity between Muslims and Hindus are centuries old. That is a strange notion. For as many years that India and Pakistan have been at war, for many more centuries our cultures have lived in peaceful co-existence. Our cultures were, and still are, necessary threads weaving the unique and vibrant cloth called South Asia.

Ladies and Gentlemen, National and world politics in the first half of the Twentieth Century was driven by geo-strategic considerations, military-territorial considerations. The great empires of the Romans, Arabs, and the British rose on territorial conquest fuelled by military strength. Fantastic economic rewards awaited victorious conquerors in the form of booty, cheap labour and captive markets. The European

Colonialism was rooted in this psychology spread over thousands of years. It concluded when the Yalta Agreement was signed between the Big Three. The Cold War era then dawned. However the collapse of the Soviet Union, brought a fundamentally new global system. It is exciting living at a time of dramatic change in history where military-territorial supremacy dissipates as the era of economic-technological supremacy dawns.

NEW WORLD ORDER

History swings from one side of the pendulum to another. With the end of the Cold War, we are back to the world where global politics was driven by economic considerations, where markets are the yardstick by which the power, size and influence of nations will be judged. Will we, the people of South Asia, be prisoners of the past or will we be able to rise to a magnificent future? The collapse of the military-territorial superpower, the Soviet Union, the rise of Germany, Japan, (South Korea Taiwan, Singapore) sent a powerful message to our generation. Brute military-territorial strength alone (like the Soviet Union) could not save it from disintegration and economic collapse. Germany, Japan and the NICs rose without military-territorial strength to become economic superpowers. We are eye-witnesses to a New World Order based upon free commerce and trade. A nation's success is measured by its ability to develop products, ideas to sell in the global marketplace, which is open to all. It is based on the quality of goods and services and global demand-supply factors. Suddenly it is possible for tiny Singapore, with a tiny territorial and population base, a quarter of Karachi or Bombay, and a virtually non-existent military base, to become an economic giant, equal to the First World Countries in the quality of life it affords to its citizens.

RULES OF THE GAME

The new rules of the game are that a nation upholds the principles of democracy, the rule of law, guarantees basic freedom and liberties to its citizens, allows free trade and a market driven economy with minimal state intervention, with a policy of non-intervention and mutual respect in inter-state relations. The concern of the state in inter-state relations is also driven by considerations of trade and commerce (again following the Japanese model), rather than by military - territorial considerations. A nation which lives in the past, bases its thinking on the old paradigm of military-territorial strength, perishes in the New World Order and is treated as a pariah state (e.g. Russia, Yugoslavia, and most recently Iraq). The success of a Nation, as we head towards a new century, a new millennium, is based upon the level of exports, hard currency reserves, its per capita GNP, and certainly not its territory, military strength, or population base. The pace in the race for economic success has become so competitive, that even First World former superpower nations such as Britain, France and Germany, felt unable to compete individually with today's economic giants, the U.S. and Japan.

The GNP of America is (US$ 8 trillion) and of Japan (US$ 5 trillion). Only after combining the 10 'First World' European economies, the combined EC GNP can compete at US$ 7 trillion. The desire for the creation of 'super-economic zones' like the EC, was driven by Britain, France and Germany seeking to effectively compete economically with the economic superpowers namely the United States and Japan. The US, in turn rushed to form NAFTA and APEC as an economic reply to the EC.

All this is accomplished, without a single bullet being fired, with no military adventures or conquests, and yet huge territories, nations and populations peacefully agreed to redefine their economic borders, and to co-exist with each other in the better interests of their future well being. The EC's formation is truly a model case of the new paradigm, where economically we enter an increasingly Borderless World while maintaining our national 'sovereignty'. The EC member states pooled their economic sovereignty in creating a free trade zone and a common currency, thus submerging their narrow national interests for the greater good of the whole European Community. Meanwhile, at the other extreme, a closed nation, closed by sanctions or voluntarily, such as Libya, Iran, Iraq, Afghanistan, Somalia and Sudan suffered economically even when they had huge oil reserves and a tiny population.

Ladies and Gentlemen, if we close our borders and live in the past, our region risks suffering a similar fate to that of the Soviet Union, Yugoslavia and other such countries.

THE POPULATION BOMB

Our two nations (India and Pakistan) are now home to nearly one-fifth of the total human population. The United Nations currently estimates the entire human population to be just shy of six billion people. Given current rates of population growth, by the year 2015, our two nations' combined population will surpass the population of China. As our populations grow, so too must our capacity to manage precious natural resources. The path to resolving our conflict lies within these unsettling figures and how we address the very real daily problems of population growth, economic opportunity, healthcare, education and stewardship of our environment.

SOUTH ASIA - A HOUSE DIVIDED

But our conflict also reflects dynamics akin to a large and unruly family. In the final analysis, South Asia is a house, but a house divided. The history of humankind clearly shows that brothers can have the greatest love for each other, but are also capable of the most venomous hatred and spite. So it is in the Middle East between the Jews and the Arabs. So it is in Ireland between the Catholics and the Protestants. So it is in the former Yugoslavia between the Muslims and the Serbs. So it is in the horn of Africa between the Ethiopians and the Eritreans. Within our South Asian house, we are no different. We are warring South Asian brothers and sisters. Personally, both my grand parents lived in the area around present Mumbai (or Bombay). Our ancestral homes remain there today. In the registers of Ajmer Sharif and Hazrat Nizamuddin Auliya, you can see the signatures of my ancestors. Indo-Pak enmity denied me the opportunity to see my grand parents' home, to offer prayers at my grandmother's grave, or my aunt Benazir after whom I am named or to take my children to a place that is a part of their history. Will I be able to do so? Will our generation have the chance to build peace or will we become another Soviet Union, with the largest land mass territory in the world, encompassing two continents, an advanced space programme, enough nuclear warheads and ballistic missiles to destroy the whole world, and a 'superpower' status, ultimately ending up having to beg for food from the EC to feed its population? Ultimately having to ask (relatively) 'tiny' Japan, with no military might, for economic aid?

Ladies and Gentlemen, this is a turning point in history, a different place from 50 years ago. We can strut around the stage pretending we are great powers in the world. Reality tells us that the Russian giant nation is considered an economic minnow today, with even tiny Singapore better off than Russia. 'Giant' India or Pakistan, with all our nuclear bravado, need to face the reality that we are economic pygmies on the world stage, and have a population base of 1.3 billion of the world's poorest people, with the worst standard of living. Once we understand these objective facts, we can address the problem and find the solutions.

FOREIGN POLICY

Ladies and Gentlemen, In this final year of the second millennium, it is time not only to take stock but to take action, not only to plan for dialogue but to engage in dialogue, not only to talk peace but to make peace. Could there be any more fitting denouement to the second millennium than a peaceful resolution to the Indo-Pakistan dispute? I think not. But if we are to proceed, it will take courage and leadership on behalf of our governments. For, in the words of the philosopher Spinoza, "peace is not mere absence of war, but is a virtue that springs from force of character."

THE NUCLEAR CRISIS

We are today in perhaps the most unsettling and dangerous situation since partition itself: a full-blown nuclear race. I am convinced that none of us know the true horrors of these weapons, nor the devastation nuclear weapons can inflict upon our people when used. None of us have truly comprehended the dire consequences of a nuclear and ballistic arms race in our land. With our close knit ecological systems, weather patterns, and dense populations, one nuclear explosion on either side of the border would have the most tragic of consequences for all. Entering the nuclear arena requires a wisdom and a patience from leaders that, to date, none of us have shown much of. I admit, I too, in my two terms followed the path of hawkishness. But that was before India and Pakistan shook the World with their nuclear blasts and brought forward many questions specifically on these weapons of mass destruction.

I ask our current leaders: Do we have adequate controls over these dangerous weapons? Have we built clear-cut lines of communications between those who watch these weapons, and those who would decide for their use? In this new nuclear era, we, Pakistan and India, no longer have the luxury to ignore our suspicions, our mistrust and our foreign policy misadventures. Both of our nations must step forward cognizant of our political realities. Both of our nations must step forward, understanding the threat to our people, our region, and the entire world, and declare South Asia a nuclear free and missile free zone.

Today I call upon India and Pakistan to jointly or singly;

(1) Adhere quickly to the CTBT Treaty;

(2) Declare a moratorium on fissile material production;

(3) Resist the development, flight testing and storage of ballistic weapons;

(4) Strengthen export control on nuclear technology

Ladies and Gentlemen, We must step forth and together change the direction of history

ON KASHMIR

Ladies and Gentlemen, all of our problems, all of our disputes, all of our disagreements can be resolved quickly to mutual satisfaction if we address the question of Jammu and Kashmir. Yes I know that some in India say this is an internal matter that Kashmir is as much a part of India as Texas is of the United States. I have heard this before. In fact, I have heard it all my life. And I know better. The issue of Jammu and Kashmir is a problem that has brought us to war before and could very well bring us to war again, this time with the most catastrophic consequences. In India, extremists say never, no compromise. In Pakistan, extremists say never, no compromise. The stakes, my friends, are much too high to let our policy be driven by our political margins.

It is time that our policy be driven by reason, and by our commitment to our children's future.There must be a resolution of the Jammu-Kashmir problem that accounts for the political sensitivities and political desires of the people of that princely state. It is not useful to hear about what a Maharaja did fifty years ago, or where an army attacked, or another army counterattacked. The fact remains that Jammu and Kashmir is a largely Muslim state, between two nations that were created in a religious partition. The fact remains that the people of Jammu and Kashmir are politically alienated and disaffected. The fact remains that an intifida has raged on the ground, and continues as we speak. The fact remains that Jammu and Kashmir is the densest and largest militarily occupied territory on earth. And the fact remains that over fifty thousand people have been killed, thousands of women raped, thousands of children kidnapped never to be seen again, scores of villages wiped off the face of the earth.

It is a record that cannot make one proud, and a record that causes us the greatest pain. No process leading to the fair and equitable resolution of the fifty-year Kashmir conflict can move forward, however, without concrete steps by both Pakistan and India. The Simla Agreement recognizes this. On India's part, there are a number of confidence-building measures that could be taken immediately, including:

— a dramatic reduction of the nearly 600,000 troops now stationed in Kashmir;

— Ceasing all forms of torture, intimidation and extra-judicial killings;

— Opening Jammu-Kashmir to monitoring by international human rights groups.

Ultimately we would like to see India begin a dialogue with the All Parties Hurriyat Conference (APHC). Likewise, for my part, I will vigorously pursue the following initiatives in Pakistan:

— Dialogue with India for open borders between Azad Kashmir and Jammu and Kashmir as a prelude to open borders between all of South Asia;

— Talks for mutual Arms reduction and redeployment of Forces.

I recall that after the end of the Second World War, President Harry Truman faced a dilemma. Europe was in physical and economic shambles. The Soviet Union had engulfed eastern and central Europe and threatened Greece, Turkey, Italy, even France. Obviously, the burden was on the United States to lead in the economic reconstruction of Europe and the political and military containment of communism. But the American people would have no part of it. Their sons and daughters had spent four years saving Europe, and the American people had had enough. They wanted to return home, build their houses, have their children, and raise their families. They wanted to turn inward. But Harry Truman was a leader. Despite public opinion polls that showed only 15% support for a massive U.S. engagement in Europe, he created the Marshall Plan and the NATO alliance, and then went out to his people and day by day, month by month, sold the necessity to a sceptical electorate. He convinced them. He convinced a Congress controlled by the opposition, and he ultimately was re-elected. And the programmes that he initiated structured foreign policy for forty years, ultimately resulting in the destruction of the Berlin Wall and the triumph of Democracy and the free market.

Why do I relate these points of history, now fifty years later? Because, Ladies and Gentlemen, it is this kind of foresight and courage which is required now, by leaders in both Pakistan and India, to begin a process of constructive dialogue and conflict resolution and hopefully consensus building. Extremists on both sides of our border might resist, but the masses of our people are looking for compromise. Our people want peace even if they cheer and scream when they are egged on by demagogues with the rhetoric of war. So let us begin.

I recall quite vividly that the problems of the Middle East were viewed as intractable, unsolvable by men and women of less than grand vision, until Anwar Sadaat broke open the debate by bold action, and began a process that is still unfolding. Like in the dispute between India and Pakistan, the dispute between the Israelis and the Arab nations was manageable and addressable when, and only when, the core issue - the issue of the political rights of the people of Palestine — was successfully addressed. And President Sadat and Prime Minister Begin won the Nobel Prize for Peace.

I recall vividly that the problems of Northern Ireland were viewed as intractable and irreconcilable by men and women of limited vision, until John Hume, David Trimble, Bill Clinton and George Mitchell restructured the debate, resulting in the extraordinary Good Friday peace treaty which we all pray, Inshallah, will lead to a final peace on that troubled, divided island. And the two men who risked the most, and fought the hardest — Mr. Hume and Mr. Trimble — won the Nobel Prize for Peace.

I recall vividly that few on earth ever thought we would live to see the day that South Africa would flourish under democracy, and the dreaded cancer of apartheid would be eradicated from the body politic. But justice prevailed, and leaders with political vision and courage prevailed. And Nelson Mandela became the President of a United South Africa, a black and white South Africa. And the two leaders who made that possible, President Mandela and President DeKlerk, won the Nobel Prize for Peace.

Ladies and Gentlemen, in Oslo, there is another set of Nobel Prizes that wait to be awarded to people of courage, to true leaders. They are reserved for leaders of peace in India and Pakistan. Prime

Minister Rajiv Gandhi and I took significant steps to promote peace between 1988-90:

(1) We signed non-attack agreement on each other's nuclear facilities

(2) We had a defence Secretaries agreement for a settlement in Siachin

(3) We expanded the trade list between our two countries.

(4) We exchanged delegations on the Wullar Barrage issue.

(5) We explored the Sir Creek matter.

But then he called for elections and death took him away before he could return to office.

It was at that time - December 1988 - that the other SAARC countries accepted the proposals of the world's youngest elected chief executive to:

(*a*) Declare 1989 the year of the Girl child;

(*b*) Allow Parliamentarians and Judges to visit SAARC countries on a SAARC Pass which required no visa;

(*c*) Allow for a common SAARC pre-stamped Mailing System so that families could remain easily in touch with each other.

It is time to pick up the threads again .

A SHARED PAST TO BUILD THE FUTURE

The South Asian region encompassing Pakistan, India, Bangladesh, Nepal and Sri Lanka, has a common and shared history. We speak the same language. Our colour is the same. Our thinking, values, pre-1947 history and culture is the same. We have a multi-religious society with Muslims, Hindus, Sikhs, Christians, Parsees, Buddhists, and others. Each in our countries believes in freedom of religion, in safety and security resisting outside coercion or intervention. In Dubai, Singapore, or London, a representative sample of the entire gamut of our population and religious spectrum has learnt to co-exist peacefully. The post nuclear era in the sub-continent calls upon us to define a new paradigm and a new set of rules for the game in South Asia.

NEW RULES FOR SOUTH ASIA

The essence of the new paradigm for South Asia is to organize government and economic affairs in a manner which delivers the maximum progress to the regional population in the shortest period of time, with the least wastage in resources. The fastest route to economic development and growth for our suffering people is the generation of critical economic mass through formation of larger 'economic free zones'. Unless South Asia pulls itself out of the quagmire of poverty, prejudice and the past to change, our people will remain slaves in the global economy carrying out menial low paying tasks for the rich citizens of the First World.

Our nations are faced with the choice: either continue as warring sovereign states who continue to carry the "Third World" label for the next 100 years, or pool our resources to create an Asian economic powerhouse comparable to the EC. Should we embark upon the logical route (not necessarily a foregone conclusion given our history of taking the path of greatest resistance), and decide on pooling economic sovereignty and creating an EC type South Asian economic free zone, then we need to ask: what obvious partners are available for India and Pakistan?

AN ASIAN FREE ZONE

The disparities in per capita income between India and ASEAN are too great. China and India are different in per capita income, in GNP, and at different stages of their economic evolution cycles. There are differences too in the economic and legal systems (Capitalists/ Communists). Pakistan, Bangladesh, Sri Lanka, and Nepal are the obvious candidates for India as partners, for these countries:

(1) Have similar per capita income;

(2) All are in similar stages of their economic development life cycles;

(3) All share a common legal system based on English Law;

(4) All have free market based economies;

(5) All share English as a common language for Government and business;

(6) All share a common history and culture.

From Pakistan's perspective, the Gulf Arab States (GCC) are a far cry as they yet have to partner with common Arab countries such as Egypt and Syria. ECO (and RCD before that) has yet to take off due to the different historical backgrounds, per capita incomes, and different stages of economic development (with Turkey wooing the EC). Afghanistan and CIS States, are behind Pakistan in their growth cycles, with a host of other problems such as language, legal systems, per capita income, and the fact that the CIS States are bound together under the Russian CIS confederation system. Pakistan cannot economically integrate with China for the same reasons as India. Therefore for Pakistan too the logical choice for a long term EC style partnership, are the South Asian nations.

Had the South Asian nations been Muslim countries, our partnership would have taken place long ago. Yet, if religion was the criteria which bound States together, then Bangladesh would still be East Pakistan and Pakistan would be free of provincialism, sectarianism, and every other kind of 'ism'. Based on this analysis my recommendation is that in Phase I, the South Asian nations agree to form a free economic zone. This zone could comprise all SAARC countries, plus Iran (or even all the ECO States if they are willing to join).

Phase I can conclude in a decade allowing the founding members to reach a critical phase in their economic development and in their per capita income. In Phase II, China could be included in the Free

Zone. This is a vision of an Asian Free Zone which by 2010 can be in existence with 2.5 to 3 billion people, and with a GNP of US$ 7 trillion (based upon 1998 'Purchasing Power Parity'). Of this GNP, roughly 2/3 would be China, and 1/3 SAARC States. Our Asian Free Zone could then be at the same level, in GNP terms, as EC, US or Japan. With roughly 50% of the World's population located in the Asian Zone, this zone in terms of an economic market would have the greatest influence, voice and clout in the Twentyfirst Century.

As one of America's Senators, Barbara Mikulski, recently said, "demography is destiny." And if demography is destiny, the future belongs to Asia. In terms of demographics, in terms of production, in terms of consumption, in terms of markets, in terms of an expanding capital intensive middle class, the Asian continent will set the tone, set the pace, and dominate the economic and geopolitical trends of the coming era. The states of the 'Asian Free Zone' would be independent sovereign nations on the pattern of the EC sharing (1) a free economic trade zone (2) a common Central Bank with a common trading currency (3) a common security policy and ultimately (4) a common revolving Presidency and Parliament (like the EC Presidency and Parliament) Even the smallest member state, such as Sri Lanka through this cooperation could have a chance to be the President of the 'superpower' Asian Zone.

PRINCIPLES OF THE ASIAN FREE ZONE

Let's see what is considered "In" and what "Out" in the proposed Asian Free Zone:

In	Out
— Free trade.	— Protected and closed markets.
— Democratic systems down to province/state level with maximum provincial and local rights.	— Centralized govt., with limited provincial rights
— Free movement of people.	— Closed borders
— Rule of law, guarantee of civil liberties.	— Authoritarianism
— Respect of all religions, castes, creeds.	— Old religious hatreds
— State is servant and economic facilitator.	— State has a 'raja' mentality
— State spends budget on health, education, etc.	— State spends budget on defense
— Close cordial & friendly state relations.	— Cold war in South Asia
— State creates environment for a new NIC.	— State creates environment for a new Russia
— Ultimately aim for the European state model of a supra-structure of independent states.	— Aim for the Soviet State model domination and hegemony by the Centre

THE FUTURE

Ladies and Gentlemen, we are the ones who have to reach to transform our people's future in a single generation. South Asia combined with Iran and China can comprise the largest population concentration region in the World with 2.6 billion people, over 50% of the global population. We can choose to become a super economic zone, enjoying a life style similar to the European people or we can cling on to our Third World status and continue to blame "foreign powers" for our miseries. The choice is in our hands. Not in the hands of our fathers. Not in the hands of Nehru, Bhutto, Bandaranaike or Mujeeb. The choice is not in the hands of the coming generations. Not in the hands of our children. Our hands will shape the destiny of South Asia, that course, that history which will flow for the next hundred years. We are gifted to be at this special time, at this special place, in this special representative capacity as one-century wanes and another dawns. Our thoughts, ideas, and deeds can make the difference.

Let me tell you about my country. Pakistan has paid a very heavy price in the spin off from the Afghan War. This includes the Kalashnikov culture in Karachi, the rapid and alarming rise in the number of drug addicts who are estimated at over four million, the spill-over of militants from trainee camps across the border, which has exacerbated tensions with our neighbours and disturbed internal security. Many Pakistanis were amazed to learn when the US Cruise Missiles hit Khost that six of the dead were Pakistanis. According to the UN, when Bamiyan in North Afghanistan fell, Pakistanis were amongst the prisoners taken. Threats of terrorism and militancy to Pakistan from across the border are real. Drugs, terrorism, extremism and violence are dangers which call for Pakistanis to pay greater attention to what is happening in Afghanistan and could happen in Pakistan. Let me tell you about our polity. In Pakistan there are different kinds of political parties. Some proclaim an Islamic system to win power. Some claim provincial autonomy/nationalism as the answer. Others pursue the politics of sectarianism to achieve their goals. Still others believe the politics of ethnicity will lead to deliverance. A few without electoral support cling to the notion of climbing into power through a military backed interim government.

The Pakistan Peoples Party believes in the politics of the people. Our goal is the economic emancipation of our people. We want our peoples to have freedom to choose, to practice. They are free to follow any sect, speak any ethnic language, practice their beliefs as they interpret religion. It is not our job. Our job is to provide freedom and economic emancipation. Quaid-e-Awam Zulfikar Ali Bhutto saw socialism as the route to economic emancipation in the seventies. His daughter led the drive for economic emancipation through decentralization, deregulation privatization and free market. For the coming decade, given the global realities, the path to economic salvation, to economic emancipation, to opportunity, prosperity, dignity, hope and success lies in a free economic zone.

Fellow Parliamentarians, will we be condemned to the miseries of an unfortunate past or will we demonstrate the courage and conviction to seize a fantastic future? Will we allow the frenzied calls of fanatics to dictate the agenda or will we allow the cool logic of the information technology world to drive an agenda of change? Will we choose the path of Satti and Karo Kari or will we break free of outmoded traditions? Will we torture and suppress our people, in fear, or will we respect people's dignity and self determination, in confidence? Will we blind ourselves to old battles or see the new ones, the real ones that need to be fought. My father, whom I loved deeply, was born in the British Raj. He lived through an epoch period of the Second World War, the freedom struggle, the collapse of Colonialism.

As a young student I heard his brilliant address at the United Nations. I heard him say, "Mr. Secretary General, realities change. The reality was that German troops were at the gates of Stalingrad". Realities change. Indeed, realities change. But I would say definitions change too. The people of South Asia are an honourable people, a self respecting people. Honour and respect through the centuries have carried different definitions. There was a time when we honoured the warriors who raped, looted and plundered calling them great Conquerors and Emperors. Today we honour a Nelson Mandela who makes peace and are appalled by those who rape, plunder and pillage. There was a time when we honoured a man who took revenge for the murder of his family or tribe. Today we are shocked and punish those who take the law into their own hands. There was a time when honour demanded that we lock up our wives in women's quarters. Today we consider it barbaric. Realities change and with them definitions. There is no honour when people commit suicide because they cannot afford to live. There is no honour when a child is born burdened with its country's debt. There is no honour when a sniper's bullet kills a father on his way to work destroying a family's joy.

Since the Berlin Wall fell, we have seen the First World move towards larger economic entities. We have seen that mighty armies could not save Communist or Third World Countries from disintegrating into Warlords who dishonoured humanity with bloodshed and carnage. Warlords ruled and ruined Lebanon at a time. Warlords ruled and ruined Somalia. Warlords ruled and ruined Afghanistan. Warlords ruled and ruined Chechnya, Bosnia, Sudan and parts of Central Asia. Armed Mafias ruled and ruined parts of Russia. Mighty armies watched helplessly as warlords or armed Mafias took over. The IMF and World Bank are not charities to help South Asia survive. They can give us loans for a time to keep us afloat. But if we fail to learn to survive, who will take us to shore.

Ladies and Gentlemen, Honoured Parliamentarians, will we learn from the First World Countries with trillion dollars economies or will we condemn the coming generations to warlords and armed Mafias who will fight and kill. The unipolar world has no reason to act as a policeman unless its vital interests are involved. The carnage in Bosnia continued for years in the heart of Europe. The killing in Kosovo has yet to push the world into action. You and I, we, the people, we the elected representatives have to police our own world by ensuring democracy, human rights, good governance and creating a macro-economic framework where our people can compete successfully and where South Asia can go on to make its mark in a new century, a new millennium Parliamentarians, in just over 300 days, we will witness, only for the third time in recorded history, the turning of the millennium. Where, and what, will we be when the year 2000 lights up the night sky? Will we be liberated to the endless possibilities of a remarkable new future?

Ladies and Gentlemen, I see a Twentyfirst Century of miraculous opportunity. I see a Twentyfirst Century where temples are not burnt nor mosques razed to the ground. I see a Twentyfirst Century where Human Rights are universal and self-determination reigns supreme. I see a Twentyfirst Century where civil dialogue replaces the rhetoric of war and consensus guides the South Asian debate. I see a Twentyfirst Century where people's trust in Government is restored, and

Government gets on with alleviating the miseries and hardships of the people. I see a Twentyfirst Century where every child is planned , wanted, nurtured and supported. I see a Twentyfirst Century of tolerance and pluralism, where religions respect other religions. I see a Twentyfirst Century of equal rights for women and men. I see a Twentyfirst Century where the birth of a girl is welcomed with the same joy as the birth of a boy.

This can be the moment of Change. This can be the moment of Hope. This can be the moment for Leadership. The stakes will never be more important. The risks never more dangerous. In the words of the UNESCO Constitution, "since wars begin in the minds of men, it is in the minds of the men that defences of peace must be constructed." Our ancestors watch. Our children and grand children's future awaits. And long after we are gone, and the pages of this keynote address has turned first to sepia, and then to dust, let the history books of India and Pakistan declare that, in the last year of second millennium, moderate and reasonable men and women seized the moment, seized the day, and through courage and conviction shaped a permanent peace for generations yet unknown. That is the Twentyfirst Century I see, for my children and for yours.

Thank you Ladies and Gentlemen.

— First Indo-Pak Parliamentarians Conference
Islamabad,13-Feb-1999

Can Indo-Pak Relations be Reinvented

It is a privilege for me to join you this evening at India Today's Conclave in New Delhi, to discuss the Challenges for the Brave New World.

I first came to India as a teenager visiting Simla with my Father in 1971.

I still remember the warmth and affection with which the people of India greeted me although we were supposed to be the enemy.

Following the Simla Agreement signed between Prime Ministers Indira Gandhi and Zulfikar Ali Bhutto in 1972, I came away with the strong feeling that peace between India and Pakistan must endure.

It gives me great satisfaction that since the signing of the Simla Agreement thirty five year ago, India and Pakistan, although engaged in conflict, did not go to full war against each other.

The enormity of this is better understood when we appreciate that between 1947 and 1971, a period of twenty five years, India and Pakistan fought three wars.

As Prime Minister of Pakistan, I worked with Prime Minister Rajiv Gandhi to build on the spirit of Simla. Our governments signed the first major agreements since Simla, the agreements not to attack each other's nuclear installations in 1988 amongst others. In 1988, at the SAARC leaders' summit at Islamabad, I proposed that we transform SAARC from a cultural organization into an economic one. The South Asian Preferential Tariff Agreement was born as a consequence.

In 1999 at the Indo Pak Parliamentarians Conference in Islamabad I proposed that India, Pakistan and all the countries of South Asia put aside their differences to create a common market to eliminate poverty, hunger, unemployment and backwardness, through soft borders. So, ladies and gentlemen, I believe that Indo Pak relations can be creatively re-invented.

Time stands still for no one. The moving finger of history writes and having written, moves on.

We have a choice. The choice is ours to write a success story of free markets, liberty, human rights, gender equality, common values of tolerance and understanding.

The Pakistan Peoples Party and I, even in Opposition, have tried to write a success story co-authored with all the intellectuals, political parties and leaders of both our countries who truly believe that the future welfare of humanity in our part of the world lies in cooperation.

I see the world in terms of competing economic blocs that can best function in an environment of peace and security. I see the world as one where the have-nots can conquer poverty if we come together in an economy of scale as Europe has done. For these ideas, and for seeking peaceful relations with India, I was once called, a "security risk" by my critics.

But ideas cannot be killed by character assassination or by repression. In time, my political opponents as well as the military establishment of my country realized the importance of peace as a quality that makes or breaks a nation.

I am proud that today India and Pakistan are discussing ways and means to have open borders, trade and travel. We still have a long way to go, but the journey has begun.Of course the danger is there of the derailment of the peace process. Both our countries nearly came to war in 1999 in the icy glaciers of Siachen. Both our armies stood eye ball to eye ball in a deadly year long confrontation following a terrorist attack on the Indian Parliament in December 2001. The recent attack on the Samjhota Express this year once again demonstrated the fragility of a peace process which can be disrupted by a deadly act of violence. We know now that there is a consensus amongst the political parties of India and Pakistan, a consensus between our military and security establishments that peace must be established. We also agree that the one serious danger to the peace process comes from militants and terrorists. Therefore the challenge for us is to dismantle the militant cells so that they cannot hold the foreign policy of two independent nations hostage to their acts of terrorism.

In this connection, I welcome the decision by both India and Pakistan to work together on anti-terrorism efforts and to share information in this regard. This is a positive step forward. I commend Prime Minister Manmohan Singh and the Government of India for refusing to rise to the terrorist bait in blaming Islamabad when a militant strikes its target. The militants are the enemies of peaceful relations, peaceful relations that both our countries want and desire.

Both the governments of India and Pakistan are declaring their deep desire to resolve the Kashmir Dispute, to build peaceful relations and to work for greater economic cooperation. I welcome this effort to re-invent our relations.

Many wellwishers advised me to oppose the present peace process between India and Pakistan for two reasons. First, they saw it lacking legitimacy as Pakistan is presently governed by a military regime which holds on to power by virtue of its army constituency. Secondly, since Indo Pak relations and the Kashmir Dispute excite passions easily, it was felt that opposing the peace process as a, "sell out" would help mobilize public opinion against the military dictatorship and facilitate the restoration of Democracy. The restoration of Democracy is a cause dear to my heart. It is a cause for which my Father and brothers laid down their lives as did hundreds of our party workers and others belonging to the democratic opposition.

It is a cause for which my husband cumulatively spent eleven years in prison without a conviction and for which my brothers, mother and I spent long years in exile. However, my Party and I did not seek the easy route to create mass frenzy. We believe that the future happiness of the people of South Asia, a happiness flowing from a peaceful environment providing opportunities for our, youth was too important to be lost in an internal political battle in Pakistan.

I do agree that there are issues of legitimacy involved when a nonrepresentative government negotiates as the people are not co-opted. The tribal situation in Pakistan, where the Taliban have regrouped is an example. Despite 80,000 troops being sent into the area to clear the militants, a peace treaty was signed with them.

This proves the point that without political participation, it is very difficult to make lasting advances. Today it is a matter of satisfaction for those of us who envisaged open borders, trade and travel between India and Pakistan, before it became fashionable to do so, to witness the Pakistani military dictatorship sign on the peace process and commit itself to resolving issues with India in a peaceful manner without prejudice to our differing views on Kashmir. There are voices that claim that the present peace process with India is an eye wash meant to cover the regime in election year to neutralize the Indian lobby. They argue that after stage managing the election schedule in Pakistan later this year, all it will take is one more militant attack to recreate the tensions that have marred Indo Pak relations in the past.However, once again I do not believe that we should base our political policies on fear.

I believe the challenge for the future is to re-invent our policies so that we build them on hope.

For that hope to be formalized we will have to deal with the issue of both militancy and terrorism.

Militancy and terrorism are the roots of violence, senseless destruction and loss of lives. We have to protect the innocent people of our countries by each one of us working for the dismantlement of militant groups, the elimination of terrorism and the promotion of interfaith tolerance and harmony. These objectives are all the more important in this the 60th anniversary of the Independence of both of our countries.

I wonder how many in this audience were present when the British set midnight of August 14, 1947 as the hour for the clock to strike freedom.

It was an exciting moment in history when the people of India and Pakistan gained their separate Nations. Yet it was also one of pain. Innocent people were killed because they were either Muslims fleeing to Pakistan or Hindus fleeing to India. And more blood was shed of our citizens who died in the many wars and acts of terror experienced since we both got our freedom from the British.

In this the 60th year of our Independence, I propose that the leadership of India and Pakistan put an end to this destructive chapter in the lives of our countries. I propose that on the 60th anniversary of our Nations this August they meet to declare their commitment to bring us the permanent tranquility and progress and prosperity that two neighboring countries must have.

Ladies and Gentlemen, I have made trade, not conflict with India, a top priority of my forthcoming electoral campaign in Pakistan. At 60 years we must pledge an end to war, terrorism and death. Sixty years of freedom gives us the maturity to change our direction dramatically.

I am committed to bringing peace between our two countries. My commitment to peace began when I was a young child. I lived through the bombings of the 1965 war between our countries. I heard the stories of the dead and of the homes destroyed, of the terrible destruction of infrastructure putting both our developing countries further back in their quest to modernise.

I saw my Mother rushing to help the soldiers and their families, help the wounded and the injured.

As a student at Harvard University in America, I joined up with fellow students to protest the Vietnam War, a war that they felt was unjust and did not want to fight.Since then I have seen many more conflicts on television in the Middle East, in Afghanistan, between Iran and Iraq and in Iraq. The more I see of the devastation of war, of how the vultures descend to feed on the bodies of dead children, the more I am convinced that we must keep our region secure and peaceful. We cannot fail our children. India and China both have a dispute but they do not go to war against each other. We must learn from this model to develop our own relations. As an undergraduate at Harvard University, I met your late Prime Minister Indira Gandhi. I witnessed the first peace agreement signed by our two countries. In the words of the famous American Secretary of State Dean Acheson, I was "Present at the Creation" of the peace movement between our two countries.

I am proud of the fact that during my two tenures in office, neither of our peoples or armies had to face a Kargil-like situation.

I am proud of the fact that during both of my tenures in office, there were no terrorist attacks on Indian targets such as the Bombay Blasts or the Indian Parliament Blast. It is not easy to keep the peace but my government did so and reined in the militants too.

On a separate note, we brought peace to Karachi taking on the militants there and we brought peace to our tribal areas taking on the militias of the narco barons in those mountains. My Government had the capacity to build nuclear weapons but we chose to remain a nuclear capable state instead of turning ourselves into a nuclear weaponised state. We had the confidence in our people and in our ability to defend ourselves without involving ourselves in adventures, which could only turn the clock back on the pursuit of progress for all the people of South Asia, who are shackled with backwardness and poverty. One of the ways that I tried to re-invent the relationship between Pakistan and India was to involve military and intelligence personnel in the process. In this connection, we established intelligence to intelligence contact with a view to help formal diplomacy. Additionally we proposed the induction of retired military officials in the track two discussions. With terrorism now a global issue, cooperation between India and Pakistan to work on eliminating terrorism from the region offers an important opportunity to reinvent the relationship. Therefore it is a welcome development that following the summit meeting in Cuba last year in September, both Islamabad and Delhi have agreed on an exchange of terror-related intelligence through quarterly meetings. I know that the hotline established by Prime Minister Rajiv Gandhi and myself, between the military headquarters of our two countries, has played no small part in preventing escalation of tensions in the relations between the two countries. Ladies and Gentlemen, we live in societies where there are islands of opulence amongst oceans of misery.

It is wrong, morally wrong that the gap between the rich and the poor should be so huge that some people do not have food to eat or a job to give them dignity. I find it so difficult to understand how in the third millennium so many should die, because they do not have drinking water or the water they have is contaminated. We should band together to fight hunger and disease. We should band together to fight discrimination and bigotry against minorities. We should band together in a political and economic condominium that could be a model to the entire world of the what the future holds. These are the real issues that confront our masses. There is much that the countries of South Asia can learn from each other.

All the countries of South Asia, except Burma and Pakistan, have civilian control over the military and therefore over the conduct of their nations in foreign policy. As the Cuban Missile Crisis of 1962 proved in America, civilian control of the military is essential to the safety and development of a country. Bringing peace between our two countries will help make that happen. The Cuban Missile Crisis showed that if the American military had had its way, the Americans would have made war against the Soviets. American President John F. Kennedy prevented a war that could have killed 100 million Americans. Former Prime Minister Nawaz Sharif and I have signed a Charter of Democracy committed to a framework of peace and justice for the people of Pakistan. The Charter of Democracy commits both our parties to friendship and peace with India.

Last year American President George W. Bush said in his annual State of the Union address. "Dictatorships shelter terrorists and feed resentment and radicalism, and seek weapons of mass destruction. Democracies replace resentment with hope, respect the rights of their citizens and their neighbors, and join the fight against terror." I agree with President Bush on the nature of dictatorships. I have dedicated my life to working for the restoration of democracy in Pakistan. In the last election of October 2002, I was not allowed to fight that contest. Yet despite international observers calling the elections "flawed", the Pakistan People's Party (PPP) which I head, was still the largest vote getter at nearly 26 per cent of the votes, almost similar to that of the Congress Party in the elections of 2004. Unfortunately the Parliamentary session was indefinitely postponed to fracture my support. If not I would have formed a government like Mrs Sonia Gandhi did after the 2004 election.

I am fully on the side of the people. My late and beloved father, Zulfikar Ali Bhutto, named our party - the Pakistan People's Party. We have a long history of fighting for the people of Pakistan. I have fought dictators and oligarchs before. I will fight them again in the election campaign of 2007, and I intend to win. Some have asked why I am returning to Pakistan. The answer is very simple, Pakistan is my home. And I have long ago accepted my responsibilities of leadership. I did not choose this life. It chose me. I have been honored by the people of Pakistan to be twice elected their Prime Minister. During the time of my service in that role, the religious parties never had more that 3 per cent representation in our National Assembly.

A democratic Pakistan standing next to a democratic India and a democratic Afghanistan can start to turn around our part of the world.

On the issue of Kashmir, we must make a viable peace. This is a solvable problem that must not take further lives. Pending a final settlement, I agree with the statement of your Prime Minister supporting an autonomous Kashmir running much of its own affairs. A Commission can be established between the two countries and the leaders of Kashmir themselves to work out what should be done in foreign and defense affairs. While working out the solution to Kashmir we should not allow slow progress on it to be an obstacle to work in other cooperative matters.

There are several ways to reinvent our relations. These include through economic integration and trade, business cooperation, media exchanges, transportation links between our two countries, the energy requirements of our economies, sports and entertainment events, cooperation in the Information Technologies, the peaceful uses of nuclear energy, in medicine, education and agriculture.

Let us remember:

(1) Economic integration and trade brought Europe the peace and prosperity it has enjoyed since World War II concluded. The Europeans started the European Coal and Steel Community. Jean Monnet, a French economist and Robert Shuman, the French Foreign Minister, saw this vital industry as critical to those wishing to wage war.

They brought the major European countries together to control steel and coal, thereby stopping the war making capacity of the individual European nations, especially of France and Germany. It was the first step that the Europeans took to blunt the instruments of war-making within their continent. There is no reason we in this sub-continent cannot do the same. A dear friend who helped bring China and the United States together told me that the total two-way trade between the US and China before 1972 was just $25 million INDIRECT trade mostly through Hong Kong.

Now in 2007 US-China direct trade is over $200 billion. That trade and other factors have made China the huge economic engine it has now become. That is the kind of future that awaits our people if we can reinvent our relations.

(2) Regarding transportation links: a start has been made with the bus journey between Srinagar and Muzzafarabad and the train between New Delhi and Lahore. We must increase those links, eliminate visa restrictions and remember that when we can travel between France and Germany - two old enemies - the train or bus does not stop any more for police

and customs checks. Energy resources are vital to our economies. The closest readily accessible energy source of hydrocarbons is in Central Asia. My government implemented my Father's proposal to build Gwadar Port in Balauchistan, Pakistan's largest province, to bring Central Asian gas and oil to world markets through Pakistan. My government agreed to building pipelines for oil and gas to be pumped across Pakistan to India.

I intend to make these plans a top priority of my country -to bring these gas and oil pipelines from Central Asia to the people of Balauchistan in Pakistan and to export them to India. It is vital to our economies and our industry.

(3) The political instability of Afghanistan hampers trade with Central Asia. Therefore controlling terrorism in the tribal areas of Pakistan is a priority for my people and for the government we hope they will elect us to make. A peaceful and democratic India, Pakistan and Afghanistan can bring enormous benefits in this programme of bringing new energy resources to all of our economies.

In addition, Pakistan has one of the richest shale deposits in the world. A new low-cost technology now is available to get useable energy from the shale and the residue in water. We will share both the technology and the product with you.

(4) We have all seen the excitement of our peoples when our sports teams visits each other's countries. These exchanges must happen frequently without governmental interference. Let the fans from Lahore come and cheer their teams playing in Bombay or Calcutta or visa-versa. The Prime Minister of Pakistan controlled Kashmir Sardar Attique has welcomed investment from all regions and religions of the world, including from Indian controlled Kashmir. He has offered gas and electricity across the Line of Control. Discussing such proposals can help bring us closer.

The devastating earthquake in 2005 demostrated that disaster recognizes no geographical borders. People on both sides of the Line of Control in Kashmir were killed, injured and lost their homes and loved ones. It was a terrible tragedy and awoke in our minds the need for us to work together even on issues such as disaster control. The entertainment industry is huge in India and growing in Pakistan. There must be no boundaries between our countries in this area too.

(5) Both of our countries exploded nuclear devices in May 1998. We have now proved to each other and the world that we are firmly in the group of elite countries that have nuclear weapons. We do not have to prove our military prowess anymore. We do need to continue investing in an area that brings little economic return to our peoples and countries. Let us turn our investment and co-operation towards the peaceful uses of nuclear energy.

The people of France get 80 per cent of their power generation of electricity from nuclear methods. I have just mentioned a very few of the areas in which we can co-operate. Many more exist. Across from the United Nations Headquarters in New York City there is a small peace park with an inscription that says:

"They shall beat their swords into plowshares, and their spears into pruning hooks: a nation shall not lift up sword against another nation, neither shall they learn war anymore." Or, as Mahatma Gandhi said, "An eye for an eye only makes the whole world blind."

Let us serve the people we all love by bringing peace to these lands we all love!

Thank you for the honour of speaking before you.

— India Today Conclave - New Delhi
March, 24, 2007

Asian Political Parties

Distinguished delegates:

I am privileged to visit Manila and address this distinguished audience at the historic first conference of Asian political leaders.A tribute to the organizers, in particular former Speaker Jose de Venecia, for inviting us to discuss the challenges of the Twentyfirst Century. The leaders of leading Asian political parties, irrespective of political affiliations, meet this morning as Asians committed to the welfare of this great continent. We reach out to create a culture of cooperation even as enormous changes sweep over our planet. Many of us gave years of our lives battling dictatorship. I congratulate the Asian countries that have won that battle of freedom. But freedom is still under assault in parts of Asia, including Burma and my own country Pakistan. Winning freedom is the start of another journey—the journey for our people to lead a life, free from want and hunger, from slums and squalour. The promise of our tomorrows awaits fulfilment. Globalization has placed us in a new political storm. Today Asia declares its readiness to face the brave new world dominated by regional trading blocs. Whilst the goal of an Asian Parliament, an Asian trading currency and an Asian Monetary Fund appear a distant dream, this morning's first step indicates our will to adjust to globalization forces dictating the pace of change.

Asia's middle classes are groaning under the world of deregulation and free currency flows that move with ruthless speed bringing both fortune and failure in its wake. With our response, we can meet the threat of a new class of marginalised underprivileged, unable to compete with modern ideas, technology and markets. We can do this by identifying common institutions, laws and procedures enabling our nations to move forward in an Asian rhythm, benefiting from the New World Order. Market forces demand a computer literate work force. Surely we have the will to prioritise our budgets to equip our people with new skills. Investment runs from, and ruins economies based on the old paradigm—a paradigm built on geostrategic concerns held up by missiles and military might. Today's might is the might of markets. Influence flows from the call of commerce and of capital markets. We can see, from Philippines to Pakistan, that economies suffer, miseries increase and helplessness sets in where markets are threatened by bombs, wars, insurgencies, terrorism, corrupt practices and narcotics trade.

Let us share building a new paradigm for Asia, beyond terror to safety. Let us light the path for Asians to compete successfully in creating wealth and prosperity. Agricultural economy dominates many Asian societies. We can create a class of agricultural entrepreneurs by investing in the rural community even as our urban force benefits from the services sector, commerce and labour export. There's a hungry world out there, looking for software engineers and biogenetic scientists. Their training and export can lead to capital transfers and huge opportunities. We need to move fast—for opportunity does not knock twice. But progress needs political parties that can promise political stability. Lack of proper funding undermines the ability of parties to combat the interests of an entrenched establishment. State funding can assist parties in establishing secretariats, facilitating policy research, establishing media offices and contesting general elections. Bribes offered to parliamentarians to switch sides is another problem. I faced it when my opponents moved a no confidence move funded by Muslim militants opposed to a woman in politics. Open balloting makes cheating more difficult. And those who switch sides can be forced to resign. The President my party elected switched sides, plunging Pakistan into a downward spiral on the rocky road of nuclear explosions, economic implosion and, finally, martial law. Fanatics challenge stability too. They do it under the cloak of religion. In promoting interfaith dialogue, the chances of a clash of civilizations can be averted.

Ladies and Gentlemen, I come from a country rich in weapons of mass destruction—a country that nearly went to a nuclear war over the frozen wastelands of an area called Kargil. A country where bomb blasts ruin lives and desperate young men, commit suicide because they cannot afford to live. It is unethical, when a regime is deaf, dumb and blind to the agonies of its own people. All of us, as Asians, can raise our voice when rules we set, in the ink of humanity, are violated. We have done this in the United Nations. We can do it as an Asian association in this, the third millenium. Picture the Asian woman, shorn of her most basic rights. Picture the Asian child, robbed of the innocence of childhood. Our women and children deserve better. The irrevocable market forces can be compensated for by human conscience. Together we can raise our voices for compassion—a great human quality. Asia can argue for debt relief. I argue for debt relief tied to good governance. And for amounts saved to go into a special anti-poverty programme. Away from the bright lights and the consumer world of Malls, MacDonalds and Mercedes, we, that God blessed as the privileged, need to measure up by reaching out to that dark underworld where poverty, hunger and squalour stalk the lives of millions, nay billions, of Asians.

Distinguished delegates, I come from a land of mystic saints who preached the message of love. I bring here that message of love and peace—for hatred is only born of fear. A new future awaits us. A future where computers have replaced combustion as the catalyst for change. Where information has replaced ideology as the idiom of action. It is time for the sleeping Asian giant to awaken.

Thank you, Speaker de venecia and organizers of the Conference, for setting the alarm clock by inviting us here to face up to the reality that: "If you always do what you always did, you'll always get what you always got."

Thank you, distinguished delegates.

— Conference of Asian Political Parties Manila
17-Sep-2000

Saving South Asia from War and Terrorism

Ladies and Gentlemen,

I am grateful to Count Albi for inviting me to speak before this distinguished audience of the Eminent Persons Advisory Group. I come to speak here at an extraordinary and dangerous time for South Asia and the larger world community.

My country Pakistan is critical to the direction that South Asia takes in the Twentyfirst Century. It is an ally of international forces in the war against terror. It is also a country that has dangerous tensions with its nuclear neighbour and rival India. It is a country where a military dictator threatens to rig elections and create greater internal instability. A series of suicide bomber attacks since this year began indicate the fragility of Pakistan's internal situation. The brutal kidnapping and execution of Danny Pearl the Wall Street Journalist, underscores the treacherous lack of ground rules in the war against terror. Danny Pearl's murder was followed by a series of devastating attacks on hospitals, churches and diplomatic missions. Meanwhile, in Afghanistan, the remnants of Al-Queda managed attacks on international forces as well as pro-Karzai supporters.

It is difficult for terrorists to operate without a base, without logistics and without re-supply. Clearly, someone somewhere is supporting them. According to the bazaar talk in Pakistan, the aim of the terrorists is to kill one hundred members of the international forces to drive them out of Afghanistan. Then, they claim, they will deal with those who supported the war against terror.

International forces do come in and are needed for short term support in areas where security is threatened. In the long run, the war against terror needs sustained commitment. It needs allies who can meet the terrorist threat locally. Long term stability depends on a world community sustained by countries and systems with the strengths to police their own countries and to work together to police their regions. Clearly Pakistan's military regime, while claiming to be a strong man regime, failed to deliver a single prize during the war against terror. The fall of Kabul came because of the Northern Alliance even as Pakistan's military dictator pleaded with President Bush to stop their advance. Islamabad continued to recognise the Taliban despite the fall of Taliban for some time. The much talked about security cordon established to stop fleeing Al Queda after the bombing of Tora Bora failed to capture Bin Laden, Mullah Omar or any of the key leadership which waged war against the international community. A key Al Queda leader, Abu Zubaydah, found himself a home in the Pakistani heartland of Punjab. His arrest came because the FBI intercepted telephonic communications from the remote areas of Afghanistan to that particular house. The investigation of the Danny Pearl case succeeded because the FBI found the internet café from where the video of the Danny Pearl capture was sent.

Islamabad has done little to contribute to ground realities except for two exceptions. Firstly, joining the war against terror and second allowing military bases. It could be argued that Islamabad joined the war because it had little choice after President Bush asked Nations to be counted as friend or foe. As for the military bases, they serve a dual purpose. While mollifying the world community, they act as a warning to neighbour India that taking on Islamabad means taking on the world community.

The country's military leader makes comments that border on the bizarre. For example, he claimed that Danny Pearl was kidnapped because he got involved in intelligence games. This almost amounted to blaming Danny for his own kidnapping. This month in the *New Yorker*, General Musharraf almost exonerated Bin Laden from the attack on the World Trade Center. He said he found it hard to believe that a man in the mountain could have planned such a sophisticated attack. Clearly the man in the mountain had the support of powerful elements to plan that attack. Clearly the escape of the top leadership needed support. Al Queda and other militant groups were formed during the war against the Soviet occupation of Afghanistan. The West gave the money and the Pakistan military did the recruiting and the training.

There are many linkages between individual officers and the men they trained. It was thus less than surprising to find that Islamabad's strong man and the terrorists have common friends. One such friend is the home secretary of Pakistan's largest province of Punjab. Omar Shaikh, the self confessed conspirator in the Pearl kidnapping, turned himself over to his friend the home secretary who also happens to be a friend and appointee of Musharraf. And while Omar Shaikh was in the custody of Musharraf's friend, the General was claiming that India did the Pearl kidnapping.

Many of General Musharraf's friends have close intelligence ties. Musharraf himself was chosen by pro-Mujahideen leader General Zia as his military secretary. Last October, as the war against terror unfolded, Musharraf sacked two hardline Generals who had brought him to power. However, the entire apparatus they put into place continued. For example, two Governors worked for the powerful ISI which oversaw the Afghan Jihad. Two diplomats worked for the same organisation. They are presently posted to the critical countries of Saudi Arabia and Morocco. Other officials from the organisation that recruited and trained the pro-Mujahideen forces today are members of the Federal and provincial cabinets and administrations.

And so I would like to ask: will the real Musharraf stand up? For years the Musharraf regime coddled the Taliban. When the war against terror started, the Musharraf regime claimed it was born again. Yet it has done everything in its power to block and marginalise the moderate forces. That it failed has more to do with the wisdom of the Pakistani people and their political awareness. There are only two powers: the power of the ballot and the power of the bullet. When the power of the ballot is marginalised, the power of the bullet gains in strength. This is why I believe that dictatorship fuels militancy.

When political parties are prevented from participating in politics, the Mosque becomes the only safe meeting place.

Yesterday General Musharraf personally met with the head of the religious party Jamaat e Islami. He sought their support to stop the Pakistan Peoples Party from winning the forthcoming General Elections.

The Pakistan Peoples Party is the only civilian and political structure in Pakistan with the popular support and the organisation to form a government outside the influence of the intelligence agencies and the military. The attempts to stop it and crush it are dangerous for the people of Pakistan as well as for the region and the wide world community in which we live. There always ought to be alternatives that are peaceful, available to the people of a country, as well as to the larger world we live in. When the alternatives wither away and power is concentrated in a clique, the balance that makes for civilised society and peaceful change is lost.

I caution the world community from putting all its eggs in one basket and that too the basket of a military dictator. The Pakistan Peoples Party is opposed by military hardliners. Its two elected and democratic governments were destabilised in the past because the military hardliners found that their hawkish policies were undermined by the presence of a political force with an independent base. The military hardliners are today looking for a dummy parliament and a dummy prime minister so that their policies can continue unabated.

I may add that I am proud of the Pakistan Peoples Party record in office in combating terrorism and in building peace in the region including with India. Each major act of international terror was organised when my Party and I were in the Opposition. During my first stint in the Opposition, Islamabad was on the verge of being declared a terrorist state. When I took over, it became one of the ten emerging capital markets of the world. When the PPP was decreed out of office, the economy collapsed and militancy forced President Clinton to curtail his time in Islamabad to a few hours, in contrast to India, which he visited for five days.

During my second stint in the Opposition, the forces of terror launched their attack on America on September 11. The two attacks on the World Trade Center, the attacks on the two U S embassies in Africa, the attack on the Cole ship in Yemen, the Bombay blasts of the nineties; the Indian Parliament attack, all took place when the Pakistan Peoples Party was in the Opposition.

The Taliban did not take control of all Afghanistan until my government was eclipsed. Bin Laden failed to show up in Afghanistan when I was Prime Minister of Pakistan. His finances were exhausted in 1996. It was only after the overthrow of the government I led that Al Queda were invited into Afghanistan by the Taliban and allowed to train militants for terror attacks across the world.

The military hardliners oppose the PPP under my leadership. They oppose my policies of building peace within and building peace without. They did everything to destroy my reputation and standing amongst the people of Pakistan and the larger world community. Once they recruited a twice convicted British slum lord to claim that my husband tied a bomb on his leg and held him for ransom. The outrageous stories were made to destroy my leadership and my Party. More dangerously they were made to destroy democracy in Pakistan and the empowerment of its people.

Mullah Omar could seize Afghanistan only after the people there were denied all chance of self-expression. It is when people are denied the right to representation and to determine their own future that their destiny can be controlled through fanatics and bigots.

The military hardliners believe they beat the Soviet Union and they can beat the West. They are determined to stop democracy in Pakistan seeing in it a danger to their world view to export revolution through the central Asian republics. Their politics threaten to destabilise South Asia as well as create greater misunderstanding between the great religions of the world. Since the tragedies of September 11, the international community rightly focused on eradicating the Taliban regime, destroying Al-Queda, building a stable government in Afghanistan and reducing tensions between nuclear-armed India and Pakistan. But nuclear tensions still remain between India and Pakistan. Pakistan's military dictator chose Independence Day on August 14 to make an important declaration. He stated that Islamabad could defend each inch of its territory as well as "take the war across the border".

It is this belief that Pakistan can win a war with India and militarily dictate its terms that worries me. Perhaps military men are trained to think of wars. Perhaps that is why it is said that war is too serious a business to be left to Generals. It is politicians that calculate the different political, diplomatic, financial, legal and other aspects of a situation. Military men look at it through one dimension.

Since my government was overthrown in 1996, India and Pakistan nearly went to war three times. My concern is that unless my Party returns to power, the pattern could be repeated again. For 15 years, the unanimous consensus amongst the leading security experts of the world community has been that the place most likely to trigger a nuclear confrontation is South Asia. The issue is Kashmir. Nuclear deterrence - the centrepiece of military strategy for both of South Asia's nuclear powers - was designed to prevent conflict. Yet since India detonated nuclear devices in 1998, and Pakistan responded in kind, South Asia has thrice come to the brink of war. Intelligence estimates, backed by published reports, suggest that a nuclear exchange between Pakistan and India over Kashmir, even if limited to five or six primary targets on each side, would cause millions of immediate deaths, and millions more after long and dreadful suffering from ensuing cancer on both sides of the border, for decades to come. With the military in Pakistan and Hindu nationalist hardliners in Delhi firmly in control, the options for dialogue and confidence-building appear remote. When two sides believe they can both gain from a military conflict, it makes the world a much more dangerous place. The danger to the region increases with a military dictatorship in Pakistan unaccountable to the people.

History teaches us that democracies do not start wars. Each war that took place between India and Pakistan took place when Islamabad was under a military dictatorship. The concern is that with a military junta in Islamabad, and the world distracted by the US-led war against terrorism, the "public check" on political decision-making in the country has ceased to exist. The Pakistan Peoples Party believes the people of South Asia deserve a future that is better than the recent past. If India and Pakistan disagree on the territorial nature of Kashmir, we can still move ahead without prejudice to our long-held beliefs. The nuclear war threat can recede if the leadership on both sides of the divide has the courage to promote safe and open borders to socially unite the Kashmiri people. The Kashmiri people are central to the dispute and it is the responsibility of the leadership on both sides of the divide to put these people first. If China and India can have a border dispute and still trade, India and Pakistan can do the same. In the absence of an elected civilian leadership in Pakistan that is accountable to the people, however, the possibility of such a dialogue is remote. The worry is that the pattern of militant acts provoking a near-nuclear confrontation will continue, at regular intervals, until it erupts into a full-fledged nuclear war. In the post-nuclear-detonation region that South Asia has been since 1998, those who live there can ill afford a military conflict. In the post-September 11 world, the Kashmiri people can ill afford a world community where terrorism and armed conflict by an occupied people is still to be distinguished. Catastrophe could also be triggered by accident: with artillery shells whizzing over the line of control when tension rises, hundreds of thousands of troops poised to strike, and elements on both sides willing to throw a match on to the fire, the situation is precarious.

Press reports indicate that nuclear weapons could be given to individual commanders with independent launch control. It is not clear whether these reports are accurate, but if so, the probability of an accidental launch jumps sharply. And with tension so high, an accident could never possibly be explained away and controlled. The genie would be out of the jar for the first time in 57 years. With the doomsday scenarios in front of us, what can be done to prevent the insanity?

I believe democracies do not start wars; democracies do not provoke wars and democracies do not promote terrorism. Each of the three wars between India and Pakistan was fought under military dictators in Pakistan. The last three major incidents that brought the world to the precipice of nuclear war surfaced after my democratic government was overthrown and the military established ascendancy in the political arena. The best prospect for peace in South Asia is to support the democratisation process in Pakistan. Political power must be transferred legally, peacefully and subject to the will of the people. Commentators believe that my party and I would be re-elected if transparent elections were held in Pakistan in October. The military regime has decreed several new laws in an attempt to prevent that from happening. Those matters are now before Pakistan's judiciary. The people of Pakistan and my Party want me to lead them again. They want me to contest the coming October elections. I want to contest those elections. I am trying to cross each hurdle that is put in my path. General Musharraf has vowed to stop my return through edicts. His attempts to do so are making a mockery of the electoral process and threatening the legitimacy of the new Parliament.

In the higher national interest, my Party kept the doors of dialogue open with the military regime to facilitate the process of democratisation in Pakistan. That dialogue remains inconclusive due to the inability of the regime to address our core issues. These concern the respect for fundamental human rights and the restoration of the democratic process guaranteed by a mutually agreed third party.

Security in South Asia — and as September 11 showed, security for the world — is in grave jeopardy. Only a democratic Pakistan can eradicate the forces of extremism, militancy and terrorism. The Pakistani people, when given the opportunity in brief interludes of democratic rule, consistently opposed policies that promoted extremism in Afghanistan and tension with neighbouring India. With militants regrouping in Pakistan the need to crack extremism in society is necessary. It is necessary to domestic peace and global stability.

Political parties can play an important role in preparing Pakistani society for such a clampdown. The parties representing broader public (beyond the army) support are needed to mobilise the man in the street against the forces of extremism. Democracy and elections are important for more than Democracy's sake. As the Presidential referendum held last April demonstrated, public discontent in Pakistan is high. A representative parliament provides the right forum for involving the people in the national debate. The danger is that a rigged electoral process plays into the hands of the militants. They depend on the bullet, rather than the ballot.

Significantly, under Musharraf's writ, the militants manage to calibrate events on the troubled Afghan and Kashmir borders. When the bombing on Tora Bora gets heavy, or when the noose on Al Queda tightens in Pakistan's tribal areas, a militant strike complicates relations with India. The Indian diversion plays to the advantage of the militants who manage to escape as international energies are consumed in averting a conflict between two nuclear armed nations. The Musharraf regime held unrestrained power for nearly three years. Their inability to raise revenues domestically despite heavy new taxes reduced living standards. Pakistanis today are further impoverished with a lower per capita income than when their democratic government was in power in 1996. As friendly as General Musharraf may have been to the War on Terrorism, he has failed to offer hope to the legions of disenfranchised in Pakistan.

Specifically, the world community could ask Musharraf to withdraw controversial constitutional amendments taking power from the legislature and concentrating it in an individual. The checks and balances of a pluralistic society are a prerequisite for consensus and tolerance. Giving Pakistan's Presidency dictatorial powers including the unilateral dismissal of the Prime Minister, Cabinet and Parliament without elections is a prescription for extremism. The world community could:

(1) Establish an international election monitoring force ensuring that the October 10 Pakistani elections are transparent and open to all parties and candidates. During the recent Referendum to elect the President, the military regime allowed eight year olds to vote while conveying busloads of

coerced citizens to different polling stations to vote numerous times in numerous places.

(2) Pressure Musharraf to free political prisoners and allow the return of political exiles, including myself, who are victims of a discredited and politically motivated process. It is time for closure on the past to allow the nation to focus on the future.

The world community could make it clear that it predicates future aid, international loans and debt relief to the holding of transparent and internationally verified elections that respect the fundamental and democratic rights of the Pakistani people. The world walked away from Afghanistan when the Soviets withdrew in 1989 without promoting the politics of consensus. That neglect contributed to the rise of the Taliban and Al-Queda. The world must avoid walking away from Democracy in Pakistan. The nightmare of the Taliban and the terrorists who on September 11 rained such unspeakable destruction on the world must never be allowed to happen again. For the security of South Asia and for the security of our global village, it is important that the people of Pakistan freely determine their own destiny on October 10. Pakistan's elections are important for the empowerment of the Pakistani people as well as their hopes of fighting terrorism, poverty and unemployment. Pakistan's elections are also important for the world community with the disappearing Al-Queda on one side of the border and one million men mobilised on the other border with India. The ball is in the international community's court. The stakes are nothing less than making the world safe from nuclear war and terrorism.

— London
16-Aug-2002

Indo-Pak Summit 2001

As General Musharraf and his delegation prepare to leave for New Delhi airport, my thoughts go back to another airport and another tarmac. I recall Prime Minister Rajiv Gandhi's visit to Islamabad on a chill December day as the sun shone warmly. The hope for peace and freedom filled the air as the band struck up the music and the Pakistan Army Guard smartly marched passed. The military and its political supporters sabotaged that spring in Indo Pak relations. It is with a sense of personal moral vindication that I watch the army chief, twelve years later, realize the wisdom of my politics and seek to follow my footsteps in defusing tensions with our larger neighbour.

I do feel a sense of national loss. Twelve years, and many thousands of deaths later, Islamabad begged for a meeting "any time and any place" when a dignified opportunity was available earlier. The Musharraf visit is controversial for three reasons: legitimacy, military history and Kashmir history. As an unelected and unrepresentative leader, Musharraf lacks legitimacy. The very army he leads can turn around tomorrow and make this argument when he joins the ranks of former chiefs. Moreover, he lacks the moral and political authority to co-opt the people. Pakistan's military history bodes ill for his visit too. Each military dictator was anxious to offer a no war pact to India which India rejected. Both countries believe that Islamabad can afford an insurgency but needs to avoid war. True to military history, Musharraf made the same offer.

Then there is recent Kashmir history. Musharraf was the architect of the Kargil crisis where thousands of Pakistani soldiers and Kashmiri militants lost their lives. Musharraf, like Lady Macbeth, finds it difficult to wash the stains of their blood from his hands. When he flies into Agra with his seventy-man delegation, the ghosts of three thousand Pakistani soldiers, buried secretly, fly with him. He will see their faces as they starved to death in the icy peaks of Kargil when supply lines stopped. There are the faces of the living, those forced to retreat when America ordered the unilateral withdrawal from Kargil. Can Musharraf offer something to compensate the earlier humiliation?

For what the martyrdoms, for what the operation and unilateral withdrawal, for what the refusal to salute if the conclusion was an embrace two years later in Delhi. A new, elected, government is free of the constraints of the burden of Kargil. And Kargil was a heavy burden. That is why, it is argued, that peace was better left to an elected and representative government. That is why, it was argued, far better for Musharraf to focus on the democratization process. But it seems "making up with Vajpayee" was a better option than "making up with the Opposition".

Much of the debate on the Musharraf visit focuses on the intentions of the man as he makes his way to Agra. His accommodation overlooks the famous Taj Mahal, the monument of love built by a Muslim Emperor for his Queen. New Delhi hopes the vision can inspire a fresh romance between the two countries.

But are such hopes well founded? There is a thinking in New Delhi that more is squeezed from a dictator than a democrat. Pakistanis may believe that democrats pioneered the lasting peace moves between the two countries but Delhi hears other arguments. They remember Zia who defended the loss of Siachin posts as "worthless ice where flowers cannot grow". Premier Vajpayee can lose little in sounding out a Musharraf who pleaded from every platform for "a meeting, any time and any place". There is much that Premier Vajpayee can gain. Entertaining Musharraf to tea and pastries, showing him his old home, the shops and the shrines, pausing to mention Kashmir and moving on, morally vindicates Vajpayee. His policies bring the Kargil architect to his door on his terms.

What of Musharraf? Four explanations come to mind for the Musharraf visit. First, that Musharraf was reborn the day he seized power from Premier Nawaz. The commando, who refused to salute the hated Indian enemy, and masterminded Kargil to highlight Indian impotence, died the day the coup took place. Instead, like a butterfly emerging from the chrysalis, a soldier for peace was born yearning to replace the medals on his chest with a Nobel Prize. The difficulty in the "rebirth" theory is that Musharraf's base is the military Establishment and the religious parties. We are yet to see signs of change in a military establishment smarting from its Kargil retreat after winning the peaks and facing Indian pounding.

The second explanation is that the Musharraf visit is a tactical move on the lines of Kargil deception. Catching the enemy unawares is the name of the game. The third explanation is that the hourglass is ticking away for Musharraf. The way to win international approval for his continuation in power, Musharraf needs to show he is a man the Indians can do business with. The fourth explanation lies in Pakistan's Northern Front. Embroiled with the Taliban, under pressure from UN sanctions, Islamabad desperately needs to release the international pressure from the Afghan front. What better way to mitigate the bad cop image than tactically playing good cop in New Delhi?

The press speculated on the agenda of the talks between the two leaders when they hole up in the Retreat together. Islamabad's press speculated on non-papers, of far reaching and secret understandings reached by both sides. That appears doubtful. More likely are continuation of the PPP led agreements. The PPP agreements that could be taken up in New Delhi include:

First, a continuation of the non-attack on each other's nuclear facilities agreement. Given the nervousness of the international community over nuclear affairs, nuclear risk reduction measures can come under discussion.

Second, the re-deployment to Kargil negotiated in the summer of 1989 can be considered.

Third, the expansion of trade for which much work was done by Commerce Minister Mukhtar.

Fourth, greater travel facilities between the two countries in the light of the PPP proposal at SAARC conference in December 1988 for visa relaxation.

Fifth, mutual reduction of troops that was discussed by the two sides during the 1989 talks and for which much progress was made by the intelligence chiefs of both sides.

Sixth, the Iran-Pakistan-India pipeline project sanctioned by the second Benazir government.

The Middle East Peace talks and the Good Friday Agreements on Northern Ireland sparked a flurry of speculation that the Pakistan's military dictator could make a dramatic breakthrough on Kashmir.

That appears unlikely. However, the foundation for a continued dialogue at the highest levels between the two countries could be laid. The regional association SAARC was to provide that opportunity to India and Pakistan. But its meetings were irregular. Musharraf goes to New Delhi as Islamabad's weakest ruler. Lacking legitimacy, internal unity and fiscal manoeuvrability, his visit to New Delhi is full of pitfalls. Lacking good advice, or foreign policy experience, he failed to build the internal consensus that was so necessary to ensure a better base. Some tested his will to build internal consensus, but he found it hard to swallow the release of ten political dissidents and a date for elections in exchange for political support on his perilous New Delhi journey.

And if it is difficult to swallow the release of ten political dissidents, we can imagine how much more difficult it is to swallow the death of three thousand innocent soldiers, who gave their lives in the mountainous glaciers for their Motherland's honour on the Commanders' orders.

— INDO-PAK SUMMIT 2001

Benazir Bhutto, 12-Jul-2001

Might Can Crush, It Cannot Conquer

The Oslo peace process lies stained with blood in the dusty streets of Ramallah and Jerusalem. The excessive use of force by the Barak regime against Palestinian protesters has sparked anger across the Muslim world. Too many human lives have been lost, including those of Palestinian children. The recording of the brutal death of a small child nestled in the father's shadow, whose protection he sought, was cruel and inhuman. For many, it shocked and symbolised the senseless violence that has gripped the Middle East for more than half a century. The inability of the Israeli regime to order an inquiry into that brutal murder, or to reign in the security forces, reinforced old stereotypes and led to the lynching of Israeli soldiers.

The inability of the world community to step in quickly enough to prevent the loss of almost 100 lives, mostly Palestinian, in two weeks shook the peace process. It also re-ignited memories of the killings of Muslims in Bosnia, Kosovo and Chechnya played, and replayed, on television screens. Once again, the international community was found slow in responding to a crisis that could lead to far and wide ramifications. To many, it appeared that the unfortunate lynching of the two Israeli soldiers was the catalyst that moved the world community to finally seek to politically intervene.

The perception within the Muslim community, whether right or wrong, that the lives of two Israeli soldiers are more valuable than the lives of ten score Palestinians is what feeds anger and fuels extremist movements across the Muslim world. The United Nations, Washington and the foreign capitals of the G-8 are too far away. Most people vent their sentiments on their own rulers, seeing them as weak and inept. This undermines the politics of moderation.

The Cold War world was built on the structure of two superpowers. Countries, and people, who felt aggrieved could look for solace and hope towards one of the superpowers. The end of the Cold War has led to a unipolar world. That unipolar world is still to construct the pillars upon which the foundations of redress can be laid. Most of the international community looks towards America. The United Nations, or even the Security Council, is still to come into its own.

Global institutions for conflict resolution and conflict prevention are necessary to enable quick responses. Otherwise the danger is that the politics of blood will feed the politics of hatred. The politics of elections, and of ratings, also determines the ability of governments to respond. Or not respond. America, caught in a presidential election, was less focused on international affairs. Electorally, the weight of the American Muslims was too weak to pressure a stronger response in the face of the early killings. Meanwhile, the violence curve provoked by the visit of controversial Israeli leader Ariel Sharon to Jerusalem had profound electoral results. The sagging political fortunes of Prime Minister Barak more than doubled. His ratings went up from 20 per cent to 50 per cent. More and more, in the world of Gallup polls and influential groups able to articulate their views effectively, leaders respond to ratings. Statesmen are too few and far between. Yet, a peaceful world needs more statespeople, those leaders able to look beyond today to take decisions that may be unpopular but necessary.

Changing the status quo requires courage. It also requires the capacity to absorb a momentary loss of support for a permanent place in history. Perhaps the recent wave of violence will lead to a review of the geographical unit and religious composition that can better police peace. The segregated and non-contiguous Palestinian enclaves, surrounded by Israeli-controlled borders, have kept tensions running high. It might have been right at the time when the Palestinian Authority had yet to be established. Now a better rationalisation seems in order.

The road to peace is difficult. Extremists on both sides demand too much. And inflame passions. President Arafat and Prime Minister Rabin both demonstrated courage in moving towards peace. In a world of instant information the expectation is of instant solutions. Yet, the world is based on human passion. Human Passion has yet to allow for instant political solutions. Yes, there are unresolved issues. It takes time to deal with each one Pakistan and Bangladesh, both Muslim countries, are yet to resolve the outstanding issues springing from their separation in 1971. Those who blame President Arafat for accepting a less than perfect initial resolution are harsh. The foot has to get in the door before the house is accessible. In accepting a torn and tattered peace, President Arafat opened the door to a solution. To expect that was the solution is simply short-sighted.

There are one billion Muslims in the world today. The demographic pressure creates a power of its own. But many within the Muslim community are caught in a cycle of cynicism and bitterness. That cycle began with the Palestinian dislocation in 1948. It deepened into frustration when large numbers of Muslims perceived themselves as caught between injustice and helplessness. Violence was a by-product.

As we enter the Twentyfirst Century, the peace process that promised so much in the last century, is in danger. It rests on the ability of the ailing President Arafat and the intractable Barak regime to move forward. The use of helicopter gunships and heavy artillery hardly helps. It gives the impression that, rather than seek peace, the Barak regime is seeking to intimidate a surrender. Israel is militarily more powerful with a suspected nuclear arsenal. That military might ought to give Barak the security to surmount fear and take steps to reach out to the Palestinians. In the ageing Palestinian leader, peace has a chance. It ought to be taken. Otherwise, the danger is that the past ghosts will come back to stalk the Middle East again. If history has a lesson, it is that might can crush but it cannot conquer.

— The News
17-Oct-2000

Social Development and Women's Empowerment

Ladies and Gentlemen:

By your focus on the essential rights of woman in society, you support the voice of the powerless, the exploited, and the abused. For women, despite the strides taken in the last century, are still the most powerless and exploited group in the world community. For me, the cause of women, is God's most noble cause, the cause of justice, equality, and life. So I thank the Indian Chamber of Industry for inviting me to New Delhi.

We meet today in challenging times. I feel myself privileged to speak to the captains of trade and industry of one of the biggest growing markets of the world community. Those major markets promise to make your country a major decision maker in the world. India's emergence in the post Cold War period shows the importance of the force of free markets in the political landscape of the global community. That force of market politics, when applied to my country in 1993, made it one of the ten emerging capital markets of the world.

Ladies and Gentlemen, this is my second visit to New Delhi. I came here first to take part in the funeral ceremonies of Prime Minister Rajiv Gandhi. I came to pay respects to a leader with whom I had worked to build a safer South Asia. Prime Minister Gandhi and I signed the most important bilateral agreements in 1988 since the signing of the Simla Agreement by our parents in 1972. We signed the first nuclear confidence building treaty, the nonattack agreement on each other's nuclear facilities. We established, for the first time, hot lines between the General Headquarters of both our countries. We opened our borders for better trade. At SAARC, we determined to work for a common SAARC travel card and a common SAARC pre-posted mailing card. We understood that Europe triumphed over hate and war and that we could do so too. We reached draft agreements on redeployment of troops to Kargil without prejudice to our view points on the icy area. We reached a draft agreement for the mutual reduction and redeployment of troops between our two countries.

But both our governments went and with it the brief spring when two young leaders stood at the brink of historical change. The hope born then was rekindled under the leadership of Prime Minister Vajpayee. He visited Lahore in 1999 and invited the country's military ruler to Agra in 2001. His Home Minister Advani agreed to talk unconditionally with the All Parties Hurriyet Conference. The Indian Government announced a unilateral ceasefire in Kashmir and met with the militant groups. These were important steps taken. They required vision and strength. The vision to build a South Asia free of tension, where the people of South Asia would have the strength and the courage to reject tension and embrace peace to build a better world for the coming generations.

Ladies and Gentlemen, I was planning to visit India for some time. I planned to come here in 1999 but the fighting in Kargil broke out. I planned visiting India this October, but fighting in Kabul broke out. It was with some trepidation that I accepted the invitation by the Confederation of Indian Trade and Industry. This time the stars were right, I am here with you and it is a special privilege for me to speak before you today. Too few political leaders from India and Pakistan, particularly from the political field, visit each other. I am here to break that precedent and set a new precedent. I hope that can be the start of new precedents that our two Nations are able to achieve as we enter the Twentyfirst century.

The Pakistan Peoples Party, which I lead, trusts in relationships of a political nature. We invited the Opposition leaders of the SAARC to Karachi in 1992 to build closer political links between the elected representatives of our region.

Ladies and Gentlemen, it is impossible to separate women's rights from human rights, just as it is impossible to separate economic justice from political liberty. In the modern era, these issues are the essential operationalizations of morality, of civility, of a just society. I come before you with a unique double focus. On one level, as the victim of human rights violations today and in the past, and on another level as someone who has had the extraordinary opportunity to address women's rights in my own country. I am no stranger to the issues of women's empowerment. I wear the scars, on my body and my soul, of the abuse of basic human rights, and thus I view oppression through the eyes of the victim.

We do not live in a perfect world, and even amongst the rapidly expanding democratic community there often seems coldness, indifference, hypocrisy and lingering prejudice. Many thought heaven would appear on earth with the crumbling of the Berlin Wall. A decade later we find that Europe may be united, but the cause of justice of the discriminated people in many countries is far from complete. Let us be truthful, the world will be a fair place when each and every human being on our planet is treated equally. And there is no human right more fundamental, and more universal, than equal rights for women in the new century. Democracy is the first step toward humanity's liberation. But it is not an end in itself. Liberty depends on social and economic justice, and above all on the universal, non-selective application of human rights to all citizens of the world. Economic development and political development are surely linked, but both are predicated on guaranteed human rights.

As the first woman ever elected to head an Islamic nation, I feel a special responsibility about issues that relate to women. I am often asked about the place of women in the message of Islam. For me, the discrimination against women has little to do with Islam and more to do with custom and tradition. Here in South Asia, many of the women in the ethnically and religiously diverse countries suffer similar fates. Too many are denied the right to live fully. Too often, women are seen as extensions of the male rather than as individuals in their own right. One of the difficulties I encounter is the prejudice born of centuries that a woman is the property of the man.

Here I am an independent woman, educated in modern universities, the daughter of an emancipated leader and I find myself the centre of controversy in the minds of the traditionalists. For them, my husband is to blame for letting me work. Traditionally respected men did not allow their wives to work. By that definition, in their eyes, my husband must be something other than a respectable person. They punish him, to punish me, and in seeking to punish us, they seek to punish women, and men who see women as separate legal entities, everywhere. The battle with the traditionalists is a battle that has dogged my political career. During the general elections in 1988, the opposition claimed that those voters who cast their vote for me would have their marriage vows dissolved in the eyes of God. Such hysterical denunciation of a woman seeking the highest electoral office highlights some of the prejudices that women in South Asia face as they seek political and economic empowerment.

South Asia is home to some of the deepest prejudices that exist against women. Honour killings and gas stove murders of women are the extreme manifestations of the prejudices against women. Yet South Asia is home to the largest number of women elected in any place and at any time in the world community. Sri Lanka's Mrs. Bandaranaike led the way with her election as Prime Minister. This was followed by the election of India's Mrs. Indira Gandhi. Pakistan and Bangladesh came next. Bangladesh went one step forward in having a leader of the house and leader of the Opposition from the same gender.

The rise of women leaders in South Asia often reinforces the traditionalist view that women are extensions of their men folk. We are often told that we got where we did because of who we were related to, rather than inherent qualities. The leading men in our fathers' lives called Mrs. Gandhi "Guryha" (doll) and I was called "that girl". Certainly, who we were was important to why we entered the political minefield. Our political backgrounds enabled us to network better whilst our family names gave us the charisma that comes with the legend that the men in our lives were. Yet it would be half the story to write of us as extensions of the male members of the family. There were other men in our families, some of whom did come forward to contest and compete.

It is important to recognise that each woman leader in South Asia had something within her which enabled her to succeed. Family name is important and character is important too. In South Asia, the rights of women have more to do with the social class they belong to. Women from privileged classes live life according to different standards from those of other classes. For me, the empowerment of women lies less in laws and more in economic independence. And it lies also in men. Our Fathers who encourage us. Our male colleagues who stand by us. Our male followers who support us and the male citizens who vote for us. Dependent women, like dependent nations, are not free to take the decisions they may like to take. For them survival becomes the code with which to address their situation.

I was reminded about this starkly when Pakistan's military regime justified joining the international coalition against terror on grounds of survival. The military regime said it feared that its nuclear assets and other strategic concerns could be endangered if it failed to join up. That is not the way I would have put it. Yet it illustrates two points. First that, women often make pragmatic choices because they are yet to become free. Second, that even men put survival before other issues, which shows that the strength of the social background matters where freedom is concerned.

We are all born free, as Rousseau said, yet too many of us are in chains. These chains come from the state or they come from the mind. These chains can be broken if we will it. It is important for South Asia to break the chains that hold its women back. Women bear children, feed and look after infants. Women, by nature, learn to nurture. This is a time when women's leadership, at all levels of society, is all the more important. It is when we learn to nurture that we can free our societies from warlike thoughts, aggression and other characteristics that forced us onto dangerous paths. For women to succeed, job opportunities and avenues are needed. Respect for the fundamental rights for women will flow when women have the economic means to stand up for themselves.

The government I led did its best for women. We recruited Lady Health Workers, an army of them, to reduce population growth rate and infant mortality rate. We hired new teachers for our primary schools and seventy per cent of them were women. We set up a women's bank run only by women for women although men were allowed to put their money in the accounts. We ran advertisements asking women to report husbands who beat them to the police stations. We appointed women judges to the superior judiciary for the first time in our history. We established women's police stations which women could visit with confidence. We lifted the ban on women taking part in sports. We hosted a Women's Olympics and held the first meeting of the Parliamentarian for Muslim women. And because I was a woman, every woman felt protected.

Not a single case of honour killings was reported during my tenure after we arrested a man who burnt his wife with electric wires in 1994. My Government signed the Convention Against Discrimination Against Women as I led the delegation to the Beijing Conference of Women in 1995. It was a remarkable time in the lives of Pakistani women. In tens of thousands they joined the work force. I remember a meeting with the women in the rural background of a place called Toba Tek Singh in central Punjab. "What's the news?" I asked the women as we met to chat about the changes taking place. "The rate of divorce has gone up", I was told. For a person of my generation, this was a shock. Divorce was frowned upon when I was growing up. "That's terrible", I said. In return, they were shocked. They wanted to know why it was terrible. I spoke of broken families and the suffering that divorce would cause, to which they replied. "We have too much self respect to now accept what we were prepared to accept in the past".

Having jobs had liberated them. The opportunity to earn enabled them to make free choices. For me, independent means is the most powerful weapon in the empowerment of women. Today in Pakistan, the veil of repression has descended across our people. The cause of human rights is being set back decades. But the cause of women's rights, I am sad to say, is being set back a century. The attempt to turn back the clock on women's rights, on liberal society, on pluralistic democracy focused on me, on destroying me politically at home and destroying my reputation abroad. Only recently did the world learn, first from the *Sunday Times* of London and then Zee Television that the charges brought against me were concocted and contrived and the judges that tried me and my husband were ordered to do so, were threatened to do so. The tape recordings of these orders from the Prime Minister's Office to the courts may have shocked the world, but they certainly did not shock me and the forces of democracy in Pakistan. We have become accustomed to all and every attempt to use the politics of personal destruction to turn back the course of democracy, human rights and women's rights in our homeland. It did not work then. It will not work now.

It saddens me to see the price the women of Pakistan paid for the dismissal of the democratic government I led. It is particularly heartbreaking to see the dismantlement of the array of special programmes that I instituted in my two terms as Prime Minister to raise the quality of life of women in Pakistan. My departure led to the collapse of national revenues, investment and growth. And the money for people's welfare programmes was simply not there. Of those programmes, the programmes for women, the weakest of the social classes, were hit first. The women of South Asia cannot be expected to struggle alone against the forces of discrimination, exploitation and manipulation. I recall the words of Dante who reminded us that "The hottest place in Hell is reserved for those who remain neutral in times of moral crisis."

Today in this world, in the fight for the liberation of women, there can be no neutrality. Our outrage at violence and discrimination directed at women cannot be selective. Hate, bigotry and violence have no international borders. Every shamed, abused girl, wherever she lives, is a mute witness for all women, everywhere in the world.

Ladies and Gentlemen, I speak at a time when new forces shape the new century, the new millennium. We shape a world committed to universal social, economic and political values - this triangular definition of comprehensive human rights for the future. We must shape a world free from exploitation and maltreatment of women. A world in which women have opportunities to rise to the highest level in business, diplomacy, and other spheres of life. Where there are no battered women. Where honour and dignity are protected in peace, and in war. Where women have economic freedom and independence. Where women are equal partners in peace and development. Repressive forces always will stand ready to exploit the moment and push us back into the past. Let us remember the words of the German writer, Goethe: "Freedom has be re-made and re-earned in every generation." The women of South Asia will not be free, until we determine to empower them. Empower them with words, with laws, with awareness, with economic opportunities and with role models.

Ladies and gentlemen, we are not free if girls cannot read. For a girl who cannot read has no future; and a girl with no future has no human rights. In this elegant city, we must remember that in the time it took for me to address you today, over one thousand children have starved to death on this planet. As long as these basic violations of human rights are allowed to continue, none of us – regardless of where we live, regardless of how civilized our life-styles, regardless of our own personal circumstances and comforts — none of us are free. A growing number of women enter the world force even as I speak with you today. They change the social complexion of the market force. Women change consumer patterns of the past. This is a world where gender and markets determine the power of a backward or forward nation. This is a world where economic interests drive nation states into new political alignments.

I am told there are 51 multi-national corporations that comprise the world's 100 largest economies. The remaining 49 are countries. The sales of General Motors and Ford are greater than the GDP of sub-Sahara Africa. The American superstore —Wal-Mart— has a higher turnover than the revenues of many Asian countries. Corporations are fast assuming the responsibilities that states failed to meet. Health, housing, education are some of the sectors where corporations are stepping in for their employees.

Ladies and gentlemen, we live in a new era. An era which witnessed the break up of many countries, including the all powerful superpower the Soviet Union. An era where the earth has shrunk into a global village. An era where the social conscience of the world is still to develop as ruthless market forces push their way across the capital centres of the world. Global Capitalism promises much in terms of changing lifestyles. Yet, unless its forces are matched by organised and articulate regional responses, the repercussions could be dangerous for those of us still living with high rates of poverty. And our rates of poverty are high. South Asia has one quarter of the world's population. But it lives in 4 per cent of the world's land area. One Quarter of humanity – and its income is less then 2 per cent of the total income of the world. One quarter of humanity – and its per capita is only 10 per cent of the world average. These figures do not make me proud. They cannot make you proud. This is a time for the countries of South Asia to reduce tension, acknowledging there are disputes, to focus on meeting parallel challenges.

My Party and I are committed to conflict management over the Indo Pak dispute of Jammu and Kashmir. We witnessed the fall of Yugoslavia into a multitude of ethnic and warring states. Nations that fail the test of economic viability can collapse into bloodshed and civil war. Globalisation changes cultures, geographies, social organizations and the way we live, think and conduct ourselves. Globalisation is freeing individuals from state control, making travel easier and business transnational. The over-regulated state suffocates businesses forcing decentralisation to achieve growth. Capital flees at the first tremor. As states de-regulate, they abandon their authority. The weakening state authority enables individuals to open up to new ideas and new values. The sweeping changes that are occurring can occur rampantly. Or they can be fashioned by states that have the wisdom to put their priorities right. The old trade associations are giving way to new ones. The World Trade Organisation is emerging as the key structure.

We, the countries of South Asia, are yet to hold meaningful discussions on how South Asia should approach the different issues raised at this important forum. The WTO will fashion the economics of the next half century. I hope it is a better half century than the one which we saw with GATT and UNCTAD. I was concerned to see the United Nations report that more than 30 per cent of the real per capita incomes have fallen over the last 35 years. I am concerned that the disparity in per capita income between the poorest and the richest countries is over 300 hundred per cent today. Half a century ago, it was much less. The countries that prospered were the countries that lived in peace. Countries that suffered were countries caught in conflict. The gap between the rich and the poor grows as long as we fail to signal the social climate of a success story. A Harvard Professor (David Landes) wrote in "Poverty is inextricably linked to armed conflict".

Ladies and gentlemen, globalisation is restructuring our planet's economic and political arrangements directly affecting humanity on a scale unwitnessed since the Industrial Revolution. Tremendous changes thunder past with little joint attention from the countries of South Asia. Our populations are the largest. The impact on us the greatest. Yet our voices most feeble. That could be otherwise were we, the great countries of South Asia, to realise our potential and wrest the control of our destinies into our hands for a better future. The debate, for our future, yours and mine, and those of our neighbours is raging right now.

This new world, this new century, this new millennium is a strange one. On one side life beckons with the brightest prospects since the dawn of time. On the other hand, young men fall prey and inflict hell in the hope of going to heaven. Life is a precious gift, to be lived. For too long South Asians instead embraced death. When death becomes beautiful, one can understood how living life has become impossible. It is for the leaders, the captains of the ships of state as well as of trade, to chart a new course for a new destination. A destination that gives premium to life which is the most precious gift bestowed by God. So precious we are told that to kill is the worst of crimes.

Our part of the world too has been teetering on the verge of doom and disaster too often. We have been at each other's throats. We have fought four wars. Troops on both sides continue to fire at each other and we have nuclear bombs too. A push on the button can end life before we realise what was done in desperation. We owe it to our children to build a world free of the threat of nuclear annihilation.

Ladies and gentlemen, my commitment to the rights of women was inspired by the categorical position taken by Pakistan's founder, Quaid-e-Azam Mohammad Ali Jinnah. In his address to the university students in 1944, he said, "No nation can rise to the heights of glory with half its population shackled. It is a crime against humanity that our women are confined within the four walls of their homes like prisoners; they should be side by side with men as their companions in all spheres of life."

Ladies and Gentlemen, I will end with a quote from Alexander Pope who said:

"What war could ravish,

Commerce could bestow

And he returned a friend

Who was a foe"

Thank you

— New Delhi
26-Nov-2001

Terror in Karachi

In a deadly suicide attack on May 8, bombers in Pakistan struck at foreign targets again. A naval bus was blown up killing fourteen people including eleven French engineers. The suicide bombers narrowly missed hitting the New Zealand cricket team staying at a hotel in an elite Karachi neighbourhood. The cricket team left by the next available flight while French President Chirac's celebrations over a grand electoral presidential win were cut short. France joined America as the latest foreign victim in the third suicide operation under Islamabad's military dictator since this year began. As blood, bodies and metal blew across the road, a clear pattern was emerging for the terrorist actions. Following the rout of the Taliban and Al-Queda, the militants are re-grouping in Pakistan. This is hardly surprising. Many of them were initially recruited and brought to Pakistan when fighting the Soviets in Afghanistan was fashionable. Once the Soviets withdrew from Afghanistan, so did the international support for the fight to win Kabul. The freedom fighters decided they had defeated one super power and could defeat another. So was born extremism and militancy.

Militancy found an expression in the post Soviet period in Kashmir. There Indian occupation was bitterly resented. The Kashmiris were ripe to rise and they did in 1989. Their movement was hijacked by the Afghan based elements in late 1996 even as Kashmiri leaders in the All Parties Hurriyat Conference were sidelined. Now the extremists moved seamlessly through the three borders, Afghanistan, Pakistan and Indian held Kashmir. The death of Pakistani democracy in 1996 enabled the military hardliners supporting the Afghan elements to control Pakistan. They rigged the elections and dominated the administration. As Mr. Sharif grew increasingly unpopular, they backed the coup of General Musharraf to retain their grip on power. Ironically, even as the international community views Musharraf as the Great White Hope in defeating extremism, many in Pakistan doubt that he can. Depending on a military regime backed by hardliners is like banking on an arsonist to put out the fire. The terrorist actions occur in an interconnecting pattern between Pakistan's Northern and Eastern hot borders. This inter-connection was made clear by Islamabad's coup leader when he defended the decision to join the war against terror last September. Addressing the Pakistani people, he said he was "joining the lesser evil (America) to fight the greater evil (India)".

The Northern Borders with neighbouring Afghanistan are hot due to escaping Al-Queda and the international force that is after them. The Eastern Border with India is hot given the massive troop deployment that accompanied New Delhi's demand that Islamabad hand over men it wanted in the Indian Parliament bombing. When the Americans put the heat on Islamabad to chase Al-Queda, the border with India heats up. Islamabad then says its military is pre-occupied with the Indian threat and unable to help effectively. This gives the dual advantage of highlighting the Kashmir Dispute.

Last winter, the Americans wanted Islamabad's military to seal the border with Afghanistan and capture fleeing Al-Queda. Militants successfully relieved the pressure by conducting the Indian Parliament attack. The threat of a possibly nuclear war became real. The international community was pre-occupied defusing it. As summer approached, American pressure on Islamabad to control its wild Northern Frontier with mountains and fierce tribesmen sympathetic to Al-Queda grew. Against the growing pressure, the Karachi terror attack near a five star hotel killing the Frenchmen and others took place shocking the city. Quickly an attack followed on May 14 killing women and children in disputed Kashmir sending the Indo-Pak war temperatures sky rocketing again. Once again Islamabad's military will find itself pre-occupied with India. And the international community will find itself pre-occupied with defusing the war threat.

The pattern is evident on the political field too. For example, when the Agra Summit heralding Indo-Pak talks took place, General

Musharraf seized the hour to boot out President Tarrar and seize the Presidency for himself. As Musharraf packed his bags for his Washington trip in February, the Danny Pearl kidnapping and murder took place. If any one doubted whether a military dictator was a proper alternative to a democratic dispensation, the kidnapping dealt with the doubts.

Then came the dictator's Referendum. Supporting Opposition calls to register a negative vote through boycott, ninety five percent of the population refused to go to the polling booths. Even as the military leader smarted from the setback of the Referendum, popularly called the Joke-dum, the Karachi attack took place.

Recently General Musharraf released twelve hundred militants into the anarchic streets of the country. He said it was wrong to keep them behind bars without court convictions. Yet such compunctions disappear when it comes to keeping his political rivals behind bars without conviction. They suffer in the sixth year of imprisonment without relief in a country where colonels sit in court rooms to pressure the courts. Released from prison on the eve of the Karachi terror attacks were one hundred and thirty convicted militants from the nineties. Experienced in rocket attacks, political assassinations, mass murders, sabotage and subterfuge, they know the streets of Karachi well. They have hideouts and finance their schemes through thefts. They have access to buried armed caches and gun smugglers. They have the experience and the capability to mount and spread terror. That they were released is mind boggling. The excuse offered was that their release could deliver Referendum votes that Musharraf needed.

Musharraf says he is unable to reach accommodation with the democratic parties because they are corrupt. Yet those charges are denied and those leaders unconvicted. The only logical explanation is that Musharraf is controlled by hardliners determined to crush the democratic forces through another rigged election. If this is the case, his continuation is a serious threat to the unity of Pakistan as well as regional peace and global security.

Pakistan invests billions in its intelligence workforce through salary, pensions and perks including lucrative land grants. Elected local leaders and junior police officers find it hard to operate with Big Brother from the powerful Inter Services Intelligence, Military Intelligence, Corps of Intelligence and a panoply of other intelligences breathing down their necks. In such a situation, there is little explanation as to why this huge internal army with eyes and ears everywhere is unable to monitor militants, extremists and terrorists.

Opposition groups believe hardliners control the intelligence as a state subsidized political party. The Major General controlling the intelligence political party is busy making and breaking political alliances at the behest of the Presidency. At the cost of poverty alleviation, officers travel frequently, taking extra daily allowance, contacting politicians. Their goal is to create a King's Party and hold on to power by rigging the promised October elections to keep out those they threw out in 1996. Islamabad's descent into madness can stop when the military hardliners who seized power in 1996 are replaced through transparent elections that bring a political change. This is possible when the military and the judiciary join the people in supporting implementation of electoral reforms ensuring Democracy. Otherwise the war that started in Kabul last September could end up in Delhi on the back of militants determined to play a high stakes game with human lives.

— **24-May-2002**

Pakistan and Free Market Objectives : A Course of Action for the Twenty-first Century

Ladies and Gentlemen:

Good evening. I am honoured to be invited to speak here before this distinguished group of business executives, and I would like to thank the D-Group and all assembled here for extending me such warm hospitality. I am sure that all of you gathered here today are no strangers to either the business realities of present day Asia, or the explosive growth in global economic integration we have experienced during this decade. All companies — and countries — are racing to keep pace with the revolutionary power that the new technologies of communications and transportation afford us. We are, in every sense of the word, entering a century to be dominated by the rules of a global market. And as we enter this new and exciting era, this new century, I am convinced that the new rules of the game are simple and concrete:

In the Twentyfirst Century, nations must uphold the principles of democracy and the rule of law;

In the Twentyfirst century, governments must guarantee basic freedoms and liberties to their citizens;

In the Twentyfirst Century, regions must promote free trade with minimal state intervention, and with a policy of non-intervention and mutual respect in inter-state relations;

In the new century, the concerns of the state will be driven more by considerations of trade and commerce, rather than by our traditional military - territorial considerations. And the success of a Nation will be based upon its level of exports, hard currency reserves, its per capita GNP, and the creative genius of its citizens.

It is becoming very clear, as we enter the coming century, that the distinguishing feature between those nations that achieve success, and those that continue to fall behind, will be the degree to which they adopt the principles of free market economics. And it is the free market economies that are now most open and positioned to fully participate in the increasingly competitive but interconnected global economy.

PAKISTAN'S CURRENT ECONOMIC CRISIS

Pakistan, as with the other nations of South Asia, is desperate to be a more active participant in the emerging global economy. Thus far, our economic capacity to do so has been weakened, principally due to the conflicts that plague our region, and the resources these conflicts take away from our infrastructure, our education, our human and technical development, and our creative capacities.

However, while South Asia's conflicts, in particular the seemingly intractable animosity between Pakistan and India, have had a large role to play in hindering our region's economic growth, most devastating of late has been the domestic economic and political actions taken by the Nawaz Sharif regime. Of most pressing concern has been the Sharif regime's attack on the Independent Power Producers in Pakistan. My previous Administration's creation of this investment mechanism, whereby the global investment world would underwrite power projects for Pakistan was a bold and decisive move, one that brought Pakistan finally into the Twentyfirst Century.

And, I know that there are many in the United Kingdom who have been watching these developments with an uneasy eye. The current regime's refusal to abide by legal contracts and normal codes of business conduct has done more to harm Pakistan's economic prospects than any economic sanctions might hope to achieve. Let me give you an example: During my last administration, we sought and accomplished an economic agenda with foreign investment and privatization as our chief goals. By 1996, direct foreign investment into Pakistan was up to $3 billion per year. Since the Sharif regime took power, attacked the IPPs and froze foreign currency accounts, direct foreign investment into Pakistan has fallen to zero.

We had a choice then and continue to have one now: either continue down the path of living off aid and hand-outs from the global economy, or open our doors, our policies and our practices so that we, too, may participate in the benefits and competition of this new era. But, Ladies and Gentlemen, before I continue down this path of criticizing the Sharif regime — a topic some would say is too near my heart — let me turn to how Pakistan can reopen to the world, and the steps that are needed to revitalize our economy.

THE PATH TO ECONOMIC RECOVERY

First and foremost, it is critical for Pakistan to again establish the trust and confidence of the international investor community. As we have seen in Mexico, Thailand and other nations of late, receiving and retaining the confidence of fickle investors is no easy task. However, as sovereign governments the world over become less able and have less resources for hand-outs, there is no other road for Pakistan to pursue. To achieve this confidence and trust, Pakistan must ease the economic constraints imposed upon it, and here I lay out the programs of my party, the Pakistan Peoples Party:

Privatization: We must increase the pace of privatization, but do so with a human face, and within this theme, we must reduce and eventually eliminate subsidies to bloated industries.

Reducing Public Debt: The government is borrowing too much, leaving the private sector starved for loans for growth, inventory, education or infrastructure. To reduce the public debt, it is paramount that our tax base be widened to include even the current Prime Minister and his cabinet.

We can achieve a higher total tax return by increasing attention to vigilant collection rather than higher rates. Too much of our economy is now in the 'black market', and our next government will take active steps to bring this back into the mainstream.

Education, Health and Human Development: As many of you know, Pakistan remains burdened by a high rate of population growth, as well as high illiteracy. Channelling our scarce resources from military expenditures at or above 7,000 metres into education and family planning is the first step.

Reduced Tariffs: We can increase trade by reducing tariffs. As it stands now, too much of the goods and services entering Pakistan are doing so illegally. Thus, by reducing tariffs, we feel we can actually increase revenue to federal programmes, as well as stimulate more economic exchange.

Lastly and perhaps most difficult, is a radical restructuring of our ingrained business habits. These less tangible but perhaps most critical notions include fostering sound business practices, transparency, promoting efficient and good governance, eradicating corruption, and most important of all, fostering an unshakeable faith in the rule of law, not the rule of graft.

Ladies and Gentlemen, Pakistan is facing one of its hardest and most pressing economic crises in our history. But there is hope. We have in the past and can in the future, with the right policies, the right direction and the right intention, turn our crisis into opportunity. And I hope, when the people of Pakistan make those decisions, this group and your colleagues will again be there to grow with us. I thank you for your time, and I look forward to hearing any comments or questions.

— London
15-Apr-1999

JASHAN-E-AZADI

Ladies and Gentlemen:

It is a pleasure for me to be in Dewsbury at the invitation of the Savirya Foundation. I congratulate Savirya Foundation under Syeda Hussain for the excellent work it is doing in supporting women and children in Pakistan and Kashmir.

I am asked to share my experiences as a woman elected to a leadership position in a traditional Muslim society. I want you to know that the gauntlet of leadership was thrown down before me. I had no choice but to pick it up. Leadership is not easy. The road to leadership can be difficult and sad. Leadership is born of a passion, and it is a commitment. A commitment to an idea, to a people, to a land.

I travel, never knowing when I will see my husband again. He was arrested the night my government was overthrown in November 1996 seven years ago. I miss my children. They are all under fourteen. It is difficult explaining to little children why their mother can not be with them, why their father is a political prisoner. I am reconciled to the fact that the needs of my 150 million people come first, and will always come first.

Women have to make difficult choices, often choices that men are not forced to make. But we do it for all the women who came before us who gave us this opportunity. And most of all, we do it for all women who will come after us — the baby girls yet unborn!

I am asked often why I continue on a journey that is difficult and painful. I do so out of the belief that my leadership changed much, and can change more, for my country and for those denied the right of choice. I do it because I must, this is my life, and this is my mission.

I was brought up in a political family. In a way, I was groomed for politics. Yet, a political role was not one that I actively sought. It came to me through an accident of fate. I had just completed my education and returned to Pakistan in 1977 when the tanks rumbled up the road in Rawalpindi and troops took over the Prime Minister's House. I was pulled into the political campaign by the arrest of senior party leaders. My father was arrested, released, re-arrested, and, finally hanged. Two of my brothers were killed . Together my family has spent 25 years behind prison bars.

The military coup of 1977 put an end to my career goal to join the Foreign Service in Pakistan and become High Commissioner to England, a country I had studied in and knew well. Fate took over my life and my destiny was no longer in my hands. As a child of my age, in the late sixties, I was influenced by the social ferment around me. The worldwide student movement, from Rawalpindi, to Washington, were important factors in my youth. The fight against apartheid shaped the ferocity of my commitment to stand up for principle. The burgeoning movement for women's rights empowered and emboldened me. As an Asian I protested against the Vietnam war, a war that shook the world in the sixties.

These important steps helped shape my outlook on life, helped me focus on fighting injustice, promoting freedom and safeguarding the rights of the weak and dispossessed. But above all, as a student in the West, where there are free elections, I saw the awesome power of the people changing policies, changing leaders, and changing history.

I came to Oxford at a time when the British politician, Enoch Powell, was threatening to throw all Asians into the sea. While I was at Oxford, the Conservative party chose a woman, Margaret Thatcher, as the Leader of Opposition. The idea of the first female British Prime Minister became a topic for student discussions. It was a thrilling moment for me, as a student, when Mrs. Thatcher, then leader of the opposition, invited me to the House of Commons for tea. I entered the oldest Parliament in the world. I walked on flag stones that could tell a thousand tales of Kings, Queens and ordinary Mortals that walked on those same steps for centuries.

At Oxford, I was the first female foreigner to be elected as President of the Oxford Union. The Oxford Union reflects the British Parliament. It was there that I learned to debate, slowly gaining confidence before an audience. And while I took part in debates, I was surrounded by statues of British Prime Ministers including Gladstone who had been President of the Oxford Union.

I had been told that as a foreigner, I could not win the Presidency and should not run. I had been told that as a woman, I could not win, and should not run. But I did run and did win and overcame my fear of losing. I learned to overcome fear and to take risks. I learned never to give in when the task seemed formidable or impossible. I had been told that as a woman I could never be elected Prime Minister in a Muslim country. I had been told that, at 35, I was too young to run for the premiership.

But I had learnt to overcome my fear of losing. I did run. I did win. I won because I refused to take "No" for an answer. And that is my message to young people here tonight. Do not take "No" for an answer. Do not be disappointed with a setback. Do not let the obstacles stand in your way. As the Prime Minister of Pakistan I appeared before an historic Joint Session of the United States Congress in 1989. In that address, the most meaningful line to me was my simple message to the women of America, my message to the women of the world. Three simple, powerful words:

YES YOU CAN!

Yes, you can achieve any goal you want to reach, if you do not accept the status quo. Do not accept traditional roles and traditional constraints. Women have made progress since I went to University. We smashed many glass ceilings. But there are thousands left to break, many battles left to fight. Sadly, the greatest obstacles to progress for women in the third millennium is the bigotry of some men, and nowhere is that bigotry more difficult than in the Taliban and the fanatics that ruled in Afghanistan.

Women fight on several fronts. We fight against terrorism. We fight against dictatorship and intolerance. We are threatened with a clash of civilizations. These are difficult times. Freedom is under assault. Democracy is under assault. The solutions will not be quick or simple. But we shall prevail.

In my father's last letter to me before he was murdered by one of Pakistan's earlier military tyrants, he quoted Tennyson:

"Ah, what shall I be at fifty if I find the world so bitter at twenty."

So, be strong but do not be bitter.

I remember the words of President George Washington who said: "May the children of the stock of Abraham who dwell in this land continue to merit and enjoy the goodwill of the other inhabitants-while every one shall sit in safety under his own vine and fig tree and there shall be none to make him afraid".

These words spoken centuries ago ring so true now. Today there is terror, war, death destruction and fear. I dream of a world where we can live in peace, a world with out violence. That is what I dream of – a world free of fear, a world at peace.

I believe women have an important role to play in building a world free from fear. To me, women are not just the building blocks of the family; they are the building blocks of society. They are responsible for the family's household budget. They bear most of the responsibility of child raising They are more sensitive to social issues like education and health. They — far more than their husbands and brothers — are cautious about committing the lives of their children to war. Women are the principal educators, not just of literacy but also of morality. And once mobilized, once organized, once unleashed, the power of women to change their societies can never again be contained.

This is an age around the world where thousands of citizens, especially youth and women, can hold governments accountable to law and public trust. This is an age of civic groups and civil society.

Savirya Foundation is a civic group. It has a role to play. I wish it well in playing that role and am delighted to have had this opportunity to share Jashan-e-Azadi with you.

I wish you all success, happiness and Jashan-e-Azadi. Mubark!

— Savirya Foundation London
16-Aug-2003

My Country

On August 14, 1997, my country Pakistan, will be fifty years old. As we approach our golden jubilee, my mind wanders over the landscape of the past. Sometimes people say that very little has changed. But that is not how it seems when we look at the past through the telescope of five decades. When I was a child, my hometown of Larkana, like many other villages, was a sleepy little place. Travelling to a village was a real adventure. It took a day and a night by train to Larkana. (Now it takes only an hour by airplane). Larkana did not have Roads, Telephones, Gas or any of the modern amenities, as it does now. When we travelled, we took with us tinned sardines, baked beans, tissue paper, insect spray to help us cope through the long summer days and the hot summer nights.

There was so much poverty in small towns and villages most people were shirtless and shoeless, faces, feet, legs, caked in mud. Often the only place to bathe was mighty river Indus which flowed nearby.

Now the complaint is about unemployment. Then the complaint was about food. Food was scare. Most families survived on one meal a day. Many did not even have one meal a day. I remember as a child how the big doors of my father's home in Larkana, Al-Murtaza, would be opened on special occasions to the public. While my father met the men in one part of the house, my mother met the women and children in another. Several women would be pleading with my mother to take their children into our home in exchange for work. My mother would look helplessly at the pleading women and the hungry children. She did her best to help. But it was npt always possible to help everyone.

Seclusion was part of the social fabric of the society. Men lived separately in their wing, where women were not allowed. The women lived in the family quarters with the children, which only male relatives could enter. Women wore Burqa, or the veil. Marriages in the big, tribal families, only took place between relatives. So, if there was no male relative available, the women simply did not marry. Or married a much younger or much older cousin. It was a man's world then.

When I see the girl students at Chandka Medical College studying alongside the boys, I wonder if they realize how much life has changed. In the old days, villages did not have colleges. Now there are plenty of places of learning. In the old days, girls stayed at home. Now they work, if they wish too.

In the first decade of its existence, no one could have dreamt that by its Fiftieth Birthday, our traditional society would have transformed itself to such an extent that it would twice elect a woman as Prime Minister in fair free and impartial elections. In 1988, Pakistan became the first Muslim country to elect a woman Prime Minister. Muslim women everywhere crossed a historic barrier on that December Day. Today women in Pakistan sit in Parliament, run banks, fly airplanes, have their own business.

When America's First Lady visited Pakistan in April 1995, I hosted a modern day Hen Party for her. We invited over a hundred outstanding women, including judges, police officers, educationists and advocates. We invited a housewife too, to demonstrate that women, and not society, should determine a woman's life choices.

When I was growing up, men had often two to three wives. We would visit them all in the women's quarters. Every wife would often be addressed by the name of her eldest son. No wonder the Girl Child was not welcome.

But all this is changing now, particularly in the urban parts of the country. Television has played a key role in opening up people's minds. In the old days, a woman often had twelve to fourteen children. As a woman politician, women often confided to me about the physical hardship of bearing so many children. They wanted less children but did not know how to go about it. From these conversations grew the idea in my mind to formulate a population control programme based around women. So, we launched the Lady Health Visitor's Programme, Pakistan's population growth rate came down from 3.1 per cent in 1988 - to less than to 2.8 per cent. It will be 2.6 per cent when the course is completed. It is a record, and Pakistanis are proud of it.

But we still have to cross the historic barrier when Pakistanis can take Democracy for granted. For too long our country has seen the strong establishment unseat governments by overt military coups or by covert intelligence operations. Fundamental human rights remain a concern. Our former High Commissioner to Her Majesty's court, Wajid Shamsul Hassan, was arrested despite a serious heart problem. He is still in hospital due to the heart problem. He has been granted bail by the court but he can not leave the hospital under advice of the doctors. Many other languish in prison cells including officials who worked for the democratic government and my family members. My husband Senator Asif Zardari has been held for nine months and the trial has not even started.

But then that is the price so many pay as countries all over the world, which became independent with the sunset on the colonial era, strive to establish the rule of law. My own life, like that of Pakistan's, has been marked by tragedy and triumphs. But, despite the slander campaigns, I have resumed my role as leader of the opposition in the Pakistani Parliament. When I look at my children, I think of all the children in Pakistan, and wonder: what will life be like for them when they are 25?

I remember my Father writing to me from prison and ending with the verse, "Ah what shall I be at 50 When I find the world so bitter at 25?" What will life be for them and for all Pakistani children, in the year 2020? My generation, which reads books and works with the pen will be old-fashioned, computers will play a key role in every individual's life from reading, working, shopping, learning and even studying. Perhaps parents will have more time with children. As a working woman I have always felt bad for not seeing my children off to school every day or fetching them back. Now in London it is such a joy to take them to Trafalgar Square and watch them feed the pigeons as my parents took me Or walk with them to Hyde Park and buy them an ice-cream cone. I pray that my children, and all Pakistani children live in a Pakistan free from persecution where the peace of family life is not broken by the midnight knock taking a loved one away.

But as we approach the third Millennium Pakistanis need not dwell on the set backs but on the achievements. We are a country of 140 million people. The only Muslim country with nuclear knowledge and missile capability. A country at the strategic crossroads to trade in East Asia, the Gulf and Central Asia. The oil and gas reserve of the future are landlocked in Central Asia and the only access is through the shores of Pakistan. As an Asian and Muslim country Pakistan is working for a global understanding between the Christian and Muslim worlds. We may have our difficulties. Who does not? But men, women, and nations are judged not on the basis of difficulties they face but the dignity and courage with which they seek to overcome them.

As we approach the third millennium it is time for us to fashion a new vision, based on the values emerging from the post cold war international situation. As a Pakistani I feel a special responsibility to make that vision a reality for my country as we move to that moment, less than one thousand days from now, when the sun sets in the black winter sky of one millennium and dawns the next to proclaim the birth of a new one. I see a Third millennium where human rights are universal, and self-determination unabridged on the planet. I see a Third Millennium where civil dialogue is restored, where victimization of political adversaries is ended, where consensus and comity once again guide the national and international debate. I see a Third Millennium of tolerance and understanding. I see a Third Millennium where every child is planned, wanted, nurtured and supported. I see a Third Millennium where the ruthless forces of market politics do not condemn a whole segment of people to live as the discarded forgotten.

And, above all, I see a Third Millennium where the birth of the girl child is welcomed with the same joy as the birth of a boy.

This is my vision. This is my hope. This is my dream.

— **BBC Radio Talk Show Ms Benazir Bhutto**
7-Aug-1997

UNIQUE LIVES AND EXPERIENCES

(Lecture Series)

Ladies and Gentlemen:

I recall the vivid images of Dante's Divine Comedy, and his characterization that "the hottest place in hell is reserved for those who remain neutral at times of moral crisis."

This is not time for neutrality or inaction. The special demands of this extraordinary historical moment requires great action from men and women of great vision and courage. In that regard, I cannot but be uplifted and empowered by the recent accord signed in Belfast on Good Friday to end the conflagration in Northern Ireland. The agreement was reached after years of backbreaking negotiations jump started by President Clinton and former Senator George Mitchell. They saw a situation where men and women of moderation and good will needed a champion willing to take risks to bring the parties together.

Clinton acted in the great tradition of President Harry Truman, who with George Marshall shaped and defined the modern era with a bold economic plan to contain communism in Europe called Marsahll Plan, and a political and military alliance called NATO. But President Harry S. Truman was a leader, and not a follower. He chose to convince a reluctant public, and built a national consensus in America and the West that was maintained through forty years of Cold War, and ultimately led to the triumph of freedom and market based economics that has swept over this planet with the implosion of communism.

There is a lesson to be learned in this. Nothing ventured, nothing gained. We hope that the path to reconciliation in Northern Ireland through honest mediation by the world's sole superpower can be repeated in other areas of the world where the problems look equally intractable, equally impossible, but where men and women of goodwill look beyond fear and loathing to reconciliation and resolution.

If Northern Ireland can be settled, why not a new initiative to save the frozen peace process in the Middle East. If Northern Ireland can be resolved, cannot the world turn its attention to the horrors in Kosovo before Kosovo becomes another Bosnian genocide. If Northern Ireland can be settled, why not a new and credible initiative to bring India, Pakistan, and the Kashmiris together to finally resolve the Kashmir issue, which hangs like the sword of Damocles across not only South Asia, but the entire world. The valley of Kashmir has been occupied by India and denied the basic right of self-determination. Tens of thousands of men, women and children have lost their lives in the quest for freedom. Villages have been burnt. Women and children targeted. Three wars over Kashmir have wrought devastation in their path. Today, 600,000 troops hold the people of Kashmir hostage. We who support freedom in the world ought not to remain silent when freedom is threatened.

That is why I say, it is time now, consistent with President Clinton's stated policy of pre-emptive crisis management, to facilitate an agreement between India and Pakistan so that the people of Kashmir and Jammu are finally allowed to determine their own political futures on the basis of the right to self determination. This is the moment of opportunity. This is also the moment, as we cross the millennium, for the world to finally become sensitive to and tolerant of different cultures, different religions, different peoples. The West needs to appreciate and understand the East, for we are all part of the same Judaic, Christian, Muslim Civilization. We are all people of the Book.

I would ask leaders in the West, not to think of the people of the East as terrorists or fanatics. No doubt there are extremists in each society in each country. However, it is the misfortune of the

Information Age that while we think we have more information for each other in fact we have less. The reason we have less knowledge is that the Information Age often broadcasts the extreme rather than the mainstream. The mainstream in the East is very much the mainstream in the West if not more so. The mainstream in the East is grounded in faith, in family, in our dreams for the future.

Ladies and Gentlemen, I have attempted, throughout my career, to combine the best of many cultures, the richness of disparate experiences, to build for my people the ability to compete and thrive in the challenging new technological era. Introducing the world of modern communication into Pakistan was one of the goals of my party. We heralded the information revolution by introducing fax machines, digital pagers, optic fibre, cellular telephones, satellite dishes, internet, the e-mail and even CNN into Pakistan. We implemented a policy which guaranteed to 95 per cent of our urban population and 70 per cent of our rural population adequate sewage facilities. We constructed over 30,000 new primary and secondary schools in three years and renovated an additional 9,800 ones. Of these new schools, approximately 70 per cent were for girls. We recruited 53,000 new teachers, 70 per cent of whom were women. We increased the health budget by 60 per cent and the WHO gave me a gold metal in recognition of Pakistan's effort to eliminate polio and provide basic health facilities to our people. We recruited and trained an army of women, 50,000 strong, to tackle the problems of infant mortality and population control. In my two terms as Prime Minister of Pakistan, one of the nine most populated countries in the world, we brought down the population growth rate from 3.1 per cent to 2.6 per cent. We brought our energy revolution directly to the people of Pakistan ending 16 hours of daily power shut downs which had crippled the economy and stunted growth. We brought the fruits of the energy revolution to the villages which had lived in darkness for centuries, electrifying over 18,000 villages in three years. All this needed money. And we pumped in resources toward the social sector while cutting the countries deficit and reducing its national debt. We built 10,000 kilometres of roads and 100,000 homes per year for the needy and deserving.

The social revolution we had launched came to a grinding halt the day I was dismissed. Today, education, health, population and the environment are starved for funds while Big Bank defaulters, led by the Prime Minister, seek to enact laws meant for personal benefit and neglect the people of the land.

My friends, I am proud that the government I led brought about a miraculous transformation of a society. We opened up markets and we opened up minds. We attacked prejudice and discrimination. We carved out an entrepreneurial society where young men and women had the freedom to choose their careers, and to embark on business ventures to compete with each other and with the world.

— Boston – USA
1-May-1998

Mother Courage

Pakistan is no ordinary country. And mine has been no ordinary life. My father and two brothers were killed. My mother, husband and I were all imprisoned. I have spent long year in exile. Despite the difficulties and sorrows, however, I feel blessed that I could break the bastion of tradition by becoming Islam's first elected woman prime minister. That election was the tipping point in the debate raging in the Muslim world on the role of women in Islam. It proved that a Muslim woman could be elected prime minister, could govern a country and could be accepted as a leader by both men and women. And while the debate between the modernizers and the extremists continues, women across the Muslim world have made great strides since I first took the oath of office on December 2, 1988.

Few in this world are given the privilege to effect change in society, to bring the modern era to a country that had only the basic infrastructure, to break down stereotypes about the role of women and ultimately to give hope for change to million who had no hope before. It is not necessarily the life I would choose, but it has been a life of opportunity, responsibility and fulfillment. Twenty year ago, in the light of the developments in my life-my father's assassination, my imprisonment, the responsibility of picking up his political mantle-I had little expectation of finding personal happiness, of finding love, marriage and of having children. Like England's Queen Elizabeth I, who had also endured imprisonment and remained single, I thought I would never get married. Yet my personal life defied these narrow expectations. I found joy and fulfillment in marriage despite difficult circumstances. I am proud of my husband for his courage and loyalty in standing by me through 19 years of marriage. During these years, he lived either in the Prime Minister's office or as a political prisoner held hostage to my career. And I found our relationship strengthened despite the physical separation and attempts to turn us against each other.

No, life is not what I would have predicted, but I do not think I would change places with any woman in history. However, I do believe my career has been so challenging because I am a woman. Clearly it is not easy for women in modern society, no matter where we live. We still have to go the extra mile to prove that we are equal to men. We have to work longer hours and make more sacrifices. And w must emotionally protect ourselves from unfair, often vicious attack made on us.

Nevertheless, we must be prepared not to complain about th double standards, but to overcome them. We must be prepared to d so even if it means working twice as long as a man. I am greatful my mother for teaching me that pregnancy is a biological state being, which should not disrupt the normal routine of life. Trying live up to her expectation, I almost ignored any hint of physical emotional limitation during my pregnancies. Yet I was acute conscious that what should have been a family matter became a to of intense political discussion from military headquarters to editor boards. Aware of this, I kept the exact details of my pregnancies sec

I have three lovely children: Bilawal, Bakhtwar and Aseefa. Th give me much joy and pride. When I was expecting my first chi Bilawal, in 1988, I was 35, and the then military dictator dismis the parliament and called for general elections. He and his top ar men believed a pregnant woman could not campaign. They w wrong. I could and I did. I went on to win the elections held sho after Bilawal's birth on September 21 1988. Bilawal's birth was of the happiest days of my life. Winning those elections that y despite predictions that a Muslim woman could not win the he and minds of her people, was another.

Shortly after I was elected Prime Minister, my mother told m "hurry up and have another child". She believed that a mother sh quickly have children before she realized the challenges of raisi family and fulfilling other responsibilities. I took her advice.

Once the political opposition learned I was pregnant, all hell broke loose. They called on the President and the military to overthrow me. They argued that Pakistan government rules did not provide for a pregnant Prime Minister going on maternity leave. They said that during delivery I would be incapacitated and therefore the government machinery would irretrievably break down for that period of time. This, to them, was unconstitutional, necessitating the President, backed by the military, to dismiss the Prime Minister and install an interim government to hold new elections.

I rejected the opposition's demands, noting that maternity rules existed in the law for working women (my father had legislated maternity leave). I argued that the law implicitly applied to a Prime Minister even not stated in the rules for conducting government business. The members of my government stood by me, noting that when a male leader was indisposed, it did not translate into a constitutional crisis. Nor should it when a female leader was indisposed.

Hardly mollified, the Opposition drew up a plan of strikes to pressure the President into sacking the Government. I had to make my own plans.

My father had taught me that in politics, timing is very important. I consulted my doctor who assured me that my child was full term and, with his permission, decided to have a caesarean delivery on the eve of the call for strike action. I did not want to encourage any stereotypes that pregnancy interferes with performance. So, despite my condition, I worked just as hard, and probably a lot harder, than a male Prime Minister would have done. In the end, I chaired a meeting of my cabinet and then left for Karachi. I woke up early in the morning and with a friend left for the hospital in her car.

It was a small car, very different from the black Mercedes used for official duties. The police on security duty hardly gave it a second glance. They concentrated on cars entering my house rather than those leaving it. My heart was beating fast as we raced to the hospital, where my doctor was waiting for us. I could see the surprise on the faces of the hospital staff as I got out of the car. I knew the news would begin to spread fast through the mobile phones and pagers that my government had introduced (we were the first country in South Asia and the Middle East to have mobile phones). I hurried down the hallway to the operating theatre. I knew that my husband and my mother would be on their way, as we discussed earlier. As soon as I began to wake from the mists of anesthesia as my hospital trolley was wheeled from the theatre to the private room, I heard my husband say: "It's a girl." I saw my mother's face beam with pleasure. I called my daughter Bakhtwar, which means the one who brings good fortune. And she did. The strikes fizzled out and the opposition's movement collapsed. I received thousands of messages of congratulations from all over the world. Heads of governments and ordinary people wrote to me, sharing the joy. It was a defining moment, especially for a young woman, proving a woman could work and have a baby in the highest and most challenging leadership positions. The next day I was on the job, reading the government papers and signing government files. Only later did I learn that I was the only head of government in recorded history, actually to give birth while in office.

Bakhtwar was born in 1990. Seven months later, on August 6; the President undemocratically dismissed my government, while world attention was diverted by Iraq's occupations of Kuwait. My husband was arrested and as my mother suggested I sent my children abroad. It was heart-rending for me to be parted from Bilawal, who had turned two, and Bakhtwar, who was not yet one. My sister, who lives in London, lovingly took them into her home. My in-laws chipped in, too, by shifting to London. Back at home I had nightmares where I heard my children cry for me. My sister would tell me not to worry during our many telephone conversations. Yet those dreams never stopped. With the sacking of my government, the port city of Karachi was gripped by anarchy and chaos. Terrorism was rampant. Innocent civilians were massacred while riding in public transport or outside their homes or in their offices. I knew it was safer for my children to be in London. Yet I found it hard to sleep, night after night, only to wake with those nightmares.

My mother and I were now living largely in the capital city of Islamabad. My husband, elected to Parliament in the 1990 elections, was also kept under house arrest in our residence during parliamentary sessions. I confided to my mother and husband how draining it was that the children were living away from me. I felt I was abandoning them, and worried that it could hurt their emotional wellbeing and growth.

By 1991,Bilawal had started attending a pre-kindergarten school in London. Bakhtwar was still one year old: I could keep her hidden safely in our house in Pakistan, I reasoned. I flew to London and could hardly wait to get to my sister Sanam's flat. As soon as I knocked on her door, I heard my daughter crying, the same cry that had sounded in my dreams. I quickly gathered her in my arms and pulled my son towards me "I had decided to take Bakhtwar back with me," I told my sister. She was relieved. "I did not want to upset you," she said, "but that child has not stopped crying for months."

Without words being spoken, it seemed that both children knew what was to come. I shell never forget as long as I live the sight of Bilawal sitting in white shirt, blue striped trousers, white socks and black shoes on the floor of the corridor with his back against the wall. He was staring at me silently and stoically with the saddest brown eyes in the world, as I took Bakhtwar with me and left him behind. No mother should ever have to leave her two-year-old son behind. No child should ever feel his mother has taken one child with her and left the other behind.

With the fall of Pakistan People's Party (PPP) government in 1990, the election campaign, the separation from my children, the witch-hunt against my party and my family, I had lost a lot of weight. In the spring of 1992 I found I was expecting another baby. As one of four children, it gave me great pleasure to know our family would grow. Yet it was a time of uncertainty, civil strife and bloodshed. The Prime Minister wanted to turn Pakistan into a Theocratic State, the idea that was opposed by majority of Pakistanis. But powerful elements in the military backed the Prime Minister who had gained a two-thirds majority in the lower house of the Parliament with their support. The Opposition party came together in a grand alliance known as the Pakistan Democratic Alliance (PDA), and called for a protest meeting in Rawalpindi on November 18, 1992. I was so thin no one suspected that I was to have a baby. Despite the weight loss, or perhaps because of it, I felt healthy and energetic. Our protest call re-energized me. People across the country responded to it. From the four corners of Pakistan the caravans were getting ready to move to Rawalpindi to display of people's power. The aim was to restore Democracy, stop Theocracy and address the bread-and-butter issues of the people.

On the eve of the protest meeting we heard that the regime had decided to use brute force to stop us from gathering. "That means the regime might use teargas." I said to my political secretary, Naheed Khan. I was worried for my baby. Someone promised a face mask similar to those used by the army, but failed to show up the next morning. So we took the wet towels with us. The crowd had gathered outside my house overnight. The next morning we awoke to barbed wire barrier around my house. As I left the front gate, with party leaders, we were baton charged. A small group managed to cross the barbed wire, find a vehicle and make our way towards Rawalpindi from Islamabad. Periodically we would come across police vehicles looking for us and we would drive slowly with our heads down to prevent identification.

Later the police told me that when a report was sent to them of my presence in Rawalpindi, they laughed it off. But within minutes they received so many calls that they decided to check it out for themselves. The found the reports were correct. Now the mad chase started in the Rawalpindi streets.

Our single jeep was tear gassed from all sides. Police sirens were blaring away. There was pandemonium. The car chase was like something from a James Bond movie- or perhaps like a Bollywood movie.

The crowd was cheering us on, their slogans filling the air. More and more police reinforcements were called in and different streets blocked with police cars and vans. Now the police were lobbing tear gas directly at the car windscreen and aiming at us. The windscreen cracked. Finally our driver had had enough. He braked, jumped out of the car and melted into the shadows. The police surrounded the car and arrested all of us. Later we were released, but the day's events had weakened the regime.

Although the two may be unconnected, after this tear-gassing incident, I began suffering from gall-bladder pain. I took homeopathic medicine but the pain continued. It was often excruciating. If I had an operation to fix it, I risked losing my child. I did not want to take the risk. As the pain got worse and worse, I flew to London. The doctors advised that I should have a caesarean as soon as possible, followed by keyhole surgery to remove the gall bladder. On February 3 1993, my little daughter Aseefa was born. I cuddled my adorable little baby.

Although I did not know at the time, with the birth of Aseefa my family was complete. Soon, on October 24, 1993, the PPP was re-elected. In the repetitive cycle of Pakistani politics, the second Government was undemocratically dismissed in 1996 and my husband Asif arrested. Sadly by the time he was freed in November 2004, I was too old to have another child.

As I write this in London, I must confess my life is as difficult as interesting. I live from suitcase to suitcase traveling the world lecturing on Islam, Democracy and women's rights before universities, business associations, women's organizations and foreign policy think tanks. I continue to pound the halls of the House of Commons and Congress. I remain the Chairperson the Pakistan Peoples Party. I visit my husband, who is having medical treatment in New York. I prepare my children for their examinations in Dubai.

And I lead the combined democratic opposition of the secular political parties of Pakistan in fighting for free and fair elections, as mandated by the Constitution of Pakistan, in 2007. It may seem much too full a plate. But that is the nature of my life and I accept it.

Epilogue

Benazir Bhutto (1953), Pakistani political leader, who served as first female Prime Minister of a Muslim country, served Pakistan from 1988 to 1990 and from 1993 to 1996. Born into a wealthy land-holding family with a tradition of political activism in a southeastern Sindh province, Bhutto enjoyed a privileged childhood.

Bhutto was educated at Harvard's Radcliff College in the United States and at the University of Oxford in England, where she excelled in studies as well as other activities including debating competitions; she was the first Asian woman to be elected President of the Oxford Union. The daughter of an intelligent and Charismatic Prime Minister, Zulfikar Ali Bhutto (1971-1977), she returned to Pakistan in June 1977, planning on a career in the foreign service. But only two weeks later, however, military officers led by General Muhammad Zia-ul-Haq, capitalizing on preplanned public protests of disputed parliamentary elections overthrew Prime Minister Zulfikar Ali Bhutto in a bloodless coup. Benazir Bhutto spent the next eighteen months in and out of house arrest as she struggled to rally political support to force Zia to drop fallacious murder charges against her father. The military dictator ignored worldwide appeals for clemency and had Zulfikar Bhutto hanged in April of 1979.

Bhutto's persecution began in earnest after the dismissal of her father's government in 1977 and his execution in 1979 as she intensified her denunciations of Zia and sought to organize a political movement against him. Repeatedly put under house arrest, she was finally imprisoned in solitary confinement in a desert cell of Sukhar Jail in Sindh province during the summer of 1981. Bhutto described the hellish conditions in her wall less cage in "Daughter of Destiny":

"The summer heat turned my cell into an oven. My skin split and peeled, coming off my hands in sheets. Boils erupted on my face. My hair, which had always been thick, began to come out by the handful. Insects crept into the cell like invading armies. Grasshoppers, mosquitoes, stinging flies, bees and bugs came up through the cracks in the floor and through the open bars from the courtyard. Big black ants, cockroaches, seething clumps of little red ants and spiders. I tried pulling the sheet over my head at night to hide from their bites, pushing it back when it got too hot to breathe."

Released in 1984, she went into exile in Britain until 1986, when martial law was lifted in Pakistan. She returned with a huge crowd numbering in the hundreds of thousands who turned out on the streets to greet her, by then the leading symbol of the anti-Zia movement, when she returned to Lahore in April of 1986. Formally elected Chair in the following month, Bhutto lost no time in organizing mass protests and civil disobedience campaigns to pressure Zia to relinquish office and call national elections. Bhutto's stirring oratory, familiar name, and striking appearance helped to give her a strong mass appeal, but she had to struggle to wrest real power from the PPP's old-guard leadership, members of which were wary of her gender, youth, and political wisdom. Supported by tumultuous crowds, Bhutto again called for fresh elections, resulting in another short prison term that same year. She also had to contend with internal dissension among the anti-Zia forces.

In 1988 Zia was killed in an airplane crash, less than three months after announcing that elections would take place. In the November elections the PPP gained huge popularity in the National Assembly, and in December 1988 Bhutto, (35) became Prime Minister of Pakistan, the first woman to hold this office in any modern Islamic state. During her first term, her objective was to return Pakistan to civilian rule and oust the men who executed her father; she also started the People's Programme for economic uplift of the masses. Benazir Bhutto lifted a ban on student and trade unions. The PPP. Government hosted the fourth SAARC Summit held in Islamabad, in December 1988.

In August 1990, however, President Ghulam Ishaq Khan dismissed her, charging her with so called incompetence and corruption. The President and the Caretaker Prime Minister filed a series of references against Mohtarma Benazir Bhutto. Her husband, Mr. Asif Ali Zardari was arrested and imprisoned for over two years on a number of charges.

Her party was soundly defeated in the engineered elections that followed in November 1990, and Bhutto became an opposition leader in the parliament. Subsequent attempts to oust the ruling party resulted in Bhutto's deportation to the city of Karachi in 1992, and she was temporarily banned from entering Islamabad, the capital of Pakistan.

In July 1993, the President of Pakistan dismissed the Government of Prime Minister Mian Nawaz Sharif on corruption charges and called for fresh elections. The Pakistan Peoples Party went to the people in October, 1993 with a new "Agenda for Change". The programme envisaged government at the door-step of the people and priority to the social sectors. Mohtarma Benazir Bhutto was again elected Prime Minister with a broad mandate after achieving strong popular support in all the four provinces of Pakistan.

Bhutto's platform has been leftist, including food for the hungry, health care, jobs, slum clearance and a monthly minimum wage.

She has been opposed by Islamic fundamentalists who have been suspicious of the PPP because of its alleged leftist leanings.

Due to Benazir's personal world popularity, during her term, Pakistan's relations with other countries improved her, moderate foreign policy had been credited for righting the wrong image of Pakistan around the world. However enemies of Democracy and forces with vested interests have widely blamed her and her party for excessive corruption.

On November 5, 1996, the President of Pakistan Farooq, Leghari dismissed Prime Minister Bhutto and dissolved the National Assembly.

President Leghari also charged that Zardari was responsible for "extrajudicial killings" in Karachi, where Bhutto rivals had been killed by police. She denounced all charges as politically motivated, and went into self-imposed exile. In 2001 the Supreme Court of Pakistan suspended a High Court's 1999 conviction of Bhutto, ordering a retrial. She is currently still in self-exile and faces charges if she returns.

She has been mentioned as "The world's most popular politician" in the New Guinness Book of Records 1996.

The "*Times*" and the "*Australian Magazine*"(May 4, 1996) have drawn up a list of 100 most powerful women and have included Benazir Bhutto as one of them.

She has received many honorary degrees and awards from several countries.

She also lectures and takes part in several major world events.

DR. IQBAL NAREJO
Iqbalnarejo@yahoo.com

THE HERITAGE OF INDIA SERIES (11)

A HISTORY OF TELUGU LITERATURE

BY

P. CHENCHIAH, M. L.

AND

RAJA M. BHUJANGA RAO BAHADUR

GYAN

Published by

Gyan Publishing House
5, Ansari Road
Daryaganj, New Delhi-110002
Phone: 011-47034999, 9811692060
E-mail: books@gyanbooks.com

Distribution Network
gyanbooks.com
India, USA, Canada, UK, Australia, France

ISBN: 978-81-212-8279-6 (HB)
First Published, 1928

2nd Impression 2023

Printed at: Gyan Press, Delhi.

THE HERITAGE OF INDIA SERIES (11); A HISTORY OF TELUGU LITERATURE

Authors: P. CHENCHIAH, RAJA M. BHUJANGA RAO BAHADUR

THE HERITAGE OF INDIA SERIES

A HISTORY OF TELUGU LITERATURE

BY

P. CHENCHIAH, M.L.

AND

RAJA M. BHUJANGA RAO BAHADUR

FOREWORD BY

THE HONBLE MR. C. R. REDDY, M.A.

VICE CHANCELLOR OF THE ĀNDHRA UNIVERSITY

CALCUTTA: THE ASSOCIATION PRESS

(Y.M.C.A.)

LONDON: OXFORD UNIVERSITY PRESS

NEW YORK TORONTO MELBOURNE

BOMBAY CALCUTTA MADRAS

DEDICATION :

KRĪSTĀRPAṆAM

FOREWORD

I HAVE cursorily glanced through the *History of Telugu Literature* by Mr. Chenchiah and Raja Bhujanga Rao, and have been much struck by the authors' grasp of the subject and broad illuminating views.

Mr. Rice's book on *Kanarese Literature* opened what to South Indians must have appeared as a new way of treating literary histories; and the present authors have benefited to the full by Mr. Rice's example. Doubtless the critical student may find in this work occasional omissions, which are inevitable in view of the enormous growth of new matter as a result of recent events and researches.

Vīraśaiva literature is now being reclaimed. And if the libraries of the various mutts of His Exalted Highness in the Nizam's Dominions are ransacked, it is very likely that more books belonging to the same group may be discovered, as also perhaps books having a special bearing on Buddhism and Jainism. The ruthless manner in which Buddhist and Jain literature, in Sanskrit as well as the vernaculars, was suppressed and destroyed through the Brahminical reaction is the greatest tragedy of Indian culture. Today, much of that vast treasure has to be imported from Tibetan and Chinese renderings. Though the outlook as regards possible finds in our own country is almost blank, I am still in hopes of occasional good fortune in this line, if a diligent and systematic search is instituted.

One of the merits of the present work is the historical background presented, and the suggestive manner in which literature is linked up with the general social and political history of the Āndhra Dēśa. Literature is life, either in its growth or its decadence; and unless it is correlated with life, it cannot be properly appreciated. And literature is, not infrequently, propaganda. Years ago, I suggested that the real motive underlying the translation of the *Mahābhārata* into Telugu, with all its pro-Brahminical interpolations, was propaganda through the vernaculars, as a counterblast to the Buddhist and Jain propaganda, which all through was carried through Māgadhī and other vernaculars of India. Indeed, Errāpragada, in one of his verses, suggests that his illustrious predecessors, Nanniah and Tikkanna, undertook the translation of the *Mahābhārata* in order to rectify the erroneous views that were widely prevalent. These 'erroneous views' could have been only the Jain version of the *Mahābhārata*, popular in the Kannaḍa language, with which in its early days Telugu seems to have had a closer relationship than at present, as is to be inferred from the fact that a number of Āndhras were the pioneers in Kannaḍa literature and grammar, and that poets of the distinguished rank of Nannechōdu Nāchana Soma, and Nārāyaṇa Bhaṭ were celebrated for their attainments in Kanarese. In Jain literature, the *Mahābhārata* appears under the name of Ārjuna Vijaya. It is a frankly secular poem, in which there is hardly any trace of the deification of Kṛishṇa.

The kernel of the *Mahābhārata* seems to have been an ancient book famous under the name of *Jaya.* And how this simple book *Jaya* expanded into the encyclopædia of the post-Āraṇyaka, but pre-Purāṇic, Aryan civilisation has yet to be investigated. When I say 'pre-Purāṇic,' I am not unmindful of still later interpolations, pertaining to the worship of Śiva and Vishṇu, such as the *Daśavatāra Stōtra* by Bhishma, interpolated in the *Śānti Parva.*

Similarly, there is a Jain version of the *Rāmāyaṇa* which is very different from the poem of Vālmīki. If it is further remembered that in the *Kathā Sarit Sāgara* ('the Ocean of Indian Legends') the stories of the *Mahābhārata, Rāmāyaṇa,* and *Bhāgavata* do not figure prominently, the idea must suggest itself to any historical student that here is a vast field of research, with a view to find out how and when, for what reasons, and with what objects, the legendary lore of Hindu India developed into its present form.

Unfortunately, this wider field of cultural investigation is beyond the scope of the present book, which deals only with Telugu literature. And Telugu literature is to a certain extent, though not to such a large extent as hasty critics imagine, imitative of Sanskrit.

A separate history may have to be written on the indigenous elements in Telugu literature, such as the lyrics or Paṭalū, the Yaksha Gānams or village dramas, and the great reformer-poets, like Vemana, a star of the first magnitude in our firmament, and all those who have given expression to the true Telugu spirit and soul. Men of genius like Kona Buddha Reddy, the author of the *Rāmāyaṇa*, which has been spuriously attributed to a mythical Raṅganātha, were able to Dravidianise the *Rāmāyaṇa* itself. A critical comparison with the poem of Vālmīki would reveal how deftly and with what consummate art Kona Buddha Reddy incorporated South Indian legends into that Aryan poem, and with what passion and imagination he treated those soul-stirring themes. The story of Sulochana and the legend of Rameśvaram, the story of Rāvana's *Pātāḷa Homam*, and the magnificent manner in which he executes the arresting transfiguration of Angada, Mandodari and Tāra are amongst the instances in point. No mere bilingual pandit could have given us Kona Buddha's rendering, which is so popular as to have become the domestic possession of every family in the Ceded Districts.

Perhaps there is also a geographical distinction between the Telugu literature of the Aryanised 'Circars,' and the predominantly Dravidian 'Ceded Districts.' If lists of works produced are prepared on a geographical basis, this distinction will come into relief. Nor can we omit from the catalogue of the books expressive of the true Āndhra soul, ballads like *Palnāti Vīracharitra*, attributed to Śrīnātha.

If I may venture on an observation, I rather think that, under the influence of a robust nationalism and Bengali literature, the Telugu soul is again finding itself in its own literature, and expressing itself in its varied moods and accents. The number of contemporary men of genius seems to be very large, and the varieties of literature produced are also large. Simplicity of expression, sincerity of emotion, natural figures of speech are again becoming the prevalent literary mode, and our literature has emerged from the unnaturalisms and idiosyncracies of the Prabandha period, which is the period, generally speaking, of our decadence.

How I wish that some competent scholar, with enough sympathy and imagination in him, would write an exhaustive history of contemporary literature, of the social drama, the lyrics, the narrative poems, the satires, the social and psychological novels, the humorous stories, the histories, etc., which have been added to our literature within the last twenty-five years.

I welcome the present book as one of the best of its kind—and, considering how rare that kind is, as a most important contribution to the history of Telugu literature. I trust that this will encourage further histories being attempted, and also histories dealing with special periods or special subjects.

C. R. REDDY.

PREFACE

THIS volume is the first attempt in English, and probably indeed in any language, to present to the reader a concise and continuous history of Telugu literature. It is too much to hope that such a book can escape the limitations and defects incidental to a first effort. Our object has been not only to make a comprehensive inventory of poets and their productions and to supply accurate information, but also so to reconstruct the past as to enable the reader to assess the literary heritage of the Telugu people at its true worth. With this object in view, we have given concise biographical details of the Telugu poets, critical estimates of standard Telugu works, and a general survey of Telugu literary tendencies, in their proper historical setting. The chapter dealing with contemporary literature is of necessity incomplete, but we hope enough has been said to show the promise for the future which the intellectual ferment of the last few decades holds. The views expressed in 'Retrospect and Prospect' are put forward as our own, though the approval of a large and rapidly growing school of literary men can be claimed for them. For dates and authorship, we have on the whole followed the lead of Mr. Vīresalingam, except where later research demanded departure.

Where obligations are extensive and varied it is invidious to particularise. We should like to place on record our special indebtedness to Mr. Vīresalingam and Mr. Vanguri Subba Rao, among authors, and to the *Āndhra Parishad Patrika*, and *Bhāratī*, among periodicals. Our thanks are also due to friends who have read through the book in manuscript and offered their valuable suggestions and criticisms.

CONTENTS

I

INTRODUCTORY

TELUGU is one of the four important languages that are spoken in South India, the other three being Tamil, Malayalam and Kanarese. According to the Census of 1921, the Telugu-speaking people number 23½ millions in the whole of India, 18 millions of whom inhabit a continuous block of territory, 117,000 square miles in extent. A semicircle, drawn with the line joining Rajahmundry and Madras as diameter, includes most of the Telugu country. Within this area are to be found a considerable number of Muhammadans and a sprinkling of naturalised Tamils known as Podur Dravidas. In almost every district of South India Telugus numbering over many thousands are to be found. They are the descendants of the colonists who settled in Tamil-land, when that country was ruled by the Telugu emperor, Kṛishṇadevarāya of Vijayanagar, and the deputies appointed by him. The Presidency of Bombay, and the Native States of Mysore and Hyderabad, contain a Telugu population of nearly six millions in all. It is said that those who add 'Telang' to their names in the Bombay Presidency are of Telugu extraction. The Telugus are an enterprising people and were among the first in India to emigrate to countries outside, such as Java; in recent years they have migrated in large numbers to Burma and Assam.

Origins. The origins of a people and their language are largely matters of speculation, incapable of certainty. Many writers on ethnology hold that the Dravidian races of South India were the inhabitants of the country before the Aryan invasions and that in race and culture they are unrelated to the Aryans; but this theory, so far as the Telugus are concerned, is purely of antiquarian interest. The Telugus may have been in the remote past a Dravidian people possessing a non-Aryan culture, but they seem to have lost their Dravidian identity very early in their history. In historical times they were so completely Aryanised in religion, language and literature, that for all practical purposes they may be treated as Aryans; although the indigenous Dravidian influence continued to make itself felt.

Andhra Desa—*the land ot the Āndhras.* The classic and historic name for the people now known as Telugus is Āndhras, a word which is variously derived, but almost all the derivations contain the idea of darkness. It is generally believed that the territory originally inhabited by the Āndhras was a part of Daṇḍakāraṇya of the *Rāmāyaṇa*, a dark and inaccessible region in the wild forests of South India. In the *Aitreya Brāhmaṇa*, *Rāmāyaṇa*, *Mahābhārata* and *Skanda Purāṇa*, the term is used as referring to a race. In one place in the *Rāmāyaṇa* it has a territorial significance. The *Bhāgavata* states that the country was named after King Āndhrudu. The early references on the whole make 'Āndhra' to be the appellation of a race, and we may take it that the name was first applied to a people, who in turn impressed it on the country they lived in, and on the language they spoke.

Āndhra Deśa was also known as Veṅgī Deśa. It is, however, probable that Veṅgī was a part of the Telugu country—the part which lay between the Godāvarī and the Kṛishṇa. The name 'Triliṅga' was often applied to the Telugu country. This may have been used to signify either the country which contains the three shrines (liṅgas), namely, those at Kāleśvaraṁ, Śrī Śailaṁ and Draksha Rāmam, or the country between these shrines. The suggestion that 'Triliṅga' is a contraction for *Trikaliṅga* does not appear to be sound. For administrative and other purposes the country was differently divided at different times. The earliest division was into *Vishayās*; a later one was into *Nādūs*, the modern one being into 'Districts.' As references to Nādūs are of frequent occurrence in literature, it may be useful to notice the prominent Nādūs:

1. *Veṅgī Nādū*, the territory between the Godāvarī and

the Kṛishṇa, which was the original homeland of the Telugus, with its capital at Rajahmundry.

2. *Muliki Nādū*, beginning with the Cuddappah District and extending to Mysore.

3. *Pottipi Nādū*, from Cuddappah to Pennar.

4. *Renādū* and *Mānādū*, Kurnool District.

5. *Palnādū*, West of Guntur.

6. *Pākanādū*, the coastal tract from Nellore to Kṛishṇa.

7. *Kammanādū*, in Guntur District, from Konidena to Kammamettu.

8. *Velinādū*, in Guntur District, with Chandavolu as capital.

Andhras. Like the Aryans, the Āndhras are divided into four castes: 'Chatur Varna'—Brahmins, Kshatriyas, Vaiśyas and Śūdras. The Brahmins fall under two main heads: Vaidikīs, those who once followed the priestly profession; and Niyogīs, the laity. The Kshatriyas among Telugus are represented by the Rāchavāru. The Śūdras are subdivided into Velamās, Reddis, Balijās and Kāpus. Beneath these there is a large submerged population of Pañchamas. It is interesting to note that while literary writers are not restricted to one class or section of the society, the honour of making by far the largest contribution belongs to the Niyogīs. The Kshatriyas and the Reddis have been patrons of art. The Dvijās or Twice-born among Telugus follow the Vedic ceremonies and Aryan Saṁskāras. In religion, the Telugus have been, on the whole, staunch adherents of Hinduism in its three later variations—Advaitism; Śaṅkara's Śaivism, including Liṅgāyatism; and Vaishṇavism. Jainism and Buddhism, though they have gained temporary successes, did not leave any abiding mark on the people or their literature. The same may be said of Muhammadanism and, in some measure, of Christianity.

Andhra Bhasha—*the language of the Āndhras.* This is known as Telugu, or *Tenugu* (*tene* = honey, *agu* = is), meaning, sweet as honey. Telugu is numbered among the Dravidian languages, of which four are of importance in South India, namely, Tamil, Telugu, Malayalam and Kanarese. Dr. Caldwell, in his *Comparative Grammar*, has given currency to the theory that they are unrelated to Sanskrit. Sharply opposed to this theory is the view, maintained by all Telugu grammarians and Sanskrit philologists, that Telugu is Vikṛiti—that is, a language formed by the modification of Sanskrit and *Prākṛit.* An analysis of the language as it has been for centuries confirms this traditional view. Dr. Caldwell's view may be true, if applied to the condition of the language at its origin; while the traditional view accounts for its present form. There are groups of words in the language, which are common to Telugu and other Dravidian languages, indicating their descent from a common parent in the remote past. It would appear that very early the Āndhras adopted a form of Prākṛit which, in the course of development, became the immediate ancestor of Telugu and Kanarese, aptly termed Kanarese-Telugu by Dr. Caldwell. From this archetype the differentiation into the modern Telugu and modern Kanarese must have taken place. For this view there is ample justification in the vocabulary and the syntax of the language. Telugu contains very few original words of its own. Its vocabulary is classified by grammarians under five heads:

1. *Tatsamamulu*, Sanskrit equivalents.
2. *Tadbhavamulu*, Sanskrit derivatives.
3. *Deśīyamulu*, indigenous words.
4. *Anyamulu*, foreign words.

Many words in Telugu are 'synthetic'—that is, are made up of initial letters of Dravidian languages and final letters of North Indian tongues. This composite structure indicates that people of many races have met, in the Godāvarī-Kṛishṇa Delta, under the stress of historic circumstances, and were fused into a single community. The language, also, was evolved when the racial fusion was taking place.

The Telugu language does not seem to be as ancient as Tamil, though it is more ancient than Malayāḷam, and at least of equal antiquity with Kanarese. It is not possible to say with any certainty when the language now known as Telugu came into vogue. There is no available literature before the eleventh century A.D. All the inscriptions before this period are either in Prākṛit or Sanskrit. The Āndhras ruled practically the whole of middle India in the beginning of the Christian era. But the information at our disposal does not enable us to say whether they used Telugu in any form. It is probable that they spoke a form of Prākṛit, from which Telugu has descended.

The lack of antiquity in the Telugu language is felt as a reproach by some writers, who believe that the greatness of a language depends on its age. This has given rise to later legends, one of which, tracing the origin of Telugu to the fourth quarter of *Kṛita Yuga* (the Golden Age), is as follows: Agnimitra lost his eyes owing to excessive heat. He prayed to the sun-god, who, pleased with his devotion, taught him a language so potent that it restored him his eyesight. This language was called Āndhra *Bhāshā*, as it dispelled darkness. We are also told that each *yuga* had its particular form of Telugu and that in *Kāli Yuga* (the Present Age), Kaliṅga Āndhra and Raudra Āndhra were established by Nandivardhana and his disciple, Devaḷa Rāya, in the reign of Śātakarṇi.

Andhra Lipi—*the Telugu script.* In its current form this was stereotyped about the thirteenth century A.D. Palæologists have traced the growth of Telugu script from remote ancestry. About the fourth century B.C. a type of character known as *Brāhmī Lipi* was evolved in Northern India, and gradually spread to the southern portion of the continent under the name of *Draviḍa Brāhmī*. This Dravidian Brāhmī, different in some respects from the Mauryan script of Aśoka inscriptions, is the common parent of all South Indian scripts. It has undergone modifications in different places and at different times, of which we may mention a few important variations that are in the line of modern Telugu script. One modification is found in the Guha Śāsanas (cave edicts) of the Āndhra kings, another in the inscriptions of Veṅgī Deśa, the original homeland of the Telugus. There is not much difference between the Guha and Veṅgī Lipis. The letters are crooked, though curvilinear. In the time of the Chāḷukyā kings we find a further change in the characters. It is in the eleventh century A.D. that we find the script taking a shape which, to the untrained eye, seems to have clear affinity to modern characters; and Nanniah, the first poet of the Telugu language, wrote in these characters. Between A.D. 1000–1300 Telugu and Kanarese had the same script; but about the time of Tikkanna the Telugu characters separated themselves from the Kanarese, and assumed their current shapes. A theory is propounded that the letters of the Telugu alphabets are all carved out of a circle. This view, though not historical, may not be altogether fanciful. The beautiful circular final form of the present alphabet is, probably, due to the influence of this view.

Telugu has a complete and scientific system of letters to express sounds and is phonetically satisfactory. It has more letters than any other Dravidian language, some of them specially introduced to express fine shades of difference in sounds. We have full zero (*Anusvāra*), half-zero (*Arthānusvāra*) and *Visarga* to express the various shades of nasal sounds. L and Ḷ, R and Ṛ are differentiated; we have a CH and JH, which are not represented in Sanskrit, and an S, SH, and KSH, not found in Tamil. Telugu has made its letters expressive of all the sounds it had to deal with, borrowing from Sanskrit, Tamil, and Hindustani, when necessary.

Sources. The sources for the history of Telugu literature are:

1. *The Prologues to the Poems.* Following the Sanskrit model, it is customary for the Telugu poets to give in each introduction a genealogy of the writer, the history of the king to whom the book is dedicated and of the dynasty to which he belongs, the names of the books composed by the author, and the names of the important earlier poets in chronological order. Valuable historical information can be extracted from this source.

2. *Inscriptions.* Telugu literature is concerned more with local history than with the major movements of Indian conquests. It is to the inscriptions that we are indebted for detailed information as to the history and chronology of the events referred to in the poems.

3. *Grammars and Anthologies.* There are several grammars, treatises on poetics, and anthologies, which give illustrative stanzas from the poets of the day. As many as one hundred poets, otherwise unknown, have

been recovered from oblivion through references in these treatises.

4. *Tradition.* Though not of much value as history, the importance of tradition for recovering the atmosphere and local colour cannot be over-estimated. Tradition also embodies a critical impression of the poets, some illuminating biographical touches, and a large fund of interesting anecdotes.

5. *Lives of Poets*, and histories of literature, written in the vernacular by authors of ripe scholarship and critical acumen, furnish in an intelligible form the net results of modern research.

Periods of Telugu Literature. The usual division is the chronological one, into early, middle and modern epochs. This classification is unsatisfactory, as it gives too much importance to the decadent period and too little to the modern renaissance. A division based on literary modes and tendencies is also sometimes adopted. This gives us four periods:

1. The period of translation.
2. The period of expansion.
3. The period of abridgement.
4. The period of imitation.

If we combine these two classifications, we may divide the history of Telugu literature into the following periods:

1. The period of early beginnings.
2. The period of translations.
3. The Prabandha period.
4. The period of decadence.
5. The modern renaissance;

and this classification will be adopted in the following pages.

II

HISTORICAL AND RELIGIOUS BACKGROUND

THE Āndhras have an ancient and illustrious history, though the beginning of the race is clouded in legend and mystery. In the *Rāmāyaṇa* and *Mahābhārata* they are referred to as a primitive tribe, inhabiting the wild and inaccessible southern forest, Daṇḍakāraṇya. The inscriptions of Aśoka mention them as a community on the fringes of the empire. During the decline and fall of the Maurya Dynasty, the Āndhra 'protected state' was among the earliest areas to revolt; and it rapidly grew into a powerful independent kingdom, stretching right across the middle of India, with its base touching the great Tamil kingdoms in the south. There were two great branches of the Āndhras; the sovereign, ruling over the eastern territories with his capital at Dhānyakaṭaka; and the heir-apparent, governing the western dominions, residing at Paithan. The Āndhra period was one of considerable prosperity. After a duration of four and a half centuries, Āndhra dominion came to an end about the middle of the third century A.D., though it is not known how or why. It is a remarkable instance of national loss of memory that Telugu literature is silent of the glories of the Āndhra Empire. The kings and heroes of this period are not celebrated in epic, *kāvya* or song. As far as Telugu literature is concerned, the Āndhra Empire might as well not have existed at all. The only memory of the Āndhra kings, dimly echoed in this literature, is associated with the seventeenth king of the dynasty, who is either the author or *Krutipati* of *Saptaśatī* in Prākṛit. Śrīnātha says that, in the prime of his youth, he translated *Sālivāhana Saptaśatī*, but the book has not come down to us. There is also the tradition that a Kāṇva composed a Telugu grammar, just as Agastya is said to have composed the first Tamil grammar. When we remember that the Āndhras succeeded the Kāṇva Dynasty, we may reasonably conjecture that this Kāṇva was a member of the supplanted dynasty, and that his grammar was in Prākṛit.

The Āndhras were Buddhists by religion, and it is possible that the literature of the day existed in Prākṛit, one form of which is considered to be the immediate literary ancestor of Telugu. The Pallavās, who conquered the country, must have exterminated Buddhism and Buddhistic literature, of which not a vestige has survived.

The immediate conquerors of the Āndhras were the Pallavās, who seem to have risen to power suddenly in the south. Starting from Kāñchī, their capital, they extended their empire northwards till it included Veṅgī Nādū. Very little is known of the Pallavās in general, or of their rule in the Āndhra country in particular. All that we can be certain of is that, after the Āndhras, they ruled the country from A.D. 230–550 and were in turn ousted by the Chāḷukyās. The early Pallavās were Jains and the country adopted the Jain faith. The only fugitive glimpses preserved for us of the Jain culture are Atharvaṇa's *Bhārata*, (said to have been burnt by Nanniah), the name of Padmakavi, and *Kavi Janāsrayam*, a treatise on poetics.

About the middle of the sixth century the Chāḷukyās, a Rajput race from Ayodhyā, imposed their power on the Deccan tableland. There were two branches of the Chāḷukyās—the western, having its capital at Badami; and the eastern at Rajahmundry. We are directly concerned with the eastern Chāḷukyās, who continued to be the rulers of Veṅgī Nādū for nearly six centuries—a period during which they were engaged in ceaseless warfare with the Pallavas, and afterwards with the Choḷas on the south, and the other branch of the Chāḷukyās on the west. The conflict with the Choḷas was eventually composed by the usual expedient of royal marriages. Vimalāditya (A.D. 1005–22), the twenty-fifth reigning sovereign of the Eastern Chāḷukyās, married the daughter of Rāja-Rāja-Choda. Rāja-Rāja-Narendra and Rāja-Rāja-Vishṇuvardhana, the son and the grandson respectively of Vimalāditya, married Choḷa princesses. Thus three generations of royal unions effected a coalition of the two great rival kingdoms; and Kulottaṅga Choḷa Deva (1063–1112) transferred the capital from Veṅgī to the south. From this time forward Veṅgī Nādū sank into a province, ruled from the south by a deputy. The result of the union with the Choḷas placed in the hands of the Chāḷukyā king, Rāja-Rāja-Narendra, an empire as extensive as that of the Āndhras in the second century. It also marked an era of peace and prosperity. It was in the reign of Rāja-Rāja-Narendra that Nanniah began the translation of the *Mahābhārata* into Telugu.

The early Chāḷukyās were Jains, but the later Chāḷukyās were champions of Hinduism, and naturally enemies of Jainism. The reforms of Śaṅkara dealt a fatal blow to the power of Jainism, and by the time of Rāja-Rāja-Narendra it is clear that the conflict had ended in the victory of the former. The opening verses of the *Mahābhārata* reveal an aggressive Hinduism in the act of consolidating its victories and taking precautions against possible attacks of the enemies in the future. The religious revival intended to achieve this end is known as the *Vaidikī* movement—a movement which, much to its credit, adopted a spiritual means of fortifying the Telugu mind in its faith. While in the Kanarese and Tamil countries the conflict had degenerated into mutual persecutions, it was the *Vaidikī* movement that gave a peaceful turn to the struggle, though it cannot be said that persecutions were altogether avoided. The first effort of the new movement was to guard against the possibility of future internecine quarrels between the followers of Śiva and Vishṇu by a judicious compromise. The Advaitic background rendered such a reconciliation possible. The devotion of the *Vaidikīs* was not directed either to Hari or Harā, but to the composite deity, Harihara-nātha. There is reason to believe that this eclectic cult had obtained extensive acceptance at the time. The other feature of the movement was to flood the country with Aryan culture, and it was in pursuance of this object that extensive translations were systematically undertaken from Sanskrit into Telugu.

The interval between the change of the capital of the Chāḷukyā-Choḷa Kingdom to the south and the establishment of the Kākatīyas in the Veṅgī Nādū, presents a confused medley of events. The deputies of Kings Kulottaṅga I and II, known as Āndhra-Chodas, seem to have carved out small provinces for themselves, and ruled them as practically independent sovereigns, with nominal allegiance to the Choḷa kings. One of these had Kandukur, in Nellore District, as his capital; another, Konidena in Guntur; yet a third, Pottipi in Pākanādū. These Āndhra-Chodas had no touch with the south, except that they cherished the name of their ancestors, and kept alive the memories of their ancestral homes. Nannechōdu (1150–70), son of Ballichoda, king of Pottipi Nādū, wrote the recently discovered *Kumāra Sambhava*—the first contribution of a naturalised southerner to Telugu literature.

The Kākatīyas of Warangal, who ruled large portions of what are now called the Nizam's Dominions, and were the feudatories of the Eastern Chāḷukyās, declared independence and by A.D. 1175 conquered the Telugu province of the Choḷa king. Pratāparudra I (1140–96), the most celebrated of the Kākatīya rulers, was a patron of letters, and himself the author of *Nītisāra*, a book on politics. Pālakuriki Somanātha was attached to his court. Buddha Rāzu, the collaborator with Raṅganātha in the production of *Dvipatha-Rāmāyaṇa*, was a Samanta or minor chief of Pratāparudra. Pratāparudra was succeeded by his brother's son, Gaṇapati Deva (1199–1257). Manumasiddhi, at whose court Tikkanna flourished, was his vassal. Gaṇapati Deva was succeeded by his daughter, Rudramma. Beddanna, author of *Sumati Śataka*, was an Āndhra Choda feudatory chief of her day. Atharvaṇa, the Jain grammarian, also belongs to this period. The last king of this dynasty, Pratāparudra II (1295–1323) was defeated and taken captive by the Delhi emperor, Ghiyaz-zid-din, in 1323. Mārana dedicated his *Mārkaṇḍeya Purāṇa* to Naya-ganna Mantri, a commander of Pratāparudra II. Vydyānātha wrote an Alaṁkāra Śāstra, by name *Pratāpa Rudrīya*, during this reign. Hul̤l̤aki Bhāskara, the author of *Bhāskara Rāmāyaṇa*, dedicated it to Sāhiṇimāra, a cavalry officer of the king. The early Kākatīyas were Jains, but Pratāparudra and his descendants were Vīraśaivas. This faith was a 'protestant' reaction against popular Hinduism, and was avowedly anti-Brahman, though curiously enough its founder was a Telugu Brahman, Basava. It was an aggressive propagandist faith, and obtained a considerable following among the Telugus. The literature of the twelfth century is pronouncedly Vīraśaiva. Pālakuriki Somanātha, the zealous missionary of the creed and a prolific writer, has given us the scriptures of Liṅgāyatism, *Basava Purāṇa, and Paṇḍitārādhya Charita.*

Out of the ruins of the Kākatīya kingdom three principalities arose, which exercised an important influence on Telugu literature.

1. **The Reddi Dynasty** (A.D. 1328–1427). On the capture of Pratāparudra II by the Emperor of Delhi, Vemā Reddi set up a kingdom with Addamki as capital. Yerranna, the last of the *Kavitraya* (the Great Three)[1] dedicated his *Harivaṁśa* to him. On his death, his eldest son, Anapota, and after him his second son, Anavema, succeeded to the kingdom, and changed the capital to Kondavīdu. Kumāragiri, son of Anapota, inherited from his uncle a kingdom which comprehended Palnādū and Veṅgī Nādū. He gave to his Prime Minister and brother-in-law, Kātayavema, the province of Rajahmundry, and made him the representative of the Reddi Dynasty in Veṅgī. After the death of Kumāragiri, a grandson of Māchā Reddi, brother of Vemā Reddi, usurped Kondavidu, and ruled as the lord of Palnādū. His son, Rācha Vema, was the last of this dynasty.

The Rajahmundry Branch. Kātayavema, the recipient of the province of Rajahmundry from Kumāragiri, and his son, also called Kumāragiri, had to defend their kingdom against the aggression of Komiti Vemā Reddi, the grandson of Māchā Reddi, and they were able to repel the aggressor through the able help and disinterested services of Allāda Reddi, who acted as the regent of Kumāragiri dur-

[1] See p. 42.

ing his minority. Kumāragiri was succeeded by his sister, Anatalli who married Vīrabhadra Reddi, son of Allāda Reddi. Pedda Kōmati Reddi, and his son, Rācha Vema, and Vīrabhadra Reddi of Rajahmundry, were all great scholars. Śrīnātha was the court poet attached to all these and he commemorates the dynasty in his *Palnādū Vīracharitra*, aptly called *Reddi Bhārata*. After 1427 the Reddi kingdom was absorbed into the kingdom of Vijayanagar.

2. **Padma Nayaks.** The officers of the army of the Kākatīya kings carved out petty kingdoms for themselves near Warangal. Of these, Sarvajña Siṁgama Bhūpāla was far-famed for his learning and literary attainments, which made him the terror of the poets. We find Śrīnātha, a poet of eminence, uttering a prayer for protection to Sarasvatī as he entered his council chamber. Bammera Pōtana, the author of the *Bhāgavata Purāṇa*, lived in his territory and was persecuted because he would not dedicate his *Bhāgavata* to him.

3. Of the three kingdoms which emerged out of the ruins of the Kākatīya Empire, that of **Vijayanagar** (A.D. 1327–1565) was destined to play an important rôle. It was called into existence by the imminent danger of annihilation with which the Hindu kingdoms were threatened by Muhammadan aggression. The first rumblings of the Muhammadan invasion were heard in the reign of Alla-ud-din Khilji, who sent an incursion into the country south of Narmada, which reached as far as Devagiri. The attack and fall of Warangal, and the captivity of Pratāparudra II, brought home to the Āndhras the meaning of the new menace. The establishment of the Bahmanī Kingdom, with its capital at Gulbarga, was a challenge which could no longer be neglected. The constant pressure, exerted by the invader across the border, united the Hindu kingdoms under the leadership of Vijayanagar, which attained its zenith under Kṛishṇadevarāya and kept the conqueror at bay for a good part of the century. The kingdom of Vijayanagar was founded by Harihara and Bukka Rāya with the assistance of their able minister, Vidyāraṅya Swāmi. The conflict with the Muhammadan powers went on with

varying fortunes, in the course of which Vijayanagar (1509–30) was more than once besieged and sacked. Kṛishṇadevarāya figures as the memorable king of the dynasty. The southern kingdoms submitted to his lordship, and he became the emperor of most of Southern India, from Veṅgī Nādū down to the modern Trichinopoly District. Kṛishṇadevarāya is known as Āndhra Bhoja, for his constant support and encouragement to Telugu literature. At his court there was a circle of eight poets, called the Ashṭa-Diggajās, who led a new literary movement known as the Prabandha movement. Kṛishṇadevarāya was succeeded by Achyuta Rāya, and in his reign the Hindu kingdom began to fall to pieces. After a few years of confusion, Rāma Rāya came to the throne. It was during his reign that a trio of great poets, Piṅgaḷī Sūranna, Rāmarāja Bhūshaṇa and Tenāli Rāmakṛishṇa existed. Rāma Rāya was defeated by the five kings of the Bahmanī kingdom in the battle of Tālikota, A.D. 1565, which marks the downfall of Vijayanagar's Empire. Kṛishṇadevarāya was a Vaishṇavite, and during his reign and that of his successor, the Vaishṇavism of Rāmānuja was practically the State religion, and a constant stream of Vaishṇava literature (corresponding to the Vīraśaiva literature of Kākatīya's reign) was kept up. Kṛishṇadevarāya wrote a prabandha called *Vishṇu Chittīya*, celebrating the saints and doctrines of Vaishṇavism.

The Bahmanī kings, on account of dissensions among themselves, were not able to take full advantage of their victory. Ultimately they were absorbed into the Moghul Empire, during the reign of Aurangzeb, in 1687. After the death of Aurangzeb in 1707, Nizam-ul-Mulk founded a hereditary dynasty, with Hyderabad as capital, which exercised a nominal authority over the entire south. The Carnatic was ruled by a deputy of the Nizam, the Nawab of the Carnatic. In the south, deputies of the Emperor of Vijayanagar declared their independence, and ruled their territories practically as their own. Thus Madura, Tanjore and Pudukkota became independent sovereign states. As in these three territories the deputies were Āndhras, we find, in the seventeenth and eighteenth centuries, considerable literary activity in Telugu. The literature of the period is known as the Southern School of Telugu literature.

The eighteenth century was marked by the wars between the French and the English. An event that has left a deep mark on the people and literature of the times is the struggle between the Marquis de Bussey, one of Dupleix's ablest subordinates, and the king of modern Vijayanagar in 1757. The story forms the subject-matter of Dittakavi Nārāyaṇa's *Rangarāya Charitra*, A.D. 1790, a popular version of which is still sung by troubadors all through the country. The issue of the struggle with the French was that the British power was finally established in South India. The Moghul Emperor, Shāh-Ālam, granted them the Dewani of Bengal, Behar, Orissa and the Northern Circars in 1764. In 1858, the Government of India was vested in the British Crown. The latter portion of the nineteenth and the beginning of the twentieth century are marked by the absorption of Western culture by the Āndhras, and the birth of the modern renaissance in Telugu literature.

The position of internal affairs, between the fall of the empire of Vijayanagar and the establishment of the British dominion, deserves notice, as it is with these conditions that Telugu literature is closely associated. The march and counter-march of the Muhammadan armies, the struggles of the French and the British, did not touch the Telugu poet so intimately as the rise and fall of minor principalities. During the rule of the Muhammadans and the British, the country was divided among Zamindars, some of whom were Reddis and others Padmanāyaks. These practically held their territory under the sovereigns of the day. Of these, the Rājas of Veṅkatagiri, Bobbili, Pithāpur and Vijayanagar deserve mention as the special patrons of literature from the seventeenth century up to the present time.

Religious Background. In order to follow the religious motive in Telugu literature, it is necessary to have a broad idea of the nature of the original faith of the Telugus, and the subsequent modifications which it underwent. The Supreme Being is regarded as having manifested in a Trinity of Power, Creation (*Sṛishṭi*), Maintenance (*Sthiti*) and Destruction (*Laya*), personified in

Brahmā, Vishṇu and Śiva. Of these, Brahmā has no temples and is not worshipped at all. The worship of Vishṇu and Śiva in their personal aspects may be said to constitute the basic elements in the faith of Hindus in general, and of the Telugus as participating in the general Hindu faith. The cults of Śiva and Vishṇu were carried on side by side, without any sense of conflict or animosity. It is on this background that the three movements, namely, those of Śaṅkara, Basava and Rāmānuja, began to operate. Śaṅkara's Advaitism, which had obtained general acceptance among Brāhmans, tended towards impersonalising both Siva and Vishṇu, and in consequence attenuating the personal element. It must, however, be said that on the Telugu mind Śaṅkara's philosophy produced rather a somewhat unexpected effect. It created a tendency towards eclecticism, in which Śiva and Vishṇu are regarded as equal, and equally worthy of worship. The Hari-Harā cult, which was expressly professed by some of the major poets of the first period, not only comprehended in its catholic outlook both Śiva and Vishṇu, but regarded the hyphenated deity as a necessary object of worship. In short, it attempted to combine two streams of religion which, till then, were flowing in separate and parallel lines. This cult held on for a time, but proved unsatisfactory to the old followers of either cult, and hence we soon find the Liṅgāyat movement on one side and the Rāmānuja movement on the other, exalting with renewed fervour Śiva and Vishṇu, each as an exclusive object of worship. Mādhvism, the third great religious movement, is a branch of Vaishṇavism, and exerts very little separately discernible influence. Islam—after the fall of Vijayanagar—and Christianity entered the country as religious influences in the eighteenth century, but exercised very little influence on literature.

III

THE LIFE OF A POET

THE poet in Telugu literature has played many a rôle in his time. In the twilight of society, he was the prophet specially endowed with powers of potent blessing and cursing. He was respected because he was feared. Bhīma Kavi curses Kaliṅga Gaṅgu, and he loses his throne. He blesses the widow of Potha Rājū with wedded happiness, and her dead husband comes back to life. When we next get a glimpse of the poet, we find he has shed much of his divinity, but has gained in dignity. He is a priest, learned in the *śāstras*, and versed in ritual. Kings rise from their seats to do him honour. Nanniah illustrates the type. The poet has scaled greater heights. He adorns the throne. Nannechōdu, Peddi Bhūpati, Kṛishṇadevarāya are royal poets whom a modern caricaturist would represent with pen in one hand and sword in the other. Descending a step, he may figure as a minister—the power behind the throne. Tikkanna heads the poets (of whom there are not a few) who have added the title 'Amātya' to their names. Śrīnātha was a courtier basking in royal sunshine. He was a pioneer of the peripatetic poets, who went from place to place, exhibiting skill and challenging rivals. They were of the order of knight-errants, who attended tournaments, engaged in combats—soldiers of fortune in the service of Sarasvatī. The poet attained to the zenith of his glory in the days of Kṛishṇadevarāya as the first citizen and foremost counsellor, honoured and respected by the king and the people. Peddana might well sit for a portrait of the happy poet. The seventeenth and eighteenth centuries mark the eclipse of the poet. Fallen from his high estate, he has taken refuge with petty

Poligars. Inspiration deserts him; he spins endless verses and holds the audience by literary acrobacy.

Kṛishṇadevarāya was a king after a poet's own heart. He delighted in the company of poets, and was never so happy as when a great poet came to his court. He enjoyed a good poem, honoured a true poet, made fun of the proud one when the mood was on him, and not infrequently himself entered the ring for a literary bout. The king's court was a royal academy, which weighed the poet in the balance and sent him forth with the imprimatur of approval. There, honour, riches, and above all true appreciation, awaited the poet. The informal durbars of the *literati* held by the emperor were the paradise of the poet.

The reward of the poet was honour, fame and the gratitude of his readers. He was not only immortal, but could confer immortality. Kings knew this well, and hence their attachment to him. Many a king lives in our memory because a great poet dedicated his poem to him; otherwise he would have been swept into oblivion. The poet did not disdain earthly honours. When a king sought the dedication of an epic or kāvya, he took care to pay the reward in advance, lest the poet's enthusiasm should wane. He gave him money, silk, musk, rubies, and gold ornaments. Occasionally, poets of first rank received largesses from the sovereign in the form of endowments. Sometimes the rewards took strange shapes. Śrīnātha speaks of the bath of gold he received in the court of Praudha Rāya. The poet was made to sit in the pearl-hall and *dīnars* and *taṅkas*—gold coins of the day—were poured over him. But more than money was the honour. It was a proud day for the poet when the king delighted to honour him. Kṛishṇadevarāya carried the palanquin of Peddanna, just to show his appreciation. It should not be supposed that all poets were rich, or that the poet had only to write a poem to be endowed with a village. No; by no means. Poverty was the normal badge of the Telugu poet. It is this touch of poverty that makes the world of poets akin. Ayyala Rājū Rāmabhadriah, unable to support his family, contemplated suicide. Śankuśāla Nṛisiṁha had to hawk his poems in the open street to pay his landlady. It was a strenuous life that the poet had to live. He had to undergo years of apprenticeship at his master's feet, then toil at his masterpiece, and finally effect an entry into the royal presence. This was by no means easy. Vested interests had to be propitiated and jealousies to be composed. His merit was his worst enemy. Atharvaṇa saw his lifework burnt to ashes by the jealousy of Nanniah. Śankuśāla Nṛisiṁha had to cool his heels in the corridors of the royal court and leave the place in disgust because Peddanna blocked his way. The poet's trouble did not end even with his entry into the coveted circle of royal poets. He had to be vigilant and maintain his position against rivals who challenged him and enemies who plotted against him. The Telugu poet, like his brethren all the world over, was a Bohemian and lived an unconventional life. Śrīnātha, Pinavīriah and Dhūrjatī were notorious for the riotous life they lived in their youth. They were a gay lot. They took the sweets and bitters of life as they came, and with the same serene composure feasted one day and starved the next. Śrīnātha in the stocks, Peddanna in tears, remind us of the tragic in the poet's life.

'Even great Homer nods at times.' Now and then we get a vivid glimpse of the poet's struggles. Tikkanna struggles for the right word, and his stenographer, a potter, comes to his aid. Potana wanders distraught for lack of a suitable phrase and finds his daughter has it before him. Pinavīranna stares at his palm leaves in despair. Tomorrow he has to read his *Bhārata* in the king's assembly, yet not a word is written. His lady-love saves him from dishonour and disgrace.

Romance, too, came in the poet's way. The queen, who has incurred the displeasure of her lord, seeks his mediation. Nandī Timmanna writes his *Parijātāpaharaṇa* to settle the imperial lovers' quarrel. Nṛisiṁha sells his stanzas in the street. The casement opens; the king's daughter enquires the price. 'A thousand a line,' cries the poet amazed. Money is paid on the spot. The starving poet goes back with money in his pocket, praise on his lips, and the image of the king's daughter in his heart.

The poet had his lighter moments too, when he delivered

his *obiter dicta,* in impromptu verse, on men and manners. He had his merry time, when he laughed with others and allowed others to laugh at him. He enjoyed a joke or a pun as much as any schoolboy. We see him poring over a 'limerick' (*samasya*) with the same devotion with which a modern reader wrestles with a crossword puzzle ; and was there not among them a 'wag'—Tenāli Rāmakṛishṇa ?

IV

LITERARY MODES AND FORMS

The Substance of the Literature. The substance of Telugu literature is preponderatingly religious. The epics, *Rāmāyaṇa*, *Mahābhārata*, *Bhāgavata*, and the *Purāṇas* are a vast storehouse of national culture from which the poets drew their material. The prodigious expenditure of time and talents which the translation of the epics involved led Śrīnātha to choose easily manageable portions of the epics for treatment. Episodes from the *Purāṇas*, under the name of Ākhyāna or Khāṇḍa, became popular. Of these the stories of *Nala* and *Harischandra* are easily the best favourities. From the sixteenth century onwards, the less known episodes from the *Purāṇas* are taken as the basis for kāvyas. Thus, the fortunes of a single hero under the title of Charitra, Vijaya, Vilāsa and Abhyudāya became a common subject-matter of poetry. In the eighteenth century, the canvas contracted still further and the marriage of heroes, under the designation of *Pariṇaya Kalyāṇa*, *Vivāha* became the order of the day. The avowedly religious literature consisted of biographies of the founders of religion, compendiums of religious teaching (*Sāra*), panegyrics of sacred places (*Mahātmya*), philosophical treatises and commentaries (*Bhāshya*); secular literature occupies a secondary place. The sciences, especially astrology, law, grammar, statecraft, archery fall under the latter head. Story and song, moral aphorisms, devotional psalms, are characteristic features of the popular literature. The drama is conspicuous by its absence. The Sanskrit Classics were also extensively translated. The lyric and the lampoon, though not regarded as separate departments, appear now and then.

The Literary Form. *Champu*, a mixture of prose and poetry, is all but universal as the vehicle of literary expression in verse. Tikkanna composed his *Uttara Rāmāyaṇa* completely in verse, eliminating prose altogether. Though this had some vogue, champu continued to be the dominant form. In translating epics from Sanskrit, it was found necessary, in order to avoid monotony, to use a variety of metres. This practice had also the advantage of allowing a variety of language to suit the variety of action. Varied metres are therefore the general rule. For popular literature, however, a single metre is generally chosen. *Dvipada* and *Śataka* are of this nature. Prose was a later discovery and did not come to its own till the eighteenth century A.D. But in the nineteenth and twentieth centuries the relative proportions of prose and poetry are reversed.

Authors' Craft. The highest form of composition in verse is *Praudha Prabandha* or *Mahā Kāvya.* The theory of poetics enunciates the essentials for such a composition as four in number: (1) *Śailī* (style), (2) *Pāka* (mould), (3) *Rasa* (sentiment), (4) *Alaṁkāra* (ornamentation).

Style. Style is either simple or 'praudha.' The latter involves an accumulation of phrases cemented together in a complex and difficult way. The words chosen are neither soft nor very musical, but dignified (Gambhira), sonorous, and majestic. Simple style had no attraction for the critics, and 'praudha,' with its complicated structure, was the standard aimed at. In style the Telugu writers generally hold up the qualities of *Mādhurya* (sweetness), *Sukumāra* (grace and delicacy), symphony, *Saurabhya* (fragrance) as worthy of attainment. In the choice of vocabulary, vulgar speech (*Grāmya*) is to be avoided.

Pāka (Mould). Equally important is pāka, or mould. There are three important pākas: *Drāksha* (wine), *Nārikeḷa* (coconut) and *Kadaḷi* (plantain). Pāka relates to the encasement of idea in language, and the nature and the texture of the language employed. Drāksha is crystal-clear style, where the idea is seen through the transparent medium. Nanniah employs this style. Kadaḷi is a little more difficult, the soft skin has to be peeled away before you reach the core. Tikkanna's style is an example of this mould. Nārikeḷa is the most difficult style and you have to break the hard rind to get at the idea. *Vishṇu Chittiyam* of Kṛishṇadevarāya is cast in this pāka.

Rasa, or sentiment, is the soul of poetry; the sūtra runs: "*Vākyam Rasathmakam Kāvyam.*" Of these rasas, there are nine: (1) *Śṛingāra* (love), (2) *Hāsya* (comic), (3) *Karuṇa* (pathos), (4) *Raudhra* (horror), (5) *Bhayānaka* (fear), (6) *Bībhatsa* (disgust), (7) *Vīra* (heroic), (8) *Adbhuta* (wonder), (9) *Sānta* (peace).

Though in a perfect kāvya there will be occasion to express all the nine rasas, in practice only a few of them are employed. In kāvya literature, as a matter of fact, śṛingāra (love) has crowded out all other rasas.

Alaṁkāra, or ornamentation. Great attention is paid by poets to alaṁkāra. There are *Śabdhālaṁkāras* (ornaments of sound), *Arthālaṁkāras* (ornaments of thought), *Slsha* (double entendre) and *Yamaka* (alliteration) are Śabdhālaṁkāras; *Upamāna* (simile) and *Utpreksha* (hyperbole) are figures of thought. In the construction of kāvya, descriptions occupy a central place. Cities, seas, mountains, seasons, sunrise, moonrise, water, sports, love passages, and weddings, all have to be described. In the kāvya, as it was developed by the Ashṭadiggajās of Rāya's court, the story is merely the framework upon which to hang these descriptions.

The General Form of Kavya. The poet begins with a short prayer containing the auspicious initial letter 'Śrī,' and invokes the blessing of God on his undertaking. The occasion or circumstances under which the work is undertaken (usually the royal command) is next stated. Tikkanna mentions the appearance of his favourite deity in a dream, suggesting the dedication of *Bhārata* to himself. This is copied by later poets, who fondly imagine that their effusions interest both gods and men. Poets have dedicated their poems either to patrons or deities; the latter are considered to be superior to the former. Then follows a description of the lineage and achievements of the patron and his ancestors, of the poet and his ancestors. From the time of Nannechodu (though it is supposed that Tikkanna set the fashion), the practice of adding *Sastyantamulu*

—a stanza in which each word or phrase ends with the preposition 'to'—grew up. The story then begins, and is related continuously. The subject matter is generally Purāṇic. A slender Purāṇic basis, which admits room for imagination, is preferred to pure invention. Piṅgaḷi Sūranna is the first poet to take a purely invented story for his theme. Some poets add the praise of good poets and the condemnation of the bad. This gives them an opportunity to dilate upon their views of poetic composition. It is usual to bow to the *Kavitraya* before beginning the composition. The story is divided into cantos, at the end of each of which there is a short subscription containing a formal statement that such and such a poet has written the prabandha.

V

EARLY BEGINNINGS, THE DESI AND THE MARGI

AT the outset of Telugu literature, we are confronted with a problem which does not at present admit of a final solution. The earliest literary work of which we can be certain is Nanniah's translation of the first three cantos of the *Mahābhārata* in A.D. 1020. Nanniah's *Bhārata* is a classic of the highest order. It is against all principles of literary evolution that a 'classic,' so sublime in its conception, and so faultless in composition, should have emerged without antecedent stages of development. So the theory is urged, with much cogency and force, that there must have existed much pre-Nanniah literature, probably Jain in authorship, which was destroyed by those who were responsible for the Brahminical reaction known as the Vaidikī movement. This theory, towards which the modern mind, imbued with notions of growth and continuity in literature, naturally inclines, is, however, beset with difficulties. The case against it may be stated thus: The researches of well-nigh a quarter of a century, in the course of which hundreds of Telugu books have been recovered from oblivion, have not produced a single work for which an earlier date than Nanniah can be assigned. Nannechodu's *Kumāra Sambhava* is now regarded by an increasing number of competent critics as post-Nanniah. Nor have the labours of epigraphists and palæologists brought to light any Telugu inscription earlier than A.D. 1020. In further confirmation of this fact is the persistent tradition that Nanniah is the pioneer of Telugu literature and the legislator of the Telugu language, '*Vagānu Śāsana.*' It is very significant that tradition does not retain the memory of any earlier poet. The argument that the earlier Jain literature was destroyed by Brahminical jealousy lacks historical confirmation; and, even if true, it is insufficient to explain the extinction of an extensive literature without leaving any traces behind. In the Tamil country, where the conflict between Jainism and Śaivism has been far more intensive, we find that Jain literature has survived all attempts at deliberate destruction. Moreover, fanaticism may account for the destruction of books, but not for the effacement of the memory of poets. The evidence against this theory is not merely negative. We have the positive testimony of Ketana that there was no Telugu grammar prior to his. Further, a study of the poetry of the period between Nanniah and Tikkanna leaves the impression that the poets were mastering, with various degrees of success, a regulative science recently inaugurated. Of lesser probative value are the following facts: (1) that Telugu scholars, before the eleventh century, used to go to the Kanarese country and write in Kanarese; and (2) that the earliest existing grammars are in Sanskrit, which are hardly to be expected if there was in existence any literature in Telugu. To crown all, there is reasonable probability that the Telugu script in the current form took shape in about the eleventh century A.D. Weighty as these considerations are, we are not driven to choose between a state of facts against all canons of literary evolution and a theory for which no verification is possible. A clue to a mediatory theory is afforded by the existence in Telugu literature of two streams; an earlier one called *Deśī*, and a later one called *Mārgī*. The indigenous Deśī type exists mostly in song and sonnets and is independent of Sanskrit. It is essentially a rural literature unsuited for elaborate forms of composition. The religious revival of the eleventh century A.D. necessitated the translation of the major epics from Sanskrit for which the resources of the Deśī type of literature were inadequate. An artificial system had to be manufactured to meet the new contingency. A new grammar, a new prosody and a new rhetoric, mostly borrowed from or fashioned after the Sanskrit model, had to be forged. It was the Telugu-Sanskrit scholars who were expected to lead the new movement, and this explains why the early grammars were in Sanskrit. The Sanskrit-Telugu literature is thus pre-eminently an artificial system, and hence has neither growth nor continuity. There is no natural transition from the epic to the kāvya. Living things, like trees, have origin and growth, a beginning and an end. Artificial structures, like pyramids, do not grow but are built. In translating from a foreign literature, the elaborate may precede the simple, an epic may be translated before a sonnet. There is nothing unnatural in the artificial system having its origin in Nanniah, or a few decades earlier. This does not exclude the existence of *any* pre-Nanniah literature, but only the existence of Telugu-Sanskrit literature before Nanniah. We may, on the basis of the foregoing conclusions, formulate tentatively the following propositions:

1. That here was originally a literature called Deśī, indigenous, and having affinity with the Dravidian rather than the Aryan literature. The bulk of pre-Nanniah literature was of this type.

2. That Nanniah was one of the earliest representatives, if not the founder, of the Mārgī literature, which dates from the eleventh century. It is unlikely that we shall be able to trace Telugu-Sanskrit literature further up than the middle of the tenth century. The earlier attempts are represented by the two *Śāsanas*, (inscriptions) of *Yuddha Malla*, and *Mopur*.

3. That the two currents have run parallel in Telugu literature.

4. That the growing influence of Sanskrit-Telugu literature diverted literary efforts to itself, and grew in volume and range, imposing its prosody and rhetoric on Desi literature.

The Pre-Nanniah Literature. The Deśī, as already pointed out, is the native literature of the Telugus. It lets us into the world of thoughts and ideas of the unsophisticated Telugu mind. In form and context, the Deśī stands in clear contrast to the Mārgī literature. The latter is essentially court-poetry—artificial and complicated in structure, and elaborate in technique. The former is fundamentally rural in outlook, simple in its structure and sentiment, and natural and graceful in expression. The verse rarely exceeded seven or eight lines; the metre is built on a syllabic basis and not on *mātra* or tone values of Sanskrit prosody; *Yati* and *Prasa*[1] are observed, in common with other Dravidian languages. Vemana's quartets and dvipada, from which Nanniah in all probability composed his *Taruvoja*, *Akkaras* and *Sīsam* represent the higher reaches of Deśī metrical art. It consisted of song, sonnet and story, and never rose to the complexity of a kāvya or epic. It may be characterised as the poetry of the simple mind in vital touch with nature, expressing itself in sharp, brisk lines touched with colour and animation.

What did it deal with? It dealt mostly with the domestic life of the cottage and the communal life of the village. Kings, palaces and wars were beyond its range. The maids at the well, the mother at the cradle, the lovers in the moonlight, the labourer in the field, and the local hero of the tribal wars were some of its themes. We may classify this literature under the following heads:

1. Songs of the Cradle (*Lāli-Pāṭalu*).
2. Songs of the Dawn (*Melu Kolupulu*).
3. Songs of Festivity (*Mangaḷa Hāratulu*).
4. Songs of Love (*Zavaḷīlu*).
5. Songs of Devotion (*Kirtanas*).
6. Songs of the Harvest (*Ūdupu Pāṭalu*).
7. Songs of the Teamster (*Kūli Pāṭalu*).
8. Songs of Wine (*Kaḷḷu Pāṭalu*).
9. Songs of Play (*Āta Pāṭalu*).
10. Proverbs (*Samitelu*).
11. Stories (*Kathalu*).
12. Sagas of Local Chiefs (Ballads).

In these we have Telugu poetry in its purest strain—not the hybrid Sanskrit collations of post-Nanniah literature. This is a literature racy of the soil, and full of lyrics of intense realism and concentrated power.

[1] The central and the vertical rhymes.

VI

PURANA YUGA, OR THE AGE OF TRANSLATION

The first stage in the development of Telugu literature—a period covering five centuries—is marked by the introduction and extension of Sanskrit culture, mainly through translations. The impulse for translation had its origin in the revival of Brahminism and the zeal to spread the Vaidikī movement, which it originated. This religious movement had the support of the kings, the approbation of the *literati*, and above all the sympathy of the people. The long-drawn struggle between Jainism and Hinduism had ended in the victory of Brahminism and the triumph of the worship of Śiva in the Tamil and Kanarese countries. That this triumph of Hinduism spread its contagious spiritual impetus to the Āndhra-land hardly admits of doubt. The victory of Hinduism, now assured beyond dispute by the decay of Jainism, had to be consolidated and the hearts of the people rendered immune to the possible renewal of assaults by the vanquished faiths. The opening of the flood-gates of Sanskrit culture was the final act of insurance against relapse in the future. This explains why, in Telugu literature, translations mark the initial, and not, as in other Dravidian vernaculars, the later, stage. This also accounts for the preponderatingly religious character and the extensive range of the translations.

The Aryan religion in its popular and non-philosophical form is embodied in three classics: the *Mahābhārata*, known as the 'fifth Veda'[1]; the *Rāmāyaṇa*, the story of Rāma; and the *Bhāgavata Purāṇa*, the story of Kṛishṇa.

[1] Often referred to simply as the *Bhārata*.

The solid achievement of this period is the translation of all these three epics into Telugu.

The Translation of the Mahabharata. This colossal undertaking, rendered all the more onerous and sacred by the circumstances which made the translation necessary, took three centuries to accomplish. It was begun by Nanniah in the eleventh century A.D., continued by Tikkanna in the thirteenth century A.D., and concluded by Errāpragada in the fourteenth. A grateful posterity enthroned them together in its memory and crowned them with the title 'Kavitraya'—the Great Three. No subsequent poet, down to our times, ever attempted to invoke the muse without paying his tribute to the three great masters.

Nanniah (Title,' Vagānu Śāsana').—Nanniah, who began the translation of the *Mahābhārata* at the command of the Chāḷukyā king, Rāja-Rāja-Narendra (1022–63), was a Vaidikī Brahmin of Mugdala Gotra, from Tanuku, in Veṅgī Nādū. He was the family *purohit* or priest of the reigning monarch, and had a reputation for great piety and scholarship in Sanskrit. He relates, in the prologue, the circumstances under which his royal master desired him to translate the epic. Rāja-Rāja-Narendra, like many monarchs of his day, claimed to be a descendant of the lunar kings, whose progenitors, the Pāṇḍavas, are celebrated in the *Mahābhārata.* He was fond of hearing the epic and emulating its heroes. Having heard the story in many languages, probably in Tamil and Kanarese, he was desirous to perpetuate it in the language of the country of which he was the ruler. There was no man of his day better qualified, by his learning and piety, for this task than Nanniah; so it was entrusted to him. He composed the Ādi and Sabhā cantos, and a portion of the Araṇya Parva. Various stories are told to account for the non-completion of this canto. One story is that Atharvaṇa wrote a *Bhārata* and showed it to Nanniah before he took it to the king. Nanniah, fearing that, if Atharvaṇa's superior composition reached the king, his own might not be accepted, set fire to the house in which Atharvaṇa's manuscript was deposited. Atharvaṇa, seeing his labour of years reduced to ashes, cursed Nanniah and he became mad. But as Nanniah and Atharvaṇa were not contemporaries the story is not worthy of credence. There is also the fact that stanzas from Atharvaṇa's *Bhārata* are given in later anthologies. Five other books are attributed to Nanniah, namely: (1) *Āndhra Śabda Chintāmaṇi*, otherwise known as *Prakriyākaumudī*; (2) *Lakshaṇa Sāra*; (3) *Indra Vijaya*; (4) *Chāmundī Vilāsa*; and (5) *Rāghavābhyudaya.* But, in all probability, none of these were written by him. As Chāmundī was the titular deity of the Chāḷukyās, it is possible that he wrote *Chāmundī Vilāsa*; but the existing work differs so much in style from Nanniah's that we may well doubt his authorship of it.

Nanniah's style is in Drāksha Pāka,[1] simple, sweet and graceful. Language delicately responds to emotion and gracefully adjusts itself to the changing action of the story, and to the varying moods of the actors. The poet employs a variety of metres suitable to the wide range of passions and events so characteristic of the epic. Though a translation, the Telugu *Bhārata* is really an independent work of art, superior to the original in many respects. Nanniah wrote the *Bhārata* in 'Champū.'[2] His prose is of two varieties, one simple and the other more complicated, but always less artificial and cumbrous than the stilted stateliness of kāvya prose. In his vocabulary, he employs two-thirds Sanskrit and one-third Telugu words. Jakkanna, a later poet, characterises his poetry as '*Rasabandhura Bhāvābhi Rāmamu*'—'beautiful ideas in bright emotional setting.' Nanniah began his epic with a Sanskrit sloka of praise. His example was copied by Raṅganātha and others, till Tikkanna set a new fashion.

Narayana Bhat. A contemporary of Nanniah, Nārāyaṇa Bhaṭ deserves mention, if for no other reason than for the praise which he has received from Nanniah. He says, 'Just as Kṛishṇa assisted Arjuna in the great war, Nārāyaṇa Bhaṭ helped me in my labours.' It is not clear what exactly were the nature of the services which Nārāyaṇa Bhaṭ ren-

[1] See above p. 34. [2] Ibid.

dered to Nanniah. It is suggested that he really composed the major portion of the *Bhārata*, now wrongly attributed to Nanniah. This is unlikely, because if Nārāyaṇa Bhaṭ had been a poet of equal eminence with Nanniah he would have continued the translation of the *Bhārata*; unless it be that he pre-deceased Nanniah ,for which we have no evidence. Nor do the first three cantos manifest any signs of a joint composition. It is more likely that Nārāyaṇa Bhaṭ helped Nanniah in his efforts to inaugurate the Vaidikī movement, as Śrī Kṛishṇa helped Arjuna to establish *Dharma*. It is possible also that Nanniah was engaged in a conflict with the Jains on the one hand and the orthodox reactionaries,who opposed the translation of sacred literature, on the other. Though no work of his has survived, Nārāyaṇa Bhaṭ was evidently a poet of eminence. He was well versed, as stated in the Nandimapūdi inscription, in Sanskrit, Karṇāṭaka, Prākṛit, Paiśāchika. As a reward for his learning the emperor made him the gift of the village of Nandimapūdi. He is said to have defeated many a proud poet and earned the title *Kavibhāva Vajrāṅkuśa* (The Terror of Rival Poets).

Tikkanna Yagvi (A.D. 1220–1300. Title 'Kavi Brahma'). For nearly two centuries the *Bhārata* was where Nanniah left it, till a great poet, worthy to continue it, came into the literary world in the person of Tikkanna. The reasons for the long delay in the emergence of a competent poet were many. There was a school of obscurantists who regarded the translation and the consequent publication of *Bhārata* to the world as sinful, especially because it was regarded as the fifth Veda, the reading and hearing of which is prohibited to non-Brahmins. The madness which befell Nanniah, who set at naught this theological injunction, strengthened the superstition that those who touch the *Araṇya Parva* would come to grief. But, above all these fears, there was the natural reluctance on the part of poets to challenge comparison with Nanniah by continuing his work. Nanniah was a poet much in advance of his age, and the art of composition which he evolved was a science which few had yet mastered. It was, therefore, natural that, in spite of the efforts of rulers, few ventured to come forward to undertake the task. Tradition, which regards Nanniah and Tikkanna as contemporaries, has an interesting story to relate, which, though not of any historical value, throws much light on the difficulties which the rulers, with all their wealth and influence, had to face in inducing competent poets to continue the translation of the *Bhārata*.

With a view to discover whether a poet of Nanniah's eminence would be forthcoming, Rāja-Rāja-Narendra caused to be circulated a stanza, considered to be Nanniah's best, throughout his realm, with a request that other poets should compose a similar stanza embodying the same idea. Various attempts were made, but all of them were rejected by the king's council of pandits as below the mark. But there was one poet who simply copied the stanza and coloured it red and sent it to the king. The council construed the act of the poet as an announcement that he could not only compose like Nanniah, but even excel him, by adding a new lustre to his composition. Enquiries showed that the poet's was no empty boast and that his learning was equal to the task set to him. The emperor commanded the feudatory chief, in whose jurisdiction the poet lived, to send him to the imperial presence. The order was sooner given than obeyed; for the poet refused to leave his native place, in spite of persuasion and promise of tempting rewards. The chieftain, vexed at the obduracy of the poet, threatened him with punishment, and swore that if he did not go to the emperor, he would have him shaved, led through the street in procession on a donkey, would make him live outside the city in a hut, and disgrace him by forcing him to eat flesh. Threats proved as unavailing as promises of gifts. The emperor, anxious that the translation of the *Bhārata* should begin at once, was willing to allow him to remain in his native place if only he would commence the work. The local chief was placed in a dilemma by the condescension of the emperor, between keeping to his threats and reconciling himself to the poet. The expedient he struck upon was to request the poet to perform *Yajña*—a purificatory sacrifice, in the course of which, according to the prescribed ritual, he had to shave himself, live outside the city and eat flesh. The poet who caused so much embarrassment to his chieftain was none other than Tikkanna.

Tikkanna was a Niyogī Brahmin attached to the court of Manumasiddhi, the ruler of Nellore, a tributary chief under the Kākatīya king, Gaṇapati Deva. He came from a family illustrious in the annals of the district, as having given to the country warriors of renown and poets of repute. The Kottaruvu family, to which the poet belonged, came originally from Vellatūru in the Kṛishṇa District, and settled in Guntur. His grandfather, Bhāskara, was a poet of eminence and is reputed to have written a Telugu *Rāmāyaṇa* which is lost. His father, Kommanna, was the head of the army of the local chief in Guntur. His 'second cousin,' Khadga Tikkanna, or 'Tikkanna of the Sword,' more than once saved his master by his valour on the battlefield. Tikkana, on account of his family influence, was more of a minister than a mere poet, honoured by his master and treated by him as his equal. On one occasion, when his master was driven out of his country by his relatives, Akkana and Bayyana, Tikkanna was entrusted with the mission of securing for him the good offices of Kākatīya Gaṇapati; and it was to Tikkanna that Manuma owed his reinstatement.

Before Tikkanna began the translation of the *Bhārata* he composed *Nirvachanottara Rāmāyaṇa*, an all-verse composition relating the story of Rāma after his coronation, and describing his reign, his conquests and his death. It will be remembered that Nanniah wrote in Champu. Tikkanna seems to have thought the all-verse composition very difficult of attainment. For some reason or other he did not finish the last canto, but Jayantī Rāmabhut completed it later on. It is said that Tikkanna was the author of *Vijaya Sena*, and a treatise on prosody called *Kavi-Vākbandhana*, but of this we cannot be sure, as these works are not available.

The poet's title to fame rests on his translation of the *Bhārata*. Afraid of beginning where Nanniah had left the story, that is, from the middle of the *Aranya Parva*, lest some evil should befall him, Tikkanna commenced with the *Virāta Parva*, and finished the remaining fifteen cantos.

Many interesting stories are told to illustrate his extraordinary learning and unfailing inspiration. He undertook to dictate his verses in open court, without referring to the Sanskrit original, and made a vow that if ever he hesitated for a word he would cut off his tongue. Tikkanna composed so quickly that it was difficult to get anyone who could take down what he delivered, till at last a competent amanuensis was found, at the suggestion of the poet himself, in one Kumāra Gurunātha, a potter by caste, who was not only an expert stenographer, but a pandit of some attainment, as the sequel showed. It was under these interesting conditions that the translation proceeded, much to the wonder of the pandits, who were astonished at the unbroken flow of verse. Once, and once only, did Tikkanna hesitate for the right word, and as the right word did not come he gave up the effort and exclaimed, 'What shall I say, Gurunātha?' The poet was disconsolate; but the amanuensis was equal to the occasion and finished the stanza with the very words which Tikkanna uttered in despair, and which, by a strange coincidence, exactly fitted the context, as an exclamation to the Kurunātha (Lord of Kurus). When this was pointed out, Tikkanna's joy knew no bounds, and he was all praise for the potter. This story, though probably apocryphal, illustrates the popular estimate of the poet's incomparable versatility. Another story, related in this connection, is that the pandits of the court, who observed that Tikkanna used common metres and simple style, began to murmur that he knew no better. Indignant at this insult, he composed *Sauptika*, and *Strī Parvas* in such difficult metres and Sanskrit compounds that it was beyond the comprehension of his erstwhile critics, who, chastened, implored him to return to his original style.

Tikkanna, in his prologue, shows considerable originality, and gave currency to certain conventions which were copied by others. He began with a condemnation of incompetent poets and a praise of the competent ones. This was necessitated by the literary conditions of the day, when many poets sought recognition who paid little attention to technique and composition. The second feature is the introductory dream, in which his grandfather appeared and delivered him a message from Harihara Nātha, that he should dedicate the *Bhārata* to him. The third is a hymn of praise, with every word ending in the possessive case (*sastyantamulu*). Later poets have mechanically copied these features.

The qualities of style which procured Tikkanna the title of 'Kavi Brahma' are twofold. The first is his conciseness of diction. He always studied economy in the use of words. It is difficult to alter a single word of his compact phrases without seriously impairing their value and richness of meaning. He was a very conscientious stylist and spared no pains in refining his verse. The second quality is his realism. Unlike the Prabandha poets, whose 'characters' move like puppets cleverly manipulated, Tikkanna inspires his heroes with life. At his touch the past springs up into life. The dead cities awake once more and the streets throng with busy crowds. Ancient palaces become alive with kings, courtiers and courtesans. The famous battle-fields echo to the tread of warriors, the rumbling of chariots and the cries of combatants. The poet attained the height of his art in *Vīrāta Parva.*

Errapragada (A.D. 1280–1350. Title, 'Śaṁbhudāsa' or 'Prabandha Parameśvāra'). Fifty years after Tikkanna, Errāpragada completed the portion of the *Araṇya Parva* still remaining unfinished. So potent was the belief that the poet who touches this Parva would come to grief, that Śaṁbhudāsa made it appear that it was Nanniah who completed it, by dedicating it to Rāja-Rāja-Narendra. Errāpragada was a Niyogī from Gudlūru in Kandukur Taluk, Nellore District, and was attached to Proliah Vemā Reddy, the ruler of the district. He says in *Harivaṁśa*—his second work—that his father, Śrī Sūrya, was a poet in two languages and a *yogī* who became a *siddha.* He relates how Tikkanna appeared to him in a dream and encouraged him to complete the *Bhārata.* Not satisfied with his contribution to the *Bhārata*, he began *Harivaṁśa*, which is in the nature of an epilogue to the *Bhārata*, and traces the fortunes of the heroes of the epic after the fateful war. Other poems attributed to him are, *Rāmāyaṇa*, *Lakshmī Nṛtsiṁha Purāṇa*, known also as *Ahobala Mahātmya.*

Errāpragada is a staunch Śaivite, a disciple of a yogī, Śaṅkaraswāmī. In points of literary merit he is worthy of being ranked with Nanniah and Tikkanna. His ability as a poet is manifest from the fact that he begins his work in the style of Nanniah and, imperceptibly, passes into that of Tikkanna. He was able to simulate them so well that the reader does not, till he is told, realise that between Nanniah and Tikkanna a third poet had intervened. His control of language and his variety of style are remarkable. His style is more difficult than that of Nanniah and Tikkanna. He writes in Kadaḷi Pāka.[1] His devotion has earned him the title of 'Śaṁbhudāsa' (Servant of Śiva), and his command of versification the title of 'Prabandha Parameśvara' (Lord of the Verse). Śrīnātha admires his felicitous combination of phrases (*Sūkti Vaichitrī*). He uses Sanskrit and Telugu words in equal proportions.

Bharata Translators. In order to complete the story of the translation of the *Bhārata* we have had to anticipate two centuries. We will now return to the chronological order. Before doing so, we may make a few general remarks about other translators of the *Bhārata*, which, like its sister epic, the *Rāmāyaṇa*, has been variously interpreted. The Brahminical version, which is also the widely accepted and popular one, regards the hero, Kṛishṇa, as a divine incarnation, and the whole story as having the sanctity of a supplementary Veda. The Jains, who renounced the theological system of the Brahmins, gave currency to a version in which all the heroes are regarded as merely *Kāraṇa Purushas*—men of destiny—sent into this world to fulfil a special mission. It is probable that Atharvaṇa's *Bhārata*, which Nanniah is said to have suppressed, is a Jaina *Bhārata*; and it is all the more likely that it was so, as the author was a Jain by faith. Jaiminī gave a slightly different version of the story, known as *Jaiminī Bhārata*, which only deals with the portion of *Bhārata* relating to the *Aśvamedha Yāja* of Yudhishṭhira, and differs in many details from the

[1] See above p. 34.

Sanskrit original. This has been translated by Pillala Marri Pinavīra Bhadriah in the fifteenth century A.D. The epic is continued under the name of *Harivaṁśa*, which relates the fortunes of Kṛishṇa after the war. Errāpragada translated it into Telugu, and Nāchana Soma versified a portion of the story, under the name *Uttara Harivaṁśa*, in 1380. There are any number of prose versions of the story written by recent authors.

Eleventh Century Poets. The eleventh and twelfth centuries are *terra incognita* in Telugu literary history. The literature of the time is being slowly recovered by the indefatigable energy of research scholars. We are sure, from the references in subsequent poems, that these centuries must have been most fertile, and yet tradition has transmitted to us the names and works of only a few of the poets. The dominant poet of the eleventh century is (as we have said) Nanniah, whose translation of the *Bhārata* inaugurates the era of translations. There is only one other poet, who, though not his contemporary, yet belongs to his century, and his name is Pāvalūri Mallanna (1060–70), a Niyogī Brahmin and the *karṅam* (accountant) of the village Pavalūr, near Guntur in Kamma Nādū. He translated into verse a mathematical treatise of Mahāvīr-āchāryalu in Sanskrit. The author follows Nanniah's example of placing a Sanskrit śloka at the beginning of his book—an example not generally followed by the poets after him. Though the Sūtras are taken from the Sanskrit original, the mathematical calculations are his own. In Sanskrit literature the names of Brahmagupta, Vīrāchārya, Bhāskārāchārya and Jagannātha stand out as eminent mathematicians. Of these, Vīrachārya's treatise has been translated into Telugu by Mallana, and into Kanarese by Rājāditya in the same century. Eluganṭi Peddanna translated *Lilāvatī* by Bhāskārāchārya under the name of *Prakīrṇa Gaṇiṭa*. There is a *Sūtra Gaṇita*, composed, during the reign of Pratāparudra, by an unknown author.

Mahāvīrāchārya's book contains chapters on mensuration, the measurement of shadows, proper and mixed fractions and the theory of numbers. It is natural that the author, who was a karṅam, should turn his attention to mathematics. It is said that he also wrote *Bhadrādri Rāma-śataka.* This is doubtful; for, though the names of the authors are the same, the names of their fathers differ.

Twelfth Century Poets. The twelfth is a century of royal poets and state religions. The dominant note of the century is the intensification of the religious consciousness of the people and the consequent birth of aggressive and propagandist creeds which sought the aid of kings for their expansion. Rāmānuja began his missionary tours about the middle of this century. The Vīravaishṇava faith gave rise to the Vīraśaiva faith associated with Basava. Religions ran into extremes. It is in this century that Telugu literature began to be influenced by Liṅgāyatism. The three poets of this period are all supporters and propagandists of this faith.

1. **Prataparudra I** (A.D. 1140–96) was a Kākatīya prince who made his reign illustrious by extensive conquests. He was a Vīraśaiva by faith and used his power for the spread of his religion by giving largesses to propagandists, poets and preachers. He is the author of *Nīti Sāra* in Sanskrit and in Telugu. It is natural and appropriate that a king should write on king-craft. In Sanskrit there is an extensive literature on Political Ethics, of which *Śukranīti*, *Pañchatantra* and *Chāṇakya Nītisāra* are the outstanding examples. It does not appear whether this treatise is a translation or an original composition. In the next century Beddana, another king, wrote a book on the same subject, and refers to Pratāparudra as his predecessor in the line.

2. **Palakuriki Somanatha,** a Liṅgāyat propagandist, flourished in his reign. Somanātha was a prolific writer on Śaivism. He composed his poems in three languages: Telugu, Kanarese and Sanskrit. Through books and pamphlets, polemics and disputations, he carried a missionary campaign which had the support of the court. Of his Telugu books, *Paṇḍitārādhya Charita*, *Dvipada Basava Purāṇa* and *Anubhava Sāra* may be mentioned.

The first of these books was utilised by Śrīnātha for his work of the same name. Piduparti Somanātha composed the *Basava Purāṇa* in verse some time later (1510). Somanātha had for his disciple the minister of Pratāparudra, Nindutūri Yannayāmātya.

3. **Nannechodu.** (A.D. 1150– . Title, 'Kavi Rāja Śikhāmaṇi,' 'Tenkaṇamātya') was an Āndhra Choda of Pākanādū. He was the author of *Kumāra Sambhava*, a Mahākāvya. He is also said to have composed another book called *Kaḷāvilāsa*, which, however, is lost. In the prologue of his *Kumāra Sambhava* he states he is the son of Chodaballi, Lord of Pākanādū, and describes the capital of his kingdom as Orayūr on the Kāveri, in the Trichy District, in which place we are told in all seriousness that stone trees blossom and stone cocks crow! It cannot be maintained that Orayūr was really the capital. As the family originally came from Kāveri, the convention was cherished, in defiance of geography, that their ancient family abode was the capital of the Telugu dominion.

The *Kumāra Sambhava* is a recent discovery, unearthed by the industry of Mr. M. Rāmakṛishṇa, M.A., who claims that the poet belongs to the tenth century A.D.—a claim not confirmed by critical examination. It is dedicated to Jaṁgama Mallikārjuna, a Liṅgāyat of renown. *Kumāra Sambhava* ranks high in the literature of the day. In Sanskrit, Kālidāsa and Udbhaṭa had written on the subject. Our poet has not followed either the one or the other exclusively, but has taken them both as his basis. Certain characteristic features of the poem are noticeable. Nannechodu is the first poet to employ Kanarese and Tamil words in Telugu poems. Though this practice is not objectionable in itself, and is even commendable where it adds to the beauty of verse, the poet cannot be said to have been discreet in the use of foreign words. His style, too, is not faultless. *Sandhis* not approved by standard grammarians are used by him. Notwithstanding these minor faults, there can be hardly any doubt of his extensive and massive learning in Sanskrit and Kanarese. In his composition he shows a perceptible partiality to Kanarese metres. Atharvaṇa, the grammarian, has instanced him as one who courted death by using inauspicious metres. It would appear that he had no knowledge of auspicious and inauspicious *gaṇas* and, as a result, employed metres which proved calamitous in the end. He began his poem with *sragdharā*, in which, according to the rules of prosody, he had to use *magaṇa* followed by *ragaṇa*,[1] which is inauspicious. Nannechodu lost his life shortly after in the internecine wars of the period. Another interesting fact is that Nannechodu used in his prologue the praise of good poets and *sastyantamulu*.[2] Posterity associated these features with Tikkanna. But Nannechodu robs Tikkanna of his laurels in this respect.

Thirteenth Century Poets. Raṅganātha and Bhāskara, one at the beginning and the other at the end of the thirteenth century, remind us that this was pre-eminently a century of *Rāmāyaṇa* translators. Tikkanna continued the translation of *Bhārata*. We need hardly say that the age of Rāma's worship is the age of Vaishṇavism as well. The story of Rāma, in its popular and literary appeal, excels the sister epic, the *Mahābhārata*. While we have in Telugu literature only one translation of the *Mahābhārata*, which took three centuries for completion, there is a surfeit of renderings of the *Rāmāyaṇa*. From the time of Nanniah, down to V. Subbā Rao in the twentieth century, there is hardly a century which did not witness several attempts at the translation of this epic. As for the incidents and episodes of the *Rāmāyaṇa*, the literary efforts they have called forth are innumerable.

Vālmīki's classic has always been the basis of these translations. Vālmīki was not only a historian of Rāma, but a champion of Aryan culture and Hinduism, and naturally his version, with all its theological implications, has been accepted by Hindus all over India. The Jains, who had renounced Brahmin theology, had their own version of the *Rāmāyaṇa*, wherein, as in the case of the Jain *Bhārata*,

[1] In verse the prosodical unit is a gaṇa—so many gaṇas of so much tone value making a line. A gaṇa is made up of the prescribed sound elements, the short ones being called *laghus*, the long ones *dīrghas*.

[2] See pp. 35 f., 48.

the hero and the heroine are represented not as incarnations of God, but as persons of destiny, and the mythological and miraculous elements are more or less excluded. The Jain version is not represented in Telugu. The story of Rāma after the recovery of Sītā, relating to his reign, the birth of his children and his death, forms as it were an epilogue to the epic, and is known as *Uttara Rāmāyaṇa.* This has been translated, as we have already indicated, by Tikkanna in all-verse, and by Kāchavibhudu in Dvipada, and by Kāṁkanti Pāparāju in Champu. The story has been allegorised and spiritualised under the names of *Adhyātma* and *Vasishṭha Rāmāyaṇa.* The characters of the story are regarded as symbolising the various incidents in the 'Pilgrim's Progress of the Soul'; Rāma as God, Sīta as the individual soul, Rāvaṇa as *Māyā.* Madiki Siṁganna, in the fifteenth century, translated the *Vāsishṭa Rāmāyaṇa.* Kaṇāda Peddana Somayājī composed the *Adhyātma Rāmāyaṇa* of Viśvamitra in verse in 1750. Another school of thought, which conceived of life in cycles, in each of which the main events are reproduced in a more or less reduced form, maintained that the *Rāmāyaṇa* was enacted in various *yugas—dvāpara, tretā,* and *kāli*; and has assayed to give the story as it happened in a previous yuga. One of such versions is represented in Telugu by the *Śatakaṇṭa Rāmāyaṇa,* attributed to Bhīma Kavi. In the thirteenth century we have two translations, one in two-feet metre by Raṅganātha, and the other in Champu by Bhāskara. In Kṛishṇadevarāya's time a lady, belonging to the potter caste, Molla by name, composed the *Rāmāyaṇa* in verse. In the seventeenth and eighteenth centuries, literal prose translations began to appear. Then we have a translation in pure Telugu by Kūchimanchi Timmanna Kavi, and translations adapted to the stage and set to music. Without being a literal translation, the story of Rāma is told under the name of *Rāghavābhyudaya* by Nanniah, and Ayyala Rāzu Rāmabhadriah. There is no epic which has been so often or so variously translated as the *Rāmāyaṇa.*

1. **Ranganatha** (A.D. 1230–40). The century opens with a translation in couplets of *Rāmāyaṇa* by Raṅganātha.

Though associated with the name of Raṅganātha, it was really composed, as the internal evidence and the explicit reference in the *Colophon* show, by Buddha Rāzu, a *samanta* or chieftain of Pratāparudra II, who held sway over a district in Kṛishṇa. It is not possible to say with any certainty whether the epic was composed by Raṅganātha, the court-poet of Buddha Rāzu, in the king's name, or written by the king and dedicated to Raṅganātha. The latter alternative seems to be the more probable; in which case Buddha Rāzu may be regarded as having continued the royal example of Nannechodu and Pratāparudra. The fact that, later in the century, the sons of Buddha Rāzu, Kachavibhudhu and Vittala Rāzu, completed this *Rāmāyaṇa* by adding the *Uttara Rāmāyaṇa*, under instructions of their father, confirms this conjecture. Dvipada, though a somewhat monotonous vehicle for an epic like the *Rāmāyaṇa*, is an easy and graceful medium. The poet's translation is simple, sweet and easily understandable by young and old. It is full of apt similes and pleasing alliterations.

2. **Atharvana** (A.D. 1240– . Title, 'Dvitiyāchārya'). Variously placed towards the beginning and the end of the century by historians, but regarded by tradition as the contemporary of Nanniah, Atharvaṇa is the author of *Triliṅga Śabdānuśāsana*, the Triliṅga grammar. The name Atharvaṇa is regarded by many as not a real name, but an assumed title. The object of the author in writing this grammar is to show the antiquity of Telugu, and he probably thought that the homely name of Nallanna was hardly dignified enough for the purpose. The name does not occur in Āndhra Desa; indeed, Brahmins belonging to Atharvaṇa Śākha are not to be found in the Telugu country, and there are not many in other parts of India. It is probable that the name is assumed to suggest that the language of which he is the grammarian is as ancient as the *Atharva Veda*. The author has the unique distinction of being the only Jain writer in the whole range of available Telugu literature. He is referred to as a standard author by later writers. The poet is also reputed to have written a work on prosody, *Atharvaṇa Chandas*, and he attempted to continue the *Bhārata* from where Nanniah had left it, and actually

finished the *Virāta, Udhyoga* and *Bhīsma Parvas*. For some reason or other, neither of these works has survived, but illustrative stanzas are given from these by Appakavi.

A grammarian is hardly qualified to be a poet; and that may be the reason why Atharvaṇa's *Bhārata* had no chance alongside the brilliant achievement of his contemporary, Tikkanna. Atharvaṇa is called Dvitiyāchārya to distinguish him from Nanniah, who is regarded as the first grammarian, and therefore the first āchārya (Prathamāchārya). The book is written in Sanskrit, though the subject matter relates to Telugu grammar.

3. **Tikkanna.** The most inspiring personality of this century was Tikkanna, who translated the *Bhārata*, to which reference has been made already. Tikkanna was an octogenarian, and saw the end of the century of which he is the most conspicuous poet.

4. **Mulaghatika Ketana** (A.D. 1250– . Title, 'Abhinava Daṇḍi'). He translated the *Daśakumāracharitra* from the Sanskrit original by Daṇḍi, and dedicated it to Tikkanna. He also wrote a grammar, called *Āndhra Bhāshābhūshaṇa*, and translated Vijñāneśvara's commentary on Yājñavalkya's *Smṛiti*, known as *Mitākshara*, the governing authority on Hindu law in South India. As there is no reference to Tikkanna's *Bhārata* by this poet, it may be surmised that he wrote his *Daśakumāracharitra* before Tikkanna began his translation. *Daśakumāracharitra* (the adventures of ten princes) contains stories of common life and reflects a corrupt state of society of that day.

5. **Beddanna** (A.D. 1261–). An Āndhra Choda minor feudatory chief of Shatsahastra land, in the reign of the Kākatīya princess, Rudramadevī. Like his predecessor, Pratāparudra, this king composed a book, *Nītiśāstra Muktāvaḷī*—the pearl chain of political truths—a book dealing with the functions and duties of kings, appointment of officers, administration of justice, functions of the executive and the protection of the country; in all, containing fifteen chapters on the science of politics. Beddanna is said to have been the author of *Sumati Śataka*, a canto of moral maxims, one of the most widely read moral text-books in the Telugu schools. This book, together with *Vemana*

Śataka, supplies in imperishable verse, pointed and pithy, the moral training of the Telugu youth.

6. **Marana,** a disciple of Tikkanna, wrote *Mārkaṇḍeya Purāṇa*, which he dedicated to the minister Nāgayyaganna, Commander of Pratāparudra II. This book ranks very high in the literature of the time. The story of Mārkaṇḍeya is the basis of the *Manucharitra* of Peddana, who has paid Māraṇa the compliment of imitation in many places.

7. **Manchanna,** a contemporary of Tikkanna and a resident of Rajahmundry, wrote *Keyūrabāhucharitra* and dedicated it to Nanduri Gundanna, a grandson of the minister of Pṛithvī Rāja, the last of the Velanādū Chodas.

8. **Hullakki Bhaskara** translated the *Rāmāyaṇa* of Vālmīki into Champu, and dedicated it to Sāhiṇimāra, literally a horseman. This unusual dedication is explained by a story which, as usual, is interesting, though unhistorical. The ruling prince, Buddha Rāzu, asked Raṅganātha to compose the *Rāmāyaṇa*. On hearing this, his minister, Bhāskara, undertook to have a better translation of the same epic done. The king promised that he would accept whichever poem was brought to him first. Bhāskara gave the commission to the poet attached to him, Huḷḷakki Bhāskara. Both Raṅganātha and Bhāskara finished and brought them to the king on the same day. The king, who favoured Raṅganātha, received his composition with his right hand and insulted Bhāskara by receiving his with the left hand. Chagrined at this lack of courtesy, the poet took back his book with the words that he would rather dedicate it to a horseman or a coachman than to a rude king. The king's horseman, hearing this and desiring to have his name perpetuated, requested the author to keep to his word. The story is no doubt a later invention, because, for one thing, Raṅganātha and Mantrī Bhāskara and Huḷḷakki Bhāskara are not contemporaries. Moreover, Sāhiṇimāra is not a coachman, but the son of Buddha Rāzu and a cavalry commander in the imperial army. The story, however, does contain two elements of truth. The dedication to Sāhiṇimāra seems to be an afterthought, and something must have occurred to have changed the poet's mind. The book was obviously written against time. It is a joint product

of Bhāskara and his disciples, written with record speed, probably to overtake a rival in the race.

Fourteenth Century Poets. Five poets, stars of the first magnitude, adorn this century, and it is a pity that the major portion of the heritage they have left is lost and has not come down to us. **Vemalavada Bhima Kavi** is a poet of mystery in Telugu literature. Tradition has been busy weaving stories round his name, so many and so incongruous, that we may well despair of coming to anything like an accurate determination of his date. Variously placed in the twelfth, thirteenth, fourteenth, fifteenth and sixteenth centuries A.D., it may be that he is one of our earliest poets. But the attempt to determine his date by reference to historic persons associated with him by tradition has not been productive of any solid results. The cycle of legends which surround this poet belong to an age when the poet is regarded as an inspired prophet. Such stories in other literatures indicate generally that the poet who has gathered these myths and legends around him, belongs to the twilight of literary beginnings. Moreover, Śrīnātha places him before the Kavitraya; an inexplicable error if he belonged to his own century.

The mystery and uncertainty that hangs round the life of this poet extend to his poems as well. We are not in a position to state with any certainty that he is really the author of any of the books attributed to him. Apart from the fact that he was a staunch Śaivite, nothing is known of him. Five or six books are attributed to him. They are: (1) *Rāghava Pāṇḍavīya*, the story of Rāma and Kṛishṇa, in a double-meaning verse. This book was lost and became a mere memory by the time of Piṅgaḷi Sūranna. (2) *Kavi Janāśraya*, recently printed, is said to be the work of a Jain Komaṭi, Rāchanna. (3) and (4) *Śatakanṭa Rāmāyaṇa* and *Nṛisiṁha Purāṇa* are not extant and are known only by illustrative stanzas given in anthologies. There is an inherent improbability in a Śaivite writing a Vishṇu Purāṇa. (5) It is exceedingly doubtful if the poet wrote the *Vāsava Purāṇa* in Telugu, as there is a Sanskrit work of the same name associated with his name.

Bhīma Kavi flits across the stage like a strange shadow, the centre of myth and miracle, never materialising into a concrete figure of history.

Nachana Soma and Amaresvara. Two other poets, worthy to be ranked with the Kavitraya, have transmitted their reputation to posterity, but without transmitting much of their work which entitled them to fame.

Nachana Soma (A.D. 1355–77). A court poet of Bukka Rāya, an ancestor of Kṛishṇadevarāya, is the author of *Uttara Harivaṁśa.* Probably dissatisfied with Errāpragada's achievement, this poet wrote it in what is considered to be a style worthy of the theme. Competent critics have adjudged that the claim of the poet is made good by the excellence of his composition, which all through maintains the high level of the Kavitraya and, in portions, even surpasses them. The same may be said of Chimmapūdi Amareśvara, whose work, *Vikramasena,* celebrating the victories of King Vikrama of Ujjain, is lost. It is said that we should have had a Kavi Chatushṭa, including this poet with the three translators of the *Bhārata,* had not that name been reminiscent of the memory of the 'wicked four' of the *Bhārata.* The loss of *Vikramasena* is a great literary calamity.

Errāpragada, the third poet who completed the translation of the *Bhārata* ; Vinnakota Peddana, author of a grammar, *Kāvyālankāra Chūḍāmaṅi* ; and Ravipati Tippanna, author of *Tripurāntakodāharaṇa* ; *Madana Vijaya* and *Ambikaśatakam* all belong to the same century.

Srinatha (A.D. 1365–1440). The poet who overshadows all others of his age is Śrīnātha, who lived in the latter part of the fourteenth and the first half of the fifteenth century. Impartial criticism assigns to him a position equal to that of the Kavitraya, and there are many who hold that he is the supreme poet of Telugu literature. Unlike Nāchana and Amareśvara, his reputation is not built on unverifiable tradition or fragmentary remnants, but on extensive writings available for criticism. The Telugu language has not produced a poet who had such a phenomenal linguistic command over Telugu and Sanskrit. His *Śṛiṅgāra Naishada* is a crown set with dazzling diamonds on the brow of Sarasvatī. Born of humble parentage in an insignificant village, he carved out a name for himself by the excellence of his genius. His inspiration was unfailing. He never stumbled for a word, nor strained for a sentiment. The peculiar qualities of his style may be said to be majesty and stateliness. The rhythm and cadence of his words have something of the surge of the sea and, like the waves, they roll in serried ranks crested with white. Śrīnātha lisped in verses. While still an infant playing childish games he composed *Marutrat Charitra*. Barely out of his teens, he published *Śālivāhana Sapta Śatī*. In the prime of his youth he gave the world *Naishāda*, his *magnum opus*, and *Bhīmeśvara Purāṇa*. In his mature old age, when the weight of years sat heavily on him, he brought out a kāvya, *Kāśikhāṇḍa*, worthy to be compared in all respects with the productions of his youth. Other Śaivite works of his are *Paṇḍitārādhya Charitra*, which had for its basis Pālakuriki Somanātha's book of that name; *Śivarātri Mahātmya*, recently discovered and published by the *Āndhra Parishad; Vallabhābhyudaya*; *Haravilāsa* and *Śṛiṅgāra Dīpikā*—a work on poetics, which, though purporting to be the composition of Kumāragiri Reddi, is held by many to be by Śrīnātha. In two other poems attributed to him, *Palnāti Vīra Charita* and *Vīdhināṭaka*, he is the pioneer of an untrodden field of literary effort. The first is a saga of the Reddi kings—a romance of love and war among the local tribal lords of his days. Literary history of this type is rare in Telugu.

A far more interesting departure from the beaten track was *Vīdhināṭaka*.[1] Though the existing work of that name is a disgusting combination of high art and low morals, there can be no doubt that the original conception, of which it is the degenerate descendant, had its birth in the fertile imagination of Śrīnātha. *Vīdhināṭaka* in Telugu literature has no resemblance to its namesake in Sanskrit drama, described in the *Daśarūpa*. *Vīdhināṭaka* contains mostly descriptions of street scenes of Rajahmundry in

[1] The standard work on drama in Sanskrit.

light running verses. The poet gives us an insight into the familiar scenes of city life in his own inimitable way. Then comes a vivid description of the ladies the poet has met in the streets of Rajahmundry in a live-long day.

Of his numerous kāvyas two, which reflect his genius at its best, deserve mention. In the Sanskrit language there are five books, called *Pañchamahā Kāvyas*, which every pandit, with any pretension to culture, is expected to master. They are, the three works of Kālidāsa known as *Kālidāsa Traya*, Bhāravi's *Kirātārjunīya* and Māgha's *Śiśupalavadha*. It is only after the student has studied these five books that he is supposed to be fit to undertake the difficult classic, *Naishada*. There is also a proverb which shows that two books in Sanskrit were regarded as extremely difficult for the student, viz. *Kāsīkhānda Mayahpinda* and *Naishāda Vidvat Aushada*. Few poets were willing to test their skill by undertaking the translation of what are considered by the pandits to be the most difficult kāvyas extant. Śrīnātha essayed this difficult task with remarkable success.

Naishada, which celebrates the fortunes of Nala and Damayantī, was composed in Sanskrit by Śrīharsha. Śrīharsha's book, on account of its difficult style, is called the medicine for the pandit.

'A Śrīnātha for a Śrīharsha'—so goes the proverb. Śrīnātha's translation of this remarkably high-class kāvya excels in places the original itself in beauty. Full of sonorous and sweet *samāsas*, the poem has the complicated symphony of an orchestra. Verses full of sibilant sweetness and labial liquidity abound. Descriptions of women are vivid, delicate and artistic. Lines linger in the memory like forgotten music. The book deserves all the praise which has been bestowed on it.

An interesting story is told in connection with Śrīnātha's *Naishada*. In places, the poet almost transliterates, instead of translates, the original. This gave rise to an amusing incident. Hearing of the astounding knowledge of the boy prodigy, Pillalamarri Pinavīrabhadriah,[1] Śrīnātha

[1] See p. 66.

was anxious to get his opinion of his book. Finding him playing in the street with other boys, Śrīnātha approached him and informed him of his purpose. The boy asked him how he translated the phrase, 'Gami karmi kruta Naikanī Vrutta' in the original. Śrīnātha replied that he translated it as 'Gami karmi kruta Naikanī Vruthuda.' On hearing this the boy critic observed, 'Your only contribution seems to be the syllable "da."' We cannot, of course, take this as serious criticism. However, it illustrates Śrīnātha's fine sense of symphony. Where the original was untranslatable he never attempted it. Moreover, by a slight change just of a letter here and a letter there, Śrīnātha could transform harsh phrases in the original into sweet ones in Telugu. It is a noteworthy fact, illustrative of the essential symphony of Telugu, that Sanskrit when transliterated into Telugu gains considerably in sweetness and music.

Śrīnātha's character seems to have been as full of faults as his style is free from them. Tradition has associated with his name many stories which do not add lustre to his character, and there are aspects of his work which seem to confirm the traditional impression, though much of it may be gross exaggeration. Nevertheless, in Śrīnātha we have a poet worthy to be ranked with the Kavitraya, and one at whose hands Telugu poetry attained a majesty and dignity unapproached ever since.

Fifteenth Century Poets. The closing century of the period of translations witnessed the rendering of the Purāṇas into Telugu, of which the most important is *Śrī-Mad-Bhāgavata*, dealing exclusively with the history of Śrī Kṛishṇa as an incarnation of Vishṇu. It is said that Vyāsa, who composed the Sanskrit *Bhārata*, was not satisfied with the incidental mention of Kṛishṇa therein, and wanted to write an epic exclusively celebrating Kṛishṇa as the hero, and so produced the *Bhāgavata*. The *Bhāgavata* has been regarded as the main sacred book of the Bhakti school and is specially held in high veneration by Vaishṇavites. We may therefore regard the translation of the *Bhāgavata* as the first literary symptom of the influence of Vaishṇavism, which is more perceptible in the second stage of the development of Telugu literature in the reign of Kṛishṇadeva-rāya.

The word Purāṇa means an ancient story or legend, but in course of time it has come to indicate a literary medium suitable for semi-didactic and semi-devotional themes. As a matter of fact, the subject-matter of a Purāṇa is varied. There are in Sanskrit eighteen chief Purāṇas. All these deal with the cosmogony of the Universe, with incidental references to the history of the world, including India and its future development. Most of these Purāṇas belong to the realistic school of philosophy, which regard creation not as *Māyā* but as the *Līla* of God. We owe the reconstruction of the Āndhra dynastic story to the *Vāyu* and *Vishṇu Purāṇas*. Sometimes a Purāṇa is merely a philosophic exposition of a religion, such as Śaivism or Vaishṇavism, in the form of a dialogue or story narrated by a *ṛishi*. Not infrequently it is the story of a sectarian religion with distinctly mytho-poetic tendencies, like the *Basava Purāṇa*. The proper function of a Purāṇa is said, in the *Mahābhārata*, to be the narration of the genealogy of any great king of antiquity.

We have already seen that in the thirteenth century A.D. Mārana translated the *Mārkaṇḍeya Purāṇa*; and in the fourteenth, Errāpragada translated the *Nṛisiṁha Purāṇa*; Śrīnātha, the *Bhīmeśvara* and *Basava Purāṇas*; and Kamalanābha, grandfather of Śrīnātha, *Padma Purāṇa*. The outstanding poet of the first half of the fifteenth century was Bammera Potana, who translated the *Bhāgavata*.

Bammera Potana (A.D. 1400-75). The author of the *Bhāgavata Purāṇa* was a Niyogī Śaivite. His birthplace has been the cause of a protracted controversy. The honour is claimed by Warangal, capital of Pratāparudra in the Nizam's Dominions, and Ontimitta in Cuddappah. Potana was honoured in his day for his purity, integrity and independence. In this he was a striking contrast to his brother-in-law, Śrīnātha, who lacked the subtle sense of self-respect. Śrīnātha basked in the sunshine of royal favour; Potana avoided kings aud courts. Śrīnātha knew how to turn rhyme into rupees, Potana preferred poverty with honour to riches and wealth;

Śrīnātha dedicated every one of his poems to a king or a rich man; Potana spurned to wed the damsel of poesy to wretched kings for money; Śrīnātha was a courtier, Potana a devotee. Many stories are told of Śrīnātha'a attempts to induce Potana to befriend the mammon of unrighteousness, but he preferred to live and die a poor man, and disdained to bow the knee to kings while he had Śiva to worship and Kṛishṇa to celebrate.

Potana was a self-made and self-taught man. He appears to have had no formal schooling. This is why some defects, counted as such by pandits, are found in his style. It is a signal proof of the devastating influence of criticism on literature that his *Bhāgavata* should not have been regarded by some as a standard work, notwithstanding its bewitching beauty of style and sentiment. It is said that while grazing cattle the poet met a yogī called Jītānanda, by whose blessing he obtained his intellectual awakening and the gift of poetry. In his early days, Potana was a gay young man, a favourite in the court of Rao Singhama, in praise of whose courtesan he composed a rhapsody called *Bhoginī Daṇḍaka*. This was the work of Potana before his conversion. After conversion, he began the translation of *Bhāgavata*. We have already said that the *Bhāgavata* deals with Kṛishṇa. In narrating the incident of Dhaksha Yāga it was necessary to relate the Rakshasās' enmity to Śiva and the words of contumely used by him. As a staunch Śaivite, Potana felt this very much, and by way of atonement is said to have written *Vīrabhadra Vījaya* in praise of Śiva.

Potana's life was devoted to the translation of the *Bhāgavata*, which he dedicated to Rāma. Rao Singhama wished that the book should be dedicated to him, but it is said that Potana, in spite of the persecutions to which he was subjected, would not consent to dedicate his poem to a mere man, though a king. The Telugu *Bhāgavata*, unlike the Telugu *Rāmāyaṇa* and *Bhārata*, is much bigger than the original; and, unlike them also, portions of it are very popular even among the illiterate. *Gajendra Moksha* and *Rukmaṇī Kalyāṇa* are perhaps the most widely read and recited portions in Telugu literature. The style of

Potana is full of Sanskritisms but, for all that, rich in topical interest and local colour. As an inspirational poet he is not excelled by any other, and his *Bhāgavata* is regarded and utilised as a standard manual of devotion.

It would appear that Potana did not publish the *Bhāgavata* in his life-time. He was disgusted with the worldliness of his day and concluded that the public of the time were unworthy to hear his poem. He left it as a heritage to his son, Mallana, with instructions that he should give it—the Pearl of Great Price—to a pure man who had devotion in his heart. Potana's son did not open the box in which the manuscript was deposited, but bequeathed it to his friend, Veligandala Nārayya, who discovered that portions of it were destroyed by Bana worms. The portions so destroyed were completed by Erchūri Siṁganna and Veligandala Nārayya. Later, Haribhaṭ (1660) translated portions of the *Bhāgavata*. We have also the *Bāla-Bhāgavata* by Koneru Kavi. Apart from the *Vishṇu Bhāgavata*, we have another *Bhāgavata* called *Devī Bhāgavata*, which was translated by an early poet, Dammanadora, and later by Śrīrāma Pantulu and Mulugu Pāpayya. Tirupati Venkateśvara Kavulu has also recently published a translation of this work.

Among the contemporaries of Śrīnātha and Potana, the following may be mentioned:

1. Jakkanna (A.D. 1410–). Translated or composed *Vikramārka Charitra*, celebrating the victories of Vikramārka, the King of Ujjain, a patron of Sanskrit literature and a hero much celebrated in history and song.
2. Madiki Siṁganna (A.D. 1420–). Translated the *Padma Purāṇa*, and *Vāsishṭa Rāmāyaṇa*, the tenth canto of *Bhāgavata* and a treatise on politics, called *Sakala Nīti Sammatamu*.
3. Nissenka Kommanna (A.D. 1430–). Wrote *Śivalīlā Vilāsa* and *Vīramaheśvara*.
4. Anantāmātya (A.D. 1434–), author of *Rasābharaṇa*, *Bhoja Rajīyā*, a book of wonder tales, *Ananta Chandas*, a book on prosody.
5. Gouranna Mantri, a minister who composed *Harichandropākyāna*, the story of the prince who never spoke a lie and who, for the sake of truth, lost his throne, wife and liberty; and *Navanātha Charitra*, remarkable as an early instance of the short story. Both of these are in Dvipada.

6. Vinukonda Vallabha (A.D. 1420–). Vinukonda Vallabha was the son of Ravipati Tippanna. This Tippanna was the ruler of a few villages in Muliki Nādū, besides being the keeper of the crown jewels of Harī Hara Rāja. The poet's *Krīdābhirāmamu*, though it purports to be a translation of a drama in Sanskrit by name *Premābhirāmamu*, is really an original composition. The author is the first Telugu poet to translate a drama as a drama, whereas till then Sanskrit dramas were translated as mere kāvyas. *Krīdābhirāmamu*, like Śrīnātha's *Vīdhināṭaka*, is a unique piece of literature in Telugu, an original literary mode exceedingly rare. The scene is laid at Warangal. It is the story of the travels narrated by Govinda Māchanna to his friend Komati Vitagrāmaṇi, informing him of the scenes he had witnessed and the adventures he had met while in Warangal. He gives a delightful description of a cock-fight in the streets of Warangal.

Pillalamarri Pinavirabhadriah (A.D. 1450–80). The second half of the fifteenth century produced one poet of outstanding merit, who stands at the close of the era of translations, summing up in himself extraordinary learning in Sanskrit, encyclopædic knowledge of the Vedas and Vedāngas, and a widespread reputation for sanctity. Pillalamarri Pinavīrabhadriah takes his place in the rank of inspired poets who owe their achievements not to laborious training, but to native talents, imparted by the favourite deity. Pinavīra's family tree is adorned with many poets; and if tradition can be trusted, the boy-prodigy had in his tenth year all the massive learning of a pandit of forty. We are told that Śrīnātha, who wanted to have the poet's criticism of his *Naishāda*, had to seek him among boys playing in the street, and could hardly bring himself to believe that the poet whom reputation had made so formidable was a young lad in his teens. Yet, with one shrewd question and a sharp comment, the boy-poet sent Śrīnātha about his business a sadder and wiser man and rejoined his playmates, all unconscious that he had sat in judgment and condemned the greatest poet of the age.[1]

Pillalamarri Pinavīrabhadriah was the court poet of Sāḷuva Narasiṁha Rāzu, who was for some time the commander of Vīrupaksha Rāya, whom he supplanted, and became an independent ruler of Ana-Gonda in Bellary District. The poet was the disciple of Bhāratītīrta Svāmī, through

[1] See p. 61 f.

whose favour he obtained the gift of poetry. Many works are attributed to him, of which the following may be mentioned:

1. *Jaiminī Bhārata.*
2. *Sriṅgāra Śākuntala.*
3. *Avatāra Darpuṇa.*
4. *Nāradīya.*
5. *Māgha Mahātya.*
6. *Purushārtha Sudhā Nidhi.*
7. *Mānasollāsa Sāra.*

Of these, only the first two are extant. A story current in connection with the *Jaiminī Bhārata* illustrates the popular idea of the poet's versatility. Vīrabhadriah, like many a great poet, led a wild life in his youth, wasting his substance among women. His brother, a very pious Brahmin, had to admonish him very often, but without effect. Having promised the king to compose *Jaiminī Bhārata*, he neglected the task till the last day, notwithstanding the remonstrances of his brother. On the last day he had a room cleaned and purified, and locked himself in. The members of the family could hear the scratch, scratch of the stylo on the palm-leaves. His brother, curious to know what was happening, peeped through the keyhole and found, to his astonishment, a lady furiously writing at great speed. She stood up and went away when she saw the poet's brother. The story is that Sarasvatī was the consort of the poet and she completed the whole epic in a night. The next day he read his composition in the court, and when the pandits applauded the grace of his diction he openly claimed Sarasvatī as his queen—a claim which the audience regarded as blasphemous. But a woman's voice was heard from behind the curtain which justified the poet's claim. It is possible that among the lady-loves of the poet was a poetess of extraordinary ability, who assisted him in his labours. Whatever value may be attached to this story, it was generally believed in his day that the poet had Sarasvatī at his command.

The court poets correctly characterised his style as the lily that gently unfolds its petals and suffuses the air with its soft aroma.

Among Pillalamarri Pinavīrabhadriah's contemporaries the following may be mentioned:

1. Praudhakavi Mallana (1450–), author of *Rukmaṅgada Charitra* or *Ekādśi Mahātya*—a poem of considerable merit. The poet is said to be the son of Bammera Potana, but this is doubtful.

2. Bhairavakavi wrote *Śrīranga Mahātya*, *Kavi Gajaṅkusa*, a treatise on prosody, and *Ratna Śāstra*. The last is a purely scientific work, in verse, on precious stones.

3. Vennela Kanti Sūranna (1460–), author of the *Vishṇu Purāṇa*, which he dedicated to Raghava Reddi, a Vaishṇavite like himself.

4. Dūbagunta Nārāyaṇa (1470–), translated *Pañchaṭanṭra* in verse. Venkatanātha, who lived a little later, translated the same book. Though this author's *Pañchatantra* is inferior to Venkatanātha's, yet it is an exceedingly readable book. The stories are related in an easy fluent style, at once simple and clear.

5. Namdi Malliah, and Ghanṭa Siṁgiah (1480–). These two poets composed together. Of their work, the more important are *Prabhoda Chandrodaya*, a curious drama of divine knowledge, expounding various systems of philosophy, and *Varāhā Purāṇa*.

6. Duggupalli Duggiah (1480–). This poet is the brother of Śrīnātha's wife. He wrote *Nāchiketopākyāṇa* and *Kāñchīpura Mahātya*.

7. Manu Manchi Bhaṭ. Though his date cannot be fixed with certainty, he probably belongs to the close of this century. He wrote a book on veterinary science—*Haya Lakshaṇasāra*. This book, dealing with the treatment and training of horses, is a translation from Sālihotra's book in Sanskrit. Particular interest attaches to this book, as it deals with a subject supposed to be quite modern.

VII

THE PERIOD OF THE PRABANDHAS
(A.D. 1509 - 1618)

The Reign of Krishnadevaraya (A.D. 1509–30) is a proud chapter in Āndhra history. Politically, under his able leadership, the Āndhras began to revive the glory of Rāja-Rāja-Narendra. The imperial grandeur of Kṛishṇadevarāya's reign was reflected in the republic of letters, by the birth of a literary movement, by far the brightest in history for originality and independence, known as the Kāvya or Prabandha period.

The poet, too, had inspiring themes to perpetuate in song and verse. The Muhammadan wave of conquest, moving downwards, was exercising its irresistible pressure on South India. The invader was at the gates. The defender, whom Providence put forward as the saviour of the country, was none else than Kṛishṇadevarāya. Springing from a petty dynasty on the banks of the Tungabhadra, Kṛishṇadevarāya shot into fame by his remarkable military career. He stemmed the tide of foreign invasion on one side, and on the other consolidated, expanded and established an empire as wide and glorious as any witnessed in the annals of South India. Those were stirring, spacious times, of great heroes and glorious battles, of love and valour, and of splendid victories and spreading dominion—a period altogether cast after the heart of a poet.

The Emperor Krishnadevaraya was a patron of letters, and himself a poet of no mean order. He was also a scholar in three languages—Sanskrit, Kanarese and Telugu. In the intervals of his wars he plunged into literature. The imperial court became the resort of the wandering minstrel and the peripatetic poet. It resounded to a battle of wits and competition of poets as momentous in the history of letters as the glorious military conquests were in the political history of the land. Thus was born, under the most propitious stars, a literary movement which in its youth was the glory, and in its decadence the humiliation, of Telugu literature. This new chapter in our literary history, was inspired and led by Kṛishṇadevarāya.

Up to A.D. 1500, Telugu literature may be characterised as belonging to the age of translations, wherein the poet borrowed his theme both in substance and in detail from the Sanskrit original. The reign of Kṛishṇadevarāya marks the beginning of a new era of literary freedom. Under his insdiring leadership, imitation was exchanged for self-expression. Released from the leading-strings of Sanskrit, the Telugu language celebrated its coming of age by inaugurating the literature of freedom. The kāvya is essentially descriptive, while the epic is fundamentally narrative. The epic depends for its appeal on the events and situations in the story, and the kāvya on the wealth and variety of the descriptive element. The kāvya afforded considerable room for the display of imagination and individual taste. The plot, generally thin, is woven round a significant, but little known, Purāṇic episode. The chief interest lay in the painting of character, the portrayal of passing moods and moving passions, and the analysis of emotion. The epic crowded the canvas with innumerable figures; the kāvya cleared the stage of all but the hero and the heroine, it traced the birth and growth of their love and held a mirror to the changing moods and the elusive hopes and fears of their romance. Another noticeable characteristic is the studied employment of a decorative style, in which certain figures of speech, such as the simile and the hyperbole, play an important part. Allied to this feature is the use of *slesha*, the conjunction of words which give a double meaning. The style is sonorous, with a distinct bias for massing Sanskrit compound words.

Kṛishṇadevarāya most appropriately leads off the movement with his *Amuktamālyada* or *Vishṇuchittīya.* This kāvya is remarkable, not only as the firstfruits of a new movement, but also as a clear indication of the influence of Vaishṇavism on Telugu literature. The works of the first period are predominantly Śaivite; but in *Amuktamālyada* we have a purely Vaishṇavite story, marking the stage when Vaishṇavism has become the source of poetic inspiration. The plot relates to the life-story of a Vaishṇavite *bhakta*. In the sacred city of Śrī-Villuputtur, in the Pāṇḍya kingdom, there lived a pious Brahmin, Vishṇuchitta, whom the gods chose as the triumphant champion of Vaishṇavism. He found on the banks of a lotus-pond a female child of surpassing beauty, whom he received as a gift from God and reared as his own daughter. This child, Amuktamālyada, was the light of his house and the pride of his heart. When she grew up to womanhood, she began to pine away, for some unknown reason. The secret of her sorrow was her love to Raṅganātha, the deity at Śrīraṅgam. The father, on divining his daughter's affections, took her to the deity, who condescended to receive her as his wife. The celestial household spent the rest of their lives in bliss divine.

The style of Kṛishṇadevarāya is so high and the diction so complicated that the reader is at first repelled rather than attracted. But the persevering student reaps a rich reward. He will find therein customs and religious beliefs of a bygone age vividly portrayed. He will gradually feel the tonic effects of a vigorous style and the glow of a new inspiration. There is hardly a book in Telugu where there is such a continual flow of ideas, seeking an impetuous outlet in language which, though rich, is yet scarcely equal to the task of full and adequate expression. For insight into human nature, and for facility in depicting elusive moods by some striking phrase, Kṛishṇadevarāya has no superior, and scarcely an equal.

Kṛishṇadevarāya was deeply versed in Sanskrit, and he is said to have written the following works in Sanskrit, though none of them are available:

1. *Madālasā Charitra.*
2. *Satya Vadhū Preṇanamu.*
3. *Sakala Kathā Sāra Saṅgraha.*
4. *Jñāna Chintāmaṇi.*
5. *Rāsāmañjarī.*

Rāya's services to Telugu literature are manifold. He composed in Telugu himself, and encouraged other poets to do so, often supplying them with materials and themes for composition; above all, as the hero of many battles, he was the inspiration of his age.

The royal court was adorned with many eminent poets, of whom eight, called the 'Ashṭadiggajās,' or eight elephants supporting the world of literature, have become famous. They are:

1. Allasāni Peddana.
2. Nandī Timmanna.
3. Ayyala Rāju Rāmabhadriah.
4. Dhūrjati.
5. Mādiahgāri Mallana.
6. Piṅgaḷi Sūranna.
7. Rāmarāja Bhūshaṇa.
8. Tenāli Rāmakṛishṇa.

It is almost certain that the last three poets did not write in the reign of Kṛishṇadevarāya, though it is unquestionably true that they, along with the rest, are the classic exponents of the kāvya type of literature.

1. **Allasani Peddana** (Title, 'Āndhra Kavitā Pitā Mahūdu') was the Poet Laureate of Kṛishṇadevarāya's court, and the most illustrious and prominent of the poets of the day. The author of a classic which was regarded as the ideal of kāvya literature, honoured by the king, looked up to for guidance and help by the *literati*, Peddana occupies a unique position in the literary world. His great influence in the royal court, his undisputed eminence as a poet, made him the autocrat of the world of letters. What he laid down was law; what he approved of was fame. While to Kṛishṇadevarāya belongs the honour of being the founder of Prabandha literature, it was Peddana who, with his *Manucharitra*, deflected the course of Telugu literature and made the kāvya the archetypal literary mode for centuries to come.

Peddana's celebrated kāvya, *Svarochisha Manucharitra* (shortly *Manucharitra*), has easily eclipsed all other poetical efforts of the day. The story is an episode from the *Mārkaṇḍeya Purāṇa* relating to Svarochisha Manusambhava. A pious Brahmin of Aruṇāspada, on the banks of the Varuṇa, visits the heights of the Himālayas, traditionally reputed to be the abode of a higher order of beings than men, with the aid of a *mantra* imparted to him by a *sidha*. In his wanderings he attracts the attention of a Gandharva damsel, who falls in love with him, but he does not reciprocate her feelings. A male Gandharva, taking advantage of the situation, assumes the form of the Brahmin, consoles the love-lorn maiden and lives with her. Out of the union was born Svarochisha, who in time becomes a ruler and meets many an adventure, in each of which he rescues a maiden whom he weds. The son of Svarochisha is the second Manu, ruler of Jambudvīpa. The story, as will be seen, is slight, but the main interest lies in the varied descriptions of the natural beauty of the Himālayas, and the delineations of character.

In literary form, *Manucharitra* is of composite structure. The poem reveals in many places the characteristic touch of Śrīnātha, for whom Peddana seems to have entertained great respect. In the description of the hunt, Pillalamarri Pinavīrabhadriah is followed. In the conception of situations, Mārana's inspiration is traceable. In the development of the theme, Kṛishṇadevarāya sets the model. *Manucharitra* well illustrates what we may call 'eclecticism in composition,' a very noticeable feature in latter-day poetry.

Peddana's learning in Sanskrit and Telugu was prodigious and his flow of inspiration sustained. In the weaving of words his skill was extraordinary, as Kākamāni Mūrti justly observed. And yet one or two defects are noticeable. Unities are lacking, and the various parts of the story do not properly articulate. Sweet imagery is meagre, though descriptions are delightful, and conversations cunningly managed.

Peddana followed the royal example of laying under tribute foreign words, especially Kanarese, whenever necessary. This practice, though condemned by purists, is a welcome departure, as it adds to the beauty and symphony of the verse. *Hari Kāthā Śāra*, which is attributed to Peddana, is not extant.

Manucharitra was dedicated to Kṛishṇadevarāya, who

honoured the poet above all others, lavished praise and gifts on him and conferred on him the title of 'Kavi Tāpitā Mahā.' The position which Peddana occupied in the royal court was something akin to that of Nanniah in the Chāḷukyā Court, i.e., that of a personal friend whom the king had made his confidant. Like Nanniah too, he had the privilege of inspiring a new literary movement. Nanniah's fault was his also—jealousy of any rising poet who promised to attract the royal attention.

Many stories are told of the king's regard for Peddana. Kṛishṇadevarāya was so much pleased with *Manucharitra* that he insisted, as a mark of his appreciation, on being one of the pole-bearers of his palanquin. On another occasion the emperor insisted on fixing a golden bangle on the poet's leg with his own hands, as a reward for victory in a literary contest. We find Peddana on his retirement, broken down with age and sorrow, bemoaning his desolation at the loss of his royal friend and patron.

2. **Nandi Timmanna** (popularly known as Mukku Timmana) was the second great poet of the royal court. He was a Niyogī Brahmin of the Aruvela sect and a staunch Śaivite by faith. The life-work of the poet was *Parijātā-paharaṇa*, which he dedicated to King Kṛishṇadevarāya. The story celebrates an incident in the life of Śrī Kṛishṇa, whose efforts to satisfy his rival wives often placed him in embarrassing situations. On one occasion he incurred the displeasure of Satyabhāma, by giving Rukmaṇī the flower from Paradise known as Parijāta. It is said that when Śrī Kṛishṇa fell at Satyabhāma's feet in an effort to appease her, she spurned him with a kick. The tactful husband, pocketing the insult, turned her wrath with the soft answer that he was more sorry that her tender feet should be hurt, than that he should be insulted. To satisfy his angry spouse Śrī Kṛishṇa goes to Svargalōka, and after a desperate battle with the heavenly hosts of Indra, who jealously guard the Parijāta, succeeds in removing the tree to Satyabhāma's palace. The lovers' quarrel was soon composed, and the curtain drops over the happy pair rejoicing in each other. There is a beautiful story told as to the circumstances under which the poet

wrote his kāvya. It would appear that on one occasion Kṛishṇadevarāya had a quarrel with his wife which threatened to develop into a serious breach. The queen was found sleeping wlth her legs towards the head of his portrait on the bed-sheet. This the king construed into a personal insult, and hence the quarrel. The poet, who probably came to the royal court in the retinue of the queen, was asked to intercede. This poem was written to show to the king that great freedom is permitted between lovers and that a wise husband should be slow in fancying insults where none was intended. It is said that the king caught the hint, so delicately conveyed through the poem, and became reconciled to his wife.

The poem is a rare prabandha, full of honeyed words, sweet sentiments and delicate and polished imagery. As a work of art it occupies a very high place in Telugu literature.

3. **Ayyala Raju Ramabhadra Kavi** (also known as Pillala Rāmabhadriah—Rāmabhadriah-Of-Many-Children, on account of his large family). Unable to support his growing family, the poet, it would seem, contemplated suicide, but was dissuaded by his friends. At their advice he went with his family to Vijianagaram, with the desperate resolve to earn a livelihood or die in the attempt. Providence helped him at the outset, for on his entry into the capital, he met with an adventure which brought him a friend, who introduced him to the royal court. Caught in a thunder-storm and drenched to the bone, the poet found in a garden a group of students who were struggling hard at the task set by their master—i.e., to give a description of the physical effects of *virāha* (love-sickness). The poet offered to help them if they could kindle a fire for him. Under the grateful glow of the crackling fire, he composed a stanza which the students presented to their master as their own unaided achievement. Tradition identifies their master with Rāmarāja Bhūshaṇa, author of *Vasucharitra*. The master at once realised that he was dealing with a poet of eminence and asked his students to take him to the stranger. Thus was formed a friendship which secured for the poet an entry into the coveted circle of royal poets.

The poet, at the command of Kṛishṇadevarāya, composed *Sakala Kathā Sāra Sangraha*, a poem in nine cantos containing the famous Purāṇic stories of Rāma Pururāva, etc. The poem was not finished by the time Kṛishṇadevarāya died. After the death of his patron, the poet settled in the court of the nephew of the son-in-law of Kṛishṇadevarāya, and composed *Rāmābhyudaya*.

4. **Dhurjati,** a staunch Śaivite, was also of the select circle. He hailed from Kāḷahastī, and appropriately composed *Kāḷahastī Mahātmya*, a kāvya extolling the virtues of Kāḷahastī as a place of pilgrimage. Kṛishṇadevarāya often wondered at the elegance of his characterisation. Once in the full court the emperor propounded the question, 'Whence did this worshipper of the poison-throated Śiva get this incomparable sweetness of expression?' The answer which the assembled poets gave, while confirming the royal patron's approbation, shows him to be a gay young man with rather doubtful morals. Dhūrjati managed to combine a reputation for profound piety with considerable looseness of character.

5. **Madiahgari Mallana,** another Ṣaivite poet of the court, was the author of *Rāja Sekhara Charitra*. He was so called to distinghish him from Praudhakavi Mallana.

6. **Sankusala Nrishimhakavi.** Though not counted among the 'great eight', he deserves special mention, as he ranks among the foremost of the poets of the day. The poet wrote *Kavikarṇa Rasāyana*, which he desired to dedicate to the emperor. With this object he approached Peddana, and, after reading to him portions of his work, requested him to introduce him to the emperor. Peddana, jealous of the poet's ability, and apprehensive that his own position might be jeopardised, put obstacles in his way. Disgusted at Peddana's conduct, and unable to obtain an entry into the royal presence, the poet was driven to selling his poem in the open market. One of the stanzas sold reached Mohanāṅgi, the daughter of the emperor. One day, while playing chess, she repeated a stanza from *Kavikarṇa Rasāyana*. The emperor, struck with the beauty and aptness of the stanza, enquired where she got it from and was told that a starving poet sold it in the bazaar. The

emperor was grieved to learn about the plot of Peddana, and wanted to make amends to the poet by permitting him to dedicate his work to him. But this was not to be, as Nṛisiṁhakavi had left the place for Śrīraṅgam, where he dedicated his poem to the goddess of the shrine. Whether the story is true or not, it illustrates the fact that true genius is irrepressible, and in the days of Kṛishṇadevarāya merit never remained unrecognised in the long run. Nṛisiṁha did not suffer fools gladly, and he has devoted a considerable portion of his introduction to the condemnation of incompetent poets.

7 and 8. **Kummari Molla** and **Kumari Dhurjati.** Two other poets of the reign are Kummari Molla, the potter poetess, who composed a *Rāmāyaṇa*; and Kumārī Dhūrjati, who chronicled the conquests of Kṛishṇadevarāya under the name of *Kṛishṇadevarāya Vijaya.* He also composed *Sāvitrī Charitra* and *Indumatī Vivāha.*

Of the minor poets of the time we need mention only the following: (1) Bhāskara Pantulu, who wrote *Kaṇyakāpurāṇa*, the story of the patron saint of a sect of Vaiśyas; and (2) Piduparti Somanātha and Piduparti Basavakavi—two Liṅgāyat poets—authors of *Basava Purāṇa* and *Prabhuliṅga Līla*, respectively.

The latter half of the sixteenth century A.D. was dominated by three poets, Piṅgaḷi Sūranna, Rāmarāja Bhūshaṇa, and Tenāli Rāmakṛishṇa, all of whom, while carrying forward the general movement of kāvya literature, added, by way of individual contribution, new elements and variations. Of these three poets, Piṅgaḷi Sūranna stands out easily the most prominent, by his daring originality, freedom from convention and unique variety of genius. It is natural that the fame of Peddana's *Manucharitra* should have challenged the ambition of that aspiring age. Nrisiṁhakavi, with his *Kavikarṇa Rasāyana*, tried to scale higher altitudes, by including in the range of descriptions a larger variety than Peddana utilised or the rhetoricians demanded. The new claimant for a place in the sun was Piṅgaḷi Sūranna.

Pingali Suranna was a Niyogī Brahmin of Āpastamba Sūtra. His family was originally resident at Piṅgaḷi, a petty village in Kistna District. The poet attached himself to the court of Kṛishṇa Rāzu (a contemporary of Sadaśivarāya, the successor of Kṛishṇadevarāya) of Nandayal. Piṅgaḷi Sūranna's first work which brought him fame was *Rāghava Pāṇḍavīya*—a 'Dvanda Kāvya' in which each verse is capable of giving two meanings, one applicable to the story of Rāma and the other to the story of the *Mahābhārata*—and the whole poem carrying the double story continuously. Piṅgaḷi Sūranna and Rāmarāja Bhūshaṇa may be said to be the pioneers of this kind of literary development, known as 'Slesha' Kāvya. Compared with *Vasucharitra*, *Rāghava Pāṇḍavīya* has one merit, rare in this type of composition, namely, grace and simplicity of style. It is a tribute to the genius of Sūranna that he was able to compose a Dvanda Kāvya which is at once simple and natural—an achievement unapproached by subsequent writers. A peculiarity of this book is that the poet has departed from the time-honoured custom of describing his family history in the introduction. Muddirāju Rāmanna wrote a commentary on *Rāghava Pāṇḍavīya* in the sixteenth century. Next, in order, comes *Kaḷāpūrnodaya*, by common consent a unique production in Telugu literature. We have already noticed that the Purāṇic writers followed a Sanskrit original, and the kāvya writers a Purāṇic episode. A purely imaginary story never was the theme of a great poet. Indeed, the author of *Vasucharitra* condemns kāvyas based upon stories of imagination, as 'inferior diamonds.' Sūranna, in the face of the literary traditions of the day, chose for his *Kaḷāpūrnodaya* a story of his own invention. Rambhā, the most beautiful of celestial damsels, proud of her beauty, boasts that she is peerless and unconquerable and that none can separate her from her lover, Nalakūbera. Nārada, the wanderer in the heavens, foretells her fall, and prophesies that a false Rambhā and Nalakūbera will rise, to confound her pride. Kalabhāshiṇi and Maṇikandhara are destined to play the part of the 'double' to Rambhā and Nalakūbera. The rest is a comedy of errors. Kalabhāshiṇi falls in love with Nalakūbera and Maṇikandhara with Rambhā. Maṇikandhara assumes the form of Nalakūbera, and attracts Rambhā to himself. Kalabhāshiṇi assumes the form of Rambhā and is attracted by Nalakūbera. The false and the real meet in a maze of errors. The spell is broken, everybody realises his folly and makes amends. In the centre of the plot are Kṛishṇa and his seraglio, and in the background are Kāli worshippers with dark hints of human sacrifices, and Malayāḷi magicians with mystic garlands and strange spells. A noticeable feature of this work is that the writer altogether discards slesha.

Prabhāvati Pradyumna is the last of Sūranna's works—the fruit of maturer years. In the previous work we observe that the story is novel, while the treatment follows the traditional path of the kāvya; whereas in *Prabhāvati Pradyumna* the theme is Purāṇic, as in the kāvyas, but the treatment is original. Vajranābha is a *Daitya*, an enemy of *Devas*. He is very powerful, and by virtue of his *tapas* becomes invincible. He resides in a city inaccessible to men and gods. Taking advantage of his invulnerable position, he conquers the three worlds and imperils the position of Indra, who seeks the help of Kṛishṇa to achieve the downfall of the wicked Vajranābha. How to conquer him whom gods have made invulnerable—this is the problem of the gods. See how the divine plotter sets about. Swans are neither gods nor men, and can find entrance into Vajranābha's territory. On this hangs the plot. The Daitya king has a beautiful daughter, Prabhāvati. The wily swan, so useful to the Indian poet, creates in Prabhāvati a love for Pradyumna, son of Kṛishṇa. The daughter of Daityas in love with the son of Devas, —parents sworn to eternal enmity—forms the good old situation. The artful swan sings the praises of a dramatic troupe of Bhadra, far famed in Devaloka. Pradyumna is smuggled with the troupe into the capital of the Daitya king. There follow love scenes, political intrigues; the father is killed, and the daughter is married.

In order to measure the greatness of Piṅgaḷi Sūranna and the literary value of his kāvyas, it is necessary to realise how far he has risen above the limitation of the times. The poet has endeavoured, though not with complete success, to escape the allurements of the kāvya type of literature, then rendered irresistible by the striking successes of a procession of great poets. The besetting sin of the kāvya literature is that it detaches art from life. The characters of the play are so many pegs to hang elaborate descriptions upon. There is neither life, development nor *dênouement*. Sūranna clearly perceived the approaching doom of the kāvya, and has sought to inspire the decaying movement with life. Following the master-dramatists of Sanskrit, Kaḷidāsa and Bāṇa, he infused a strong dramatic interest into the kāvya. As we follow him our attention is attracted to the plot and its beauty, not to the poet and his dexterity, as in the kāvyas. Sūranna creates and evolves; his characters are life-like, their movements spontaneous, their conversations natural and the situations tense and vivid. Unlike the kāvya writers, who invariably follow the chronological sequence of events, Sūranna plunges into the middle of the plot, and makes his characters relate the story. *Prabhāvati Pradyumna* opens with a beautiful description of Dwārka, seen in the haze and glow of the morning sun, from the *vimāna* or flying chariot of Indra high in the sky. Piṇgaḷi Sūranna's chief title to fame is that he made a great effort (consciously or unconsciously) to turn the flood-tide of kāvya into drama—not that he succeeded altogether, but he came very near success. He gave us two kāvyas, unique in Telugu literature, which combine the learning of Peddana and the dramatic interest of Kaḷidāsa and Bāṇa. It is interesting to note that this poet was a contemporary of Shakespeare, and his two plays recall to memory the two dramas of Shakespeare—*Kaḷāpūrnodaya*, the *Comedy of Errors*; and *Prabhāvati Pradyumna*, *Romeo and Juliet*.

Ramaraja Bhushana, as his name indicates, adorned the court of Rāmarāya. The son-in-law of Kṛishṇadevarāya, he seems to have served his apprenticeship under Peddana, and keenly followed the literary career of Piṇgaḷi Sūranna. By the time the poet started his literary life, *Manucharitra* was the praise of the *literati* of the day, and *Rāghava Pāṇḍavīya* was the talk of critics. This inspired him with an ambition to take the public by storm with a work which would eclipse the fame of Peddana and Sūranna. He concentrated in his work on the reproduction of the descriptive excellence of Peddana, and the slesha novelty introduced by Sūranna. In this the poet succeeded beyond all expectations and his *Vasucharitra* became the model for the poets who followed him. The rehabilitation of Piṅgaḷi Sūranna is the achievement of modern literary criticism. Tradition makes Rāmarāja Bhūshaṇa the hero of the kāvya stage, and in the opinion of many conservative critics, the pupil is regarded as having excelled his master.

For a prabandha, the theme must be a well-known Purāṇic story. It will be realised that in such a case the freedom of the poet is considerably restricted, as he has to adapt himself to the framework given to him, and his imagination can be exercised only within the limitations of the general outline of the story. This is obvious in the construction of *Manucharitra*. Rāmarāja Bhūshaṇa strained at the leash. He wanted greater freedom than the selection of a Purāṇic story would permit. The new-born urge for freedom demanded not only liberty of expression and latitude in treatment, but complete freedom to shape the subject-matter of the story as well. On the other hand, he was not prepared to go to the extent of Piṅgaḷi Sūranna in discarding the Purāṇic story altogether. His own conception of the kāvya is stated thus: 'Purely imaginary stories are an inferior type of precious stones; but borrowed themes make artificial diamonds. I should like to take a story neither famous nor purely imaginary; but one which is insignificant in itself, while permitting considerable scope for improvement, like a rough precious stone which shines when cut and polished.'

In pursuance of his own canon, the poet chose an insignificant episode from the *Bhāgavata Purāṇa* as the basis of his kāvya. The incident chosen is the marriage of Garika, the daughter of Sūktimatī (a river), and Kolāhāla (a mountain), with the King Vasu—rather a meagre plot. But Rāmarāja Bhūshaṇa handled the theme with infinite skill, making an ingenious use of slesha.

The supreme felicity with which he handles slesha, avoiding wooden artificiality on one side and sacrifice of sense for sound on the other, makes him a supreme artist of this school. But while he owns the same command of expression and felicity of phrase, his style lacks the simplicity of his illustrious colleague, Piṅgaḷi Sūranna.

The primary defect of *Vasucharitra*—a defect inherent in the kāvya type of literature, but more apparent in *Vasucharitra* than in *Manucharitra*—is the over-elaboration of the descriptive element, which smothers the movement of the story, in itself very thin. Descriptions, delightful in themselves, stand out of relation to the immediate demands of the narrative. As one critic justly observes, 'Peddana strings his pearls into a necklace and throws it round the neck of Saraśvatī, while Rāmarāja showers them loose and unstrung on her.'

Rāmarāja Bhūshaṇa had one advantage over his contemporaries. He was himself a great and accomplished musician. This accounts for the symphony and cadence of his verse. There is not only a unique wedding of sound to sense, but also a sweet atmosphere of harmony about his poem. His poetry is song set to music. *Vasucharitra* is a gem of art. Rāmarāja Bhūshaṇa composed also another kāvya known as *Harischandra Nalopākhyāna.* In it he tells simultaneously the adventures of Nala and the suffering of Harischandra, in verse capable of yielding both stories.

There is another book, *Narasabhūpālīya*, about whose authorship critical opinion is divided. Some are of opinion that this is the work of Rāmarāja Bhūshaṇa, while others attribute it to a poet called Bhaṭṭumūrti. Two facts are clear: (1) that Bhaṭṭumūrti wrote *Narasabhūpālīya,* and (2) that Rāmarāja Bhūshaṇa wrote *Harischandra Nalopākhyāna* and *Vasucharitra.* The question that has given rise to the controversy is, whether they are different poets, or different names of the same poet. Rāmarāja Bhūshaṇa is an honorific title, meaning the ornament of Rāmarāja's court; while Bhaṭṭumūrti is a natural name. Contemporary writers have regarded them as the name and title of the same person. Internal evidence tends to the same conclusion. But the genealogies given in the books slightly differ. This is not fatal to the theory of identity.

The suggestion that the author was given in adoption to another family accounts for the difference in genealogy. Sound critical opinion inclines in favour of Bhaṭṭumūrti and

Rāmarāja Bhūshaṇa being the same person. *Narasabhūpalīya* is a treatise on rhetoric in verse. It is a Telugu rendering of *Pratapārudrīya.*

Tenali Ramakrishna. An enigmatic figure of the time was Rāmakṛishṇa, who was attached to the court of Venkatapati Rāya, one of the Vijayanagar kings, who changed the capital of the empire to Chandragiri. Rāmaliṅga, as he was originally called, is said to have been a Śaivite by birth and wrote in his youth the *Liṅga Purāṇa.* However, he became a convert to Vaishṇavism, and changed his name to Rāmakṛishṇa. He is known to posterity, not so much as a poet, but as a court jester, whose practical jokes, witty sallies and resourceful pranks have been ever since the chief source of mirth in family circles all through the Āndhra country. He is generally regarded as a mediæval court jester, with a dash of the 'Charlie Chaplin' in him. He was the contemporary of Tātachāri and Appiah Dīkshit, protagonists of Vaishṇavism and Śaivism respectively. Rāmakṛishṇa was never so happy as when he made the life of the orthodox Tātachāri miserable with his practical jokes. The saving grace of humour often stood him in good stead, as it saved him from the wrath of his royal master, who was himself not infrequently the victim of his irrepressible humour.

As a poet he reveals altogether a new personality; serious, pious and devotional. His great work, *Pāṇḍuraṅga Mahātmya,* contains a legendary account of a shrine of Vishṇu as Pāṇḍuraṅga, at Pāṇḍharpur, consecrated by the ministration of Saint Pāṇḍarika. A Brahmin, Nigama Sarma, who wasted his life in dissipation and debauchery, breathed his last at Pāṇḍharpur. A controversy ensues between the servants of Yama and the servants of Vishṇu; the former were anxious to carry him to hell, as he lived a wicked life, and the latter claimed him for heaven, as he died in that sacred place. Of course, the verdict was in favour of the servants of Vishṇu. Rāmakṛishṇa's work is a kāvya of high merit, remarkable for its sonorous dignity of phrasing, and is justly counted as one of the *Pañcha Mahā Kāvyas* (the Five Great Kāvyas).

OTHER WRITERS

Minor poets belonging to the second half of the sixteenth century A.D., who deserve mention, are:

(1) and (2) Addaṁki Gangādhara, who wrote *Tapatīsamvaraṇa*; and Ponnikanti Telaganārya, author of *Yāyāti Charitra*, a pure Telugu work. Special interest attaches to these books, as they are the only kāvyas in Telugu literature dedicated to a Muhammadan ruler, Ibrahim Mulk, the fourth son of Kutumb Shah, one of the Bahmanī kings, who ruled over Golkonda between A.D. 1512 and 1543. On the death of his father, Ibrahim Mulk incurred the displeasure of his elder brother, and sought refuge under Kṛishṇadevarāya. He was very fond of Telugu literature and was a patron of the poets Gangādhara and Telaganārya, who were attached to his court.

(3) Sāruṅgu Timmanna, the Madhva poet, who wrote *Vaijayanti Vilāsa* or *Vipranārāyaṇa Charitra*, which is a story of a Vaishṇava *bhakta*, whom two sisters of the prostitute class, Madhuravāṇī and Devadevī, tried to seduce from his chastity and almost succeeded, when Vishṇu stretched forth his hand to save him. Chadalavāda Malliah, a descendant of Errāpragada, one of the Kavitraya, also put this story into verse in 1585.

(4) Turagā Rāmakavi earned the unenviable notoriety of being the master of vituperative verse, and was counted as one of the 'cursing poets,' whose maledictions were more effective than benedictions. He dedicated his work, *Nagara Khānda*, to a rich goldsmith named Mārkaṃḍeya.

(5) Tarigopulla Mallana, author of *Chandrabhānu Charitra* (1586–1614), was attached to the court of Venkatapati Rāya. The story is about the marriage of Chandrabhan, the son of Kṛishṇa, with Kumudinī, the daughter of Rukmabahu. The poet was a Madhva.

(6) Kamsāli Rudrakavi (A.D. 1620–), a goldsmith by caste, author of a high-class kāvya, *Nirankusopākhyāna*.

The period under survey presents kāvya literature at its best. In the hands of the Ashṭadiggajās, the classic exponents of this type, it became an indigenous movement of great originality. The kāvya literature could have given us (if its early promises had been redeemed) what Telugu literature very much lacks—a nature-school and a psychological school of poetry. It has, in fact, given to our poets a splendid opportunity for self-expression and for the display of individual ability. The kāvya stands for a vivid portrayal of men and nature, a profound study of character and emotion, and for artistic decoration and choice ornamentation. In technique, it marks an endeavour to extract from the Telugu language a new music. Symphony was its soul.

The defects of the kāvya literature are stamped on its face. It is artificial and ornate, with a complicated technique. If it is to be effective, it involves a delicate balance of its component parts, a just sense of proportion, and, above all, a capacity for restraint, which is rarely to be found in any but great masters. It is a complicated machine, so nicely balanced that none but experts can handle it. Piṅgaḷi Sūranna was correct when he diagnosed the condition of kāvya as 'suffering from creeping paralysis,' and pronounced that it could only be saved by an infusion of new life, in the shape of dramatic interest. Unfortunately, Sūranna had no followers.

VIII

THE PERIOD OF STAGNATION

A.D. 1630–1850

THE battle of Taḷikoṭa (1565) is as much a literary as an historical landmark in the life of the Āndhras. It marked the disintegration of the empire founded by Kṛishṇadevarāya, and 'the beginning of the end' of the literary movements inaugurated by him. The Kāvya movement outlived his political downfall for nearly half a century; as the poets, born and trained during the spacious days of the emperor-poet, continued to inspire the movement and maintain it on the same high level. But from the third decade of the seventeenth century, up to the beginning of the twentieth, it is one long night. During this period we find versifiers innumerable, but poets few; literary output enormous, but quality very poor. There is a thick growth of rank vegetation, but hardly a noble tree showing itself. It is an age of stagnation and deterioration. The single redeeming feature of the situation is the extension of the field of Telugu literature to the South. The new literary output came from Tanjore, Madura, Pudukkota and Mysore, and it was marked by distinguishing features of its own. As it stands in clear contrast to the main current, the Northern school, it has been designated as the Southern school.

The primary causes for the steady decline of the Northern school were:

1. **The Disintegration of the Empire of Vijayanagar** into petty pāḷayams under chieftains incompetent to direct any literary movement, since they themselves possessed very little culture or education. Petty patrons beget petty poetry. The poets consequently lack inspiration, vision, vital energy and true ambition.

2. **The Dictatorship of the Grammarian and Rhetorician.** The great poets of the Purāṇa Yuga were the creators of grammar and rhetoric. The poets of the kāvya age were superior to these secondary arts. It is otherwise with the writers of the seventeenth and eighteenth centuries. The kāvya poetry involved a poetic architecture so technical and complicated that the poet had to be apprenticed to the rhetorician in order to learn the new craft. The free spirit of poetry was harnessed by the rhetorician, and the literature suffered under the cramping influence of the 'regulative science.' This accounts for the lack of freedom and spontaneity and for the dull mediocrity of all poetic effort.

3. **The Inherent Vices of the Kavya Style.** The kāvya is the worst literary mode for imitation; and imitation was in the blood of the Telugu poets. The virtues of kāvya are hidden, and its weaknesses glitter on the surface. The imitator caught the latter and missed the former. In its technique, apparently (though not in reality) art was divorced from life. Kāvya emphasised description, and description in turn depended on simile and hyperbole (*upamāna utpreksha̅*). Simile requires an insight into nature and a gift of imagination, if it is to be original and striking; while hyperbole, to be pleasing, has to be handled with discretion and restraint. The great masters, while they seemed to be engrossed with the technique, really kept an eye on life. Their imitators did not catch this art. They lost touch with nature. They borrowed not only art but also life from the Ashṭadiggajās.[1] The result was that the range of ideas and the nature of ornamentation became stereotyped. The only avenue possible for individual distinction lay in extravagance and aberration. The similes became far-fetched, pointless and abstruse. Hyperbole degenerated into unmeasured exaggeration. One poet said that the turrets of the city seemed to kiss the sky. Another went a step further and imagined that they pierced the vault. Yet a third outstripped these, describing them as emerging in the court of Indra!

[1] See above, p. 72.

Ornamentation was another source of degradation. Nothing is so easy, yet nothing is such bad taste, as overdoing or parading ornamentation. Slesha, alliteration, chitra, kavitva,[1] if occasionally resorted to, add to the beauty and excite interest; but as the sole basis for a kāvya, they are in execrable taste.

The literature of this period, in consequence, moves in one dead level of mediocrity, and monotony is the dominant note. The endless procession of kāvyas, one resembling the other, tire the eye. The old Purāṇic stories are told and retold with prolixity and verbosity. Thought becomes stagnant and the same similes and ideas appear again and again in new garbs. But for the incomparable grace and melody of the language, the poet resembles the 'club bore,' who inflicts on his unhappy victim his favourite story for the hundredth time. The only features which attract our attention are the aberrations, which, strangely enough, meet with the approval of the critics.

The deviations from the norm may be classified under the following heads:

1. **Slesha Kavyas.** The author of *Vasucharitra*, by producing a Dvanda kāvya[2]—a novel type of literary effort—created false tastes and diverted poetic energy into new but unprofitable channels. *Vasucharitra* became the measure of learning and the test of poetic excellence. This gave rise to a crop of imitations, some possessing the merits of *Vasucharitra*, others managing to reproduce all its defects but none of its excellence. Abbanā Mātyā's *Kavi Rāja Manorañjana* (1780), Sūrakavi's *Kavi Jana Rañjana* (1780), Kṛishṇa Kavi's *Śakuntalā Pariṇaya* (1799), and Chāmakūra Venkata Kavi's *Vijaya Vilāsa*, though not slesha kāvyas, fall under the former category. Kūchimanchi Timmanna's *Rasika Janobhirāma*, Podūri Peda Rāmā Mātyā's *Śivarāmābhyudaya*, Sūryaprakāsa Kavi's *Kṛishṇārjuna Charitra* (1850) fall under the latter. The last two are Dvanda kāvyas.

Yet others, in an effort to excel, produced poems capable of telling *three* stories simultaneously. These poems attempt to tell the stories of Rāma and Kṛishṇa and the Pāṇḍavas, and combine the *Rāmāyaṇa*, the *Māhabhārata* and the *Bhāgavata*. Of these the following deserve mention.:

(1) Elakūchi Bālasaraśvatī, *Rāghava Yādava Pāṇḍavīya*.
(2) Nellūri Rāghavakavi, *Yādava Rāghava Pāṇḍavīya*.
(3) Ayyagāri Vīrabhadrakavi, *Rāghava Yādava Pāṇḍavīya*.
(4) Origanti Somasekhara Kavi, *Rāmakṛishṇārjuna Nārāyaṇīya*.

[1] See p. 89. [2] See p. 78.

This type of literature is not easy to write; it demands infinite resource, phenomenal command of language, and extraordinary ingenuity. But the very restrictions under which the author had to work forbade any poetic quality of a high order. Though looked upon at the time as high-class literature, it does not appeal to modern tastes.

2. **Pure Telugu Poetry.** There is in the modern Telugu language only a residuum of original Telugu. This Dravidian basis is so little that it is not adequate for the composition of even a few verses. If only Sanskrit equivalents are excluded and the rest regarded as pure Telugu, it may be possible, with some difficulty, to compose an all-Telugu kāvya. Poets of the first period, as a curiosity, used to introduce an occasional stanza or two containing pure Telugu words—a feat much appreciated by the readers.

Ponnikanti Telaganārya (1578) made an attempt at opening a new field, by composing his *Yāyāti Charitra*, a kāvya of five cantos, in pure Telugu, avoiding Sanskritisms as far as possible. Curiously enough, he was able to produce a very readable book of considerable merit. Others followed, but not with the same amount of success. Adidamu Bala Bhāskara's *Rāmāyaṇa* (not now available), Kūchimanchi Timmanna's *Rāmāyaṇa* and *Nīlasundarā Pariṇaya* belong to this order.

These works are more or less of the nature of a *tour de force*. The language, involving tiresome circumlocution, is unintelligible even to the pandit. They are like letters written in cypher, unmeaning without a key. In Tamil and in English, the desire to exclude foreign words came in the wake of a purist tendency and was partly the outcome of genuine patriotism. It was not so in Telugu. These writings owe their origin to a frantic effort, on the part of the poet, to hold the flickering attention of his audience by doing something out of the way. These laborious products of misplaced zeal, never read (in fact, not even readable), may be consigned to the literary museum as momentoes of an antiquarian age.

3. **Chitra and Bhanda Kavitva.** Slesha kāvyas and 'Acchā Telugu' works may be considered as literature, though not of a high order. The same cannot be said of developments in other directions, euphemistically called 'fancy poetry,' but really a type of freak literature.

Some poets have composed kāvyas excluding labials. Kottalanka Mrutyumjaya Kavi's *Nala Charitra* and Mariṁganti Siṁgarāchārlu's *Daśaratha Rāja Nandana Charitra* are instances. Others attempted fantastic combinations and produced pure Telugu, non-labial and 'all-verse' kāvyas. Poets are not wanting who carried their self-denial further still and eschewed gutturals along with labials. Extremists of this school discarded the first twenty letters of the alphabet and used only the *apañchavargīya*, i.e., the last five letters. Kāṇāda Peddana Somayājī perpetuated this monstrosity in his *Sesha Śailesā Līla*. The climax of this form of lunacy was reached when stanzas were written in a single letter. Gaṇapavarapu Venkatakavi and Gudāru Venkatadāsakavi are said to have scaled the heights of perfection in this art.

Another variety of chitra kavitva is known as *Garbha* and *Bhanda Kavitvā*. The former involves introduction of stanzas of one metre within another of a different type ; the latter consists in fitting short poems into geometrical figures—such as serpents and chariots.

It is difficult to appreciate the tastes of an age that applauded these tongue-twisters and tumblers as poets of merit.

PROMINENT POETS

Seventeenth Century Poets. We have already mentioned some of these in connection with slesha and chitra kavitva. Very few poets of merit are found between A.D. 1630 and 1700. Elakūchi Bālasaraśvatī, a learned scholar who obtained the title of Mahāmahopadhāya, composed a drama called *Raṅga-Kaumudi*. Hari Bhaṭ, about the middle of the seventeenth century, wrote *Varāha* and *Matsya* Purāṇas ; Kākamāni Mūrti, often confounded with Bhaṭṭumūrti, is regarded as combining in his style the excellences of Peddana, Timmana and Rāmakṛishṇa. He was the author of *Pāñchāli Pariṇaya*, *Rāja Vāhanavijaya* and *Bahuḷāsva Charitra*. Nūtanakavi Sūranna, towards the close of the century, wrote *Dhanābhi Rāmamu* and a drama, *Vishṇu Māya Vilāsa*. *Dhanābhi Rāmamu* embodies the beautiful story of a contest between Manmadha, god of beauty, and Kubhera, god of wealth, as to which of these commands the hearts of men.

Eighteenth Century Poets. Paidimarri Venkatapati opens the century with *Chandraṅgada Charitra*. Kūchimanchi Timmanna, known as Abhinava Vāgānuśasana, wrote many kāvyas, of which *Rukmaṇī Pariṇaya*, *Rājasekhara Vilāsa*, *Baḷḷaṇa Charitra* may be mentioned.

Vakkalanda Vīrabhadranna, who adapted two stories from Sanskrit writers, *Vāsavadatta Pariṇaya* and *Gourī Kalyaṇa* is mentioned with evident appreciation and respect by contemporary writers. One satirist, Kūchimanchi Jaggakavi, and two Christian poets,[1] Mangaḷagiri Ānandakavi, author of *Vedānta Rasāyana*, and Pingaḷi Eḷḷanaryundu, who wrote *Tobhya Charitra*, flourished about the same time. The first half of the century closes with Ĕnugu Lakshmaṇakavi, who wrote *Rāma Vilasa* and translated into Telugu *Subhāshita Ratnāvaḷi*.

In the second half of the century, Adidamu Sūrakavi (1780), author of *Kavi Jana Rañjana*, popularly known as *Pilla Vasucharitra* ; Kanuparti Abbanāmātya, author of *Anuruddha Charitra* and *Kavi Raja Manorañjana*, generally regarded as the best book after *Vasucharitra* ; and Dittakavi Nārāyaṇa, who celebrated in verse the Bobbili war between the Rāja of Vijayanagar and the French in Northern Circars in 1756, are conspicuous.

Nineteenth Century Poets. Besides those already referred to, the following may be mentioned :

1. Pindiproli Lakshmaṇakavi, author of *Rāvaṇa Dommīyamu*, or *Laṅkā Vijaya*, (1840–).

[1] See below, pp. 105 ff.

2. Shistu Kṛishṇamūrti, a scholar of considerable learning in Sanskrit, also a musician of considerable ability. He was good at extempore composition and was exceedingly popular as a reader of Purāṇas. He wrote *Sarva Kāmadā Pariṇaya* and many other works.

3. Māda Bhāshi Venkatācharlu was an intellectual prodigy. It is said that he could repeat anything that was read to him twice, upside down. He composed *Bhāratābhyudaya.*

4. Gopīnātha Venkatakavi (1850) was the author of a translation of *Vālmīki Rāmāyaṇa, Śiśupala Vadha* and *Bhāghavatgītā.*

5. Sonṭi Bhadradri Rāmaśāstri (1860) composed *Chitra Sīma*, an original production in verse on the lines of Piṅgaḷi Sūranna's *Kaḷāpūrnodaya*, a commentary to *Ahobalīyā* and *Śrirāma Śataka.*

THE SOUTHERN SCHOOL

Kṛishṇadevarāya appointed deputies for each of the southern countries he had conquered. On the fall of the empire of Vijayanagar, they became independent rulers of the countries under their control. The task of consolidation took a good part of the century. Their political position secured, they were able to turn their attention to the peaceful arts of literature. It is fortunate that the viceroys appointed by Kṛishṇadevarāya were, like himself, imbued with a taste for literature, and their descendants turned out to be great patrons of art, zealous of their mother-tongue and anxious to conserve Āndhra culture for the colonists. The Southern school was born in a praiseworthy effort to transplant the home culture into the country of their adoption. The literature of the South belongs, partly, to the seventeenth and mostly to the eighteenth centuries A.D. The contributions came from Tanjore, Madura, Puddukota and Mysore.

1. **Tanjore.** Chavva Rāju was the chief appointed for Tanjore by Kṛishṇadevarāya. His son, Achyuta Nāyak, had for his minister Govinda Dīkshit, a Telugu pandit of great learning. It was in the court of Raghunātha (1630–40), son of Achyuta, that the first-fruits of the new harvest were gathered. The king himself composed a prose kāvya, *Valmīki Charitra.* Chāmakūra Venkatakavi, who was attached to the court, gave to the world *Sārangadhara* and *Vijaya Vilāsa.* The former of these two is admired for the vivid, tragic interest of the theme and the impressive

realism of the art; the latter is, perhaps, the last work of real merit in Telugu literature. It has been described as a heap of precious gems. The polish of the language, the delicacy of sentiment, and the melody of verse combine in this poet as in no other. His style is so uniquely his own that a new name had to be coined to express its quality and it was called after his surname, 'Chāmakūrapāka'—Chāmakūra being also the succulent Indian curry. It is probable, though not certain, that Kavi Choudappah—a moralist who stands next to Vemana and Sumati, among Śataka writers—belonged to this period.

Later, Muddupaḷaṇi, a courtesan of Pratāpa Sinha, of Tanjore (1765), composed in Telugu a kāvya under the name *Rādhikā Svantam*. Kasturi Raṅga Kavi dedicated his *Raṅgara Chandamu* to Ananda Raṅgapillai. But the greatest gift of Tanjore to the Āndhra literature is Tyāgarāja, the hymnologist and musician whose songs are sung all over South India.

2. **Madura.** But it is in the eighteenth century and in the court of Vijaya Raṅga Chokkanātha, the king of Madura, a descendant of Nigama Nāyak, appointed by Kṛishṇadevarāya, that we find the Southern school in full bloom. Viśvanātha Nāyak, father of Chokkanātha, is said to have brought many learned pandits from the north, and gave them gifts of land, thus inducing them to settle in the south. The fruits of Viśvanātha's foresight were reaped by his son, Chokkanātha, who set a good example by rendering into prose *Śrīraṅga Mahātya*. Of the group of poets whose literary output not only constitutes the bulk of Southern Telugu literature but also gives the tone to the movement, Samukha Venkata Kṛishṇappa Nāyak has to his credit not less than four books, of which *Jaimini Bhārata*, in prose, may be taken as an example of the high level of literary value attained by the Southern school. *Ahalyā Samkraṇdana*, *Sārangadhara Charitra* and *Rādhikā Svantam* are his other kāvyas. They belong, every one of them, to the erotic type. Sesham Venkatapati's *Tarāśasaṅka* belongs to the same order. The other works of the period are of a religious type. Syāmakavi is the author of *Rāmāyaṇa* in Vachana, Tupākula Ananta Rāju composed *Vishṇu*

Purāṇa and *Bhāgavatgītā*. Sumati Rāmabhadra Kavi wrote *Hālāsyā Mahātya* and Velagapūdi Kṛishṇa Kavi, *Vedānta Sāra*.

3. **Puddukota.** Puddukota's contribution under Rāja Rāghava Tondamān (1767–89) takes the shape of dictionaries and anthologies among other things, of which Nudurupati Venkatanāryudu's *Āndhra Bhāshārṇava* deserves mention. His son is responsible *for Bilhaṇīya.*

4. **Mysore.** Vīrarāju (1650–1700), whose *Bhārata* is perhaps the earliest extant instance of a prose kāvya, and Nanja Rāju, a minister of the Mysore king, author of *Liṅga Purāṇa* and *Hālāsya Mahātya*, represent the contribution from Mysore.

A bare description of the literature of the period throws into prominence some characteristic features of this school.

1. The chief merit of the Southern school is *the discovery of prose.* During the Purāṇic period we find Nanniah, the first of the Kavitraya, using prose which is simple and clear; but Tikkanna seemed to have scorned any resort to prose in his *Nirvachanottara Rāmāyaṇa*, an example which had some following. Prose is used as a literary device by the classic writers, partly as a 'pause,' to relieve the strain of composition, and partly to traverse portions of the story more rapidly with a view to economy. Writers who follow the Kavitraya, especially Nāchana Soma, and Potana, the author of a *Bhāgavata*, employ a prose style which is afflicted with all the infirmities of poetic composition—complexity, over-ornamentation, slesha and yamaka.

The unique distinction of the Southern school is that it has realised that prose is as valuable and as useful a medium of literary expression as verse. The extensive use of prose was to a large extent dictated by the necessities of the case. The third and fourth generation of Telugus in a Tamil country are not likely to have possessed sufficient education to understand the prabandha or even epic poetry. If, then, culture was to be retained at all, it had to be conveyed through a medium not altogether beyond the comprehension of the average educated man. Prose was obviously such a medium. Nevertheless, the high artistic value and the relatively important place assigned to prose by the writers themselves, show that they understood its function and possibilities. *Jaimini Bhārata* is a work of art, regarded by its author himself as of equal importance with *Sārangadhara*.

2. Secondly, *the deliberate and decidedly more extensive use of the drama* is another feature of the Southern school. During the first three centuries the Northern school did not produce more than two dramas of any importance, and even these do not occupy a noticeable position in the literature of the times. But, according to a recent writer, the dramas of the Southern school, during the eighteenth century alone, exceed twenty in number. Doubtless none of them were of any acknowledged literary value. But that is also the case with the Northern school. Here again the use of the drama may have been adopted in order to bring the Āndhra culture to those who had not even the capacity to understand prose. In any case, in one century, the Southern school produced more dramas than the Northern school in the course of eight centuries of its existence.

3. The most arresting feature of the Southern school is *the absencc of ethical principles.* To whatever causes we may attribute it, the fact is undeniable that the Southern school is essentially immoral. This is brought out by the examination of a characteristic feature of the literature of this period. Excluding directly religious topics, there is hardly a poet, whether of the Northern or Southern school, who did not write a kāvya dealing with the marriage of the heroes of the Purāṇas. We may say that ninety per cent. of the books deal with Pariṇaya, Kalyāṇa or Vivāha. This preoccupation with the question of marriage is the central fact of interest. The mystery of sexual attraction has always been the theme of the poet and the painter. But the way in which they deal with it is indicative of the culture of the age. The poets of the Purāṇa Yuga deal with it with delicacy, reverence, and a sense of its spiritual significance. The hero wins his bride either in a contest of valour or on the battlefield. He seals his faith in the nobility of womanhood by risking his life. The writers of the kāvya period fall far below the ideal. By stressing 'Ṣṛingāra Rāsa,' they have impaired the subtle aroma of

social relations. Physical attractions are described with an elaborate minuteness and a wealth of detail repulsive to delicate feeling. Even the loves of gods, forbidden to the poets by the writers on poetics, are not immune from their prying attentions.

The Northern school, even in its wildest excesses, never departs from the conventions of life. The sexual attraction finds its legitimate consummation in marriage, though marriage is regarded as the end rather than the beginning of all romance.

But the Southern school stands in painful and humiliating contrast to the Northern in this matter. The poets do not so much deal with marriage as with the violation of chastity. Their treatment of the problem recalls to the mind the unconventional modern schools of Shaw and Ibsen; only they lack the earnestness of purpose or coherent philosophy of the modern schools; and they are prurient, often putrid. These poets preach immorality as a creed, in kāvya and drama, in prose and poetry, in song and story. The prominent works of this period are *Sārangadhara*, *Tārāśaśaṅka*, *Bilhaṇīya* and *Rādhikā Svānta*. The story in the first comes very near the tragedy of incest. Rāja-Rāja-Narendra takes for his wife, in his old age, one who cherishes in her heart a love for his son. Her advances are rejected by Sārangadhara. She, in turn, trumps up a false charge against him and throws him to the wolves. *Tārāśaśaṅka* is the story of Chandra's elopement with his guru's wife. *Bilhaṇīya*, a story which counts more than five authors, relates to the same theme in another aspect. King Madanabhirāma appoints Bilhaṇa to teach his daughter, Yaminī Pūrṇa Tilaka. The teacher is beautiful and the daughter young, and to prevent complication he tells his daughter that the teacher is born blind and informs the teacher that his pupil is a leper. A curtain separates the teacher from the pupil. But, one day Bilhaṇa describes the rising moon and gives away the show. The result is not marriage but free love. It is the same with the literary stories of the period. *Śuka Saptati* and *Haṁsaviṁśati* relate the artful way in which society women violated their marital vows.

It is easy to dismiss the whole outlook as immoral putrifaction. But when we set the Southern against the Northern school, it is difficult to escape the conviction that some social upheaval has thrown into relief the problem of sexual relations, which the Northern school deals in a conventional, and the Southern in an unconventional, way. As we read we are led to ask 'Is it pruriency or philosophy?' or, 'Is the problem of the "eternal triangle" not quite so modern as we sometimes suppose?'

IX

POPULAR LITERATURE

THE impulse for the translation of Sanskrit epics and Purāṇas, with which Telugu literature begins, had its roots in a religious movement to spread the Aryan culture among the people. This was achieved to a very limited extent only, because the tone and style of Champu Kāvya was beyond the comprehension of the masses, even when read to them. So it remained essentially the literature of the educated. With the growth of time, the divergence between the literary and popular language became very marked. Literature became the exclusive possession of a select few, of considerable learning. The poet ceased to write even for the educated, but only for the pandit. The problem of bringing to the average man the heritage of the past was, however, not left unsolved. The desideratum of a popular literature, in a country where the generality of society is illiterate, is a simplicity of style and substance, an appealing rhythm, an easy swing of movement, which renders what is heard easily memorized. The new literary vehicles for the dissemination of knowledge among the people were found in Dvipada and Śataka. Dvipada means two feet, i.e., a couplet; śataka means a hundred, that is a cento of verses. Though primarily literary forms, they have by association come to signify a type of literature intended for popular use, different and distinguishable from the epic and the kāvya. When released from the necessity of translating from Sanskrit, the Telugu poet naturally turned to these two modes as most suitable to his native genius, and best adopted for self-expression.

Dvipada Literature. Nanniah employed a metre called *taruvōja*, which consisted of two easily separable halves, balanced by a central pause. We may say that the lines almost invite the reader to bisect them. If we do so and arrange the two halves one below the other, we get something like dvipada. It is necessary to observe both *Yati* and *Prasa*[1] for dvipada. In flexibility and simplicity it resembles the *anushtupa* metre in Sanskrit.

The three great epics have been put into dvipada:

Valmīki Rāmāyaṇa, by Buddha Rāzu.

Rāmāyaṇa, by Raṅganātha.

Uttara Rāmāyaṇa, by Kāchavibhudu and Vittal Rāju.

Bhārata, by Timmakavi.

Bhāgavata, by Kōnēru Kavi.

Śrīnātha's *Palnāti Vīra Charitra* is in this metre. Pālakuriki Somanātha and Madiki Siṁganna are among other writers in this field.

Sataka Literature. From about the twelfth century onwards, we have a broadening stream of śatakas, forming a parallel movement to the kāvya literature. It is estimated that there are about six hundred śatakas so far recovered. Of these only a few are translations or adaptations; the rest are original.

There are some śatakas in Telugu in which the hundred verses are divided into ten groups of ten verses each called *daśakas*. This daśaka division was probably adopted from Prākṛit. However, the standard form consists of a hundred self-complete stanzas. The characteristic feature of the śataka is the *makuta*, or crown, that is, the last word of the stanza, which consists of the name of the person or the deity to whom the preceding lines are addressed. This makuta determines the metre to be employed and thus shapes the structure of the verse.

The themes of the śataka are either outpourings of devotion or the teaching of moral truths; occasionally, humorous reflections on current events and contemporary personalities. Of the six hundred śatakas, more then three-fourths relate to religious and moral teachings. Śaivites and Vaishṇavites have resorted to the śataka, both for propagandistic and devotional purposes. Almost all the great writers have one

[1] See p. 40.

or two śatakas associated with their names. Śataka literature had its beginning in the twelfth century, its zenith in the seventeenth, its widest range in the eighteenth and nineteenth centuries. The earliest śataka we have is *Vṛishādipa Śataka*, by Pālakuriki Somanātha, in 1180. Of almost the same status is *Sumati Śataka*, whose authorship is not certain, though it is generally attributed to Peddana.

Vemana is the prince of śataka writers. Vemana was an Advaitic mystic, a *sannyāsī* who has renounced the world. His birthplace is uncertain, though claims have been made for Kondavīdu, in the Ceded Districts, and Kāturu, a village where his tomb exists; nor can we fix his date, even approximately. Various suggestions have been made, but none on convincing grounds. It is probable that he lived in the beginning of the fifteenth century. He is the greatest moral teacher of the Āndhras. For well-nigh five centuries his *Śataka* has been the text-book of morals for Telugu boys, and a better book cannot be asked for. The *Vemana Śataka* is of a very high literary order. Each stanza is a casket containing a simple moral truth. The idea is never carried beyond a single stanza. The first two lines contain the picture, the next two state the moral. The order is sometimes reversed. Every truth is incarnated in a suitable figure, so apt and just that the mind finds it difficult to separate them. The verses are easily memorized and the rhythm lingers in the memory without effort. The *Śataka* embodies much practical wisdom, shrewd judgment, and kindly advice. It is interesting to note that one verse is a fairly literal translation of Matt. 5: 43–44[1] and Luke 6: 33–35, and a third one embodies the Pauline injunction in Rom. 12: 20, 'If thine enemy hungers, feed him.'

Of devotional śatakas, *Sarveśvara Śataka*, by Yadhā Vākkula Annayya; *Kalahasteśvara Śataka*, by Dhūrjati; *Dāsarathi Śataka*, by Kancherla Gopanna, the celebrated Rāma Bhakta of Bhadrachellam and a disciple

[1] Matt. 5: 43-44, 'Ye have heard that it hath been said, Thou shalt love thy neighbour, and hate thy enemy. But I say unto you, Love your enemies; bless them that curse you; do good to them that hate you.'

of Kabir; and *Kavi Choudappa Śataka* are among the most popular.

Allied to dvipada and śataka is *daṇḍaka*, (rhapsody of praise), consisting of alliterative phrases permitting a rapid and impetuous outflow with a short prayer at the end. Composed in a single gaṇa, the daṇḍakas are half-sung, half-recited. Not infrequently, the daṇḍakas relate to the majesty, power, and justice of the deity. Wonder, fear, and horror are the sentiments expressed.

Sacred and Secular Music. In India, music is the handmaid of worship. Praises are sung, prayers are intoned, *bhajans* always performed to the accompaniment of musical instruments. Thus it happens that a considerable portion of popular devotional literature is intended to be sung, and is called *geyamulu.* This is not subject to the restraint of prosody, though it keeps to a rough measure. *Kīrtans, kṛitīs, harikathas* belong to this order.

The kīrtans of Tyāgarāja are of the highest spirituality. They breathe a spirit of fervid devotion, simple faith and reliance on Providence. Women, too, have contributed to this literature. *Melukolupulu*, Songs of the Dawn; *Mangaḷahratulu*, Songs of Festivity; *Lālipātalu*, Songs of the Cradle—all contain much true poetry.

There are in Telugu what are called *Jāvaḷis* (Songs of Love) which are looked down upon, as they are sung by public women. But, prejudice apart, the jāvaḷis merit being ranked as high-class poetry. Nowhere, in the whole region of Telugu literature, do we come across the secret longing of love so beautifully expressed. The kāvya writers have debased Śṛingāra Rāsa by identifying it with the cruder erotic sentiment of physical attraction. In the jāvaḷis the same theme has received a more subtle, refined and delicate treatment. Here we find the aroma of longing, the alternate elation and dejection of lovers, set to soft music touched with pathos of a type now made familiar to the western reader in Tagore's *Gardener*.

Prose. We have already seen that, in the South, prose has been extensively used as a medium of popular education. Another use for prose is found in devotional literature in the shape of *vinnapamulu*, or petitions, which resemble the prayers in the Prayer Book of the Church of England. Some of them rise to a high level of thought and diction.

It is much to be regretted that this popular literature has not received the attention it merits. Orthodox critics look down upon it as literature of an inferior class. This judgment will not be endorsed by the modern student. Most of it exists in the form of oral literature, not yet reduced to print. When the industry of the research scholar makes it available for the critic to sift and winnow, it will be found that this literature, scorned by the pandit, looked down upon by the learned, is the true heritage of the Āndhras—their characteristic contribution to the commonwealth of letters—their true *Gītānjali*.

X

WOMEN POETS

It is a pleasing reflection that there is no sex disqualification in the republic of letters. In the Telugu country, as elsewhere, Saraśvatī is justified of her daughters. The condition of society, the prejudices of the age, and the customs of the country, no doubt made it difficult for women to obtain the recognition they merited. Nevertheless, Telugu literature has its women poets..

The influence of women on literature is greater than the number of women poets would lead us to expect. They were patrons of letters when in power, as in the case of Rudramma, the Kākatīya queen. In the humbler rôle of silent sympathisers and gentle critics, their kindly help has always been with us. Many a poet has found hope and encouragement in the knowledge that, invisible to the eye, somewhere behind the *purdah*, are ears straining to hear his poems. Tradition has handed down many memories of cultured women whose help has been the inspiration of our poets.

There is a story of the Āndhra king, Śatavāhana, who was asked by his wife in Sanskrit not to splash water on her while they were engaged in water sports. The king, ignorant of Sanskrit, understood the word *modaka* to mean sweetmeats. His ignorance raised a laugh against him. Stung by the reproach, he set himself to study and in due time became the author of *Bṛihat Kathā Mañjari.* The impression of high culture in the royal household finds confirmation in the conditions prevailing in Kṛishṇadevarāya's zenana.

Then, there is the well-known incident of Potana. While engaged in composing the *Bhāgavata*, one day, he could not get the right line to finish a verse, try as he would. He left the manuscript with his daughter and went out, in the hope that inspiration might come in the open fields. He found, on his return, much to his surprise, the line correctly filled up. There is no need to invent a superfluous miracle, as tradition has done, when we can easily see the timely helper in his daughter.

Equally suggestive is the story of Pinavīranna and his *Jaimini Bhārata.*[1] There, again, we can easily guess that Saraśvatī was not the goddess, but a lady friend of the poet, to whom we owe the *Bhārata*, which we place to the credit of Pinavīranna.

Of the women poets handed down to us by tradition, we may mention the following:

1. Kuppamma, the daughter of Nārāyaṇa Bhaṭ, the friend and helper of Nanniah in his Vaidikī Movement, is said to have been a poetess of merit.

2. Of the same name is the daughter of Budda Rāzu, (1230–40), collaborator with Raṅganātha of *Dvipada Rāmāyaṇa*, who is said to have composed stanzas of touching pathos about her own sorrows as a young widow—which were incorporated by Ayyalarāju Rāmabhadriah in his *Sakala Kathā Sāra Saṅgraha* in the context of Damayantī's sorrow when parted from her husband.

3. Kummari Molla (1509–30), a potter-woman, is the author of the *Molla Rāmāyaṇa*, which has taken its place among the standard works of our literature; indeed, of all the *Rāmāyaṇas*, Molla's is the most widely read and popular. The general high level of her composition, as a whole, entitles her to be ranked with our best poets.

4. Mohanāṅgi, the daughter of Kṛishṇadevarāya, is the author of a Śṛingāra Prabandha, called *Marīchi Pariṇaya*, which she submitted in the full court to the criticism of the poets, who declared it to be a kāvya of merit. Though the book is not now extant, its existence is well attested. That she was passionately fond of good poetry, and that she was a keen judge of merit, is illustrated by the story of her purchase of a verse sold by the indigent poet,

[1] See above p. 67.

Sankuśala Nṛisiṁhakavi,[1] whom she was instrumental in introducing to her father.

5. Muddupaḷaṇi (1765–), a courtesan attached to the court of Pratāpasinha, of Tanjore, composed in flowing, felicitous rhymes a kāvya, *Rādhikā Svantam*, also known as *Eḷadevīya*. This work, like others of the Southern school, is marred by bad taste and utter lack of decency.

6. Tarikonda Venkamma (1839–) composed many kāvyas, of which *Bhāgavata* in dvipada, *Rāja Yogasāra* and *Venkatāchala Mahātya* are important. Her poems, full of elevated sentiments, are an eloquent protest against the debased literary tastes of the day.

7. Subhadramma (1781–) wrote some śatakas and daṇḍakas, of which *Kesava Śataka* and *Kṛishṇa Śataka* may be mentioned.

8. We find another group of women poets in the nineteenth century:

Bandi Bapamma (1850–), wrote *Mīnākshī Śataka.*

Ratnāmba (1870 ?–), wrote *Venkataramaṇa Śataka.*

Chelikāni Chellāyama (1900–), wrote *Pārthasārathī Śataka, Jānakī Sataka.*

[1] See above, p. 76.

XI

CHRISTIAN AND MUHAMMADAN POETS

Christian Poets

We have two poets, belonging to the seventeenth and eighteenth centuries A.D., respectively, who have written kāvyas on Christian subjects—Piṇgaḷi Erranārya, and Mangaḷagiri Ānandakavi. Both of them were Brahmins—the former attached to a Reddy family, and the latter to a Brahmin family of affluence. Though it is doubtful whether they were formal members of the Christian Church, it is probable that they were followers of Christ from within the Hindu community.

Piṇgaḷi Ellanaryudu (1602) is the author of *Tobhya Charitra*, otherwise known as *Sarveśvara Mahātya.* He informs the reader that through the grace of his guru, Sarabha Nāradhya, he learned the eightfold composition. In an introductory stanza he mentions the important Śaivite saints and poets to whom he offers the customary praises. The book was written at the instance of Thumma Rāyapa Reddi, a petty prince of Baktavāda, in Kondavīdu. In the prologue further details are given as to the circumstances under which he composed the kāvya. Obala Reddi, father of Kondā Reddi, received orally from his āchārya, Sanjivanādha Swāmi, an account of the life of Saint Thomas, which was subsequently reduced to writing. This appears to be the basis for the poet's kāvya.

Mangaḷagiri Ānandakavi (1750). About the middle of the eighteenth century, this poet wrote *Vedānta Rasāyana* and *Anuruddha Charitra.* *Vedānta Rasāyana* is a kāvya in four cantos dedicated to Nidimāmiḷḷa Dāsayāmātya, a member of an influential family which has adopted the

Christian faith. K. Vīresalingam judges the poet to be a writer of very high eminence, worthy to be placed among the best poets of his century.

The author approaches the subject in a devotional frame of mind and gives a clear and succinct account of the life of Christ. The teachings of Jesus are not much referred to. Of the miracles, a few prominent ones are chosen—the raising of Lazarus, the cure of the blind. The Nativity stories and the events of Passion Week are narrated in detail. In the prelude, there is a disquisition on the attributes of God and in the epilogue a discourse on the means of grace. The author shows intimate acquaintance with the scriptures and the rites of the Christian Church. The kāvya is remarkable as the solitary instance in which a Hindu bhakta, saturated with the thought-forms of his own country, has reverently undertaken to proclaim the life of Christ to the world.

The nature of the theme and the necessity of conveying a correct impression of the life of the foreign Guru brings out the best in the author. In handling thought-forms evidently not familiar to the Hindu mind, he shows considerable ability. For example, the phrase 'The lamb that taketh away the sin' is translated without the figure, as *Kalmasha Paritrāṇa* (Remover of Sins). Throughout, we come across touches of fervent Eastern imagination. 'The Holy One,' he says, 'yielding up his spirit, let fall the head on his breast, as the friend of the lotus drops behind the hill of the evening.' In one respect the book stands out as a class apart. The language is chaste and the imagery chastened. The exuberance of fancy, excess of alliteration and complexity of structure, characteristic of kāvya, are all rigorously excluded. We feel in this book the earnestness of the bhakta approaching a subject too precious to indulge in the arts of mere rhetoric.

The recent contributions to Christian literature include the lyrics used in the church—the prominent writer being Choudary Purushottam; and the devotional works of Rāja Bhujanga Rao, whose versification of the New Testament is perhaps the first attempt to present the scriptures of the Christians in a simple, appealing Telugu style.

Muhammadan Poets.

As pointed out,[1] there have been one or two Muhammadan rulers who were patrons of Telugu literature. But, curiously enough, there were no Muhammadan writers till modern times. Among contemporary writers, Ummar Āli Shah is a solitary instance of the Muhammadan poet. One, Gaṅganapalli Hussain, a Muhammadan Vedantist, is the author of *Hussain Dāsu Śataka* and *Kumati Śataka.*

[1] See above p 84

XII

THE MODERN PERIOD (1850-1925)

THE advent of the British brought the Āndhra culture into contact with the vitalizing influences of Western literatures and arts. The intelligentsia acquired a knowledge of English literature. Under its influence, literary tastes are changing, and literary ideals undergoing radical transformations. New ideals challenge attention and evoke enthusiasm; new watchwords are springing up. On one side, love for the vernaculars is being intensified; on the other side, there is a growing, almost a petulant, impatience with the old forms and ideals. The mutual interpretation of the two cultures has hardly begun. How the genius of the race is going to react remains to be seen. A new power has entered our literary life, and it is too early to forecast the possibilities of this conjunction. Meanwhile the air is thick with revolutionary creeds, anarchic tendencies, reactionary obscurantism. The twentieth century is vibrant with literary activity. It is only possible to note a few of the striking features. Broadly speaking, the activities fall under three heads: (1) Critical. (2) Creative. (3) Traditional.

Under the first head fall (*a*) literary controversies, (*b*) literary research, (*c*) literary criticism. Under the second, we have the drama, the novel, new prose, new poetry, short stories, the literature of knowledge, literary magazines, etc. Under the third head are grouped the activities which carry forward the traditional literature and use traditional methods. It is not possible, even if it were advisable, to refer to contemporary writers in detail. We propose to restrict ourselves to general tendencies and movements, referring to prominent writers only by way of illustration.

CRITICAL ACTIVITIES

Literary Controversies. One controversy, which has led to an acrimonious battle of words, relates to the rival claims of the literary (grāndika) and colloquial (grāmya) types of Telugu languages. In Telugu, unlike English, the language of literature is separated by a wide (and widening) gulf from the colloquial. Zealous reformers, anxious to make literature the living language of the people, are advocating that the 'pandit language,' with its complicated grammar, stilted style, tawdry ornamentation, and fantastic restraints of slesha and yamaka, shall be replaced by a simpler and more graceful medium. There are extremists on both sides; 'Pharisees' who regard common language as untouchable, and 'Philistines' who would sacrifice all beauty for utility. Between these extremes there is a growing consensus of opinion that it is possible to have a literary medium which is grammatical without being pedantic, and simple without being vulgar or crude.

2. Another controversy relates to the nature and function of literature. Four centuries of devotion to the kāvya type has created an impasse. With the traditional school, language and technique are everything, ideas and inspiration are nothing. The pendulum has now swung to the other side. One school, in its devotion to life, would exclude art from literature. Another school insists that everything Indian should be discarded and everything English should be admired. They have no eye for the genius of their own language. They are anarchists who desire to break down all traditional restrictions. They willingly exchange old lamps for new; priceless tapestries and jewels for the glittering glass of the foreign market. These attempts have produced the most grotesque hybrid patchwork, which has neither the beauty of Telugu nor the vitality of English. A hopeful feature of the situation is the growing number of radical reformers who realise that the mechanical adjustments of cultures will only result in incongruous medley, and consequently stand for a living fusion of culture in the realm of the spirit.

Literary Research. A few of the many lines of activity pursued by research scholars may be here indicated.

1. *The Recovery of Lost Literature.* Mānavalli Rāmakṛishṇiah has scoured the country with a view to ascertain whether there was any pre-Sanskrit Telugu literature before Nanniah. He has collected a considerable number of hitherto unpublished manuscripts, which, whether they prove the existence of pre-Nanniah literature or not, are a valuable addition to the existing stock of books. His discovery and publication of Nannechodu's *Kumāra Sambhava* is a literary event of capital importance. The Āndhra Sāhitya Parishad has for its credit the recovery of many hundreds of volumes belonging to the Southern school of Telugu literature. The Government Oriental Library represents the work done by the State in this connection. The valuable collections by Dr. Brown and Col. Mackenzie deserve grateful recognition.

2. *The Consolidation of the Results of Research.* This has been done by working the raw materials supplied by various departments of research into a coherent whole in the shape of histories of literature and lives of poets. Mr. K. Vīresalingam's *Lives of Telugu Poets* (*Āndhra Kavula Charitra*) is a standard work of reference. It is a monument of patient research and sound scholarship. *Biographies of Telugu Poets* (*Kavijīvitamulu*), by Guruzāda Śrīrāmamurti, though less reliable, contains a wealth of information about Telugu poets. Vanguri Subbā Rao's *History of Telugu Literature* (*Āndhra Vāṅgmaya Charitra*) is a study in literary evolution of considerable merit and originality.

3. *Perpetuation of Oral Literature.* As we have already indicated, pre-Nanniah literature of considerable antiquity, forming the indigenous Deśī literature, still exists in the shape of songs and stories, which have not yet been printed. The value of oral literature is gradually being realised. T. Rājagopala Rao has made investigations in Deśī metre and has acquired a collection of nursery rhymes. Vetūri Prabhākara Śāstrī has already published a volume of Chatudhāra poems and has ready for publication *Songs of the Playfield.* Vanguri Subbā Rao has made a valuable contribution in his *Śataka Poets.* Nandī Rāju Chelapati Rao has brought out a collection of songs of festivity.

Folklore is being slowly gathered aud published piecemeal.

4. A fourth line of activity relates to the exploring of Prākṛit in order to find the evolution of the Telugu language and to determine the influence of Jainism and Buddhism on our literature.

5. *Comparative Studies.* The grammars and vocabularies of Dravidian languages are being explored, with a view to ascertain their mutual relation and obligations. B. Sheshagiri Row and Gidugu Rāmamūrti are conspicuous in this field.

Literary Criticism. The primary function of criticism is to exhibit the work of an author in the best light, with a view to bring out the graces of his style and the quality of his creative art. Constructive criticism of this nature is now being pursued along two lines of activity:

(1) A co-ordination of the labours of epigraphists, palæologists and historians is being made, with a view to recover the historical background, and the spirit and atmosphere of the age. The names of Jayanti Rāmiah and Kommarāju Lakshmaṇa Rao Pantulu stand out prominent in this field.

(2) Critical editions of classical authors are being prepared, with elaborate introductions, containing discussions on the date, the social setting of the poem, merits of style and the correct reading of the text.

2. Another direction in which criticism is making itself felt is the evaluation of literary tendencies and claims. The regulative function of criticism is no less important than the constructive. According to the orthodox tradition, a place of primacy is given to the kāvya type, and the literary outlook it implies. Modern criticism, equipped with a knowledge of other literatures, is challenging this position. The assault against kāvya is led by the radical critics of this generation. The ethics of Śṛingārarāsa, the utility of ornamentation, and the worth of slesha have all come under fire. A trans-valuation of literary values is taking place. Two brilliant works recently published deserve mention: *Kavitatva Vichāraṇa*, by C. R. Reddy; *Śataka Kavulu*, by Vanguri Subbā Rao.

The latter is an attempt to restore popular literature to its true place. Among the critics of the day, Vedam Venkatarāya Śāstrī, Vetūri Prabhākara Śāstrī and the Kasī Bhatla Brothers command respect for their learning, critical acumen and sympathy for new developments in literature. They realise that a critical appreciation of our literary heritage is the only enlightened safeguard against revolution on one side and reaction on the other.

Literary criticism in its truest sense, namely, estimating and exhibiting the true excellence of a poet, is not new to Telugu literature. It is a long-standing custom to introduce in the introductory portion ślokas praising the work of the great poets. These ślokas are really models of literary criticism, expressing in neat and compact phrases the true estimate of the poet, with remarkable insight. We give two instances, supposed to have been stanzas addressed to Śrīnātha and to Kākamāni Mūrti, respectively:

(1) 'Thou canst compose now like Bhīma Kavi (p. 58 f.) in words of power, now like Nanniah (p. 42 f.) in the glory of two languages (Telugu and Sanskrit), now like Tikkanna (pp. 44 ff.) in verses glistening with rasas, now after the manner of Prabandha Parameśvāra (p. 48), in stanzas of felicitous word and phrase.'

(2) 'The word-weaving magic of Peddana (p. 72), the honeyed sweetness of Timmanna (p. 74), the majesty of expression of Pāṇḍuraṅga Rāmakṛishṇa (p. 83) are thine.'

CREATIVE ACTIVITIES

The greatest change that is coming over our literary outlook is not so much the work of conscious criticism, as the effect of the time-spirit affecting the basis of literary life. The decadence of poetry, patent during the last four centuries, has been due to the ebbing away of vital energies from literature—a fact often masked behind elaborate word-architecture. The primary cause of this anæmia has been the segregation of the poet from the vital currents of life. He lost touch with realities, and lived in an artificial world of his own making. The pandit, the grammarian, and the rhetorician presented the poet with an artificial system of cardboard men and women gaudily painted, standardized emotions, and stereotyped figures of speech and thought, unchanged through long ages. But now the new life has broken into this strongly barricaded enclosure, and has liberated the spirit of poetry from the prison-house of fixed ideas. The re-animation of fading energies, the re-kindling of hope—in short, the recovery of youth and vigour—are among the spiritual gains of this contact with world-thought. The literary output springing from the new spirit may be classified under three heads:

1. The Literature of Knowledge.
2. The Literature of Union.
3. The Literature of Rejuvenation.

The Literature of Knowledge. A craving for translation is a congenital impulse in Telugu literature. We began with an era of translations, and we are in the midst of an active recrudescence of the phenomenon. Ever since Mr. Vīresalingam translated Lamb's *Tales from Shakespeare*, the appetite for translations has become voracious. Sanskrit drama, Bengali poetry, French novels, Russian tales, science, art and history are included in the range of translations. Another branch of this type of literature is the preparation of books of reference. The Āndhra Parishad is compiling a new Telugu Dictionary called *Sūrya Rāya Nigantu*, after the name of the Rāja of Pitapur, who is financing the undertaking. The *Vijñāna Chandrikā* Series was started with the object of bringing to the Telugu reader the wealth of world-culture. Mr. C. Vīrabhadra Rao's *History of the Āndhras* (*Āndhrula Charitra*) and *Āndhra Sarvasvamu* (a Telugu Encyclopædia), edited by the late Mr. K. Lakshmaṇa Rao, are among the most notable publications of this series.

The Literature of Union. Under this class fall new modes of activity in Telugu literature, such as the drama, novel, short story, and new poetry. This literature is born at the confluence of two streams of thought, East and West, and is controlled by English-educated young men, who look at the heritage of the past from a new standpoint.

1. **The Drama.** Though drama as a department of Telugu literature is of recent origin, acted plays have existed for a long time. Cruder forms of drama were in vogue in the form of *Pagati-Veshamulu* (Daylight Plays) and *Vīdhi-*

nāṭakamulu (Street Plays). Stage-craft must have attained some development, as we find Śrīnātha mentioning the name Butchigadu as a celebrated actor of female parts in his day. Piṅgaḷi Sūranna's *Prabhāvati Pradyumnamu* (p. 79), if it can be taken to reflect prevailing conditions, throws interesting light on the acting and the staging of the drama.

The earliest drama in the Telugu language is Vallabhā Mātya's *Kṛidābhi Rāmamu* (Street Scenes) at the Imperial capital, Warangal. The author says that he had seen a woman acting portions of *Palnāti Vīra Charitra.* The next set of dramas are of the eighteenth century. They are Bālasaraśvatī's *Raṅgakaumudi* and Kaṁkanti Pāpa Rāju's *Vishṇu Māya Vilāsa.* The Southern school was more prolific in dramas, but it is doubtful whether any of them have a claim to be regarded as literature.

The origin of the modern Telugu drama is traceable to the influence of the plays of Shakespeare, often enacted in India, and the impulse given by the advent of the Dhārvada Nātaka Company and Parsi theatricals. The plays fall under the three classes: (1) Adaptations from Sanskrit and English; (2) Social Satire; (3) Historical Drama.

With the exception of one or two plays, most of them are a mediocre type. There seems to be a feud between the playwright and the producer. The popular dramas have no literary value and literary dramas are not popular.

Purāṇic Dramas. Purāṇas supply an inexhaustible store of material. Here, too, as elsewhere, a beginning is made with translations. Prominent translators from Sanskrit are: (1) Paravastu Rangāchārlu, *Śakuntalā.* (2) Kokkonda Venkataratnam Pantulu, *Narakāsura Vijaya.* (3) Veddādi Śubbārāyudu, *Mallika Māruta, Veṇī Saṁhāra, Sakuntalā, Vikrama Urvasīya.*

Other dramas belonging to this order are: *Mṛichakatika, Ratnāvali* and *Droupati Vastrāpaharaṇa.* In the present decade, these have been replaced by plays which are independent adoptions of Purāṇic stories. D. Kṛishṇamācharlu is a popular author of many Purāṇic dramas, of which *Chitra Naliyam* has had a great run. In point of literary merit the plays of Vedam Venkata Rāya Śastrī are amongst the best.

Social Satire. Mr. Vīresalingam has written light farces, more or less of the nature of interludes, which are very popular. In these, social follies and foibles are held up to ridicule in comic sketches written in a light vein. Guruzāda Apparao, who wrote *Kanyā Sulka* (dealing with the scandal of the dowry system), and Pānuganti Lakshminarasiṁha Rao, who wrote *Kantābharaṇam*, are prominent writers of satirical plays.

Historical Drama. A writer above the ordinary level is K. Śrinivasa Rao, the leader of the historic drama. *Prithivī Rāja* and *The Fall of Vijayanagar* are the most popular of his plays. Both of them are tragedies—a type not represented in the Indian dramas. *The Fall of Vijayanagar* is a study in race conflict. Rāma Rāzu, the last of the Vijayanagar kings, had an illegitimate son by a Muhammadan woman, whom he brings up as his own son and entrusts him with the command of his army in the fateful battle of Taḷikota. The hero is in love with a Muhammadan girl, a captive of war, who seeks to revenge the insult offered to her by the king and incites him to go over to the enemy. The hero is in the grip of a great struggle. The call of his race and of love points one way, but the call of duty and parental affections urge in the opposite direction. Under the stress of a great emotional conflict he turns mad on the battlefield and, after killing his father, commits suicide. Of the other historical plays the following deserve mention:

Roshanara, by K. Subbā Rao.

Pratāparudra, by V. Venkata Rāya Śāstrī.

Bobbili Battle, by Śrīpāda Kṛishṇa Mūrti.

Sārangadhara, a play of questionable morals and execrable taste, disgraces the stage.

2. **The Novel.** The novel is unrepresented in old Telugu literature and owes its birth to the influence of its English prototype. *Kādambarī*, a type of metrical romance, copied from the Sanskrit, is the nearest approach to the novel. The novel, though fast becoming popular, is still in its initial stages of development. Most of them are second-rate copies or adaptations from English. The original productions are crude, hybrid patchworks of immature

workmanship. The historic and domestic novel is represented by translations from Bengali, mainly from Bankim Chandra Chattopādhyaya and Romesh Chandra Dutt. The credit of being the pathfinder in this field belongs to Mr. Vīresalingam, whose *Rāja Śekhara Charitra*, adapted from the *Vicar of Wakefield*, is the earliest novel. The detective novel is just making its appearance, and it is too early to predict its future. In the construction of the plot and development of interest and vividness of style Ch. Lakshmīnarasiṁhan stands head and shoulders over the writers of the day.

3. **Satire.** In the eighteenth and the nineteenth centuries A.D., two poets became conspicuous by their satirical writings. Their humour, never polished, often malicious, and occasionally descending to vulgarity, was intended to hurt. Jaggakavi's *Chandra Rekhā Vilāpam*, though marred by long stretches of low humour, is of a better type. He holds up to ridicule the life of the idle-rich—the zamindars of the day—their vanity, vulgarity and crude immorality. He was a master of invective. *Ravaṇa Dommīyamu*, known as *Laṅkā Vijaya*, is an instance of satire after the manner of the *Dunciad*. Parody is represented by Gīrata.

In the twentieth century, following the example of English humorists, a new type of literature has come into existence. Mr. Vīresalingam's prahasanas lead the way for social satire. Genial and kindly, pointed but never painful, the author's light farces are models to be followed. A worthy successor to him is Pānuganṭi Lakshmīnarasiṁham, whose *Sākshi* (Spectator) is an example of clean, sparkling humour, which seeks to kill social vices without cruelty.

4. **New Prose.** Up to the eighteenth century, verse was the universal medium of Telugu literature. Such prose as existed occurred in parenthetical snatches, introduced as a literary device. The eighteenth century prose was more a creature of necessity than of literary perception. As a result of modern controversies, there is a clearer delineation of the province of prose and verse, and a clearer perception of the possibilities of prose. Modern prose, like Nanniah's, is simpler and more malleable than

the 'high prose' of the kāvya period. Mr. Vīresalingam is the pioneer, and Mr. P. Chinniah Sūri sets the model of perspicuity and grace in his *Pañchaṭanṭra.*

5. **New Poetry.** The most prominent of recent tendencies in literature, which holds the promise of a great future, is the 'New Poetry.' Unlike the new drama and the new novel, it is not imitative. Though profoundly influenced by Bengali literature on one side, and English on the other, it has neither borrowed the substance nor copied the form from outside. It is the product of literary tendencies long lying dormant, now awakened to activity by the impetus of new forces from outside. The significance of the new poetry lies in the fact that it marks a return to Deśī type of literature—the native element in which the Āndhra mind can flower and bear fruit. From the twelfth century onwards our poetry has been a wanderer in the realm of Sanskrit culture. The 'New Poetry' marks the joyful home-coming of the prodigal. Much of it is strewn broadcast in contemporary magazines, and hence it is difficult to assess correctly its value and tendency. As far as can be judged, it is expressing itself in lyric and sonnet. Part of it reflects a spirit of simple fellowship and communion with nature, and may develop into a Nature School. The honour of being the pioneer in this line of development belongs to Rāyaprolu Subbā Rao. The Sāhiti Samiti, a literary association started for the purpose of cultivating the 'New Poetry,' contains among its members most of the prominent poets of this school. D. Ramireddi's *Kṛishīvaludu* is a welcome departure from worn-out paths. It is a description of the life of the agriculturist, of the procession of the seasons, and the glory of the harvest. Some of the lyrics are after the fashion of Shelley's *Skylark.* The prominent feature is its suggestiveness. Behind the obvious value there is a suggestion of spiritual meaning. The setting sun, somehow, suggests the passing away of the soul; the music of the bangle yields some illusive song of the spirit. *Venki Songs,* by N. Subbā Rao, sums up the elusive charm of simple imagery, hinting depths of meaning. In *Venki Songs* the new poetry of this decade reaches its high-water mark.

6. **The Short Story.** We have in Telugu literature the didactic fable represented by *Pañchaṭanṭra*, prose romances represented by *Daśakumāra Charitra*, stories after the manner of *Arabian Nights* represented by *Madana Kāma Rāju* stories and *Suka Saptati*, tales of wonder represented by *Siṁhāsana Dvātrimiska* stories, and tales in verse represented by *Navanātha Charitra* and *Dhanābhi Rāmamu*. But the 'short story' in the modern sense is only now making its appearance. The following collection of short stories have already been published:

(1) Pānuganṭi Lakshminarasiṁham Rao, *Suvarṇa Rekhā Kathāvali.*

(2) Mādapati Hānumanta Rao, *Mallikā Gutchamu* (A Bouquet of Jasmin).

(3) Akki Rāju Umākānta, *Triliṅga Stories.*

(4) Śrīpāda Subramanya Śāstrī, *Phūladanda* (A Garland of Flowers).

TRADITIONAL ACTIVITIES

Alongside the new poetry the historic tradition of the epic and the kāvya is continued, though under new and vastly changed environment. The poets trained in the old learning, holding allegiance to old idols, are writing kāvyas. These represent the conservative wing of the literary advance. Though not directly influenced by English literature, the new culture is brought to bear upon them in a thousand and one channels of suggestion and contact. Their literary productions are infused with a sense of the new life. The crudities of kāvya outlook are shed, and the ornate style is replaced by a pleasing blend of the softness of the old with the vigour of the new. More attention is paid to the story and less to the description. Harmony and proportion are studied. Of the prominent authors of this school the following may be mentioned:

(1) Tirupati Venkateśvara Kavulu.
(2) Rāmakṛishṇa Kavulu.
(3) Kokkonda Venkataratnam.
(4) Veddādi Sebbārāyudu.
(5) Devulapalli Brothers, of Pithapuram.

Magazines and Newspapers. The printing press, which is pregnant with revolutionary possibilities, has transferred the power of patronage from the king and the zamindar to a reading public. In the past, kings and *sanghams* were the judges of the poet. This is fast changing. The critical function is passing into the hands of newspapers and magazines. It may not be out of place here just to note the more important of the current magazines:

(1) The *Āndhra Patrika.* This premier Telugu daily has played an important part in promoting the revival of letters. It is the supporter of new movements in literature.

(2) The *Āndhra Parishad Patrika* stands for cautious advance in literary reform.

(3) *Bhārati*, a high-class literary magazine, mainly interested in the promotion of research and encouragement of new tendencies in literature.

(4) *Sāhiti* is the exponent of new poetry and specializes in the short story.

(5) *Sārada* focuses literary tendencies and forms a link between the conservative and liberal schools.

(6) *Kaḷā* stands for the correlation of art and literature.

(7) *Saraśvatī* publishes unpublished works in instalments. It is the organ of the conservative school.

(8) *Mañjuvāṇi* (now discontinued), a literary magazine with the same object as *Saraśvatī.*

XIII

RETROSPECT AND PROSPECT

The history of Telugu literature, as narrated in the previous chapters, has enabled us to trace its development in broad outlines. Starting with the humble beginnings in the Deśī, the normal tenor of development was violently arrested by the inauguration of the Mārgī. The Deśī literature, like the pretty prattling brooks of the countryside, represented the natural outpourings of the simple-hearted indigenous poet. From about the eleventh century A.D. new ambitions have filled the literary vision. The poets have assayed to build an august 'Vidyasāgar,' for which they acquired the necessary engineering skill by arduous apprenticeship to Sanskrit writers. Having built it, they diverted into it the stagnating waters of Sanskrit culture. It is a noble achievement, imposing in its grandeur, though lacking in simplicity. Thenceforward Sanskrit-Telugu literature became the main current, the Deśī surviving by sufferance. Had it been otherwise, had the main line of development been with the Deśī, had Sanskrit been content to play the rôle of a generous sympathiser from outside, instead of being stepmother within the household, we should have had a nobler history to write, and a prouder heritage to commemorate. As it is, Āndhra literature, though wanting in originality and creative energy, is nevertheless varied and beautiful—a heritage of which the Telugu can justly be proud and to which he can always turn for inspiration.

Characteristics. What are the distinguishing features of Telugu literature, as compared with Sanskrit on the one hand, and Dravidian literatures on the other? What individual and characteristic note does it strike? The Telugu poets are not creators but artists. Theirs is not the supreme genius of inspiration, but the secondary excellence of craftsmanship. They are excellent moulders. The moulds and the materials are borrowed; but the art of melting and the cunning of casting is all their own. The images they turn out are the Purāṇic images common to Sanskrit and Dravidian literatures; but the polish of features, the delicacy of pencilling, the deftness of touch is peculiar to Telugu poetic art. The Telugu poets are worshippers of style; and their art is in the refinement of language. It is the dexterity of weaving words, the daintiness of sentiment, sweetness of phrasing that draws their admiration. In technical language, the differentia of Telugu poetry is 'pāka,' the art of melting Sanskrit and Telugu in due proportion and the knack of pouring it into the mould at the right temperature. Telugu poetry is song set to music; symphony and sweetness is its soul. The Telugu poets have grafted the wild Sanskrit onto the crude Dravidian-Telugu stock, and have evolved a luscious literary Telugu, which, like the mango, is unmatched for taste and colour. There is no more beautiful or sweeter language among Indian tongues than the literary Telugu; the guttural harshness of Sanskrit is subdued and the crudeness of Dravidian Telugu sublimated by a judicious blend. The best Telugu poets are those who have learned the secret of this harmonious blend.

Defects. This facility, almost this witchery, of expression has been alike the excellence and ruin of Telugu literature. It rendered it all too easy to separate art from life. This central weakness has prevented Telugu literature from taking its place among the great literatures of the world. The Telugu poets, though conscientious and capable artists, fall short of being creators. They have not given to the world any creations corresponding to Hamlet, Shylock, Jingle, Pickwick, or Sherlock Holmes. In the international assembly of poets' ideal creations, the Āndhra is unrepresented. Life thus divorced from art took its revenge whenever the poets ventured into paths of independence, by striking them with confusion. With regard to form and language, the instinct of the Telugu poets is unerring, and their taste cultivated. But in the realm of ideation, their instincts were perverted, taste crude, judgment clouded. In the indictment against Telugu poetry there are many counts, and all of them flow from this dissociation of art from life. The poets copied Sanskrit literature, not at its best, but just when it was decadent; not from the masterpieces of *Vaidarbhi*, but from the artificial elaboration of Gauda style. It is a humiliating reflection that they translated *Śakuntalā* as a kāvya. They avoided the drama and admired the kāvya. Their adoration of the kāvya stamps them all over with literary ineptitude. They neglected the natural beauties of the Deśī and cultivated the tawdry elaborations of the Mārgī. They exalted the sickening excesses of *Śṛingāra* over the subtle charms of the *Jāvaḷi.* The kāvya heroes are not strong men of action and achievement, but psychopathic perverts grovelling in eroticism. *Chitra Kavitva* is literary acrobacy. The love of slesha is but a primitive taste. All these defects, present in the shape of incipient tendencies in all except the major poets, become increasingly patent from the time of the Ashṭadiggajās; till at last in the seventeenth, eighteenth and nineteenth centuries, the movements of literature, like the dance of a paralytic, are stiff, uncouth, painful alike to perform and to witness. Here lies also the striking paradox in Telugu literature. The age of translations was really the age of freedom, and the so-called age of independence (the kāvya age) ushered in the period of bondage. When the poet borrowed the substance from Sanskrit, he retained the freedom of art and expression; but when he borrowed the art from Sanskrit, he lost the freedom of thought.

The mischief of excessive preoccupation with art and technique, to the neglect of life, did not stop with these disastrous consequences to literary thought, taste and judgment, but has induced a moral outlook in the poets which is detrimental to all true progress. In the first place, the poets became indifferent to what they borrowed and where they borrowed it from, so long as they were able to cast it in a sweet musical medium. Since it was easier to borrow themes from outside, than carve them out of raw life, they became chronic mendicants. They borrowed from Sanskrit literature in the Purāṇa Yuga, from Sanskrit rhetoricians in the Prabandha Yuga, from each other in Andhakāra Yuga, from all and sundry in the Nava Yuga—all this, when the life within and without clamoured for poetic expression. Hence, Telugu literature reflects very little of Āndhra life, history, culture, scenery. In the second place, the constant association with what was deemed to be a superior culture, Sanskrit, bred in the poet a tendency to develop high-brow literature, contemptuous of common life and simple emotions; and with the snobbery of parvenus, they called Dvipada 'an old hag,' and barely tolerated Śataka. The neglect of a life which was their own, the hankering after a life which was others', was the moral retribution of the severing of life and art.

Telugu literature is a flaming red symbol of warning against dissociation of life from art in literature. It is a literary transgression of the first magnitude to legislate for life, and maintain, as the authorities on poetics have done, that there are only nine 'rasas.'[1] Life is so various, mysterious, elusive that we have to say that the rasas are ninety times nine. Love is not Śṛingāra, the mephitic inhalations of lust alone. There are a thousand tenses and moods for love—the love that weeps, laughs, prattles, rollics, smiles, kills, immolates. Poetry must ally itself with the mystery of life in all its ceaseless manifestations. To force life into the cast-iron systems of grammarians and rhetoricians is to forfeit all claims to inspiration. The real danger to literature does not arise from anarchists—they damage but the body. The enemies are of the household, the pandit and the pedant—for they hurt the soul.

The Future. The future of Telugu literature depends largely upon the capacity of the new generation of poets to escape from the bondage of the kāvya ideal and outlook. Fortunately, there are unmistakable signs in the literature of the last three decades that the emancipation is already being effected. A union of life and art is being established anew. Through contact with Western literatures and the

[1] See above p. 35.

emergence of new social and political ideals, a fresh and truer conception of poetry is coming into vogue. It is realised that the poet is something more than the maker of verses, however beautiful. The poet is the seer, who sees life anew. The poet is the visionary, who imparts his visions to the reader.

The reaction against kāvya may carry the poet to the other extreme. If great art alone does not make noble literature, neither does great thought alone. Doubtless, life is the major partner; but art has a vital interest. Quarried stones must be cut and polished. The neglect of form is only a passing phase. If our poets lay firm hold of the simple truth that true literature is the *artistic expression of life*, there is no need to be pessimistic of the future. The fecundity of the last few decades inspires hope for the future. A literature that has survived four centuries of kāvya must have had a charmed life. The love of art is always with the Telugu poets. What literature stands in supreme need of is baptism by full immersion in Āndhra life. Then the modern renaissance may yet add a new chapter to the Telugu literature, which can worthily compare with the glories of the Kavitraya and the grandeur of the Ashṭadiggajās.

INDEX

Titles of books are given in *italics*